Red Advance White Defeat

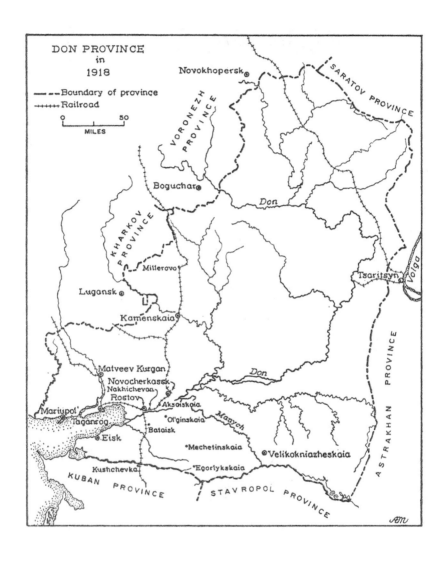

DON PROVINCE
in
1918

— — Boundary of province
++++ Railroad

0   50
MILES

Novokhopersk

VORONEZH PROVINCE

SARATOV PROVINCE

Boguchar

Don

KHARKOV PROVINCE

Millerovo

Tsaritsyn

Volga

Lugansk

Kamenskaia

PROVINCE

Matveev Kurgan

Novocherkassk

Nakhichevan

Rostov

Don

Aksaiskaia

Mariupol

Taganrog

Ol'ginskaia

Manych

ASTRAKHAN PROVINCE

Bataisk

Eisk

Mechetinskaia

Velikokniazheskaia

Kushchevka

Egorlykskaia

KUBAN PROVINCE

STAVROPOL PROVINCE

AM

RED ADVANCE
WHITE DEFEAT

Civil War in South Russia 1919-1920

Peter Kenez

New Academia Publishing
Washington, DC

New Academia Publishing
P.O. Box 27420, Washington, DC 20038-7420
www.newacademia.com - info@newacademia.com

To P. D. K. with love

Contents

List of Illustrations

Acknowledgments

Several friends helped me in my work. William Rosenberg, Barbara Clements and David Joravsky read the entire manuscript, and on the basis of their suggestions I made many improvements. William Rosenberg also called my attention to materials which I had overlooked. Isebill Gruhn, Victoria Bonnell and George Baer read various chapters. Discussions with them were useful in clarifying my thinking on a number of points and I am grateful to them for their friendship and encouragement.

In my research and writing I was supported by the Hoover Institution which twice awarded me National Fellowships, first for the summer of 1972 and then for the academic year of 1973-1974. The Hoover Institution provided me not only with a magnificent library and rich archives, but also with ideal working conditions. I enjoyed the company of my fellow National Fellows. The Research Committee of the Academic Senate of the University of California at Santa Cruz awarded me several grants. These grants enabled me to travel to New York twice and work in the Archives of the Russian and Eastern European Institute of Columbia University.

I would also like to thank Dorothy Dalby, who corrected many of my grammatical errors, Gene Tanke, whose copy editing greatly improved the final text, Lynn Mally, who prepared the index and Adrienne Morgan, who drew the maps.

Sections of this book have appeared in *Slavonic and Eastern European Journal*, *The Russian Review* and *The Wiener Library Bulletin*.

All dates are given according to the Gregorian or Western calendar, unless otherwise indicated. I have followed the transliteration system of the Library of Congress.

P.K.

Introduction

Every book on the Russian Civil War is essentially a study of the causes of the victor's victory and the loser's defeat. Even the historian who aims at nothing more than telling the story of the struggle at least implicitly provides us with an explanation of the outcome.

In Western historiography there is general agreement on the main causes of Bolshevik victory, and most historians would agree with the following summary. The Bolsheviks possessed superior leadership. Lenin was a master of political strategy and Trotskii had great organizational ability, which he showed in creating the Red Army and leading it to victory. The Bolsheviks also took advantage of the revolutionary enthusiasm of the Russian people, an enthusiasm fired by the injustices they had suffered under an outdated political and social system; the crucible of a modern war revealed just how outdated it was. Lenin's appropriation of the agrarian program of the Social Revolutionaries induced the peasants to prefer the Bolsheviks to their enemies. And whereas the Bolsheviks were relatively united, their enemies were divided by personal animosities, ideologies, and memories of previous conflicts. The Bolsheviks, who occupied the center of the country, had a great strategic advantage: their enemies had to base their movements on the peripheries, inhabited largely by non-Russians; the Red Army could send reinforcements to any segment of the front that was most directly threatened, but the Whites could not coordinate their military moves.

But such a simple enumeration of causes is hardly satisfactory. After all, what evidence do we have, for instance, that the peasants preferred the Bolsheviks, except the fact that the Bolsheviks ultimately won? Besides, is it not possible that the Bolsheviks won in spite of the attitude of the peasants? How is one to balance the importance of the favorable strategic position of the Bolsheviks against the significance of Allied aid, which obviously greatly benefited the Whites? It is true that the anti-Bolshevik camp was deeply divided, but perhaps the White advantage of having a large pool of experienced administrators and trained officers was an adequate compensation. Most important, how is one to rank the various explanations? Which cause should we consider primary?

This book, too, is an attempt to explain the outcome of the Civil War. However, I will try to develop a primary or general explanation for the defeat of the Whites, one broad enough to include a number of the others previously mentioned. In the process of describing the defeat of the Whites I hope to work out a new framework for looking at the Civil War. Instead of regarding it as a purely military contest between two opposing armies, I will approach it as a political competition between the two major antagonists in which each tried to impose its will on a reluctant people. The winner in this competition was the winner of the Civil War.

The Revolution represented the disintegration of traditional authority. The institutions, the ideology, and the leaders by which the tsarist regime governed the country at the time of an extremely demanding war proved inadequate. The March revolution gave an opportunity to the liberal intelligentsia to experiment with a new system, but the events of 1917 proved conclusively that the Provisional Government was no more able to hold the country together than its defunct predecessor. The victorious liberals not only failed to reverse the process of disintegration, but themselves contributed to anarchy. Under the circumstances, the accomplishment of the Bolsheviks in November was a slight one. Almost any small group of determined men with some support from the people could have removed the defenseless Provisional Government, which had already defeated itself. The difficult task lay ahead: the Bolsheviks had to devise a system of government which could cope with the extraordinary situation.

The Civil War was a period of boundless anarchy; but it was also a time when groups of men experimented with institutions and ideologies which would help them to overcome anarchy. One might have thought that the democratic socialists, whose program was clearly favored by a majority of Russians, would have had the best chance of rallying the people. Yet within a year the Socialist Revolutionaries and the Mensheviks had lost all positions of power and influence, proving that an attractive ideology is only one component for establishing a successful government. Most socialists drew the unavoidable conclusions and, depending on their ideologies and personalities, joined either the Whites or the Reds, the two surviving antagonists.

Russia could hardly have produced two more different groups of people than the leaders of the Reds and the Whites. On one side were the revolutionary intellectuals who had spent years in jail or in exile and who were profoundly committed to change. They were articulate, they lived their politics, and they believed it was in their power to mold society into something better than they had found. The other side consisted of army officers, men who had felt basically at home in tsarist Russia, who disliked politics, and who envisaged only military solutions to problems. They had no vision of a future Russia, yet they deeply felt that Bolshevik rule would bring only evil to their country. Obviously the two groups hated and despised one another.

However little these men shared in background and ideology, they did share common problems. For whatever their long-term goals, the immediate task for Whites and Reds alike was to create a functioning administrative machinery which would enable them to carry out their decisions, to organize an army, to collect food, and to make railroads run and factories produce; briefly, to bring order out of chaos.

The central argument of this book is that the Whites lost the Civil War above all because they failed to build those institutions which would have enabled them to administer the territories under their nominal rule. This failure can be understood only in a comparative context. After all, Bolshevik rule was also shaky in these years. Bolshevik weakness made the civil war inevitable and the survival of the Whites for three years possible. But a civil conflict is always a struggle between the weak and the weaker. In this conflict the Whites in the end proved inferior: their administrative confusion was greater, and their territories even more engulfed by anarchy.

To be able to govern means to have authority. The problem of a country in the throes of a civil war is that the two components of authority, legitimacy and force, are in short supply.[1] The task is to build authority. But how can one acquire legitimacy, and where is the force to come from? The more a government's right to rule is questioned and the less it is able to coerce, the more it has to appeal to the people. In order to stay in power it must present itself as the defender of the aspirations of the masses. At the same time it has to organize a coercive apparatus. For that purpose it must mobilize a highly motivated group of activists willing to perform often unattractive tasks, such as, for example, staffing the secret police.

Propaganda and organization are essential elements for winning a civil war. But the leaders of the Whites were military men who never properly understood the political nature of the war in which they were engaged, and thus did not understand the tasks confronting them. Their inbred contempt for politics was a fatal disability, for they were forced to compete with masters of political manipulation. It may be that the White cause was hopeless from the beginning. After all, the enemies of the November revolution could not easily outbid the Bolsheviks. No White general could have countenanced the agrarian revolution which was taking place in the villages. The Whites and the Reds had to rely on different social classes, and this reliance imposed severe limitations on their programs. Nevertheless, it is clear that the White leaders played their hand poorly.

In *Civil War in South Russia, 1918* I summarized the difficulties the Bolsheviks had to surmount during the first year of the struggle and described in detail the birth of the White movement. In November 1917 there were few people in Russia or abroad who believed that the Bolsheviks, with their outlandish ideas and utopian plans, could hold on to power and succeed where more traditional statesmen had failed. But the Bolsheviks did succeed. Their leaders possessed political talent and determination, and their enemies were weak, divided, and demoralized. Lenin's government survived one crisis after another. In January 1918 this government showed its lack of democratic scruples as it dismissed the Constituent Assembly, the fruit of Russia's only free election. In the following month the new regime had to face a far more dangerous threat: the German army. Only large territorial concessions could stop the effortlessly advancing enemy; but these concessions, made to the Germans at Brest-Litovsk, led to a break with the Bolsheviks' only coalition partners, the Left Socialist Revolutionaries, and even threatened the unity of the Party.

The worst crisis came in the last spring and early summer of 1918. The Bolsheviks' inability to feed the people resulted in such misery and dissatisfaction that their base of power was close to crumbling away completely; Russia was on the brink of total anarchy. This was the time when large scale anti-Bolshevik forces started to organize and the Civil War began in earnest. The first serious military opponents of Bolshevik rule formed a strange group. The Provisional Government had organized a small army out of the willing prisoners of war of Czech and Slovak extraction who wanted to fight for the birth of their own country. After the Brest-Litovsk peace, this army of approximately forty thousand men wanted to be transported to Western Europe in order to continue the fight against Germany. Their remarkable odyssey had an unexpected result: the Czechs rebelled against their hosts and within a short time they gained control of the entire Trans-Siberian railroad; forty thousand men became the masters of Siberia. Under Czech protection, the Socialist Revolutionaries organized a government and an army. For awhile this new army advanced victoriously and the Bolsheviks lived through very anxious days. Trotskii's defeat of the enemy at Sviazhsk, not far from Kazan, at the end of August 1918 is considered one of the decisive battles of the Civil War.

At the same time a bewildering variety of anti-Bolshevik forces organized in South Russia. The Ukraine was in the hands of the Germans, who administered it through their reactionary puppet, Hetman Skoropadskii. The newly formed Caucasian states all assumed an anti-Bolshevik stance. The Don Cossacks of Ataman* Krasnov, with German aid and protection, soon liberated the entire Don *Voisko*.† Perhaps most important, the Volunteer Army,

---

*Ataman. Cossack chieftain. The word is probably from the Turkish. Up to the beginning of the eighteenth century the Cossacks elected their own leaders. From that time until the Revolution the government named the atamans. During the Civil War some of the Ukrainian partisans also called their leaders atamans.

†*Voisko:* literally, army. In the beginning of the twentieth century the Cossacks organized themselves into eleven communities, which were called *voiska* (singular, *voisko*). The largest of these was the Don.

which had been established by Russia's most prominent generals soon after the November Revolution, in the summer grew into a serious force. The army was protected from the main Bolshevik armies by the Don Cossacks, and—ironically in view of the army's loyalty to the Allies—by the Germans. Under these favorable circumstances the Whites could organize their forces in the relative security of the Kuban. In August they captured the capital of the district, Ekaterinodar, which was to remain their headquarters for many months.

November 1918 was a turning point in the history of the Civil War. In Siberia, Admiral Kolchak overthrew a government in which the Socialist Revolutionaries had participated. After this coup, Russia's most popular party never again played a major role. Even more important for the course of the Civil War was the end of the war in Europe. This enabled the Allies to pay more attention to Russia. As a result, paradoxically, the intervention which began within the context of the European war greatly expanded after November 1918. The spirit of the anti-Bolsheviks was lifted by the prospect of large-scale support from foreign friends. They optimistically assumed that the powers which had defeated the greatest army in the world, the German, now would quickly remove Lenin and his comrades.

Yet the immediate beneficiaries of German defeat were the Bolsheviks. As the German troops withdrew from the Ukraine, the Red Army quickly occupied the country. The Bolsheviks, unlike their enemies, possessed the forces to take advantage of the power vacuum. German defeat was followed by revolutionary risings, and the Bolsheviks confidently expected that the socialist victory in Berlin was only a prologue to a communist revolution. It seemed that their days of terrible isolation were nearing an end.

This book takes up the story where the previous volume left off. In 1919 the Volunteer Army grew from a regional force into a major army which in October came close to occupying Moscow. But the success proved ephemeral, and in March 1920 the White movement was on the verge of collapse. During the period of victories and defeats the White leadership experimented with policies and institutional changes. Studying these shifts we become aware of the varieties possible even within military counterrevolution. In the spring of 1920 General Wrangel took General Denikin's place as Commander-in-Chief, but he succeeded in staving off defeat only for a few months. In November 1920 the remnants of the Volunteer Army evacuated the Crimea, and this event finally ended the three-year-old Civil War.

In deciding the outcome of the struggle, political failures were more decisive than military ones, and so I consider my main tasks to be these: to describe the administrative apparatus of the Whites, to reconstruct the world view of the men who organized and ran the institutions, and to analyze the White social and economic policies. Of course, in the chaos of the Civil War there was a wide gap between the policies agreed on by the central organs and what the people actually experienced. While it is relatively easy to relate the functioning of central institutions, such as Denikin's Special Council, it is far more difficult to reconstruct the work of the administrative organs closest to the people. For example, we can follow the development of the thinking of the leaders on the issue of land reform and the work of various commissions, but we have only a hazy picture of the effect of Wrangel's land law on the peasants, and it is hard to establish how much of the reform was in fact carried out. We are forced to conjecture on the basis of thin evidence.

Since this book must describe the defeat of an army, obviously much will have to be said about the changing military situation. However, this book is not intended as military history. I am more interested in the army as an institution, in the background and behavior of the soldiers, and in questions of morale and indoctrination than in the history of campaigns.

Similarly, I devote relatively little space to the issue of Allied intervention. I do so because I believe that the Civil War was indeed a civil war in the sense that its outcome was determined by local forces and circumstances. Also, foreign intervention is the aspect of the Civil War which has been described best and in most detail by other historians.[2] Indeed, the many books on this subject may actually have distorted our picture of the conflict by exaggerating the role of foreigners.

In the historical literature there are far better works about the Bolsheviks than about their enemies. However, from many otherwise valuable books the comparative perspective is missing.[3] It is a serious weakness. The Reds and the Whites were, of course, quite conscious of competing against one another, and therefore when the historian concentrates only on one group he cannot present a fully accurate picture. For example, in order to understand Lenin's agrarian policies it is important to know what the Whites were doing. Recently some historians have stressed the heterogeneous nature of the Bolshevik Party in the years of the Civil War.[4] Those who study the White movement will quickly see that, by comparison, the Bolsheviks were firmly united.

Although I recount the history only of the South Russian anti-Bolshevik movement, I have tried to write something broader than a regional history. I have concentrated on the microcosm of the South because it seemed the best way to pay attention to the enormous variety of forces which were at work, and thus to gain a better understanding of the White movement in general.

CHAPTER 1

The Bolsheviks

Reds and Whites competed against one another in building an administrative structure, in formulating policies which would appeal to large segments of the population, and, of course, on the battlefields. In order to place the White movement in proper perspective, let us begin our survey with a brief description of the Bolsheviks' organizational principles, their social and economic policies, and the strengths and weaknesses of the young Red Army.

Soviet historians have always given the Bolshevik Party a major share of the credit for winning the Civil War. Indeed, the Party gave an inestimable advantage to the Reds over their enemies: it provided organization and discipline at a time when these qualities were in short supply. As circumstances changed, the organization was able to meet new situations and satisfy new requirements. It was meant to be an association of professional revolutionaries, but it was transformed into an instrument of rule. However, the fact that the Bolshevik Party was originally created for tasks which were very different from those which it was forced to play during the Civil War was of relatively small significance. What mattered was that Leninist ideas, principles, and attitudes, as they were embodied in the Party, turned out to be very timely.

The central feature of Leninist political theory was the stress on organization. No revolutionary before Lenin had paid comparable attention to the mundane needs of building a party machinery. Lenin always struggled against the anarchic element in Russian socialism, and he feared and distrusted spontaneous action. In his opinion the success of the revolution depended not so much on the workers themselves as on the cohesion and skill of the Party.[1] From their experience in revolutionary underground work against the tsarist regime, the Bolsheviks had learned the same lesson: in order to succeed, the Party needed discipline and tight organization. In a period of anarchy and confusion a small group of dedicated people can accomplish remarkable tasks. In Russia, it was only the Bolsheviks who were predisposed by their intellectual and political traditions to act on the basis of this understanding.

Of course, the Party was not yet afflicted by Stalinist conformity. The Bolsheviks were members of the international socialist community, and their theoretical heritage, together with autocratic elements, included a commitment to democracy. Later, when the requirements of democracy and the need for discipline collided, the Bolsheviks would again and again choose discipline. But at the outbreak of the Civil War the Party was still creating itself, and its future was far from predetermined. In the period of underground struggle, Lenin had frequently removed those comrades who dared to disagree with him on important matters. However, the ever-pragmatic leader realized that the needs of the Party in 1917 were not the same as when it had been a small band of revolutionaries. He knew that even the occasionally unruly followers could make important contributions, and was therefore willing to overlook "errors" and forgive past "mistakes." The chaotic circumstances of the Revolution also loosened discipline. As a result, the Bolshevik Party of 1917-1921 was a more heterogeneous organization than at any other period of its history. It was faction-ridden, and its leaders held personal grudges against one another. The control of the center over party cells in outlying provinces was often only tenuous. Ambitious and strong-minded leaders could easily defy directives from Petrograd or Moscow. However, no one can fail to recognize that compared to their enemies, the Bolsheviks were disciplined and united.

Both the composition and the functions of the Party went through enormous changes in the years of the Revolution and Civil War. The growth of membership was so great that within a short time the new members completely submerged the old cadres. No reliable data exist for membership figures, but the magnitude of the growth is beyond doubt. The party had 23,600 members at the time of the February Revolution.[2] According to the most widely accepted estimates, in November 1917 the figure grew to 115,000. During the Civil War the Party experienced stages of fast expansion and purges, and at the end of the conflict, there were close to three quarters of a million Communists.[3] The periodic purges and recruitment drives were the result of the two conflicting purposes of the leadership. On the one hand, the Party wanted to attract talent to help to win the war, and to increase its influence among the workers and peasants; on the other, it did not want to be held responsible for the uneducated, irresponsible careerists who infiltrated the organization.

Indeed, many people who joined embarrassed the Party by anti-Semitic agitation, crude careerism, and corrupt practices. There is no doubt that in general, the original twenty thousand underground activists were more selfless, courageous, and dedicated revolutionaries than the new Communists. But it would be a mistake to emphasize only the political and human weaknesses of the new members. Many of the peasants and workers who acquired their membership cards at this time could really reach their fellow Russians, even though they had only the haziest notions about Marxist theory and the goals of the socialist revolution. They were able to influence the public mood; they agitated for the immediate goals of the Party; and they carried out policies made in Moscow. One of the most significant accomplishments of the Party, and a main reason for its ultimate victory, was the mobilization of large pools of talent, never previously tapped. The Party found uneducated but able men and women who acquired political experience in the Civil War. Many of them later occupied important posts in the economic and political life of the Soviet Union. The Party could be regarded as a recruitment agency; the Whites possessed no comparable instrument.

The new Party member received intangible yet important psychological rewards with his membership. He came to regard himself as a member of the elite, a fighter in the avant garde. Joining implied a serious commitment. Even if a person entered the Party for less than selfless motives, when the enemy threatened the region, he would participate in the organization of a defense because he knew that the Whites treated all Bolsheviks alike. The short-sighted White policy of immediately executing Communist captives greatly benefited the Red side in the Civil War.

It is hard to describe the functions of the Party since it was involved in every aspect of public life. It was a policy-making body, which developed the strategy for winning the Civil War; it was a recruitment agency, which brought forward cadres for important positions; it was responsible for reporting on the mood of the people, and it organized propaganda both for the distant goal of socialism and for pressing everyday tasks. Most important, it supervised the work of government, and of social organizations such as trade unions and cooperatives, and watched the loyalty of technical experts and officers who had been cajoled and coerced into Bolshevik service.

The Party's previous experience in underground work now proved especially useful. In areas controlled by the enemy the Bolsheviks quickly reorganized their secret network. The fact that the Bolsheviks had trusted agents in major cities and factories was very beneficial; underground activists printed newspapers, carried out sabotage, and in general undermined the people's confidence in the stability of the White regime. This was dangerous work, for capture meant summary execution. The Whites possessed no comparable network. When they tried to organize underground work it was usually amateurish and readily exposed without significant accomplishments.

The fact that the functions of Party and government frequently overlapped often led to confusion. The chief ailment was a lack of authority. But two sets of institutions, functioning inadequately and sometimes at cross purposes, were still better than no control at all.

The organization of the Party resembled that of an army. Although in the confusion of the Civil War discipline was sometimes violated, it was normally enforced. Democratic centralism, in which local organs would select the higher ones and in turn be bound by their decisions, remained a meaningless phrase. In practice, local leaders were almost always appointed from the center.

Although the Party was inundated by new members the central apparat remained in the hands of old Bolsheviks, who were bound to Lenin by a tradition of personal loyalty.[4] The pre-revolutionary members may have made up only a small minority of the Party, but their influence remained crucial. In addition to the Central Committee at the top and the local cells in the villages, factories, and army units, there were a number of intervening organizations at the provincial, district, and city levels. Naturally, the strength of the Party ultimately depended on the local cells. Some of these in factories and villages contained no more than four or five members. In the beginning of the Civil War, Bolshevik strength was almost entirely concentrated in the army and in the cities. The majority of villages did not have a single Bolshevik. As the war progressed, the position of the party in the countryside gradually improved. However, Bolshevik strength among workers remained far greater than it was among peasants. The crucial and difficult task was to control the countryside, and unfortunately for the Bolsheviks, it was precisely in this aspect of the work that the Party was weakest.

The new constitution of 1918 did not mention the most distinctive political institution of the country, the Bolshevik Party.[5] It did have, however, much to say about the other novel political organizations, the Soviets.

Workers created the first Soviets in 1905 to take care of the immediate problems of revolutionary action. With the suppression of the revolutionary movement, Soviets disappeared to emerge again twelve years later. In April 1917, when Lenin issued his famous slogan, "All power to the Soviets," his party was in a small minority in almost every one of them. However, as the Bolsheviks gained strength in the course of 1917 their representation increased, and in September they acquired majorities in the two most important Soviets, those in Moscow and Petrograd. These political victories were the prerequisites of the November Revolution, which was carried out in the name of the Soviets and acquired a certain degree of legitimacy when the Second All-Russian Congress of Soviets met on November 7 and passed a resolution approving Lenin's revolution.

At this time the Soviets were loosely organized bodies lacking any clearly defined sphere of competence. They were useful to the Bolsheviks because they extended the reach of the Party when it very much needed this help. In theory, the Congress of Soviets, which elected an Executive Committee to which the Council of Commissars was responsible, was the supreme power of the land, and the local Soviets practiced self-government. However, as time went on the Soviets were subverted. The Bolsheviks gradually removed their socialist competitors, the Mensheviks and Socialist Revolutionaries. The Executive Committee and the Government came to be directed by the same leaders who ruled the Party. The local Soviets, on the other hand, took on themselves the functions of local government and in practice became indistinguishable from prerevolutionary organs. In many villages nothing changed but the nomenclature; the village elder or Ataman, on Bolshevik victory, became the chairman of the village Soviet. The independence of local organs was not the result of devotion to the principle of self-government, but a manifestation of anarchy; as soon as they could, the Bolsheviks imposed control and central direction.

The purpose of political institutions is to carry out policies. Obviously, the success or failure of institutions depends not on organizational skill alone but also on the nature of the social and economic policies which they attempt to introduce.

The most difficult task for the social historian of the revolutionary period is to describe how central policies actually affected people. Obviously, many of the decrees remained dead letters, and some of the most significant social changes occurred independently of or even in spite of the wishes of the nominal rulers. Since it is relatively easy to study resolutions, proclamations, and minutes of meetings, the historian may be tempted to believe that these materials will enable him to reconstruct the full story of the period. But they cannot; the main outlines of the social history of the Civil War are clear, but the details remain elusive. It is particularly hard to appreciate what the peasants experienced in Russia's thousands of villages.

The social revolution which was sweeping the villages began in 1917, independent of the Bolsheviks. Russia was an agricultural country with a large surplus agrarian population, which the weakly developed industry could not absorb. The peasantry was ignorant of modern methods, crop yields were low, and the population was never far from the danger of famine. The peasants were rebellious; they resented the landlords, who seemed representatives of an alien culture, and coveted their lands. Some historians argue that the reforms which Prime Minister Stolypin introduced shortly before the outbreak of the First World War might have solved the problems of the country; but no one can maintain that the problems had been solved.

In the light of the experience of the peasant revolution of 1905–1906 no great foresight was needed to anticipate that the demise of tsarism in 1917 would bring new peasant disturbances. It is not so much that the war increased the misery of the peasants. Indeed, where industry had failed, the army succeeded in removing the surplus population from the villages, and the supply situation deteriorated far more rapidly in the cities than in the countryside. But the collapse of traditional authority tempted the peasants to use the opportunity to satisfy their desire for land and vengeance. In the late spring and early summer of 1917 peasant disturbances began in the form of small acts of non-cooperation, such as refusal to pay rent, but these soon escalated into violence. Insurgents burned down manors, forcibly occupied land, and even killed some landlords. "Good" and "bad" landlords suffered alike.

The attitude of the Provisional Government to this incipient social revolution had all the elements of the later policies of the White regimes. While the Provisional Government accepted in principle the need for a thorough-going land reform, in practice the moderate politicians wanted to postpone action until revolutionary passions had cooled. The government considered that land reform undertaken during the war would disrupt the already precarious supply situation in the cities, and would encourage peasant soldiers to defect in order not to miss their share. At the same time the government had neither the force nor the determination to punish the rebellious peasants. The government which could not suppress the revolutionary and anarchist acts nor satisfy the desire of the peasants found its authority undermined.

The Bolsheviks in 1917 had nothing to lose and much to gain from the spreading anarchy. They did not have to worry about the economic consequences of the expropriation of the land and so they could give verbal support to the peasants. Yet they, too, had to pay a price. As revolutionary Marxists, the Bolsheviks in the past had not approved of land distribution for fear that it would strengthen the peasant's consciousness of private property, making the creation of socialism all the more difficult. Lenin, unlike most contemporary revolutionary socialist leaders, fully appreciated the strategic importance of gaining peasant good will at the time of making his revolution. With the advantage of hindsight it is safe to conclude that without the Bolsheviks' concession to the peasants on the issue of land reform, the November Revolution would have been doomed.

The Bolsheviks knew how to take advantage of the inability of the Provisional Government to satisfy the people's craving for land and peace, and they succeeded in November in removing the liberal democratic regime. Lenin was determined to avoid the "errors" of his predecessors and on November 8 he simultaneously called for peace negotiations with all belligerent powers and issued his decree abolishing ownership of land without compensation.

The decree merely legalized and completed the peasant revolution. In name the land became national property, but the peasants regarded the nationalized land as their own. Their assemblies, which had experience in these matters from the days of the peasant commune, distributed all the available lands of landlords and frequently even lands belonging to the rich peasants or kulaks. The kulaks who had spent years saving money to buy an extra *desiatina* (2.7 acres) now found that their labors had been in vain. In villages where land was plentiful the peasants received generous allotments, while in neighboring villages there might be little or nothing to distribute. Outsiders received nothing. It would be wrong to imagine that such a land reform could have solved the age-old problem of the Russian peasantry. The landlords, who as a class had been losing their lands to the peasants for decades in any case, did not possess enough lands to satisfy the needs of the overpopulated Russian villages. In the majority of provinces an individual peasant did not receive more than a half a *desiatina*.[6] However, the political significance of the land reform did not depend on economic considerations. The peasants hated the landlords, and the new government unequivocally took their side in the class struggle.

The peasants and the Bolsheviks allowed one another to carry out their revolutions. However, within a few months the Bolsheviks realized that they needed more from the countryside than mere tolerance. In the spring and early summer of 1918 the greatest threat to the survival of the regime was an uprising of starving workers.

The supply situation had constantly deteriorated during the course of the war, and the destruction of large estates which were supplying the cities with food was bound to have disastrous results. The peasants, even when they had surplus food, had no incentive to sell since the cities had nothing to give in exchange. The Bolsheviks, in order not to be swept away by the indignant proletariat, had to take food by force.

The peasants responded by reducing production. That the attitude of many peasants toward the Bolsheviks changed from friendly tolerance to bitter hostility can be taken for granted. The Bolsheviks sought allies in the countryside; they encouraged the hatred of the poor against the not-so-poor. They designed their policies to favor the poorest among the peasants. They encouraged the poor peasants to form detachments, which together with groups of workers from the cities, took what could be taken from the richer peasants.

Assuming that the Bolsheviks' desire to stay in power was legitimate, it is hard to see what other agricultural policy they could have pursued. However disastrous the economic consequences of requisitioning, the Bolsheviks had no alternative. But there was an aspect of their policy which further alienated the peasants and which was motivated not by expediency but by ideological commitment. The land law was "provisional" because the Bolsheviks never renounced their goal of socialist agriculture. Bolshevik legislation consistently favored collectives against individual peasants; the Bolsheviks retained some estates as state farms and agitated for the formation of collective farms. But their collectivist agitation was very unsuccessful: at the end of the Civil War less than one percent of the total area under cultivation belonged to collectives.[7] Since the peasants quickly took over the valuable estates, only the less fertile lands were left for state farms. At the time of the Civil War the state, of course, could not afford to invest a substantial amount of capital in equipping these farms properly. As a result, collectives and state farms remained economically unimportant and unprofitable. Even though participation was voluntary, the peasants hated them. White propaganda took advantage of this hatred. The simple peasant could get the impression from White pamphlets and oral propaganda that most of the land under Bolshevik rule belonged to collectives.[8] The peasants associated the name "communist" with communes, and therefore often hated communists even when they were prepared to accept the Bolsheviks.

Running the nation's industry turned out to be just as difficult as making the peasants produce. Here, the Bolsheviks inherited a miserable legacy. The decline of industrial production, which reached its nadir at the end of the Civil War, had begun not in November 1917 but at the outbreak of World War I. The necessity of satisfying the insatiable appetite of the army, the mobilization of skilled workers, the disruption of transport, and the impediments to external trade had placed a crushing burden on the weakly developed Russian industry.[9]

When Lenin returned from Switzerland he did not call for nationalization but merely for an extension of the role of workers' committees, which had been formed almost everywhere. He did not immediately change his position after his victory, but it soon became clear that dividing the responsibility for running the factories between workers and managers had increased confusion. Many of the managers sabotaged the policies of the new regime. The Bolsheviks set up a Supreme Council for the National Economy (VSNKh) in December 1917, but this act did not check the slide into industrial chaos. As factories closed down, as the unemployed workers could not be fed, as the railroads stopped running and the supply of Red army materiel was endangered, the Bolsheviks took increasingly radical and desperate measures. The economic system born by improvisation in this dark period came to be called "war communism."

The essential feature of war communism was the substitution of compulsion for the workings of the market mechanism. The state outlawed free trade in grain and it assumed a direct role in running the factories. Ultimately, it was necessary to force people to work by militarizing labor. It is hard to evaluate war communism as an economic system, for on the one hand it enabled the Reds to win the Civil War, and on the other it is evident that it did not stop the process of disintegration. War communism brought untold suffering and misery to the Russian people. Statistics well express the magnitude of the breakdown. In 1921 the gross output of Russian industry was only 31 percent of the prewar figure. In the case of large-scale industry, it was only 21 percent. The production of coal between 1913 and 1921 declined from 29 million to 9 million tons, electricity from 2039 billion to 520 billion kilowatt hours, steel from 4.2 million to 200 thousand tons, and railway tonnage carried from 132.4 million to 39.4 million.[10] In real terms these figures meant that factories closed down, workers remained unemployed, apartments could not be heated. It meant that the cities could provide nothing for the countryside, and therefore the peasants had to be deprived of their products by force.

A particularly disturbing problem was the collapse of the monetary system. The main culprit was the tsarist government, which financed the war by loans and by printing paper money. The Bolsheviks could not stop inflation. As industrial production declined, the state paid its bills by printing more and more money. This was, of course, no solution. As inflation accelerated there was a shortage of paper money and ultimately money lost all value. Some Bolshevik ideologists saw in this development the first step toward socialism, but it is difficult to know whether the writers themselves believed such nonsense.

Clearly, the policies of war communism were largely responses to existing conditions. Although some leaders might have tried to find ideological justification for the disappearance of a money economy, the more clear-sighted obviously deplored this phenomenon, and saw it for what it was: a manifestation of collapse and a cause of misery. Yet it would be wrong to underestimate the importance of ideology in evaluating Bolshevik attitudes. Their intellectual background predisposed the Bolshevik leaders to choose some solutions and reject others. Radical actions, such as the militarization of labor, had a certain attraction, for they seemed appropriate for revolutionaries in a critical situation.

Russia in the years of the Civil War experienced one of the great social revolutions of history. This occurred partially as a result of Bolshevik policies, but also because of the objective conditions of the times, such as economic ruin, fighting, and famine.

The ruling classes lost their base of power. Tens of thousands first escaped to areas which temporarily appeared safe and then left the country. Many possessed managerial or other skills which the Bolsheviks were happy to use. Factory owners, counts and barons,

officers of the Imperial Guard and of the General Staff came to serv
their "class enemy," some in lowly positions but others in posts o
genuine responsibility.

The peasants, in spite of their sufferings and misery, were tl
great gainers in the Revolution. They acquired the land of the lanc
lords and often even the holdings of the kulaks. Land reform an
the committees of the poor reduced stratification in the villages; tl
efforts of Stolypin were undone. However, as a result of the sociali
revolution, the desire of the peasants to possess property did no
at all decrease. The future conflict between this majority of Ru
sians and the new rulers could be predicted.

The Revolution was carried out in the name of the proletaria
but no one suffered more than the workers and the urban poor. Ui
employment, inadequate housing, the inability of the regime t
feed the cities made life miserable. The proletarian revolution wa
accompanied by a flight of the proletarians back to the village
where many of them still had ties. From 1917 to 1920 the numbe
of urban workers in Russia declined from 3.6 million to 1.5 mi
lion.[11] The Bolsheviks were understandably concerned that the
weak social base was further undermined.[12] Yet, and this is an iron
twist on Marxist ideology, the workers remained loyal to the ne
regime not because of the material benefits they received, but b
cause of their idealistic ideological commitment. They believed tl
propaganda of the new regime and accepted it as their own.

THE RED ARMY

The Bolsheviks could not have won the Civil War without a rea
sonably well-disciplined military force. However, the difficultie
of building such an army were enormous. The country was de
astated, the people were tired of fighting, and the ingrained habi
and ideology of the Bolsheviks were a hindrance to them in cor
fronting their military tasks. They had always regarded armies an
militarism as among the most dangerous enemies of the revolutio
In the course of 1917 they made every effort to contribute to the di
integration of the army by encouraging the peasants' desire to retur
home and championing such utopian and subversive principles a
the election of military officers. They succeeded too well. The one

mighty army, the largest the world had ever seen, ceased to exist as a fighting force. After their victory, the Bolsheviks could count only on miniscule partisan-type units, which were useful against the almost nonexistent counterrevolution, but which were hopeless when facing regular forces.

Trotskii quickly freed himself from illusions.[13] He became Commissar of War in March 1918 and immediately started to create a regular army. He based his policy on the conviction that the Red Army needed organization and discipline above all. He was determined to wipe out *partizanshchina* (partisan-type warfare), a method of fighting for which he acquired a personal hatred.

When the Czech legion rose against the Bolsheviks in May 1918, it quickly became clear that the Red Army could not attract enough volunteers. The entire enormous country had no more than 200,000 soldiers fighting in irregular, partisan-type units, which had extremely low military value.[14] A few days after the rising of the Czechs, the Bolsheviks introduced conscription. The draft was first extended only to workers, then to poor peasants, and finally to all peasants, with the exception of the ill-defined category of kulaks. The kulaks, together with their urban counterpart, the bourgeoisie, had to serve in labor battalions instead. The army grew quickly. By the middle of September the Reds had 452,000 men under arms and by the end of the Civil War, five million.[15] Even though the workers who fought in the Red Army were disproportionate to their number in the population, and suffered very heavy casualties, the great majority of soliders came from the peasantry. At first the army drafted only those peasants who had had fighting experience in the World War, but before long it had to turn to those who had been too young to fight. Since in the conditions of the Civil War they received little training, the military value of the young peasants was slight.[16]

An even more difficult task than drafting peasants was providing the army with officers. It is remarkable how quickly Trotskii found the only possible solution and then stuck to it, in spite of difficulties and the opposition which he encountered. Without hesitation he abandoned the principle of election of officers and decided to gain the services of trained men—those who had already served the tsar and the Provisional Government. In November 1918, some 22,315 ex-tsarist officers served in the Red Army. By the end of the Civil War the figure was almost 50,000. In addition, the Bolsheviks greatly benefited from the service of over 200,000 men who had participated in the World War as non-commissioned officers.[17]

The proletarian state made great efforts to train "Red commanders"; ex-NCO's and even privates were hurried through crash courses and sent to the front to command battalions. Still, there were never enough of them. At the end of 1918 two-thirds of the officers had received their training in the old army, and even at the end of the Civil War their percentage did not fall below 50.[18] Even these figures understate the significance of the contribution of the well-trained officers, since the higher posts, where the crucial strategic decisions were made, were almost entirely filled by them. Without their expertise the Red Army could never have defeated the enemy.

Very few officers volunteered; most of them had to be forced into service by threats of punishment. Under these circumstances the Bolsheviks had cause to fear treason. Indeed, many officers defected to the enemy at the first opportunity. Trotskii tried to reduce the danger by providing good working conditions for those who served loyally, by punishing the guilty mercilessly, and by introducing the new position of political commissar. At the time when commissars first appeared in the Russian army, during the tenure of the Provisional Government, they were assigned only to large army units, such as fronts and armies. After November 1917 the commissars received new duties and were sent to every military unit down to the company level. They had two main functions: to supervise the work of military specialists, and to organize propaganda among the soldiers. In the first stages of the Civil War the political commissars signed the operational orders of commanders and thereby established a system of dual command. In the beginning of 1919 Trotskii did away with this system and absolved the commissars from direct responsibility for purely strategic decisions. The new arrangement led to duplications and misunderstandings. How was the commissar to prevent treason if he could not interfere in military decisions? Yet these men, most of them simple workers and peasants, played a crucial role in winning the Civil War. Their relentless agitation against "White guard restorationists" and "counterrevolutionaries" did in fact raise the morale of the troops.

Trotskii's military policies, and above all his employment of tsarist officers, bitterly divided the Bolshevik leadership. Some objected to the reconstruction of an organized and disciplined army on libertarian grounds. Others found it galling that the same people against whom the Revolution was fought were now once again placed in positions of power and responsibility. Lenin supported Trotskii and so the Commissar of War prevailed, but Lenin himself remained aloof from the day-to-day struggle. The employment of tsarist officers was Trotskii's policy, and it was he who had to bear the brunt of responsibility.[19] I. V. Stalin, who in the summer of 1918 became political commissar of the Southern front, perhaps out of a dislike of the Commissar of War, protected those who resisted discipline and disapproved of the employment of military specialists. Because of the strength of his opponents, Trotskii did not succeed in introducing his reforms everywhere in the army. Some units, notably in outlying regions, remained infested with the spirit of *partizanshchina*, and their fighting value remained extremely low. The disagreements between Trotskii and his opponents were manifested on a large variety of issues, both organizational and strategic, and the dissension within Bolshevik ranks significantly weakened the Red Army.

Aside from a shortage of skilled and reliable officers, the Red Army suffered from lack of supplies and munitions. In the first period of the Civil War the situation was not unfavorable. The army was still relatively small and the stores of the defunct Imperial army were rich. But the army grew and the supplies gradually became depleted. By contrast, the Whites began to receive valuable help from abroad. In the summer of 1919, the time of the crucial battles, the supply situation was becoming critical.

Under the circumstances the survival of the regime depended on its ability to organize the economic life of the country well enough to supply the army with essentials. The Bolsheviks held the main centers of the Russian munitions industry: Tula, Moscow, Petrograd, and Tsaritsyn, but the raw material producing districts in the Ukraine and especially in the Donets basin were occupied by the enemy. It required a major organizational feat to supply the army. The Bolsheviks, by concentrating their energies on this vital task, succeeded. Between April and December 1919 the munitions fac-

tories produced a monthly average of 28.7 million bullets. Tula, perhaps the most important center in the country, increased monthly
production from 16,000 rifles in April to 27,000 in December and
during the same period machine gun production rose from 325 to
4562.[20] In spite of these great exertions, the Whites, with aid from
the Allies, were usually better supplied than the Reds in 1919.

The Red Army also suffered from a lack of professional organization, at least during the first months of its existence. In September
1918 the Bolsheviks took an important step toward remedying the
situation. Trotskii became the chairman of the newly formed Supreme Military Soviet, which had responsibility for the conduct of
the war. At the same time I. I. Vatsetis, an ex-colonel of the Imperial
army, became Commander-in-Chief of all armed forces of the republic. On the example of the tsarist army, the Red forces were
organized into "fronts" and "armies." The ex-imperial officer General P. P. Sytin took command of the Southern front, which included the Eighth, Ninth, Tenth, Eleventh, and Twelfth armies.
The Eighth, Ninth, and Tenth armies fought on the Don against
the Ataman Krasnov, while the Eleventh and Twelfth in the Northern Caucasus faced Denikin's forces.[21] Because of the problems of
communications and logistics, the subordination of the Eleventh
and Twelfth armies to the command of the Southern front was only
theoretical. In fact, these two armies formed a separate front and
the actions of the Reds against Krasnov and Denikin were poorly
coordinated.

Without Trotskii's reforms the Red Army could not have survived the difficult year of 1919. In January the ring around Soviet-
held Russia was almost entirely closed. The Allies had troops in
Murmansk and Archangel; the Finnish army of Mannerheim was
bitterly hostile to the Bolsheviks; the newly established Baltic states
were becoming bases for interventionists and anti-Bolsheviks; Pilsudski's Poland was only waiting for a favorable moment to attack
and tied down a large number of Red troops; the French had landed
in Odessa and in the Crimea and were threatening to overrun the
Ukraine; and in Siberia Admiral Kolchak was gathering strength.
The South was the birthplace of the anti-Bolshevik movement.
Here, Ataman Krasnov's Don Cossack Army was a major force.
The Volunteer Army was still engaged in the Northern Caucasus,

but the Bolsheviks had reason to fear its potential growth and power. The Bolsheviks could field only 380,000 men against all their enemies. The bulk of the Red Army was in the South: 47,000 in the Ukraine, 117,000 on the Don, and 35,000 in the Caucasus. Some 85,000 fought Kolchak, and the rest were tied down in the West.[22] Trotskii's strategic plans envisaged a quick occupation of the Ukraine, because he feared that the Ukrainian nationalists with the aid of the French might become a great danger. Lenin, on the other hand, first wanted to destroy the Don army in order to prevent a junction of eastern and southern counterrevolutionaries.[23] The resulting compromise satisfied no one. The High Command sent reinforcements to the Don front, but not enough to gain a decisive victory. In the Ukraine, the Red Army achieved major successes and came into possession of the entire territory, but in the east and in the south the Whites were gaining strength and becoming increasingly dangerous.

CHAPTER 2
The Army

In South Russia the anti-Bolshevik movement was largely in the hands of generals. Understandably, they saw their tasks in military terms; their dream was to lead a victorious army into Moscow. Most of them were able men in their chosen profession. They succeeded in building an army which in spite of its small size was an impressive force, and often they provided imaginative and inspired leadership. Yet the dream eluded them.

In the first stages of the Civil War the opposing armies differed profoundly. The Bolsheviks had a relatively large number of men under arms, but their forces were poorly led and their soldiers were put to flight at the least sign of resistance. The Volunteer Army, by contrast, was a small band of officers whose heroism was born out of desperation. As the war progressed, the differences gradually diminished. The Bolsheviks succeeded in imposing some discipline on their men, and under the circumstances the only way the Volunteer Army could avoid certain destruction was to build a massive army. For this, there was a price to pay: as the army grew larger, its remarkable discipline, cohesion, and will to win gradually declined.

The first step in this transformation took place in March 1918, when a group of Kuban Cossacks joined a small unit of officers. At this moment the White cause acquired the services of able and experienced fighters, but at the same time the seeds of future bitter disagreements were sown, because the political ideals and background of the Cossacks differed greatly from those of the officers.

The next important event in remaking the army was the introduction of conscription. Even during the first months of its existence
the Army occasionally forced Cossacks and officers to join its ranks,
thereby violating the principle of voluntary service. Then in August
1918 the Army ceased to be voluntary in everything but name.* In
that month Denikin drafted two year groups of peasants (almost
entirely *inogorodnie*)† and ten year groups of Cossacks. Those who
had joined before and were bound only by four-month contracts
now had a choice: they could leave Volunteer-held territory within
seven days, or they could accept service without limitation. Most
of them decided to stay. As a result of conscription by the middle
of September 1918 Denikin had thirty-five to forty thousand soldiers. In the following months the army did not increase in size because the new draftees could barely make up for the enormously
heavy losses suffered during the fighting.

In January 1919 the Volunteer Army united with the army of the
Don Cossacks. The defeat of Germany undermined the Ataman
Krasnov's position. It was a great blow to his prestige that his protectors had been vanquished, but more important, his supplies had
dried up and the withdrawal of the Germans left the western boundaries of the Don Voisko unprotected. The quick deterioration of
the strategic situation brought war weariness to the Cossacks.
Krasnov, who had regarded the Volunteer Army as weaker and
less significant than his own, now could turn to no one but his rival
Denikin for help. Denikin took advantage of his improved position and expected subordination as a price for aid. The Allies, who
had no reason to feel sympathy for the pro-German Ataman, fully

---

*In January 1919 the Volunteer Army was named the Armed Forces of South
Russia. In 1920 General Wrangel adopted the name "Russian Army." The population, however, continued to refer to the White troops as the Volunteer Army,
and therefore I use this term throughout the text.

†*Inogorodnie*, literally means "people from other towns." The term refers to those
peasants who settled on Cossack territories, mostly after the liberation of the serfs
in 1861. These people did not become permanent residents, but had to retain their
passports from their previous districts. The *inogorodnie* did not share in the privileges of the Cossack estate and lived under the constant threat of expulsion. They
were much poorer than the Cossacks, and most of them rented, rather than owned,
land. See P. Kenez, *Civil War in South Russia, 1918*, pp. 38–44.

supported the Volunteer leadership. Krasnov, after some gestures
of futile resistance, gave in, and on January 8, 1919, Denikin assumed the title of Commander-in-Chief of the newly formed Armed
Forces of South Russia. In the long run, the creation of a united
army allowed a more rational use of resources and the White cause
substantially benefited by it; in the immediate future, however,
the strategic situation not only failed to improve but actually deteriorated. Denikin had to assume responsibility for an extended
crumbling front.

The final step in the transformation of the Volunteer Army occurred during the months of its great victories in the summer of
1919. The army grew rapidly: from May to October the number of
soldiers increased from 64,000 to 150,000.[1] As more territory came
under their control, the Whites could draft tens of thousands of
new soldiers, most of them Ukrainian peasants. But drafting was a
double-edged sword. The Army did not possess a powerful enough
administrative machinery to enforce draft laws, and as a result many
of the peasants, who regarded the Whites as restorationists, preferred to flee their villages and join the partisans. Thus while the
introduction of compulsory service increased the size of the Volunteer Army, it also increased the strength of the partisan movement.

Although both sides drafted tens of thousands of peasants, the
differences in social composition did not altogether disappear. Even
in the fall of 1919, when the Volunteer Army reached its maximum
size, between one-half and two-thirds of the fighting men were Cossacks.[2] Their presence was a source of both strength and weakness.

On the positive side, the Cossacks were among Russia's most experienced and skilled soldiers, and many had a burning hatred for
the Bolsheviks who wanted to destroy their beloved way of life. Further, the Cossacks provided the Whites with clear superiority in
cavalry. This was a crucial advantage when front lines were long
and thinly held, communications poor, and intelligence frequently
faulty. Up to the end of 1919 the Whites could defeat much larger
enemy forces through the mobility made possible by the horse. At
the end of July 1919 they had 43,000 horsemen against the enemy's
20,000. In the October battles, White superiority was even greater—
48,000 against 16,000.[3] Finally, with tremendous effort, the Bolsheviks succeeded in catching up, and the decisive victories at the
end of 1919 came when, for the first time, the Red Cavalry was a

match for the Whites. On both sides most of the leaders who acquired military reputations were cavalry commanders—such as
Wrangel, Mamontov, and Shkuro among the Whites, and Budennyi
and Chapaev among the Reds. (The Russian Civil War was the last
European conflict in which cavalry played an important role.)

On the other side, the High Command had constant trouble with
the Cossacks. First, the Cossack units were heterogeneous. Since
the fall of 1918 both the Don and the Kuban Cossacks had drafted
inogorodnie. Many of these peasants regarded the Bolsheviks as their
protectors and the Cossacks as their enemies, and they did not, to
put it mildly, become enthusiastic warriors. Second, not even all
the Cossacks were committed to the White cause. Those coming
from the northern and poorer areas of the Don, especially, often
sympathized with the Reds. The Cossacks constantly quarreled
among themselves, which reduced their fighting value. Third, and
most important, the subordination of Cossack troops to headquarters was incomplete. The Kuban Cossacks did not have an autonomous army, but in many units they made up the majority of fighting
men and their views could not be lightly disregarded. Their agitation for a separate army was a major irritant. The Don army retained
its own military organization. Krasnov and General Denisov, the
Commanders of the Don army, were forced by the Don Cossack
parliament (the *krug*) to resign in February 1919 because the *krug*
expected that the departure of the pro-German leaders would open
the way to increased Allied aid. The new leaders, Ataman Bogaevskii
and General Sidorin, were friends of the Volunteer leadership, but
they retained a great deal of independence. Denikin often had to
negotiate with Sidorin, as if he were leading a coalition rather than
commanding an army. The Don Cossacks fought well when they
were defending their own territory, but when Denikin ordered them
to march north against Moscow, their enthusiasm quickly faded.

Despite these conflicts and other weaknesses, the Volunteer
Army in the first half of 1919 was a remarkably able fighting force—
at least by comparison with its opponent. The army enjoyed three
significant advantages: it had a superior cavalry, it was better led,
and it was better supplied.

It started out as an organization of officers, and even in the later
stages of the struggle it retained a disproportionate number of them.
While the Reds could not find enough men to fill essential positions

of command, among the Whites colonels often commanded mere companies. In fact the Volunteer Army had an embarrassment of riches. The High Command had to reconcile competing claims: some believed that they deserved high appoitments because of their experience in the World War; others based their claims on their previous posts in various anti-Bolshevik armies, such as Skoropadskii's or the ill-fated, German-inspired Southern Army; still others had organized partisan units, which they came to regard as their private property, and when they joined Denikin's forces it was impossible to take their men away from them. There could be no single principle on the basis of which appointments could be distributed, and the principle of seniority, dear to the heart of most professional officers, often had to be disregarded.[4] Although many officers sulked and refused to take positions which they considered demeaning, the small army possessed a great wealth of talent and experience. The history of the Volunteer Army is rich with examples of imaginative and often brilliant leadership.

In 1919 the Whites were also better supplied with munitions than their enemies, but it was otherwise in the first stages of the conflict. In the beginning they could gain supplies only at the expense of their opponents, and their strategy was often determined by the need for capturing munitions stores. In the summer and fall of 1918 Krasnov helped Denikin: he passed on part of the materiel which he had received from the Germans, and also supplied Denikin from the production of the reopened munitions factories of the Don.[5] But in February 1919 supplies from the Allies began to arrive and the army did not suffer again from a shortage of munitions. The Allies, especially the British, were generous. Between February and October 1919 the Volunteers received 280,000 rifles, 4,898 machine guns, 917 cannons, 102 tanks, 194 airplanes, 28 million rounds of ammunition, 112 tractors, and 1,335 automobiles.[6] In addition, the Whites acquired a major portion of the large military stores left by the Russian army on the Rumanian front. Without this aid, the Whites would have had to concentrate all their effort on producing munitions. Their factories never could have supplied the army adequately, and investing all their resources in the munitions industry would have been a major burden.

Western aid gave the Whites superiority in certain types of warfare. Tanks, which began to arrive in the spring of 1919, had a shattering impact on the enemy's morale, and airplanes proved extremely useful in reconnaissance—they enabled commanders to concentrate their forces where they were most needed. Denikin acquired his naval fleet also with the aid of his foreign friends: he claimed the Russian Black Sea Fleet, which at the end of the war came into the possession of the British and the French. His problem was that the Ukraine also wanted these ships, but ultimately the Allies decided in his favor. Two minesweepers which the French gave in January 1919 became the beginning of the White navy. When Denikin's victory seemed likely, the Allies returned most of the Russian ships.[7] During the summer the Whites bombarded Bolshevik-held towns from the sea, and with some British help the White navy aided a rising of officers in Odessa, which enabled Denikin to take this important port on August 23.

Medical supplies which came from abroad were as valuable as military hardware. During the fall of 1918 a typhus epidemic decimated the Red Army—the Eleventh army fighting in the Northern Caucasus, was especially hard hit—and from the Reds the disease spread to the Whites. Although a large number of doctors volunteered their services, without medicine they could accomplish little. In these terrible months almost as many died of typhus as were killed by the enemy. The epidemic took its toll primarily among soldiers, but officers were not immune; General Wrangel himself came down with the disease and was once on the verge of death. Only the arrival of medicine from abroad enabled the doctors to combat the epidemic successfully.[8]

The British sent many instructors to teach the Russians the use of modern weaponry. Their government ordered them not to participate in the fighting, but the temptation often proved too great: although London officially denied it, the instructors drove tanks and flew airplanes for the Whites.[9] The British found the Russians exasperating: they did not oil their guns; they sent guns to the front without teaching the men how to use the expensive machinery properly; they did not calculate, but merely guessed the angle of sight; and they wasted munitions. The easy-going nature of the Russian soldiers and officers appalled the British. Officers took naps instead of working in the afternoon and the soldiers did not take good care of their weapons. Under the circumstances the British attached to the Volunteer Army had little faith in ultimate success.[10] They showed their contempt and preached at their hosts; understandably, the Russians reciprocated with cordial dislike. The life of the interventionist is never an easy one.

The British were most disturbed by the unparalleled corruption which they saw everywhere. The Allies sent not only weapons but also other supplies. The English journalist, John Hodgson, who stayed at Denikin's headquarters for some months, wrote, for example, that London had sent a 200-bed, fully equipped hospital, but that not a single bed had reached its destination. Beds, blankets, sheets, and mattresses all found their way into the houses of staff officers and members of the Kuban government. He reported that while he never saw a nurse in British uniform, he saw many women in the streets wearing skirts and blouses which came with the hospital equipment.[11]

Contemporary observers agreed that there was much more corruption in the White Army than in the Red. Of course there was more to steal; the bounty provided by the Allies was a great temptation indeed. However, greater wealth cannot be the only explanation for greater corruption. The real source of the difference must be sought in the contrasting world views of the two elites. The Bolshevik leadership believed in the possibility of remaking society and man, and was committed to a puritanical outlook. The Whites, on the other hand, regarded the Civil War not as a heroic period in which the foundations of a better society were being laid, but as a nightmare which they had to survive as well as they could. They cared about the outcome of the conflict just as much as their enemies, and certainly hated them as much as they were hated by them. But their hatred allowed for a degree of cynicism which led to corruption.

The weaknesses of the White army existed even in the period of its great victories, but they became all too obvious in a time of defeats. The Volunteer Army was harmed by dissension and insubordination among its commanders and declining morale among its soldiers. The Bolshevik leadership, too, was rent by disagreements over strategy and military organization. But on the Red side, only Trotskii's policies came under fire; Lenin remained above the disputes, his authority unchallenged. It was different in the White camp. Since Denikin designed the main outlines of strategy, it was he who was held accountable for the failures. Denikin never enjoyed such unquestioned authority among his fellow leaders as Lenin did; the White movement was heterogeneous, and the Commander-in-Chief could not impose his will on some of his subordinates without fear of tearing the movement apart. And Denikin himself was at least partly responsible for the disunity. He was a gentle person, and not at all power-hungry. He allowed his subordinates to defy him even when he well understood that such defiance might harm his cause. He tolerated misbehavior on the part of his generals because he wanted to avoid the unpleasantness of removing them. Often he rationalized his own failure to act by underestimating his own power.

Of all the quarrels within the White camp, none harmed the Volunteer Army more than the ever-increasing rivalry between Denikin and Baron P. N. Wrangel. Among the top leaders, Wrangel was one of the few aristocrats. He was a graduate of the Academy of the General Staff, but instead of choosing a staff appointment, as was customary among the graduates, he had preferred to serve in a guard regiment. He was undoubtedly an able man. Although he was only 40 when he joined the anti-Bolshevik army in August 1918, he was already a general with distinguished war service. He was also a charismatic leader. Aside from his intelligence and military abilities, he was helped by his remarkable height and booming voice. At the same time he was boundlessly vain, ambitious, and given to histrionics and intrigues. In spite of his talents he brought far more harm than good to the White movement.

When Wrangel offered his services, Denikin was impressed and gave him an important command post. Wrangel fought well, but even during his first weeks with the army, he distinguished himself by his arrogant behavior. In military councils he constantly demanded reinforcements, a larger share of supplies, and recognition. He could not be convinced that the situation was also critical in other sectors of the front, and that other commanders also had to fight without reinforcements and with inadequate supplies.[12] Many of

his fellow officers were incensed by his behavior and acquired a
lasting dislike for him. His style attracted some and repelled others;
he had loyal followers and bitter enemies, but no one who knew him
felt neutral about him.

It seems that Denikin was somewhat awed by this dashing and
supremely self-confident aristocrat, because he gave him one important command post after another. When Denikin assumed the title
of Commander-in-Chief of the Armed Forces of South Russia in
January 1919, he wanted to assign the most important field command, the leadership of the reorganized Volunteer Army, to his
friend General I. P. Romanovskii. Romanovskii considered the
offer for a day, but decided to remain as chief of staff to Denikin.
Then Denikin's choice fell to Wrangel. This was a curious decision,
since Wrangel was still relatively untried and was by no means close
to the Commander-in-Chief. Some of the senior officers, such as
General Kazanovich, the able veteran of the Ice March, felt so bitter
about the appointment that they resigned in protest.[13]

In time, Wrangel attacked every one of Denikin's major political
and military decisions, his tone becoming increasingly bitter and
abusive. The disputes between the two leaders were soon public
knowledge. The conservatives, monarchists, and guard officers
who disliked many of Denikin's policies rallied around Wrangel.
Denikin tolerated Wrangel's insubordination partly out of weakness, but also partly out of fear that removing the General would
alienate the conservative wing of his movement. He gradually developed an impotent and obsessive hatred for Wrangel which stayed
with him for the rest of his days.

Wrangel's mischievous work undermined confidence in Denikin's
authority and thereby harmed the movement, but other generals
whom Denikin tolerated also brought ill-repute to the anti-Bolsheviks.
Mai-Maevskii was a corrupt drunkard, Slashchev a drug addict,
Pokrovskii a sadist, and Shkuro only little better than a bandit.
Denikin, of course, knew about the wrongdoings of his subordinates
and pleaded with them, but in vain. He did not dare to dismiss them
because he needed capable leaders, and because men like Mai-
Maevskii, Pokrovskii, and Shkuro bought the fierce loyalty of their
soldiers by allowing them to loot. Denikin feared that the troops
simply would not obey new leaders. In the long run, the anti-

Bolshevik movement paid a high price for Denikin's pusillanimity. With the generals setting a bad example, the soldiers could not be expected to resist looting; Denikin issued one ineffectual order after another. Besides, the soldiers were poorly paid and not supplied by headquarters; they were expected to feed themselves at the expense of the population—a primitive supply system which encouraged looting, for it was difficult to distinguish between legitimate requisitioning and robbery. Such behavior not only alienated the peasants but also undermined the morale of the army.[14] On occasion, the mobility of the troops was restricted because the soldiers could not carry their loot. The Cossacks were especially bad in this respect, because for them looting was a matter of tradition, but all units were more or less guilty.

The main reason for the declining morale of the army in the second half of 1919 was that the newly drafted peasants had no desire to fight and did not regard the White cause as their own. The Volunteer leadership did far too little to indoctrinate soldiers; the Whites had no equivalent of the institution of political commissar. The main recruiting agency was the army itself. When the Whites occupied a town, they gave weapons to the newly drafted peasants and in a short time, without ideological or military preparation, sent them into battle. Even the prisoners of war, who were forced to change sides, did not receive any ideological retraining.[15] Only a few Orthodox priests who accompained the soldiers attempted to put the struggle into a wider ideological framework. The generals ignored indoctrination because they continued to think in conventional military terms. They hated the Bolsheviks and naively assumed that everyone shared their attitude. It was alien to their tradition and mentality to explain to the soldiers the purpose of the war and the reasons for fighting.

WINTER AND SPRING CAMPAIGNS

During 1918 Denikin pursued a cautious strategy. He was determined to avoid encountering the main forces of the Red Army prematurely and attributed primary importance to securing his rear. On the basis of these considerations, in May 1918 he rejected Krasnov's suggestion of attacking Tsaritsyn and instead decided to establish a secure base for his army on the Kuban. Even after the success of the second Kuban campaign, the Volunteer Army did not march north, but embarked on clearing the entire Northern Caucasus of Bolsheviks.

The task took several months. The local Bolsheviks had numerically superior forces, but in this outlying region, which had poor communications with the rest of Soviet Russia, Trotskii's reforms had not been introduced. Communist political organizations barely functioned and the army of the Northern Caucasus, which in October 1918 became the Eleventh army, suffered the worst manifestations of chaos. In an exhausting 28-day battle for Stavropol in October and November, the Reds were defeated.

The Bolsheviks were more successful in the nearby Terek. In November the Twelfth Red army defeated the Cossacks who fought independently of the Volunteer Army. This victory raised the morale of the Bolsheviks, strengthened their hold on the Caspian, and enabled them to transfer some units from the Twelfth to the Eleventh army.

In the first half of December, approximately three-fourths of the Volunteer Army was deployed in the Northern Caucasus. The front line stretched from Vladikavkaz in the south to the Manych River in the north. In the mineral water district, around Vladikavkaz, General Liakhov had ten thousand soldiers; in the center of the front, two Volunteer corps under Generals Wrangel and Kazanovich had thirteen thousand; in the north, General Stankevich with two to three thousand men protected communications with the Don Cossacks. Even at this time, the Eleventh Red army had great numerical superiority. Against the 25 thousand Whites, they had over 70 thousand men. However, their army was overextended and rapidly falling apart.[16]

Denikin deployed the rest of his troops outside the main battle area. General Mai-Maevskii with three thousand men went to reinforce the crumbling Don front in the strategically important Donets basin in the district of Iuzovka. General de Bode commanded two thousand soldiers in the Crimea. The Whites hoped to attract many recruits in the peninsula, and de Bode's force was regarded as the nucleus of a much larger army. Meanwhile the Volunteers defended the Perekop isthmus and protected the bases of a future

Black Sea Fleet. Because of the strained relations with Georgia, the Whites found it necessary to station three thousand men at Tuapse. Denikin feared that the Georgian army might march north on the Black Sea coast and occupy Novorossisk, which was to be his main point of contact with the Allies.

The Commander of the Eleventh Red army, V. Kruze, hoped to reverse the slow disintegration of his force by carrying out a major offensive. He decided to strike between the right wing and center of the White front, between the troops commanded by Liakhov and Wrangel. The attack started on January 2 against Batalpashinsk. Since the offensive was poorly planned and executed and the Reds lacked sufficient reserves they could not follow up their initial successes. General Wrangel counterattacked and on January 6, in a crucial battle, he took the town of Blagodarnye. The best Bolshevik unit, the famous Taman army, attempted to recapture Blagodarnye twice, but failed. From this point on, the disintegration of the Eleventh army was remarkably rapid.

The main cause of the quick collapse of this numerically still impressive Red army was the supply problem. The rich Kuban and Stavropol provinces provided adequate food for the Volunteer Army, but the Reds allowed themselves to be pushed into the barren desert near the Caspian Sea. They lacked both food and water. Their supplies came from a distance of four hundred miles on a route which was impossible to protect. In these circumstances, the loss of a few important battles led to panic: the army broke into two groups which retreated in disorder while being continuously pursued by the enemy. The raging typhus epidemics greatly contributed to the misery of the soldiers; during the winter of 1918-1919 fifty thousand men became ill. The sick, the hungry, and the demoralized gave themselves up by the tens of thousands. The Whites captured large stores of weapons and the Eleventh army ceased to exist.[17]

The defeat had far-reaching strategic consequences. The Twelfth army had to give up the fruits of its victories and withdraw from the Terek toward Astrakhan, because it was in danger of being cut off from its source of supplies. Finally the Volunteer Army achieved its goal and possessed a secure rear. The collapse of the Bolshevik Northern Caucasian front enabled the Whites to move north. From a local force the Volunteer Army was quickly transformed into the most dangerous threat to Bolshevik rule in the course of the Civil War. For the Don Cossacks, Denikin's victory came just in time; at the end of January their front was on the verge of collapse and they needed help desperately. For while in the summer and fall of 1918 Ataman Krasnov's Cossacks had fought well and managed to liberate the Don Voisko, by the end of the year the tide had turned. The Don troops lost their social homogeneity when Krasnov began to draft *inogorodnie*, who were unwilling fighters. Even the Cossacks grew tired of the war; they had no desire to go beyond their native territory. When the Germans withdrew from the Ukraine, they exposed the left flank of the Don front and Krasnov had to spread his troops very thinly. And while the Cossacks suffered from declining morale, the number of Red soldiers increased and their fighting ability improved. Trotskii's reorganization slowly began to take effect on the Southern front. The Bolshevik High Command attributed great significance to the defeat of Krasnov and sent reinforcements from other fronts, especially from Siberia.

The crucial battles took place in January 1919. At this time the fifty-thousand-strong Cossack army held a long front from the Donets basin to Tsaritsyn. Krasnov concentrated his strength at two points, moving on Voronezh in the north and fighting for Tsaritsyn in the east.[18] The Bolshevik forces consisted of the group of Kozhevnikov, the future Thirteenth army, which had twenty thousand men and fought in the Donets basin; the main forces, the Eighth and Ninth army, had fifty thousand infantry and 5,500 cavalry and held the front from Balashov to Voronezh; and the Tenth army of thirty thousand infantry and eight thousand cavalry defended Tsaritsyn. Thus the Reds had a better than two-to-one superiority. General Slaven, the front commander who took Sytin's place, developed his strategy in January. He ordered Kozhevnikov to move southeast and surround the main Cossack forces which were fighting in the north. Slaven planned to destroy the Whites at Tsaritsyn only after the operation in the north was concluded. He assumed that the Volunteer Army would continue to be tied down in the Northern Caucasus by the Eleventh army.[19]

In the following weeks the Reds achieved major successes, occupying large territories and reducing the size of the enemy army, yet they could not entirely realize their strategic plan.

The Red army was greatly helped by a series of anti-White risings which took place in the northern districts of the Voisko, the area of the heaviest fighting. In this poorest section of the Don, the Bolsheviks carried out intensive propaganda. They convinced the poor Cossacks that Bolshevik rule was directed only against the rich, the capitalists, and the officers, and that the simple Cossacks had nothing to fear. Another main theme of Red propaganda was that the Allies were not going to give substantial help.[20] The dissaffection also infected the army. On January 31 for example, five regiments of the Fifteenth division in *stanitsa** Alekseevskaia decided to change sides.[21] Under these circumstances, the Bolsheviks were able to successfully push the front southward.

In spite of defeats in the district of Voronezh, White successes at the eastern and western ends of the front prevented catastrophe. In the Donets, General Mai-Maevskii engaged the numerically vastly superior forces of Kozhevnikov, preventing the planned encirclement of half of Krasnov's army. Second, the Cossacks at Tsaritsyn fought well and in the middle of January once again surrounded the city. General Gittis, the new Red commander of the Southern front, the third in five months, had to withdraw troops from the north in order to strengthen the Tenth army. However, by the beginning of February the position of the Cossacks was critical. Neither in the Donets nor at Tsaritsyn could the Whites hold up for long the much stronger enemy. As a result of heavy losses and defections, the size of the Don army was greatly reduced. The once-mighty army numbered only fifteen thousand men.[22]

In the beginning of February, at the time when Ataman Krasnov left his post, Denikin was ready to come to the aid of the Don Cossacks. First he had to make a strategic decision: should he send his strongest forces to the right wing of the Don front in the hope of capturing Tsaritsyn and later establishing contact with the Siberian Whites under Admiral Kolchak; or should he strengthen the left wing and thereby defend the Donets, a strategically and economically important region?

Denikin's first intention was to move on Tsaritsyn. He planned an attack on Astrakhan which would cut off the Reds from the Cas-

---

**Stanitsa:* a large Cossack village.

pian Sea before taking Tsaritsyn. His staff had already drawn up
operational plans when Denikin changed his mind.[23] The advance
of the enemy in the West frightened him. It seemed that without
substantial reinforcements there, Mai-Maevskii could not hold back
the Bolsheviks, who would then threaten Rostov and might occupy
the entire Don district. Denikin, as always, was determined to defend Cossack territory. In the middle of February the best units of
the Volunteer Army, including the troops of Shkuro and Pokrovskii,
were sent to the aid of the greatly pressured Mai-Maevskii.

   General Wrangel bitterly criticized Denikin's decision. He was
willing to accept not only the loss of the Donets basin, but of the
entire Don Voisko because he believed strongly that no goal could
be more important than meeting Kolchak's advance somewhere
along the Volga river.[24] Wrangel, most unfairly, even charged Denikin with not wanting to unite with Kolchak because of a desire to
be first in Moscow.

   The disagreement over strategy between Wrangel and Denikin
was caused by their different evaluations of two factors, the importance of unification with Kolchak and the importance of retaining
the Cossack districts as the primary base for the Volunteer Army.
One of the weaknesses of the anti-Bolshevik movement was that
it grew up in the peripheries of the country and its different strands
could never be properly brought together. Contacts between the
South and Siberia were tenuous and it took so long for messages to
reach their destination that it was pointless to send strategic information. Much of the communication between the two White leaders
took place in Paris, where both had representatives.

   Denikin, as a man trained in conventional military thinking, well
understood the importance of joining forces with Kolchak. However, he was unwilling to disregard all other considerations. In the
perspective of time, it is clear that he was right. The establishment
of physical contact would not have meant successful coordination.
Both Denikin and Kolchak had difficulty keeping their own forces
together and compelling subordinates to carry out orders, and there
is no reason to believe that a physical link-up on the Volga would
have changed the course of the Civil War. Siberian counterrevolution had its own dynamics; Kolchak could not have postponed his
offensive until the fall, and Denikin with his small army was not

yet ready to embark on the decisive campaign. It is interesting that Bolshevik strategists, just like Wrangel, were mesmerized by the possibility of a link-up between their two enemies. They were determined to prevent it and sent their best troops to the East. This decision allowed Denikin to occupy the entire Donets basin and cause enormous harm to the Soviet republic.[25]

But the most important difference between Wrangel and Denikin was in their attitudes toward the Cossacks. Denikin, who participated in the organization of the Volunteer Army on the Don and then was one of those who led it to the Kuban, could not imagine the survival of his army outside of the Cossack *voiska*. He believed that the arrival of the volunteers would rekindle the fighting enthusiasm of the Don Cossacks and soon their army would start to grow again into a powerful force. At the same time he was pessimistic about the possibility of receiving support from the Russian peasants. Therefore he feared that a march northeast would be suicidal. He also felt duty-bound to defend Cossack territories; whatever the strategic considerations, he would not abandon his Cossack allies. Such arguments did not move Wrangel. He did not accept the idea that there was an unbreakable bond between the anti-Bolshevik movement and the cause of the Cossacks. Denikin's decision did not finally resolve the issue. Wrangel continued for months, in an increasingly strident tone, to demand the strengthening of the right wing at the expense of all other considerations.[26]

In the middle of March the Bolsheviks still had a crushing numerical superiority on the Southern front, approximately 130 thousand men against Denikin's forty-five thousand.[27] Near Tsaritsyn the Bolshevik Tenth army under Egorov had twenty-three thousand men. The Reds went on the offensive and advanced along the Tsaritsyn-Velikokniazheskaia railroad line. They were resisted by Mamontov's five to six thousand soldiers, who took up a defensive position in the marshy area between the two tributaries of the Don, the Manych and the Sal'. General Kutepov's ten thousand soldiers south of the Manych river served as a reserve force.[28]

At the center of the front, the Don Cossack army of General Sidorin, twelve to thirteen thousand strong, faced the Eighth and Ninth Red armies with a combined strength of fifty-five thousand. Further to the West in the Donets basin, the best units of the Whites fought under General Mai-Maevskii. His twelve thousand men engaged the newly formed twenty to twenty-five thousand strong Thirteenth Red army under Kozhevnikov. The strategic situation of the Whites in the Donets basin was complicated by the strength of the Ukrainian Bolsheviks on the northern shores of the Black Sea. The second Ukrainian army, which included the partisan fighters of Makhno and other anarchist bands, was later renamed the Fourteenth Red army and was also used against Denikin.[29] (See Map 1.)

In the battles of March and April the fighting at the two flanks was critical while the center sector was relatively quiet. The Bolsheviks were determined to occupy the entire Donets basin. To achieve this goal they sent reinforcements from Moscow and planned to regroup the Southern front in order to strengthen their right flank. The Bolsheviks failed and after two months of heavy fighting the battle line remained more or less stationary. They did not succeed because the Ukrainian partisans who made up the Thirteenth and Fourteenth armies proved unequal to the best units of the White army. They were further handicapped by the spring floods, which made maneuvering difficult. They did not succeed in bringing reinforcements from the Eighth army, because the Whites fighting at the center of the front engaged and tied down the Red units. But most important, they failed because of the remarkable performance of Mai-Maevskii and his soldiers.

V. Z. Mai-Maevskii was a complex figure. He lived a dissolute life and his orgies brought ill-repute to the cause which he served. In territories under his control, terror and lawlessness reigned. His soldiers called him Kutuzov, not because of his style of leadership, but because of his appearance: he was fat and flabby and wore a pince-nez. He did not àt all look like a soldier.[30] Nevertheless, he was one of the ablest White military leaders. Although he was trained as a career officer, he was not bound by conventional military thinking, but knew how to use the special conditions of the Civil War. He planned his strategy to take advantage of an important asset, the well-developed railroad network on the Donets Basin. He concentrated his troops not on the front line but at major railroad junctions, and sent reinforcements with great speed to the sector where they were most needed. On one occasion, one unit fought at three different places in the course of a single day. Such mobility

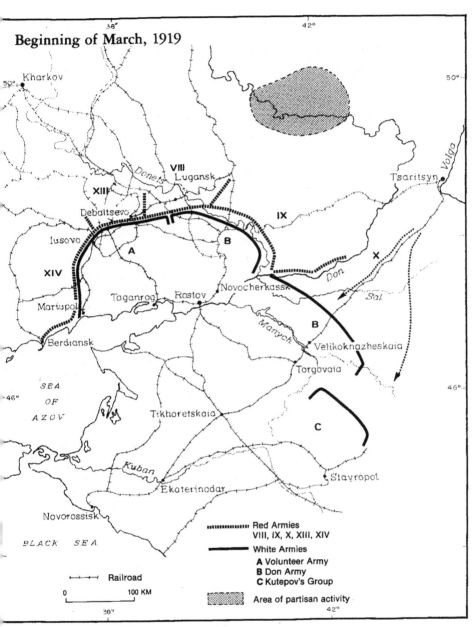

Beginning of March, 1919

MAP 1

confused the enemy. Mai-Maevskii was also among the first Russians who knew how to use airplanes; British and Russian pilots flew reconnaissance missions which enabled him to send his troops where they were the most needed.

An important element in Mai-Maevskii's success was that his soldiers idolized him. He had great physical courage. He appeared almost every day on the front, usually at the most critical sectors, and inspired his troops. The fact that he allowed his soldiers to loot may have also added to his popularity.[31]

While the front remained stable in the Western and central sectors, the situation in the east deteriorated. The Tenth Red army, in spite of the lack of supplies and munitions, carried out an extremely difficult march and succeeded in crossing the Manych river. This Bolshevik advance threatened to cut the White forces in two, separating the Don from the Kuban. Had the Bolsheviks succeeded they might have destroyed the Southern anti-Bolshevik movement.

Denikin desperately tried to save the situation. He sent all available reserves to the Manych front and quickly built up a sizable cavalry force. He wanted Wrangel to command it, but Wrangel stipulated conditions which Denikin could not accept. He wanted so many reinforcements from the Donets front that Mai-Maevskii's earlier successes would have been immediately nullified. On May 1 Denikin himself assumed command, and within a few days he managed to stabilize the front. The soldiers of the poorly equipped Tenth Red army were tired of uninterrupted fighting, and the Red command, with no reserves, had to allow Denikin to extricate his forces from a difficult situation.[32]

THE MOSCOW DIRECTIVE

At the end of May, military fortunes turned. In March and April the Volunteer Army had been on the defensive; time and again it seemed that the Reds would break through, but the Whites by determination and a skillful deployment of their forces managed to avert disaster. Then, rather suddenly, they started to advance on all fronts.

Denikin did not bring about the change himself, but was taking advantage of new opportunities. Developments outside his control had profoundly weakened the Red's Southern front. In April the

Bolshevik position in the East became increasingly critical. Kolchak captured Ufa and threatened Orenburg, Kazan, and even Samara. From Moscow's perspective, Siberian counterrevolution led by an army over a hundred thousand strong seemed the most dangerous enemy at the moment. The Military Revolutionary Committee concentrated its attention on the East and sent reinforcements and scarce supplies there. Although Kolchak's advance was checked by the end of April, the White enemy remained formidable.

At the same time the Soviet position greatly deteriorated in the Ukraine. In the beginning of May, the bandit-anarchist chieftain, Ataman Grigorev, a temporary ally of the Bolsheviks, defected. Anarchy engulfed the countryside.[33] The Ukraine, which had been a source of soldiers and supply for the anti-Denikin front, now became soft and vulnerable, ready for the new conqueror, Denikin.

The Bolshevik Southern front suffered two other heavy blows. At the end of April, General N. D. Vsevolodov, the commander of the Ninth army, after sabotaging orders, defected to the Whites.[34] More important, in the same month, not far beyond the front line, the Cossacks in the northern areas of the Don Voisko rose against the Bolsheviks. Remarkably, this was the same area in which the Cossacks a short time before had rebelled against Ataman Krasnov. The violence of Bolshevik rule and especially the persecution of the Church temporarily united all the Cossacks, rich and poor alike. The rising soon reached major proportions. Within a few weeks in the district of Beshenskaia, the insurgents had twenty-five to thirty thousand soldiers.[35] At first they were poorly supplied, but later airplanes from the Volunteer Army succeeded in bringing them essentials. The rising caused enormous harm to the Red Army: the Cossacks looted and blew up supply bases, harassed their rear, and interrupted communications. The Bolshevik used units from the Ninth army to put down the rebellion, but fighting against the insurgents greatly undermined the morale of the soldiers. On one occasion an entire regiment changed sides.[36]

In view of the changed military situation, Denikin once again reorganized his forces. The Caucasian Volunteer Army bore its name only for historical reasons; it was now fighting in the Donets basin. Denikin renamed it Volunteer Army and entrusted it to General Mai-Maevskii. Although the Commander-in-Chief was disturbed and even disgusted by Mai-Maevskii's escapades and

orgies, his brilliant performance in the previous months made him
the obvious candidate for this important post. Mai-Maevskii's army
included some of the best units and a large share of veterans from
the difficult campaigns of 1918.

General Sidorin commanded the Don army, which, after a period
of decline, had started to grow again in size. The Cossacks fought
on a long front, tying down a large number of enemy forces.

The third major unit of the Armed Forces of South Russia became the troops fighting between the Manych and Sal'. This was
the army which Denikin hastily organized to stop the advance of
the Reds. A large majority of it was made up of Kuban Cossacks,
who were experienced cavalrymen. Denikin named it the Caucasian
Army and gave its command to General Wrangel. It is remarkable
that Denikin chose a general who had bitterly attacked him, who
had declined to accept an assignment when the situation on the front
was critical, and who increasingly appeared as a rival for supreme
leadership. Denikin simply believed that among the available commanders Wrangel was the most able cavalry leader.[37]

The Caucasian army soon achieved a major victory. In a great
battle for Veliko-knaizheskaia between May 19 and 22, Wrangel
defeated the Tenth army, taking fifteen thousand prisoners. In the
following weeks the Whites continued their advance in spite of the
efforts of the retreating Bolsheviks, who blew up railroad lines and
bridges and repeatedly brought in reinforcements from Astrakhan.
Wrangel skillfully used airplanes, trains, and tanks which he had
recently received. Fresh troops brought about the fall of Tsaritsyn
on July 1. The capture of this strategically important city was one
of the greatest White victories in the Civil War; it yielded them large
quantities of military supplies, including locomotives, armed trains,
machine guns, and forty thousand prisoners, in addition to the city's
munitions factories.[38]

The Don army also advanced rapidly. In June the Cossacks established contact with the insurgents, and soon after the entire
Voisko was freed. At the end of the month Sidorin advanced victoriously toward the Voronezh. Between May 23 and June 28 the
size of the army increased from fifteen thousand to forty thousand,
and for the first time in the Civil War the Cossacks faced a numerically weaker enemy.[39]

But perhaps Denikin had his most spectacular successes in the West. There the Red army became infected by the anarchy prevailing in the Ukraine. The famous anarchist leader, Makhno, who protected the extreme right wing of the Bolshevik front, was put to flight quickly. However skillful he was as a guerrilla leader, he did not perform well in a conventional battle against a well-organized army. When the Whites broke through the front held by the anarchists, the Thirteenth Red Army was endangered and had to retreat. The Bolsheviks tried to stop the enemy advance by reorganizing their forces, but it did not help. Mai-Maevskii took Kharkov, a major industrial center, on June 25 and five days later he took Ekaterinoslav. The Reds had to retreat from the Crimean peninsula to avoid being cut off.

On July 3, on the occasion of a celebration over the capture of Tsaritsyn, Denikin issued his famous Moscow directive:

In order to gain our final goal, the capture of the heart of Russia, Moscow, I order:

1. General Wrangel to advance to the Saratov-Rtishchevo-Balashov front and replace in these sectors the Don units and continue to advance toward Penza, Ruzaevka, Arzamas, and further, toward Nizhnii-Novgorod, Vladimir and Moscow. To dispatch units immediately in order to establish contact with the Ural army and to clear the lower Volga.

2. General Sidorin, until the arrival of General Wrangel's troops, with his right wing to continue to fulfill his previous tasks and advance to the Kamyshin-Balashov front. The remaining units to develop a blow on Moscow in the directions (a) Voronezh, Kozlov, Riasan, (b) N. Oskol, Elets, Kashira.

3. General Mai-Maevskii to attack Moscow in the direction of Kursk, Orel, Tula. In order to protect himself from the West, to advance to the line of the Dnepr and Desna, take Kiev and other places of crossing (on the Dnepr) between Ekaterinoslav and Briansk.

4. General Dobrovol'skii to advance by the Dnepr from Aleksandrovsk to the estuary, in order to take Kherson and Nikolaev. . . .

6. The Black Sea fleet to cooperate in carrying out military tasks . . . and blockade the port of Odessa.[40] [See Map 2.]

The strategic idea of the directive was simple. Up to this time the Whites had advanced East and West in a fan-like movement, but

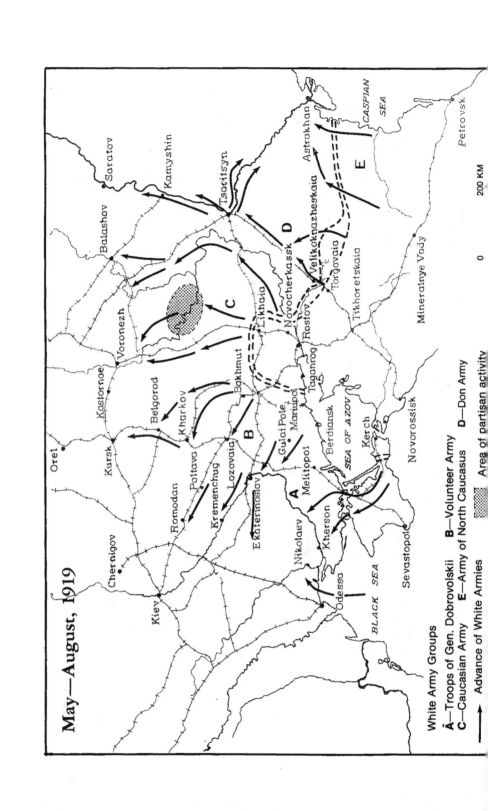

May—August, 1919

White Army Groups

A—Troops of Gen. Dobrovolskii   B—Volunteer Army
C—Caucasian Army   E—Army of North Caucasus   D—Don Army

➞ Advance of White Armies   ▨ Area of partisan activity

0   200 KM

A
B
C
D
E

CASPIAN SEA
BLACK SEA
SEA OF AZOV

Orel
Kiev
Chernigov
Kursk
Kostornoe
Belgorod
Kharkov
Voronezh
Romodan
Poltava
Kremenchug
Lozovaia
Bakhmut
E Katerinoslav
Gulai Pole
Mariupol
Melitopol
Nikolaev
Kherson
Odessa
Sevastopol
Kerch
Novorossisk
Berdiansk
Taganrog
Rostov
Novocherkassk
Likhaia
Velikoknazheskaia
Torgovaia
Tikhoretskaia
Mineralnye Vody
Petrovsk
Astrakhan
Tsaritsyn
Kamyshin
Saratov
Balashov

now, Denikin envisaged, his armies would converge on Moscow. Denikin, who in 1918 resisted all pressure and refused to face the main forces of the enemy while his rear was not properly protected, was now carried away by the prevailing optimism and planned to take Moscow in one enormous jump.

Historians and contemporaries have frequently criticized Denikin's strategy. Wrangel, the bitterest critic, called the Moscow Directive the "death sentence of the armies of South Russia."[41] He condemned the idea of issuing the order altogether, but more specifically he made two points in his criticism. He argued that the Commander-in-Chief should have chosen a primary direction of attack and should not have divided his forces. Of course Denikin did choose a primary direction, which was Kursk and Voronezh, the shortest route to Moscow. Perhaps what Wrangel had in mind was that Denikin should have chosen the direction which he had recommended and where his troops fought, the Volga. Since by this time the armies of Kolchak were retreating and therefore there could be no uniting of fronts, there was no reason whatever to prefer the eastern approach to Moscow. Nor could it be said that the plan called for an unnecessary division of forces. Denikin obviously had to protect his flanks. It was Wrangel who constantly demanded reinforcements and thereby contributed to the weakening of the central sector.

Wrangel had a better case when he attacked the Commander-in-Chief for excessive optimism. In his numerous memoranda to headquarters Wrangel suggested a temporarily defensive posture. He wanted the army to defend the Ekaterinoslav-Tsaritsyn line and take advantage of the Dnepr and Volga for the defense of the flanks. The only offensive operation he envisaged was taking Astrakhan, a thorn in the side of the Whites.[42] He believed that the soldiers were tired after months of uninterrupted fighting. He saw the disorganization of the rear and wanted to use the relative quiet on the front to impose discipline.

Would the position of the Volunteer Army have improved by postponing the great offensive? The soldiers certainly would have welcomed a rest, and undoubtedly the newly created units needed organization and the draftees more training before going into battle. Yet time was on the side of the enemy. In the summer of 1919 Kolchak still tied down a large number of Red troops, but sooner or later these were bound to appear on the Southern front. The Bolsheviks had immensely larger reserves to draw on. Also, waiting might have destroyed the momentum of victory, a feeling of optimism, which was essential for a numerically inferior army.

The Moscow directive was a gamble, one which was ultimately lost. Yet, no time in the Civil War would have been more favorable for undertaking such a gamble. By capturing enormous territories Denikin could draft thousands of peasants into his army. It is true that these new soldiers would not fight well, but the only hope of winning the Civil War lay in the creation of a mass army; had Denikin not tried to create such an army he would have conceded defeat. In short, Denikin's strategy was certainly not faultless, or very imaginative, yet we must look elsewhere for the causes of the ultimate failure of the White movement.

The great defeats forced the Bolsheviks to pay closer attention to the Southern front. Since Kolchak was already in retreat, they began to transfer some of their troops there from the East. Trotskii now spent most of his time in the South. He fired incompetent commanders and made renewed attempts to impose discipline on the Ukrainian forces, the weakest units in his army. It took time for the reforms to bring results however, and for weeks the momentum of White victories continued. One important reason for the Bolshevik's failure was their poor strategy.

The question of how best to defeat Denikin's forces gave rise to the bitterest dispute about strategy among the Reds in the course of the Civil War. The issue became entangled with personal alliances and hostilities, which made resolving it on its merits impossible. I. I. Vatsetis, the Commander-in-Chief, supported by Trotskii, planned a main blow through the Donets basin. Vatsetis, however, was removed from his post. The new Commander-in-Chief, S. S. Kamenev, a protegé of Stalin, wanted to make his left wing the strongest. He envisaged the main attack moving through Tsaritsyn, Novocherkassk, and Rostov, hoping to strike at Denikin's base on the Kuban. He argued that it was necessary to entrust the crucial task to the best Red armies, the Ninth and Tenth, rather than to those fighting in the Donets basin, the Thirteenth and Fourteenth, which were the weakest. Also, it was easier to transport troops from the East to the Volga than to the Ukraine. He further maintained that capturing Tsaritsyn would forever eliminate the danger of Kolchak and Denikin uniting.

However, as Trotskii pointed out, whatever the military advantages of the plan, it did not take into consideration the political factor. While in the Donets basin the Red army could expect a favorable reception from the large working class, in the Cossack districts it would encounter serious resistance. It was foolish to drive the Cossacks into the arms of Denikin, for they would fight best in defense of their homes. The enemies of Trotskii prevailed. He offered his resignation as Commissar of War, it was rejected on July 5, and he proceeded to implement a plan with which he disagreed.[43]

In order to carry out Kamenev's plan, the High Command organized two strike forces, the Eighth and Ninth armies under the command of V. I. Shorin, and the Eighth, Thirteenth, and some units from the Fourteenth under V. I. Selivachev. Shorin with his fifty thousand men commenced the main attack in the direction of Tsaritsyn on August 14, and Selivachev with his forty thousand soldiers went on the offensive a day later, hoping to capture Kharkov.[44]

Wrangel, facing the brunt of the enemy attack, was once again put in a difficult situation. The Caucasian army was forced to give up Kamyshin and retreat slowly to the outskirts of Tsaritsyn, where the Whites made a successful stand.[45] After six weeks of heavy fighting Shorin's troops were beaten, remaining capable only of passive defense. The diversionary attack, insufficiently coordinated, also failed. The Don army and units from the Volunteer Army first stopped the troops of Selivachev and then pursued them, capturing a large amount of territory.[46]

At the time the Reds commenced their summer offensive, the Cossack cavalry of K. K. Mamontov was carrying out one of the most remarkable military exploits of the Civil War. With his seven to eight thousand picked Don cavalry, Mamontov broke through the Red front at the junction of the Eighth and Ninth armies and raided the enemy rear. He captured major towns, including Tambov, but moved so quickly that the Bolsheviks could not catch up with him. He caused a great deal of harm: he interrupted communications between front line units and their staffs, blew up bridges, railroad lines, and munition dumps, and dispersed newly drafted

Red units. Perhaps most important, he created panic and undermined morale.[47] However, as Denikin well understood at the time, Mamontov could have accomplished more than a temporary disruption behind the Red front. His Cossacks looted so much that in the second part of his adventure their remarkable mobility slowed down; they could hardly carry their loot. And Mamontov himself was insubordinate. Instead of concentrating on disrupting the rear of the Eighth and Ninth armies, as he was ordered to do, he preferred to capture and then evacuate cities, a task which was both easier and more profitable.[48]

However Mamontov's exploits may have captured the imagination of contemporaries, the really important battles were taking place in the Ukraine and on the Don front. Kamenev's plan obviously failed. The best Bolshevik troops failed in their breakthrough attempt, and on other sectors of the front the Whites advanced at little cost, meeting little resistance. Denikin's advance in the Ukraine was the most spectacular. He took Poltava on July 31, Odessa on August 23, and Kiev on August 31. In the Ukraine Soviet authority crumbled, and the Whites met almost as much resistance from Ukrainian nationalists as from the Bolsheviks. General Bredov, for example, captured Kiev for the Volunteer Army not from the Reds but from the troops of Petliura, who had occupied the city a day before.

In September the White advance continued into the center of the country. On September 20 Kutepov occupied Kursk, and on the 30th Shkuro's cavalry in a surprise move crossed the Don and occupied the large and strategically important city of Voronezh. On October 14 the Whites occupied Orel, a town only 250 miles from Moscow.[49] Denikin was not destined to come any closer to his goal.

CHAPTER 3

Institutions

The Civil War was not decided on the battlefields. Victory ultimately depended on the ability of leaders to create an administrative structure and other institutions necessary for governing. It was easy to make declarations and policy statements in Moscow or Ekaterinodar, but only a reasonably well-functioning organization could carry out the much more difficult task of enforcing decisions, imposing discipline, and reducing chaos.

In order to understand the White movement in South Russia— the ideas which motivated it, the difficulties it encountered, and the causes of its ultimate defeat—we must first study its institutions.

THE HIGH COMMAND

Lenin and the Bolsheviks took the legitimacy of their government for granted. Theoretically, their right to rule derived from the decision of the Congress of Soviets which approved the November coup d'etat. In their mind, however, the revolution needed no justification; they believed that they had acted in the name of the proletariat to establish a classless society for the benefit of all mankind.

For the majority of the army officers, among them the leaders of the Volunteer Army, the issue of legitimacy was much more bothersome. In their eyes the March revolution had destroyed legal continuity, and therefore even the claims of the Provisional Government were murky. The Tsar in his abdication manifesto called on his people to follow the orders of the Provisional Government and thereby enabled the officers to continue to serve without a crisis of conscience until the November coup d'etat destroyed even a semblance of legitimacy. Logically speaking, the officers now had to choose: either advocate a return to the prerevolutionary order and espouse monarchism, or call for a Constituent Assembly. A. I. Denikin, who was ultimately responsible for the policies of the Volunteer Army, saw dangers in each alternative and vacillated.

Two of Denikin's closest advisers, Generals A. S. Lukomskii and A. M. Dragomirov, were monarchists. It is very likely that the great majority of the officers who made up the backbone of the Volunteer Army also wanted a Romanov restoration.[1] In any case, Denikin perceived a constant monarchist pressure from his followers. The more farsighted and moderate monarchist politicians were ready to compromise: for a recognition of the future claim of the Romanov family they promised to support Denikin as the temporary head of the anti-Bolshevik movement. This solution would have enabled the Romanovs to dissociate themselves from the everyday problems of the movement and avoid the loss of prestige from a possible defeat of one army or another, while at the same time improving the chances of eventual restoration. However tempting it may have seemed as a way to protect himself against attacks from the right, Denikin wisely resisted the monarchists. He understood that the explicit aim of restoration would dangerously narrow the social base of his movement, and would therefore be politically suicidal.[2]

Denikin was fortunate in that the most promising candidate of the monarchists, Grand Duke Nikolai Nikolaevich, scrupulously avoided giving even the appearance of encouraging his supporters. He had been the Commander-in-Chief of the Russian armies in the first year of World War I and enjoyed some popularity not only among the officers but even among the peasants, many of whom had served under him. During the war he had acquired a reputation, perhaps ill-founded, for being a champion of the common soldier. In early 1919, on Denikin's instructions, General Lukomskii visited Nikolai Nikolaevich, who lived in the Crimea. The Grand Duke behaved with great tact and promised to act in such a way as not to undermine Denikin's position. A few months later, when the Bolsheviks threatened the peninsula, he left for

Italy on board a British ship. When the military situation improved, Denikin informed him that the Crimea was again safe, but Nikolai Nikolaevich chose not to return.[3]

Although the Volunteer Army under Denikin's leadership was not a monarchist organization, the Commander-in-Chief did not unequivocally support the principle of popular sovereignty. The attitude of the Army's leadership toward the Constituent Assembly underwent subtle but important changes. In the earliest period of the movement, before the results of Russia's only free elections became known, Alekseev, Kornilov, and presumably Denikin were in favor of allowing the people to express their will. As late as February 5, 1918, L. G. Kornilov incautiously advocated reconvening the Assembly, which had just been dispersed by the Bolsheviks. At the same time the politically more sophisticated M. V. Alekseev, talking about the Constituent Assembly, left it purposely vague whether there should be new elections after the defeat of the Bolsheviks. Within a short time the official position of the Army changed. Now the officers maintained that the first Constituent Assembly had been irrevocably destroyed by the Bolsheviks and new elections would have to be held to reflect the current attitudes of the people.[4] This issue became one of the chief points of disagreement between the generals and the socialists, who were well satisfied with the election results. While the necessity of new elections was disputed, the desirability of a Constituent Assembly was taken for granted by officers and socialists alike. In the first half of 1918 every political manifesto of the Volunteer Army restated a commitment to this institution.

The Socialist Revolutionaries had won the elections of November 1917 decisively, and it is understandable that in their plans the reconvened Assembly played a great role. They insisted that the Russian people had clearly expressed its will, and that only the elected deputies had the right to make crucial decisions which would affect the future of the people. In Siberia, where the Social Revolutionaries dominated the anti-Bolshevik movement, the leaders of the Party hoped to convene the dispersed deputies.

The leaders of the Volunteer Army had a visceral dislike for socialists, and consequently for the Assembly, in which they had a majority. Among the officers the idea of *uchredilka* (from *Uchredi-*

tel'noe sobranie), as the Constituent Assembly was contemptuously
called, had always been bitterly unpopular. After Alekseev's death,
both Lukomskii and Dragomirov asked Denikin to change his position and added that they could not any longer fight in an army
whose chief goal was convening a Constituent Assembly.[5] Denikin,
who shared the prevailing anti-socialist prejudice, retreated. The
official stance of the army became increasingly vague. The army
was still fighting to "let the Russian people express its will," but
Denikin now declined to specify how this could be done. In the
fall of 1918 the proclamations of the army mention not a Constituent
Assembly but a "National Assembly," without describing how
such a body would be elected and what the limits of its competence
would be. Talk about "legal continuity" and the "rebirth of the
Russian state" further muddled the issue. Implicitly at least, the
leaders of the Volunteer Army now rejected the notion of universal
suffrage; it is hard to understand how the Russian people could
express its will if the army did not plan to call a Constituent Assembly after its anticipated victory.

Some of Denikin's advisers urged him to create some sort of a
representative organ for the duration of the Civil War regardless
of the ultimate fate of a Constituent or National Assembly. In the
summer of 1918 M. V. Rodzianko, an ex-President of the Duma,
suggested the convocation of an assembly formed by the representatives of all four previous state dumas. He argued that only
these men had the right to speak for the Russian people.[6] In view
of the extremely limited franchise on the basis of which the Third
and Fourth dumas had been elected, it is highly unlikely that the
envisaged organ would have enjoyed wide public support. In any
case, Denikin had no desire to deal with potentially unruly parliaments and without hesitation he rejected Rodzianko's idea.

At the end of 1919 some of the liberal Kadet politicians, notably
N. I. Astrov, recommended to Denikin the formation of an elected
Assembly in which the Cossack territories as well as other occupied provinces would be represented.[7] The advocates of this plan
envisaged that some appointed members could join the assembly,
and that it could play a useful role in the political life of the country by deflecting some of the criticism directed against the Volunteer Army. They argued that this organ could also help to acquaint

the High Command with the views of the people and at the same time explain the policies of the army to the constituents. The planners did not want a legislative assembly which could veto Denikin's policies; they merely suggested an advisory organ. However, even this modest plan never materialized.

The opposition of the officers to the Constituent Assembly and to any other elected organ which might have participated in directing the anti-Bolshevik movement, was at least partially based on their dislike of politics and politicians. Denikin, though a far more sophisticated man than the average officer, was nevertheless deeply influenced by this prevailing ideology and shared the instinctive anti-parliamentarianism of his comrades. He was convinced that during a time of confusion one-man rule was essential for victory, and that any restriction which a popularly elected body might impose on the leader of the army was dangerous. Unfortunately, Denikin and his ideologues, the conservative Kadet politicians, chose to call the concept of one-man rule "dictatorship." What Denikin had in mind had little to do with "dictatorship" as the term has been used since the middle of the twentieth century. It never even occurred to him to transform the life of the people by coercion or to create the means, develop the ideology, and devise the trappings necessary for a modern dictatorship.

The debate over the empty issue of "dictatorship" deeply divided the White camp. Conservative politicians rhapsodized about the virtues of concentrated power, which they contrasted with the despised Provisional Government. They naively believed that the matter of strong authority could be resolved by a proclamation. The socialists and liberals, on the other hand, were unduly disturbed by the word. They wanted the army to set up a directorate, which would decide civilian issues, and assumed that they would be represented in this directorate. Since the socialists did not succeed in mobilizing the people, they had little to offer the military leaders. Under the circumstances, it was naive to expect that the army would hand them a share in power. The real issue which they had to decide was whether or not to support the Volunteer Army; they should have been concerned with substance rather than form, and made their choice on the basis of the actual policy carried out by the army.

It is one of the great ironies of the history of the Civil War that the Bolsheviks, in spite of their democratic ideology, succeeded in establishing a centralized political system, while the Whites, who praised the virtues of one-man rule and strong government, never succeeded in creating one.

Denikin did not long have the opportunity of being considered a "dictator," even in theory. In June 1919 he decided to recognize the authority of the Supreme Ruler Admiral A. V. Kolchak, the leader of the anti-Bolshevik movement in Siberia. Although the act followed long soul-searching and much debate and drew a great deal of favorable comment, it was almost totally without practical significance.

It was evident even to contemporaries that one of the chief weaknesses of the anti-Bolshevik movement was its geographic and political disunity. If all the various factions in distant parts of Russia could have coordinated their plans, the Bolsheviks might have been defeated. In the South, the Volunteer Army followed with great interest what was happening in Siberia, even though information which came to Ekaterinodar was frequently unreliable and out of date. In November 1918 the officers greeted with great enthusiasm the news of Kolchak's assumption of power and the destruction of the Ufa directorate. They assumed that developments in Siberia now would follow a pattern similar to that in the South, and in this expectation they were not disappointed.

Although there were no longer any significant ideological differences between the two anti-Bolshevik centers, the difficulties of communication prevented any coordination of strategy. In their letters Denikin and Kolchak merely exchanged polite phrases and congratulations. Nevertheless, the very first exchange led to some embarrassment. Shortly after his coup, Kolchak informed Denikin about the situation in Siberia. In the temporary absence of Denikin, S. D. Sazonov, the director of foreign relations in Ekaterinodar at the time, responded by recognizing the supreme authority of Kolchak. Sazonov, a man experienced in international relations, meant that the Volunteer Army recognized the authority of the Admiral on areas under his control, rather than implying any subordination of Denikin to Kolchak. But the phrase might have been misunderstood and therefore had to be clarified.[8]

An even more embarrassing incident occurred a few months later. In May 1919 General A. N. Grishin-Almazov traveled from Ekaterinodar to Omsk. He was ambushed by the Bolsheviks, and in order to avoid capture he committed suicide. In his mail pouch the Bolsheviks found a letter from Denikin to Kolchak. In it Denikin discussed the desirability of creating a unified command after the link-up of the fronts and suggested a meeting of the two commanders at Saratov, a town yet to be captured. The Bolsheviks took this letter as an indication of White strategy, and in the following months concentrated great forces in the Saratov area in order to prevent such a meeting.

A worse consequence of Grishin-Almazov's misfortune was the publication of Denikin's letter verbatim in *Pravda*. Denikin, still much affected by the abrupt abandonment of French intervention in South Russia, complained bitterly to Kolchak about French policies and characterized the foreigners as merely a hindrance in the struggle. Understandably, the French were greatly disturbed to learn of Denikin's feelings from reading *Pravda*. General Dragomirov, who visited Paris in the late summer, had an interview with Clemenceau, who strongly protested Denikin's remarks. The continued hostility between the Volunteer Army and the French could be at least partially explained by this incident.[9]

Because of the dangers of the direct overland route, many of the exchanges between the two separated White areas went through Paris or London. Even the sea route, via Vladivostok, was used, although it took a messenger three months to make this journey. In view of the difficulties in communications, it did not seem to make sense to establish a united command before the linking up of the fronts. Both Denikin and Kolchak assumed that when the time was ripe, the creation of a united authority would be an easy task. There was no discussion at the time about who would take supreme authority and who would have to accept subordination.

During the spring of 1919 the pressure on Denikin to subordinate himself gradually built up. Public opinion regarded Kolchak's army as better and more powerful than the Volunteer Army, and Kolchak was more popular in South Russia than Denikin. The only explanation for this undeserved popularity must be that the population knew less about the shady side of White rule in Siberia

than they did about White conduct in their own districts. Many
expected that the Admiral would rescue them from the misrule
of the Volunteers. Agents of the secret service reported from the
Ukraine that the loyal population preferred Kolchak to Denikin.[10]
A report dated May 1919 from Armavir tells how, following the
disappearance of a picture of Kolchak from a shop window, a ru-
mor spread that Denikin had Kolchak shot because Kolchak wanted
to defend the interests of the common people.[11]

Denikin was most disturbed by the charge that he wanted to
avoid the unification of fronts because he did not want to subordinate himself. According to secret service reports, these allega-
tions were widespread, especially among officers and among the
refugees from the Crimea and Odessa, where Denikin and his army
had never been very popular.[12]

The most important argument for subordination was White Russia's international situation. On June 9 General D. G. Shcherbachev
and two public figures, M. S. Adzhemov and V. V. Vyrubov,
came to Ekaterinodar from Paris on a mission. They wanted to
persuade Denikin to recognize Kolchak's authority because such
an act would make a favorable impact on Western European governments. They argued that the emergence of a leader of a united
anti-Bolshevik movement would enable the Allies to give de facto
recognition to the Supreme Ruler. This would have been an important accomplishment, not only because it would have raised the
prestige of the movement but also because it would have precluded
Allied recognition of the Soviet government. Adzhemov and
Vyrubov implied that Allied recognition of Kolchak depended
on Denikin.[13] Denikin had received similar advice from Russian
representatives in Paris; British officers attached to his headquarters also must have intimated that the Allies would favor the move.

Denikin asked Adzhemov and Vyrubov to present their case
to the Special Council. The Special Council debated the matter
only briefly. There were many arguments against immediate recognition. K. N. Sokolov maintained that it would undermine the
ability of Ekaterinodar to deal successfully with the Cossack governments.[14] The monarchists opposed it because they hoped that
when the two fronts were linked up a Romanov would be asked
to take leadership. In general, in Ekaterinodar Kolchak had the

reputation of being more leftist than Denikin, and therefore the conservatives feared a leftward turn from him. The Special Council in its note to the Commander-in-Chief pointed out that the Volunteer Army had not been officially approached by any of the foreign representatives in this matter, and suggested sending a delegation to Paris to gain more information about international implications. For the time being, the Council reaffirmed its earlier position that the question of Denikin's subordination should be postponed.

Denikin decided not to accept this recommendation. On June 12 he himself wrote a proclamation in which he subordinated himself to the Supreme Ruler. On a dinner given in honor of the departing British representative, General Briggs, who was leaving for London, Denikin revealed his decision. It came as a complete surprise to everyone present. The choice of the occasion implies that Denikin wanted to impress his British friends.[15]

In the middle of June Denikin's armies were advancing on all fronts and Kolchak's armies were retreating. Of course no one in Ekaterinodar could have known that the Siberian army would never recover. Denikin assumed that Kolchak's reverses were temporary, no different from those which the Volunteer Army had also suffered periodically. The pressure on Denikin to subordinate himself was not overwhelming. His advisers were divided and although foreign opinion was important, Denikin himself would not have given in if he had not had his own reasons. He apparently wanted to avoid giving the impression of being power-hungry and enjoyed the pose of self-sacrifice.

The domestic response was largely favorable. The Special Council, which had just recommended against such an act, devoted a session to composing a manifesto hailing "Denikin's patriotic decision."[16] The three main political organizations of anti-Bolshevik Russia—the Council for State Unity, the National Center, and the Union for Regeneration—held a combined festive meeting in which speakers expressed their approval of Denikin's decision in the most enthusiastic terms.

There were some dissenting voices, largely among Cossack politicians. The *inogorodnie* approved because they saw in Denikin's move a step toward the reestablishment of a centralized Russia and the destruction of the Cossack governments, against which they felt an understandable hostility.[17] For the same reason, the Cossack leaders were dismayed. Denikin convened a meeting of atamans and the leaders of Cossack governments in order to explain his decision and win their support. In the course of the meeting the Cossacks indicated that they approved the idea of a unified military command, but that they believed that the formation of a national political authority must wait until a Constituent Assembly could be convened. The Cossacks worried in vain. The change in the legal basis of Denikin's authority had no impact whatever on the most sensitive political issue of the time, the issue of Cossack-Volunteer relations.[18]

Denikin sent a high-ranking delegation consisting of General Dragomirov, N. I. Astrov, K. N. Sokolov, and A. A. Neratov to Paris to establish ties with the Russian political committee operating there, and to make indirect contact with Admiral Kolchak.[19] Denikin provided Sokolov with instructions and documents and asked him to compose a report to Kolchak and work out the details of cooperation. Sokolov in his report suggested no basic change in the status quo, which in the prevailing circumstances was a reasonable position. When the answer finally came from Omsk, it was disappointing: Kolchak granted Denikin's right to issue laws, but he wanted to establish an organ which would coordinate financial and land policies. It was obvious that when it took months to send a message from Siberia to the South, such a system could not work. The chief of the department of finances, V. M. Bernadskii, considered the situation so frustrating that he threatened resignation.[20] Sokolov wrote Kolchak again, and the Admiral, whose military position by this time was completely hopeless, answered satisfactorily.

The last telegram from Kolchak, which Denikin received in December 1919, said: "The circumstances demand giving all power to General Denikin in territories under his control; please give General Denikin my complete assurance that I will not part from him on the basis of our common work for the regeneration of Russia."[21] Denikin believed that the publication of the message would exacerbate the despair caused by continuous defeats and decided to suppress it.

At the apex of the administrative hierarchy stood the Special Council. This institution was established in October 1918 and it remained in existence until the great defeats of late 1919. The Council, to which the heads of departments (or ministries) belonged, coordinated the work of these departments and passed on their budgets. It was also the highest legislative-advisory body of anti-Bolshevik South Russia: it submitted legislative proposals to the Commander-in-Chief, which upon his signature acquired the force of law. The Special Council expressed an opinion on all the major civilian issues confronting the White movement, from land reform to foreign policy.

The President of the Special Council from its establishment until June 20, 1919, was General A. M. Dragomirov. When Dragomirov headed a delegation to Paris in June, General A. S. Lukomskii acted in his stead. When Dragomirov returned he became Governor General in recently liberated Kiev, and Lukomskii was appointed permanent head of the Special Council. Before his promotion Lukomskii had been deputy chairman and head of the military department. Four other military men belonged to the Council. The first three were Vice Admiral Gerasimov of the naval department; General Sannikov, chief of military supplies; and General Tikhmenev, of the department of military communications. The fourth, General I. P. Romanovskii, the Chief of Staff and the man Denikin had secretly named his successor, rarely attended the meetings. He exerted influence through his close friendship with the Commander-in-Chief.

There was a large turnover among the twenty or so civilians who at any given time belonged to the Council. N. I. Astrov was the most able, respected, and influential liberal politician at headquarters. He did not accept a portfolio. Aside from Astrov, M. M. Fedorov, also without portfolio, was the most outspoken liberal. K. N. Sokolov, at the outbreak of the Civil War a moderate Kadet, became increasingly conservative and an apologist for the policies of the Volunteer Army. He was responsible for the department of propaganda, and also composed the most important legislative and constitutional projects. The rightist-monarchist Kadet V. A.

Stepanov headed the department of state control and played an important role in running the secret service. S. D. Sazonov and A. A. Neratov, two rightist functionaries of the tsarist regime, headed at different times the department of foreign affairs. The Kadet financial expert M. V. Bernadskii directed the department of finances to the very end of the existence of the Volunteer Army. The most articulate spokesmen for the right were two Octobrists, S. N. Maslov, head of the department of supplies, and N. V. Savich, who had no portfolio. Although V. V. Shulgin belonged to the Council from its establishment until the middle of 1919, he almost never participated in the meetings since he was rarely in Ekaterinodar. He was influential in Volunteer politics because of his close ties with Generals Dragomirov and Lukomskii.[22]

The Council was ideologically divided from the beginning, and as time went on the division became sharper and sharper. The right was in complete control. All the generals, with the exception of Romanovskii, were restorationists and it was they who set the broad outline of policies. Lukomskii and Dragomirov made the civilians feel that the army in general and the Special Council in particular belonged to the military men, and civilians were merely tolerated as long as they behaved.[23] The generals were hopelessly out of touch with the mood of the Russian people. In November 1917, 75 percent of the electorate voted for socialist candidates, yet no socialist was ever appointed to the Special Council. Several liberal Kadet advisers urged Denikin to invite at least one moderate socialist as a gesture, but he adamantly refused, saying that the army would not tolerate such an appointment. It is clear that Denikin shared the officers' hostility toward the socialists. This collection of generals and ex-tsarist functionaries had no understanding whatever of the revolutionary mentality; they were far removed from the aspirations of simple workers and peasants. To them, the revolution was a destructive force which had brought the country to the verge of anarchy. The efforts of the socialists—and Bolsheviks—to bring about a new and better society were incomprehensible to them.

The Kadets within the Council were disunited. They wanted Denikin to invite P. N. Miliukov in the hope that he might provide them with leadership, but Denikin, again referring to the hostility of the officers, refused.[24] Only a minority of the Kadets could be considered members of the left wing. Men such as Astrov and Fedorov were largely isolated, and they could play a role only because Denikin was often sympathetic to their points of view and protected them. In any case their "leftism" was very moderate: it meant only a recognition that the Civil War could not be won in opposition to the majority of the Russian people, and that therefore concessions were necessary. The left, unlike the right, was not satisfied to base the anti-Bolshevik movement entirely on conservative landowners and tsarist functionaries. Liberal Kadets were put in a difficult position. On the one hand they were determined to support the policies of the army under any circumstances, for they could not see an alternative. On the other hand, they considered those policies in many cases profoundly mistaken. Since they realized that the posture of opposition was fruitless, often they did not even find it possible to register a contrary opinion.[25]

The Special Council was not only reactionary but also inefficient. Civilian members feared responsibility. As a result, department heads reported to their colleagues on matters which they should have been able to resolve themselves. The Council became greatly overburdened with work. The Tuesday and Thursday meetings lasted far into the night. On genuinely controversial matters, the Council usually avoided taking a position by creating a commission which labored for months, usually without tangible results.[26] Members of the Council also negotiated on behalf of the army, went on assignments, and consequently had no time to take care of business within their own departments. In order to alleviate the heavy work load, in March 1919 Denikin established a Small Assembly, consisting of the deputy heads of departments, which was to discuss less significant matters. However, there could be no remedy for indecision and political cowardice, and the Council remained greatly overburdened.

In this respect, the contrast between the White and the Bolshevik leadership was striking. Stalin or Trotskii, or even men of lesser standing, such as Ordzhonikidze or Kirov, could be sent to troublespots to resolve issues immediately. This system led to some confusion and quarrels, but by and large the emissaries from the center enforced the will of the highest policy-making bodies of the Party.

It was unthinkable for a civilian to possess comparable authority among the Whites. Civilian members of the Special Council had no independent standing, and so it was not surprising that they dared not assert themselves. Also, the Bolshevik leaders shared an experience in illegal Party work, and, of course, a common ideology. The gap between the background, education, and mentality of the generals and the liberal politicians was almost unbridgeable.

In the fall of 1919 Denikin moved his headquarters to Taganrog and the main administrative offices to Rostov, saying that the move was necessary to bring the headquarters closer to the front. In fact his main reason for leaving Ekaterinodar was that he wanted to get away from the Kuban capital, which was increasingly dominated by separatist politicians. Taganrog, however, was a small town and it seemed sensible to have the main offices in Rostov, which had the communications network and office space necessary for successful work. On the other hand, having the headquarters and the Special Council in different towns led to some confusion and a general weakening of Denikin's liberal influence.

The Special Council had few partisans. It was disliked by officers, who regarded it as a bastion of Kadet influence, and it was hated by socialists, who considered it reactionary. The Cossack governments were also hostile because they saw it as an obstacle to the establishment of self-government and an example of Russian centralism. In fact, it may be that the Special Council's most useful function was to serve as a magnet for the hatred which otherwise would have been concentrated on the policies of the Commander-in-Chief.

In spite of its failures, the Special Council was a far more effective organization than the organs of local government. It was an easier and ultimately a less important task to establish a reasonably well-functioning central government than it was to influence the lives of the people in outlying provinces; it was a long step between arriving at decisions in Ekaterinodar and carrying them out hundreds of miles away.

The Volunteer Army accepted administrative tasks reluctantly. During the first year of its existence it operated almost entirely on Cossack territory, and any coordination and supervision of local institutions was carried out by the Kuban and Don Cossack governments. At this time the army did not interfere in administration, even though the generals must have been aware that the Cossacks cruelly abused the *inogorodnie*.

The first non-Cossack districts which the army liberated were the Stavropol and Black Sea provinces. During the fall of 1918 Denikin considered attaching these areas to the Kuban *Voisko* for the purposes of administration, and the Cossack government would have been happy to accept the responsibility. Denikin, however, understood that the Russian peasants were bitterly hostile to the Cossacks, and that the political price for such an arrangement would be high, and so he decided against it.[27] When in 1919 the army was rapidly advancing northward and the Don government requested that the newly conquered territories be included temporarily in the *Voisko*, Denikin once again resisted such a suggestion.[28]

Until the late spring of 1919 the area which was directly administered by the army was small, but as a result of the great victories it expanded rapidly. By October 1919 approximately forty million people lived under Denikin's rule. In these territories the Volunteer Army recreated the old tsarist administrative divisions. It established four military governorships: Kharkov, Kiev, Odessa, and North Caucasus. The military governors, who were responsible only to the Commander-in-Chief and not to the Department of the Interior of the Special Council, concentrated in their hands both military and civilian authority.[29] Denikin's closest advisers, the most prominent generals, took these important posts. The governors, who headed the provinces, came under the authority of Military Governors. Provincial administration mirrored the administrative divisions within the Special Council. Each department had representatives. Although the governors handled largely civilian matters, these jobs also were given usually to military officers. The provinces were subdivided into districts (*uezdy*) headed by district chiefs (*nachal'niki*), many of whom were officers. In a time of civil war, communications were so poor that there could be no meaningful supervision of the work of district chiefs, and they could act in any way they pleased. Some of them became petty tyrants who grossly abused their power. On the lowest level, the army resurrected the ancient office of the village elder (*starosta*).

But the authority of the Volunteer Army usually extended to the villages only when military forces were present. The code of behavior of these troops had little to do with the laboriously worked out plans of the Special Council.

Some of the liberals at headquarters, notably N. I. Astrov, believed that the army needed the help of the population in correcting the abuses. He insisted that the remedy for the anarchy prevailing in White-controlled territories must be the revitalization of local self-government (*zemstvo*). Astrov realized that the prerevolutionary *zemstvo*, in which the enlightened gentry played a crucial role, could not be recreated. He argued that during the Revolution and Civil War the nobility had lost its prestige among the population, and that the peasants would no longer accept its leading role. In any case, few nobles remained on their estates; many emigrated to places such as the Crimea or went abroad. Astrov wanted to involve other classes, notably the peasantry, in order to make self-government function. He headed several commissions and presented numerous proposals, but in vain; his views found little support among the officers and conservative politicans, who could imagine the *zemstvo* only on the basis of the old pattern.[30]

Given the attitude of the White leaders to the Russian people it is not surprising that Astrov did not succeed. The Generals distrusted self-government because they had grave doubts about the political attitudes of the Russian people. They made election to city dumas restrictive and they limited the competence of these bodies. In city duma elections, the right to vote was limited to those who had been residents for more than two years. This law disenfranchised those ex-soldiers who had fought for their country in the World War. The residence requirement was deleted, however, for those who owned property in the city, a clause which shows an explicit class bias. The governor of the province could remove elected officials without appeal. The district chief could veto any *zemstvo* election.[31] The power of the government over the finances of *zemstvo* and city dumas was so great that they could not function independently.[32] Under the circumstances it is understandable that the population was apathetic about elections. In Kharkov, for example, in October 1919, out of the eighty thousand who had the right to vote only twelve thousand chose to exercise their right.[33]

Instead of building up the institutions of self-government, the Volunteer Army based its power in the countryside on the gendarmerie. As the spread of anarchy became ever more evident and as the partisan movement grew with alarming speed, the headquarters and the Special Council paid increasing attention to strengthening these troops. In September 1919 it had twenty brigades with 77,393 men, which was about half the size of the regular army.[34] Neither the *zemstva* and city dumas nor the department of interior had control over the gendarmerie, whose leaders were regular army officers. The department of the interior did not at all like this arrangement, but it protested in vain.

The Special Council spent millions of its limited resources on these irregular troops. Ekaterinodar considered them so important that the Special Council set up skeletal organizations for cities months before they were captured. For example, the Kursk unit was organized in early July, but the city was taken only in the beginning of October. The Voronezh, Tambov, and Saratov units were also organized months before the army occupied these cities.[35]

The gendarmerie proved inadequate for the task. At the height of the successes of the White army, the partisan movement became so threatening that the Special Council decided to experiment with a new type of organization. On September 19, at Dragomirov's suggestion, the Council formed a committee—under the chairmanship of N. N. Chebyshev, head of the department of the interior, with the participation of Lukomskii, V.N. Chelishchev, N.V. Savich, and General Sannikov—to study how militia units could be formed in each district. The task of the militia was to "combat banditism"—a phrase often used to describe the partisan movement. It was to be based on "reliable local elements."[36] But reliable local elements did not exist, and the department of the interior soon expressed concern about giving weapons to men who might use them against the Volunteer Army.

The Whites failed to create a well-functioning local administration because they did not find reliable and competent men. As the army occupied towns and villages, the commander usually requested ex-tsarist bureaucrats to resume their jobs. It is understandable that officers chose these men rather than representatives of the liberal intelligentsia, who by and large lacked administrative experience, differed from them in background and ideology, and often had no desire to become identified with White rule in any case. Yet returning a class of discredited bureaucrats to power had disastrous consequences. The Special Council may have worked out some reasonable reforms, but what the peasants saw was the return of those who had been chased out a short time before. The reappearance of old bureaucrats had far more to do with the reactionary image of the army than the policies of Denikin and the Special Council. The leaders of the Army did not appreciate this danger. When Astrov or one of the liberals recommended the appointment of a candidate to Dragomirov or Lukomskii, they would usually ask how much experience the person in question had. If the answer was none, they would reject the recommendation. Dragomirov and Lukomskii believed that they were acting in a non-partisan manner, but they failed to understand that returning tsarist officials to power had the most explicit significance.[37]

A prominent feature of Volunteer Army administration was militarization. Even in tsarist times officers played a considerable role in the administration of the country. Military governors had performed civilian tasks; many officers received civilian appointments and carried out their jobs while continuing to wear a uniform; many high functionaries had not only attended military schools but also served as officers before attaining their posts. During the Civil War this tendency developed much further. The more politically ignorant an officer was, the more he distrusted politicians and believed that all problems had military solutions. In the anarchy of the Civil War the man with the gun had the power; the officers did not understand why they should share this power with civilians, who in their opinion had created the problems of the country in the first place.

The officers who assumed civilian tasks were even worse than the ex-tsarist bureaucrats in pursuing blindly reactionary policies. They lacked the tact and moderation that successful politicians and administrators must acquire. The largest number of complaints Denikin received for abuse of power was against officers. The military men put their stamp on the administration as a whole; the civilians feared them and consequently shirked responsibility.

Another unfortunate feature of White administration was the mushrooming of bureaucracy. Russia had been long notorious for this problem, and the Civil War only made it worse. It is something of a paradox that the contempt for civilians in general and for administrators in particular went hand in hand with a proliferation of committees, departments, and sections, and thousands of generally useless jobs. The wellspring of bureaucracy was always a fear of accepting responsibility, and the Civil War made administrators all the more afraid. Hostility to local self-government also made necessary the creation of many new positions. But most important, many found it more desirable to serve the anti-Bolshevik cause in an office than to risk their lives in a regiment.

The Journals of the Special Council were full of descriptions of new committees, departments, and offices. Denikin, who was concerned about the problem, once wrote on the margin of the minutes:

> In spite of the terrible growth of civil administration (at a time when the size of the territory under our control not only did not increase but contracted), in spite of my numerous requests and orders, the number of positions continues to grow constantly and without interruption.
>
> I ask the Special Council to exhibit firmness and prevent the further growth of apparatus until my special permission.
>
> Our civic duty demands exerting all our strength and getting along with the existing number of people. The front has been doing this for a long time in a self-sacrificing manner.[38]

The forces which created bureaucratization were far too strong to be stopped by such a well-intentioned order.

The administration was thoroughly corrupt. Corruption, like bureaucracy, had a long tradition in Russia, but in the conditions of the Civil War it flourished. The government paid very low salaries. Denikin was extremely concerned with economy, because he was determined not to leave a large debt to the future state. At a time of raging inflation, it was often difficult and at times impossible to live on official salaries. The civil servants and officers could choose between nobly starving themselves and their families or accepting bribes. There were some who preferred self-sacrifice. Lukomskii, one of the most powerful men in the hierarchy, wrote in his memoirs that in the summer of 1919 he received a monthly salary of 1800 rubles; this was barely enough for food, and his wife had to do the cooking and laundry. A governor complained that he could not ask an official visitor to his table because there was not enough to eat.[39] Denikin and his family lived on a bare subsistence level also.[40] Of course when the most prominent men received such small salaries, the position of less exalted bureaucrats was much, much worse.

But only the honest remained poor. The archives contain innumerable examples of corruption; men in high position as well as simple clerks were guilty of bribe-taking, theft, and extortion. The government all too rarely took steps against the wrongdoers, and the reports complain against the same individuals month after month.

A few examples must suffice. A. P. Kutepov, one of the most able commanders of the movement, became governor of the Black Sea province in the fall of 1918. Complaints started to pour in. Contrary to his instructions, he carried out blindly reactionary policies and introduced bloody terror. He was accused of taking several million rubles in bribes for giving export and import permits at the port of Novorossisk.[41] The *Stavka* disregarded the reports, and Kutepov continued to receive appointments with wide power.

A General Komissarov made money in Rostov by providing protection to gambling establishments. Colonel Fetisov, in the same town, received complaints from the population that his soldiers were taking food and wine at gunpoint. Instead of punishing his soldiers, he threatened those who complained. Some suspected that the colonel was receiving a part of the loot.[42] The most glaring and ultimately costly failure of the Volunteer Army was its inability to protect the population from itself. It is difficult to convey the appalling picture of lawlessness which emerges from the secret reports, because it is not so much the individual examples which affect the reader, as their cumulative power. The files contain dozens of letters essentially similar to the one written in September 1919 by Ivan Adamovich Schleining, a Lutheran pastor among the German colonists of Saratov province.[43]

The pastor first described the sufferings of his people under Bolshevik rule. The Reds sent punishment battalions, replaced elected officials, drafted young men against their will into the army, took hostages, and requisitioned whatever they could get their hands on. The well-to-do Germans naturally sympathized with the Whites and even staged an abortive rising against Bolshevik rule.

Under the circumstances it was understandable that the Germans greeted the Volunteers as saviors. But they were bitterly disappointed. The Whites beat up and humiliated some old men, took away the remaining horses, and treated the population as a defeated enemy. The Germans consoled one another by saying that these were not really the soldiers of the Volunteer Army, but merely bandits, pretending to be fighters for the White cause.

Schleining correctly sensed the essence of the matter. The Whites treated the area as an occupied country and regarded the population as a defeated enemy. White abuse of the people can only partially be explained by the general lawlessness prevailing at the time. A more important component was the fear and distrust which the soldiers and their officers felt toward the Russian people. Of course, in their official documents they did not say so, and very likely they themselves did not realize their true feelings. Nevertheless, the realization was not far below the surface. Oddly, for example, the basic statute concerning administration was titled: "Policies governing occupied territory." One does not usually refer to one's own country as "occupied territory." Clearly it would have been more tactful to talk about "liberated areas" or "territories taken from the enemy." Yet, the phrase "occupied territory" did accurately describe an attitude.

It was a vicious circle: the Whites abused the people because they distrusted them, and the people, who experienced terror and brutality, lived up to expectations and turned against the Whites.

THE AZBUKA

The role of a secret service in any civil war is especially important. On the one hand, because the battlefront is the entire country, receiving reliable information from every district has great strategic significance; on the other hand, it is a relatively easy task to penetrate "enemy" territory. The Bolsheviks had no special secret service because they had no need for it. The Party had trusted agents in most localities, many of them with long underground experience. Among the many crucial roles the Party played in the Civil War, information-gathering was one of the most important.

The South Russian anti-Bolshevik secret service, the Azbuka, was the creation of one man, V. V. Shulgin.[44] The Azbuka started as a private army, and though it acquired increasingly close ties with the Volunteer Army, it never became fully a part of it. The organization continued to reflect the views and personality of its creator.

Shulgin alone among the major figures of the anti-Bolshevik movement could be described as a proto-fascist. His passionate nationalism, his demagogy, his willingness to exploit anti-Semitism, and his ability to experiment with unconventional methods of political warfare made him appear a modern figure among conservatives and reactionaries. It is ironic but not very surprising that he was among the very few White leaders who ultimately made their peace with the Soviet regime.

He had been a prominent figure long before the Civil War. His father, V. Ia. Shulgin, had founded in Kiev a Russian nationalist and anti-Ukrainian paper, *Kievlianin*, which he inherited. In 1907 he was elected a member of the Second Duma and soon emerged in national politics as a leader of the right. Among the monarchists he stood out by his political acumen, his integrity, and his education.[45]

Shulgin went to Novocherkassk in November 1917, even before the arrival of Generals Alekseev and Kornilov. The independent Ukrainian government had banned his paper, and he hoped to transfer it to the Don Capital. General Alekseev, who had known him for a long time, supported him, but Ataman Kaledin realized that the publication of a rightist paper would be inflammatory and did not give his permission. Under the circumstances, Shulgin decided to return to Kiev, but before departing he promised to do clandestine work for Alekseev in the Ukrainian capital. Partly because of his work, Kiev became one of the main recruitment centers for the Volunteer Army. In the first two months Shulgin sent 1500 recruits to Novocherkassk.[46]

When the Bolsheviks briefly occupied Kiev, Shulgin, together with General Dragomirov, the future head of the Special Council, was arrested. His incarceration did not last long because the Germans soon entered the capital and freed the prisoners. Shulgin, a passionate nationalist, never for a moment was tempted to cooperate with the conquerors, the supporters of the hated Ukrainian cause.

Since he could not publish his paper, he occupied himself entirely with underground work. It was at this time that the Azbuka came into being. Shulgin recruited secret agents whom he sent into different parts of the country.[47] They signed their reports with a pseudonym, arranged in an alphabetical order—hence the name Azbuka, the Russian word for alphabet.

Shulgin naturally recruited men who agreed with his political philosophy, and so the Azbuka from its inception was a rightist-monarchist organization, faithful to the Allies and determined to support the Volunteer Army. Shulgin quickly established ties with the representatives of various Allied secret services who were already operating in Odessa. He was in touch with rightist political organizations operating everywhere in the country, but he had especially close ties with Moscow political circles. Since he was a monarchist, he took it upon himself to report on political developments to various members of the Imperial family.[48]

His ties with the Volunteer Army became increasingly close. In September 1918 he traveled to Ekaterinodar and participated in working out the "constitution" of the Volunteer Army and setting up the Special Council. Alekseev's death did not diminish his influence; Generals Dragomirov and Lukomskii both had great confidence in him.

In the middle of 1918 the Azbuka had 34 agents, all of them officers, reporting from various parts of the country. The first center of the organization was Kiev, but Shulgin, an extremely energetic man, traveled a great deal, and at this time wherever he went the headquarters moved with him. In September he visited Ekaterinodar and then went to Jassy. At the end of 1918 he traveled to Odessa. When the French occupied this city it became the center of political intrigues and therefore seemed a convenient location for secret work.

The operation of a national secret service required substantial funds. Shulgin first depended on contributions from rich friends, but this method of financing was unreliable and inadequate. Later the Azbuka's main financial support came from two anti-Bolshevik groups in Moscow, the Right Center and the National Center. So long as the politicians were far away, Shulgin had a free hand in running his organization. But during the fall of 1918 more and more politicians moved from Moscow to the relative safety of Kiev, and this created an intolerable situation for the Azbuka. Rightist politicians became increasingly seduced by the prospect of gaining German aid for their anti-Bolshevik crusade, and a German orientation implied a compromise with moderate Ukranian nationalism. Shulgin, who had spent his entire political life fighting for the great Russian cause, could not go along. In order to preserve his independence he had to look elsewhere for support.

In September 1918 he proposed to make the Azbuka part of the Volunteer Army in the hope of receiving aid. The *stavka* was hesitant. Dragomirov supported Shulgin, but Denikin was an old-fashioned man, to whom all intelligence work seemed sordid. He did not appreciate the significance of the contribution the Azbuka could make to winning the Civil War. Also, he disliked Shulgin's politics; Shulgin's rightist past and contacts with the Imperial family made the Commander-in-Chief suspicious. But finally he gave in. He extended reserve officer status to all active agents of the Azbuka, and in February 1919, for the first time, he provided some money.

This development, however, did not bring an end to Shulgin's financial problems. The Special Council officially knew nothing of the Azbuka's existence, and the money for running the organization came out of a discretionary fund at Denikin's disposal.[49] Denikin's parsimoniousness was a constant source of discouragement for Shulgin. He repeatedly had to beg for money and he always received much less than he asked for. For example, in February 1919 he hoped for 750,000 rubles, but he got only 120,550.[50] This was a very small sum. To put it in perspective, we may compare it with the budget of the propaganda agency, Osvag, which received 25 million rubles for the first three months of 1919.[51]

Still, financial support from the Volunteer Army enabled Shulgin to expand the operations of the Azbuka. In the beginning of 1919 Ekaterinodar became the headquarters of the organization. Since Shulgin was frequently away, V. A. Stepanov, a prominent rightist Kadet and a member of the Special Council, took charge of the day-to-day operations. Shulgin and Stepanov designated cities as of primary, secondary, and tertiary importance and assigned their agents accordingly. Moscow and Kiev were in the first category; Kharkov, Voronezh, and Saratov were in the second; and Odessa (this was after the withdrawal of the French), Kishinev, Lvov, Kholm, Warsaw, and Vilna were in the third.[52] The most difficult task was not gathering information but relaying it to Ekaterinodar. A large number of agents did nothing more than carry letters from one center to another: four carriers were assigned to the Moscow route, three to Kiev, and two maintained ties with the cities of Kharkov, Voronezh, Saratov, and Odessa. The work of these carriers was dangerous. Sometimes only one out of six would arrive. In the first few months the Azbuka lost 50 percent of its personnel.[53] By and large Azbuka agents were brave men, who hated Bolshevism so much that they were willing to risk their lives to defeat it. Almost all the participants were novices in underground work, and many made fatal errors. An agent in Odessa committed an indiscretion in April 1919 and as a consequence the Kiev organization was decimated.[54] Many of the men had to work in a hostile environment, where they sometimes received no instructions from the center for months. Yet, the Azbuka was an efficient organization. Considering that it never had more than a hundred agents at any one time, it accomplished a great deal.

The Azbuka's most important contribution was informing the leaders of the Volunteer Army on the mood of the people and on political developments. Denikin, Dragomirov, Lukomskii, and Romanovskii received summaries of all its reports, and the National Center was provided with political information.[55] The Azbuka often duplicated the work of the information department of the general staff, but it reached many more parts of the country and by and large provided more detailed, reliable, and frank reports. The agents freely reported on dissatisfaction among the peasants, corruption of officials and officers, and mismanagement of volunteer programs. It is evident that since these reports were the main source of information for the policy makers of the army, the point of view inherent in them influenced the perception of the generals. On some issues the agents disagreed. For example, reports from Odessa at the time of the French occupation describe the role of General Grishin-Almazov, the volunteer representative, in a contradictory way.[56] While one agent was obviously a partisan of Grishin-Almazov, the other believed that the General was mishandling the situation and suspected him of corruption. Since the summaries the Generals in Ekaterinodar received were not signed, it was difficult for them to know whom to trust. But the tone and point of view of the reports were remarkably uniform. The agents, like their chief, Shulgin, advocated land reform, betrayed a pathological anti-Semitism, denounced the nationalist aspirations of non-Russian peoples, exhibited hostility to the Germans even after their defeat, and were contemptuous of liberal politicians. Their voluminous writings provide the most detailed and best evidence for understanding the thinking and prejudices of the anti-Bolshevik warriors.

Azbuka reports from Soviet territory were based on eyewitness accounts and on the Soviet press. White agents never penetrated the decision-making bodies of the other side. Although many ex-tsarist officers defected from the Red Army and carried out sabotage while they pretended to serve, there is no evidence that the Azbuka was in touch with any of these men. On the other hand, agents did infiltrate Skoropadskii's and Petliura's armies. On occasion, the Azbuka informed the headquarters (*stavka*) that some of its men made pro-Ukrainian statements in order to cover themselves, and that they should not be regarded as traitors to the Russian cause.[57]

Aside from reporting, the Azbuka had a variety of missions. For example, Lukomskii asked the agency to gather information on the secret discussions of the Cossack Congress which opened in June 1919 in Rostov.[58] But on another occasion the *stavka* entrusted the organization with the preparation of a report for the Allies and Kolchak on the situation in South Russia. The Azbuka also carried out propaganda work for the Volunteer Army beyond Russia's borders. Shulgin attributed special importance to influencing public opinion in the neighboring countries, and so the Azbuka maintained centers in Kishinev, Warsaw, and Vilna. Sometimes the Azbuka carried out direct action. After asking the permission of the *stavka*, agents organized sabotage against Soviet munition trains and factories.[59] Azbuka agents maintained ties with insurgents operating against the Soviet regime.

No doubt the Azbuka could have accomplished more if Denikin had decided to give it full support. Shulgin would have liked to establish centers in the Caucasus and in Siberia, but he could not because of a lack of funds. He became increasingly disgusted with Denikin's stinginess and was ready to give up. In February 1919 he wrote Stepanov from Odessa that he was so poor that his family could eat only one meal a day. The Azbuka, he said, could not take any initiatives in this city at a time when the Ukrainian nationalists and even the Bolsheviks seemed very well financed.[60] In June he requested 750,000 rubles once again, but he received only 500,000, the largest sum ever given to him by the Volunteer Army.[61] In October he wanted 1.4 million, but at this time Denikin refused to give any money at all.

The Azbuka ceased to function because it ran out of money. In December 1919 it dispersed. After some negotiations, Denikin gave a paltry sum of seventy-five thousand rubles for the purpose of liquidation.[62] Shulgin, bitterly disappointed with the Volunteer Army which had provided funds so reluctantly, also lost faith in the entire White movement, and he ceased to play an active role in the continuation of the anti-Bolshevik struggle.[63]

THE OSVAG

Even the Whites realized that their propaganda was ineffective and that their enemies were much superior in this matter.

They hoped to find a solution, and therefore incessantly reorganized their propaganda agency. When the Volunteer Army set up the Special Council, it established an agitation and information section within the department of foreign affairs. The section, which came to be called the Osvag (from *osvedomitel'noe-agitatsionnoe otdelenie*), was headed by S. S. Chakhotin. He was a well-educated and diligent man, but basically a bureaucrat and totally unsuited for his new position. The members of the Special Council soon understood that the marriage of propaganda and foreign affairs was a mistake and that a large-scale reorganization was necessary. The Council decided to invest a large sum of money, to establish an independent department, and to entrust it to someone other than the inexperienced Chakhotin.[64]

At the end of January 1919, N. E. Paramonov took over the direction of the Osvag. He had impressive qualifications. He was among the most prominent Kadets of the Don Voisko and one of the leaders of the opposition to Ataman Krasnov's conservative policies. But he also had political contacts all over the country, and what was especially useful for his new position, broad editorial experience. He planned to introduce far-reaching and ambitious changes. First of all, he asked for a 50-million ruble budget for the next three months. At the beginning of 1919 this was still a very large sum of money and therefore the Special Council felt that it could grant only half of the request.[65] Even so, at this time the Osvag was well-financed.

Paramonov decided to set up his offices in Rostov rather than in Ekaterinodar because Rostov, a much larger city, had technical facilities, such as printing presses, which were necessary for successful work. Also, he did not want to give up participation in the political life of the Don *Voisko*. This arrangement, however, had disadvantages. Ataman Krasnov's price for having the agency based in Don territory was the right to name one of Paramonov's deputies. Since Krasnov and Paramonov were political enemies, it is not surprising that the Ataman named a man, F. D. Kriukov, with whom Paramonov could not work well and whose interference only hindered him. More important, Paramonov was forced to move out of Ekaterinodar, the center of power; this lessened his influence, led to misunderstandings, and allowed those who objected to his policies to work against him freely.

Paramonov fully understood that no amount of reorganization, money, or technical resources could help unless the army was prepared to change some of its policies. On assuming his job, he wrote a report to General Romanovskii, the Chief of Staff.[66] This report, one of the most liberal documents produced by a White leader during the war, was a cogent criticism of existing practices. In perspective it can be read as an analysis of the causes of the ultimate failure of the White movement.

First of all, Paramonov noted, the appeal of the Volunteer Army could be increased only if the officers succeeded in restraining the soldiers from looting and in making them behave tactfully toward the population. He wanted a clearly established chain of authority in which the lower organs would always carry out the policies agreed on in Ekaterinodar. He also saw that the lack of a well-defined program not only failed to broaden the army's appeal but also undermined it by allowing enemies to place the movement's goals in the most unfavorable light; as a result, the conservatives considered the army too far on the left and the leftists regarded it as a reactionary band. Paramonov recommended a leftist program. He wanted Denikin to make the following declaration:

1. The Russian army is fighting for the recreation of order.
2. The Russian army is fighting for the creation of an environment in which the people can choose their form of government.
3. The Russian army aims at the establishment of genuine representative government, and it is hostile to the old form of autocracy and to those limitations which were imposed on the pre-revolutionary Duma.
4. The Russian army wants to establish broad autonomy.
5. The Russian army considers it necessary to introduce land reform, legislation protecting labor, and other social reforms.

His recommendations for running his agency were also not calculated to win the support of the conservatives. Since he attributed great significance to getting cooperation from all anti-Bolshevik groups, he wanted to employ socialists in his agency. Since he had low regard for the conservative Special Council, he wanted to work without interference from that body and therefore wanted to place his agency directly under the Commander-in-Chief. He asked Denikin to exact a promise from the prominent generals that they would not publicly contradict him and thereby create confusion. He even asked Denikin to dissociate himself completely from the tsarist regime, a rejection of pre-revolutionary Russia which the Commander-in-Chief was not ready to make.

The ideological difference between Paramonov and the White leadership was much too great for successful cooperation. And since the chief of the propaganda agency obviously was not in a position to determine the main outlines of policy for the movement, it was soon clear that Paramonov could not long remain in office. Also, he continued to be involved in Don politics, which were in a turmoil after the removal of Ataman Krasnov. This rendered him unable to devote all his energies to running his agency, and defending it against the increasingly vocal attacks in Ekaterinodar. In the middle of March, after only six weeks in office, he was forced to resign.[67]

On March 17, the Special Council named K. N. Sokolov head
of the propaganda department. Sokolov, a lawyer by training,
was an able and energetic man, close to the leading generals of the
army. However, like Paramonov, he could not devote all his time
to running the agency. He remained head of the department of
justice, he continued to participate in various negotiations with the
Cossack governments, and during the summer of 1919 he spent several weeks abroad representing the Volunteer Army. With Sokolov's appointment, the ideological rift between the Osvag and the
Special Council was removed. Whereas Paramonov was on the left
wing of the Party, Sokolov was so far to the right that many of his
party colleagues regarded him as no longer a Kadet.

Sokolov found the Osvag in such disarray that he decided the
old organization should be abolished and a new one formed. He
wanted a month to establish the new agency. Denikin and the Special Council, however, believed that the army could not be left
without a propaganda organization for a full month, and Sokolov
had to be satisfied with a reorganization.[68]

Sokolov failed to improve the effectiveness of White propaganda.
He began his work by removing most of Paramonov's associates,
and in particular all Jews and socialists. In his memoirs he maintained that he was not guided by anti-Semitism, but believed it
was necessary to make a concession to the prevailing mood of the
officers and of the Russian people in general. It is interesting that
the removal of Jews did not satisfy the anti-Semites, who continued to believe that the agency was dominated by Jews.[69] Sokolov's greatest failure was his inability to attract able collaborators.
Small salaries and petty interference made the work unattractive.
But more discouraging than low pay was the low prestige of propaganda work in general and of the Osvag in particular. Even those
intellectuals who agreed with the basic policies of the army preferred to serve elsewhere. As a result, the Osvag became dominated by uneducated men whose main desire was to escape military
service.

Another important obstacle to successful work was the lack of
technical means with which to reach the people. The Civil War
had destroyed the weak communications system. Telegraph lines
did not function. Propaganda material and even personal messages

had to be sent by carriers. Traveling by railroad was a dangerous undertaking and many of the messengers were captured by the Bolsheviks and did not return.[70] To make matters worse, there was a constant paper shortage. The mills did not operate and the supplies captured from the enemy were soon exhausted. Newspapers could be printed only in very small editions and pamphlets could not be widely distributed. Since the Whites did not have enough papers to distribute, people read the smuggled Soviet papers, which were available.[71] Incidentally, the allocation of scarce paper was the most effective form of censorship: the army gave it only to organizations which supported its policies. The Osvag spent a great deal of money building a large radio transmitter, which began operating in November 1919. But, of course, the Russian peasants had no radios, and the transmitter did not turn out to be powerful enough to reach Western Europe.[72]

The chief target of White propaganda was the peasantry, a very difficult audience to reach. In January 1919 an Azbuka agent wrote a special report on organizing propaganda work in the villages. He recommended setting up a special organization which would mediate between the village and the army by explaining the policies of the Volunteer Army to the peasants. The report envisaged a cell in each village which would also serve as the main army recruiting agency; and it also recommended publishing a newspaper to be sold at a minimal cost (it was assumed that the peasants would be suspicious of anything which was given away free), and called for a peasant congress. It was suggested that such a congress would have significance even beyond the borders of Russia, for it would demonstrate peasant support for the anti-Bolshevik cause. The report recommended using refugees from the North as propagandists; these men, it was thought, would be the most convincing in describing the difficult life under Soviet rule.[73] These rather ambitious plans for reaching the peasants came to nothing, however, because the Volunteer Army lacked the means and the vision to carry out such a large-scale project. The Osvag accomplished no more than publishing some ineffective pamphlets for the peasants and occasionally sending agitators to villages; the would-be agitators, for the most part, had little knowledge of peasant life and failed to establish rapport with their audience.

It was easier to reach the workers. Agitators periodically visited factories and lectured on Bolshevik atrocities. Some of the more intelligent agitators realized that the workers were more interested in hearing about what the Volunteer Army was planning to do about economic issues, such as unemployment, inflation, and low wages; these matters, however, were beyond the competence of the Osvag and the lecturers preferred not to touch on them.

The Osvag also performed especially poorly in some other crucial areas. It did not at all penetrate Soviet Russia, and its meager efforts to influence Western European public opinion proved futile. It accomplished little among the soldiers or in newly liberated territories, where it depended on the help of army officers, who, by and large, did not understand the significance of the work.

As in other areas of Volunteer Army life, a chief problem was coordinating the work of the central offices with the efforts of the provincial representatives. Under the circumstances of the Civil War much depended on local initiatives. However poorly the men in Ekaterinodar and Rostov carried out their tasks, they were almost invariably more competent than those who worked far away from headquarters.

In order to appreciate the problems the local offices faced, it is worthwhile to look at the work of one of them, the Kharkov office.[74] Propagandists elsewhere in the country confronted similar difficulties. The Kharkov agency, operating in the largest industrial center of the Ukraine, was among the most important ones in the country. It was organized shortly after the Volunteer Army occupied the city on June 25, 1919. Only a handful of propagandists came from Rostov, and the majority of the workers had to be hired in Kharkov. Within a short time the office had sixty workers; the organizers hired everyone who asked for a job. Almost none of the applicants had previous experience in similar work. The only interference in personal matters which came from Rostov was the order to fire all Jews. The agency received no instructions and no printed material. As a consequence, the psychologically most important period of time, that immediately following liberation from the Red armies, was wasted.

The agency organized departments of information, publication, art, theater, and education. Of these the information department

was the most important. It had a double task: to report to Rostov
on the mood of the population, and to inform the people about the
goals and achievements of the Volunteer Army. Those who gathered information, however, reported only what they knew their
superiors wanted to hear, thus misleading headquarters and causing
more harm than good. Since the agency lacked people who could
write in a way that would effectively reach the population, the material they composed was not very useful. The publication department could hardly operate because of the shortage of paper. In the
course of three months it published only three short pamphlets,
pictures of Denikin, Kolchak, and Kornilov, and some proclamations. The department also published two newspapers, but they
appeared with such small circulation that they failed to achieve
much. The Kharkov agency also presented lectures, performances,
concerts, and movie shows.

The leaders of the agency realized that their greatest failure was
their inability to send competent propagandists into the countryside. To remedy the situation, they set up a school for agitators.
Out of the 52 candidates, the school accepted 26. But even the successful candidates were uneducated and had no acquaintance with
village life. The impact of their efforts must have been small. A
report of the Kharkov center concludes: "Our propaganda tried
to copy the Bolsheviks, but we did not learn from them what was
the most important: the ability to go to the masses."

By all accounts and according to all measures, the propaganda
of the anti-Bolshevik movement was a failure. It is true that the efforts of the Osvag were hindered by a lack of talented workers and
by a scarcity of technical resources, but the real source of weakness
was deeper. The leaders of the Volunteer Army had no clearly
articulated goals; the work of the propaganda agency merely reflected the confusion and disagreements within the movement.
Indeed, what could hired newspapermen and agitators do when the
leader of the Army had a predilection for postponing controversial
decisions and avoiding difficult issues? When Denikin was asked
what his army was fighting for, he could do no better than answer,
"For Russia." This was hardly inspiring.

In fact, the very notion of propaganda went contrary to the White
leaders' conception of the Civil War. It was hard for them to accept

that they were living in an age when the Russian people could not altogether be excluded from the decisions affecting the future of the country. It was self-evident that public support was essential, yet the White leaders resented the need to appeal to the people and to explain their policies. They considered propaganda as something impure and dishonest. It is hardly surprising that the Osvag did not attract the best people.

The Osvag was one of the most unpopular institutions of the Volunteer Army. Those who disliked some aspects of the Army's policies—in other words, the great majority of the people—hated the propaganda agency for espousing those policies. Although it was obviously untrue, the reactionaries continued to believe that the Osvag was run by Jews and socialists. There was more justification for regarding it as a reactionary stronghold, even in comparison with the other agencies of the Army. Monarchists succeeded in infiltrating some of the local offices, and giving jobs to their ideological comrades and often expressing views contrary to the official policy of the army with impunity. The Cossacks especially hated the Osvag, because they saw it as a mouthpiece for great Russian nationalism and as an opponent of local autonomy.

The clumsy attempts with which the Osvag tried to appeal to workers and peasants were merely a reflection of the unease with which the leaders of the anti-Bolshevik movement approached the Russian people. And to their great misfortune, in the field of propaganda they had to compete with masters of the art.

THE CHURCH

The Orthodox Church, of course, was not an institution of the Volunteer Army, but there can be no doubt about the enormous contribution of the Church to the anti-Bolshevik cause. Beyond a general expression of support, the Volunteer Army had no policy toward the Church. In June 1920, when archbishop Feofan suggested that the government should set up a department of Church affairs, Wrangel's advisory council turned down the suggestion, considering the change unnecessary.[75]

From the very beginning of the war, Churchmen recognized the Bolsheviks as uncompromising enemies and did everything within their power to defeat them. The hierarchy helped in every way it could. Church leaders repeatedly appealed to Western European public opinion and to other Christian Churches for help in the anti-Bolshevik struggle. In the early stages of the Civil War, for example, Platon Metropolitan of Odessa addressed the Christians of Western Europe with these words: "Here I lower myself on my knees with tears from my suffering soul and turn to you: 'Help the suffering Russian People.' There still is a force in the struggle against the Bolsheviks and in the organism there are still strong and healthy cells such as our Volunteer Army."[76] Church leaders participated in Volunteer propaganda efforts. When in December 1918 the Special Council set up a commission to study ways to improve propaganda, a churchman, Georgii Shavelskii joined the commission.[77] Church representatives lent prestige and credibility to the numerous committees set up for investigating Bolshevik atrocities. Priests celebrated important White victories with special services.

The leaders of the Volunteer Army were aware of the value of this ideological support and did everything to help the Church to organize and expand its influence. In the summer of 1919 Denikin suggested to churchmen that they call together an assembly in order to reconstruct the ecclesiastical hierarchy. The meeting opened on June 3 in Stavropol with 60 elected delegates in attendance. Denikin in his opening speech expressed his belief that the immediate goal of the Church and of the Volunteer Army was the same: struggle against Bolshevism with all available means. The assembly elected a seven-man presidium, headed by the archbishop of the Don, Mitrofan.[78]

The greatest help the Church provided was not through the appeals it sent to uninterested foreign audiences, but through its unique ability to reach the people. Its network of village priests covered the countryside, and they were incomparably more effective as anti-Bolshevik agitators than Osvag representatives. They denounced the atheistic Bolsheviks, decried Bolshevik atrocities against the faithful, and provided martyrs for the cause. Often they even led White partisan movements. Looking back, there is no doubt that the Bolshevik attacks on religion backfired badly. The accounts of peasant risings almost invariably mention some crude attack on the Church as a motivating force. The church gladly spread myths, such as a report from Yalta that a Jewish commissar had shot at an icon and been killed when the icon deflected the bullet back toward him.[79]

POLITICAL ORGANIZATIONS

The territory under the control of the Volunteer Army attracted a large number of politicians of various persuasions. They came South both in order to avoid persecution and in order to offer their services to the leaders of the anti-Bolshevik cause. In the cities of Kiev, Kharkov, Yalta, Odessa, Rostov, and Ekaterinodar they held meetings and conferences, organized lectures, and endlessly disputed political platforms and alliances. Ultimately they accomplished very little. Those civilians who did play significant roles in Volunteer Army administration achieved influence not as representatives of organized political groups, but through their closeness to powerful generals.

Three political organizations operated in anti-Bolshevik Russia: leftist Union for Regeneration, rightist State Unity Council, and the centrist National Center.

The Union for Regeneration was the least influential. It was an organization of moderate socialists who feared the Bolsheviks more than counterrevolution. Its activities were centered in the cities of the Ukraine, and its most articulate leaders were V. A. Miakotin, I. P. Aleksinskii, and A. A. Titov. Although the Union had serious disagreements with the policy of the army, it always remained within the bounds of loyal opposition.[80] It never attempted to rally the population against the army, but on the contrary appealed to the people to accept the Whites as liberators.[81]

The leaders of the Union for Regeneration criticized the army on two important points. They disapproved of the dilatory and hesitant manner in which the Special Council approached land reform. They wanted all agricultural lands to become national property and then be distributed among the peasants. The other issue concerned the organization of the anti-Bolshevik movement. They condemned Denikin's notion of dictatorship, and wanted a share of political power for themselves. Denikin made no concessions to them, for deep down he regarded all socialists as traitors. Years after the Civil War, when he should have known better, he still believed that socialists either supported the Bolsheviks or wanted to remain neutral, and that they were responsible for many attempts on the lives of White leaders.[82]

The most active political organization was the National Center. The Kadets, or Constitutional Democrats, dominated this body. They preferred to operate within the Center, rather than reviving the Party organization, because this course of action supported the illusion that they were rising above "petty party politics."

The Kadet Party was in great disarray. The Civil War scattered Kadets around the country: there were colonies of them in Moscow, Kiev, Siberia, the Crimea, and in Ekaterinodar. At a time when communications became difficult, it is understandable that former ideological comrades acquired different perspectives. Those who remained in Moscow lived in constant danger. They hated Bolshevism as much as anyone, but they understood better than their comrades reasons for the appeal of Lenin's regime. Consequently, the Moscow Kadets were more likely to retain their liberalism than the members of the Party elsewhere. In their smuggled letters, men such as N. Kishkin, N. Shchepkin, and P. Gerasimov warned their friends in Ekaterinodar that a military dictatorship divorced from the people could not succeed, and that there could be no return to the prerevolutionary past. They wanted to cooperate with moderate socialists, they recommended concessions to the left, and they feared a complete identification of the party with the Volunteer Army.[83]

The Kadets in the Crimea succeeded in forming their own government, and this experience greatly influenced their political judgment. Their spokesmen Vinaver and Petrunkevich also called for cooperation with the socialists and a separation of military and civilian functions in Volunteer Army administration.[84] By taking responsibility for running a government, they became more sympathetic to those who wanted to reform Russia on a federal basis and disapproved of the headquarters' uncompromising centralism. In Kiev, the conservative Kadets dominated; it was they who had been attracted in 1918 by the promise of German aid.

The headquarters of the army attracted the largest Kadet community. Although they were not at all united, they were influenced by the prevailing conservative mood; most of them came to accept the thinking and prejudices of their military colleagues. Some did so with enthusiasm, others with misgivings, but they all supported every twist and turn of the policies of the Volunteer Army. The liberal intellectuals, who had fought for civil rights, political freedom, and the rule of law during the tsarist regime now unhesitatingly supported a marauding army led by reactionary officers. The Civil War rendered Russian liberalism bankrupt.

On the right of the National Center stood the State Unity Council. This organization was established in the fall of 1918 in Kiev by amalgamating a number of conservative groups. The leader of the Council was an ex-tsarist minister of agriculture, A. V. Krivoshein. The fact that the State Unity Council, unlike the socialists or the Kadets, did have a recognized leader gave it additional power and influence. Denikin did not name Krivoshein to the Special Council, perhaps because he feared giving the right such a powerful voice, but the State Unity Council was well represented in this highest administrative body of the Volunteer Army: S. N. Maslov, S. V. Bezobrazov, D. N. Shipov, and Savich belonged to it. Behind the scenes, Krivoshein was one of the most powerful men in Ekaterinodar.

The State Unity Council opposed Denikin's policies from the right. It was a monarchist organization, which hoped that ultimately Grand Duke Nikolai Nikolaevich would assume leadership of the anti-Bolshevik movement. The right was compromised with German cooperation in 1918. After the end of the war in Europe, the group moved the center of its activities from Kiev to Odessa, hoping to exchange French protection for the lost German help. Because the State Unity Council was dominated by large landowners, it was a powerful lobby against land reform. The Council would have been willing to make concessions to workers on matters of freedom of organization and wages, but it opposed any proposal which included compulsory alienation of land.

The State Unity Council was a powerful organization because the military members of the Special Council, even though they did not belong to it, accepted its platform. Generals Dragomirov and Lukomskii were influential patrons. The Council was especially

influential on the provincial level; the ex-governors and functionaries who were returned to office by the victorious Volunteer Army,
often belonged to it.[85]

A large number of splinter groups on the extreme right completed the political spectrum of anti-Bolshevik South Russia. The
Don *Voisko* under the rule of Ataman Krasnov provided a fertile
breeding ground for extremists. The Ataman, far from restricting
their activities, shared many of their beliefs and attitudes and on
occasion supported them financially. The Russkoe Sobranie (Russian Assembly) and the All-Russian Monarchist Center were the
largest. The Monarchist Center was so extremist that it preferred
to operate underground even in Krasnov's Don. The Brotherhood
of the Life-Giving Cross, led by Father Vostokov, was especially
notorious, because this demagogic priest was unusually successful
in stirring up pogroms against the Jews.

After the Ataman's departure, the work of the splinter groups
became more difficult and many had to go underground. However, since many of Krasnov's friends remained in office, the Don
remained a hotbed of rightist radicalism. The radicals thought up
wild schemes for the removal of Denikin, for bringing back Krasnov, and for getting German aid.[86]

The extreme rightists were monarchist, pro-German, anti-
Semitic, and nationalist, but unlike the "legitimate" conservatives,
they believed in conspiratorial solutions and had a penchant for
demagogy. They had some importance not because they attracted
a wide following or because they received important posts in the
administration, but because of the support they enjoyed from many
younger and bitterly anti-Bolshevik army officers. They were also
well supplied with money.[87] The extremists established underground cells in many army units and succeeded in penetrating
some of the administrative offices. They were especially influential
in controlling some of the local offices of the Osvag, where they
used their influence to distort the basic propaganda message of the
Volunteer Army. At the end of 1919 and the beginning of 1920
the extreme rightists united in their support of General Wrangel,
with whom they hoped to replace Denikin. Their agitation contributed to the general confusion and demoralization.

The various political groups did give some aid to the anti-Bolshevik cause. The support of the three major organizations conferred a degree of legitimacy on the Volunteer Army in the eyes of many Russians, and some foreigners as well. To some extent they provided the army with administrative personnel; to a degree they did succeed in mobilizing the people in support of the army in the cities. (They remained almost completely ineffectual in the countryside.) However, all in all, politicians accomplished very little, and they themselves were responsible for the failure: they did not know how to appeal to the people on basic issues, and spent their time in useless doctrinal arguments. The exclusion of civilians from positions of influence, however, was above all the fault of the army officers, who looked down on politicians and were suspicious of them. They never understood the value of the services civilians could provide.

CHAPTER 4

Policies

The Bolshevik leaders had firmly held goals, but they were flexible. They could make concessions and temporary adjustments in their plans precisely because they believed that their long-range goals justified some opportunism. When expedience forced Lenin and Trotskii to introduce measures which could not easily be deduced from Marxism (such as using military specialists or concluding a treaty with a capitalist power), their "heresies" caused bitter debates. But the leaders of the Party did not question each other's commitment to the ultimate goals; ideology remained the chief bond keeping the Party together.

The Bolshevik leaders, as men of keen political instinct, knew that in order to win the civil conflict they had to offer their followers a vision of a better future. They understood the importance of propaganda and articulated their goals in ways calculated to appeal to the largest number of people.

The anti-Bolsheviks lacked a well-defined program. After all, the revolutionaries wanted to change Russia, but the point of departure for the anti-Bolsheviks (with the exception of the increasingly powerless socialists) was always the prerevolutionary regime. It was difficult to base an attractive program on the return to the past. The anti-Bolshevik were more or less condemned to be negative.

The diverse elements in the White camp had little in common except their opposition to the regime in Moscow. Under the circumstances, as Denikin realized, any political program was bound

to be divisive. But Denikin was wrong in believing that the problem could be avoided. Although the leaders of the Army did not
make their political and social program explicit, and insisted that
the Army stood above politics, their political views could be in-
ferred from their actions, and it did not take long for the Russian
people to draw their own conclusions.

LAND REFORM

It has always been evident, to participants and historians alike, that
the single most crucial and complex issue the White regime faced
was the peasant question. The men to whom the leadership of the
White movement was entrusted very much wanted to avoid making
a decision on this matter. Like the socialist and liberal politicians
of 1917, they had long maintained that only the Constituent Assembly could resolve such a major issue as land reform. This desire
to avoid controversial issues was a conservative stance, and sooner
than the Whites would have wished the peasants began to understand that the policy of the Volunteer Army was always directed
at avoiding or even undoing any social revolution that would benefit
the countryside.

In the first year of the Volunteer Army, agricultural policies, such
as they were, were determined by the allies of the anti-Bolshevik
officers, the Cossacks. The Cossacks of the Don and the Kuban
lived on some of the richest agricultural areas of Russia. In the nineteenth century these territories attracted a large number of peasant
settlers, who could not become members of the Cossack estate
or even acquire permanent residence; they were called "people
from other towns" (*inogorodnie*). They remained much poorer than
the Cossacks and had to be satisfied with renting land or working
as hired hands. In 1917 this nascent class struggle was exacerbated
by an increased hostility between the two halves of the population:
the *inogorodnie* coveted Cossack lands, and the Cossacks were determined to defend their wealth and estate privileges.[1]

In November 1917 the Don and the Kuban seemed an attractive base to the future leaders of the Volunteer Army because the
Cossacks were in a combative, anti-Bolshevik mood. With their
tradition of self-government, better organization, and wealth, the

Cossacks completely dominated local politics, and they cruelly mistreated the *inogorodnie*. The army officers who made no attempt to stop them became accomplices. The same army that wanted to remove the Bolshevik government from Moscow was spending its energy fighting the peasantry of the Kuban, and the reputation of the White army as an enemy of the peasantry was established in the war.

In 1919, when the Volunteer Army came into control of large areas, it was increasingly difficult for the leaders to maintain their hands-off policy on the question of land reform. The secret service, the Azbuka, was especially active in urging Denikin to develop a policy. Azbuka agents rather perceptively reported on the mood of the peasantry both in friendly and in enemy territories. They all painted the same picture: the peasants wanted to take all lands suitable for agriculture, and would support only the side that expressed willingness to accede to their demand. The agents recommended that the army first legalize previous land seizures by peasants and then work out a reform plan to deal with the landowners who had managed to retain their estates. The reports were hopeful about the possibility of winning peasant support. While they were willing to concede the urban workers to the Bolsheviks, the agents saw weaknesses in Bolshevik policies toward the peasants which they wanted the Whites to exploit. They recognized that Bolshevik propaganda in favor of communes, and especially forced food collection, alienated the peasants. The anti-religious policies of the Bolsheviks and the large number of Jews in leading positions on the Soviet side also made the peasants hostile.[2]

As a result of these reports, and with the urgings of some of his advisers, Denikin realized that the army must present some sort of program to the peasants. On April 5, 1919, he instructed the Special Council to work out a detailed land reform plan. Aware of the propaganda implication of this issue in Russia and abroad, Denikin gave his instructions to the White propaganda organization to publicize. N. I. Astrov was instrumental in drawing up the order, but it was Denikin himself who put it in its final form; it was his only proclamation on land reform.

In his order Denikin pointed out that while the issue should ultimately be resolved by the Legislative Assembly of a reconstructed Russia, the state of agriculture was so bad that immediate steps were necessary. The land program of the Volunteer Army, he wrote, should be based on the following principles: (1) It must safeguard the interests of the working population. (2) It should strengthen small and medium-sized holdings at the expense of the treasury and the property of large landowners. (3) It must preserve the proprietors' right to the land; in every district, committees should determine the size of maximum holdings, and lands in excess of this maximum would become subject to forcible alienation for compensation. (4) Highly productive estates, forests, lands unsuitable for cultivation, and Cossack lands must remain inviolable. (5) Landowners should receive all possible aid from the state to stimulate production. Denikin added that class hatred and vengeance must not be tolerated.[3]

Meaningless verbiage aside, the important point in Denikin's proposal was the compulsory alienation of land with compensation. From the point of view of the landless peasants, it certainly did not compete with Lenin's simple land decree, but no White leader whose support came from the landowning class could offer more. Even if Denikin had wanted to, which of course he did not at this time, he could not have carried out uncompensated land seizures.

While Denikin cannot be blamed for the timidity of his proposals, he certainly can be faulted for not providing leadership and for allowing the issue to be neglected by his subordinates. Denikin's proposals were not radical, but even so nothing ever came of them.

It took almost a month for the Special Council to form a land-reform commission of 55 members. It did not bode well for the future of a meaningful reform that the chairmanship of the commission was assumed by V. G. Kolokoltsev, the head of the department of landholdings in the Special Council and a former minister in the cabinet of Hetman Skoropadskii. The commission formed three subcommittees which were headed by V. N. Nikitin, P. N. Sokol'nikov, and M. I. Goremykin. After weeks of work in the subcommittees and in 17 plenary meetings, the Commission completed its assignment at the end of July.[4] The plan it presented was restorationist and contrary to Denikin's desire for a meaningful land reform. It called for the immediate return of land seized at the time of the Revolution and envisaged some compulsory alienation only three years after the Civil War should have ended. Committees of landowners would then establish the value of the land, which of course only rich peasants could afford to buy, because the buyer would have to pay one-half of the purchase price at the time of the transfer. The plan also set extremely high limits (300–500 *desiatina*, 810–1350 acres, depending on localities) on the size of the holdings which the landowners would be allowed to retain.[5]

Denikin rejected the proposal, and as a result Kolokoltsev resigned. A. D. Bilimovich, a friend of Shulgin and a well-known agrarian expert, took his place as minister of landholdings. At the same time the Special Council formed a new commission, under minister of justice V.N. Chelishchev. The Chelishchev-Bilimovich commission worked for another four months. The debates within the commission were sharp and even the newspapers reported on the disagreements. Finally, six members (A. I. Chelintsev, V. A. Burnet, N. I. Astrov, B. P. Granskii, M. M. Fedorov, Bernatskii, and Lebedev) submitted a separate opinion in which they criticized the majority for not making more substantial changes in the Kolokoltsev plan. Indeed, the changes were rather minor. The new plan, too, envisaged the beginning of the reform only after the end of the Civil War. It proposed that the landlords should first be encouraged to sell their lands, with compulsory alienation to begin after the passage of two years. The maximums were reduced from 300–500 to 250–400 (675–1080 acres), which was not a very significant reduction.[6]

According to a calculation by A. V. Peshekhonov, a member of the Union for Regeneration, because of the high maximums and numerous exceptions (forests, highly cultivated estates, etc.) this plan if implemented would have affected only 25 percent of landlord property in European Russia. Since the peasants were buying 2 percent of landlord land yearly even before the war, the introduction of the reform would not have made a substantial difference. In the North, compulsory alienation would have been more important than in the South. In provinces which in fact were under Denikin's control, the peasants had little to gain by this plan.[7]

At the end of November, the commission submitted its revised plan to Denikin and to the Special Council. Denikin wanted the opinions of *zemstvo* leaders and also wanted the proposal discussed in the newspapers. Since Admiral Kolchak claimed jurisdiction in matters of agrarian policy for his "Russian government," Denikin hesitated to introduce the reform. In any case, it was probably too late for any agrarian policy to affect the fate of the White movement; the White army was retreating on a broad front and it seemed the wrong moment to publish a land reform plan.[8]

Agrarian policies became a divisive issue partly because of Denikin's lack of leadership. Had land reform been elaborated and actually implemented on the basis of Denikin's principles, it might have found support among most politicians. But as long as the Army did not announce a policy it was inevitable that the various political organizations which had mushroomed in Russia would debate the issue and make contradictory recommendations.

The monarchist State Unity Council, a pressure group of landowners, fought land reform from the very beginning. A. V. Krivoshein asked Denikin to postpone the publication of his declaration on land reform, which Denikin refused to do.[9] The rightists argued that discussions on land reform would divide the anti-Bolshevik camp, undermine respect for private property, create economic ruin, and destroy the morale of the army. Although Kolokoltsev belonged to the State Unity Council, even his modest proposal was rejected by the rightists. In its July 27 resolution the State Unity Council denounced the principle of compulsory alienation; it recommended instead strengthening the peasant land bank which would enable the peasants to buy land on the open market. The All-Russian Council of Landowners took the same position. Understandably, the right disliked the Chelishchev-Bilimovich proposal even more. Some members of the State Unity Council saw in it the destruction of landowners.[10] Wrangel, close to many of the leading figures of the State Unity Council, expressed his belief that there should be no compulsory alienation of land, and that land sales should be encouraged instead.[11] M. V. Rodzianko, the ex-President of the Duma, wrote Denikin, protesting the idea of transferring the land before convening the Constituent Assembly. He insisted that a land reform plan would ruin the finances of the state.[12] Opposition from the right had special significance because of the great power of the conservatives in local administration. One district chief, for example, refused to publicize Denikin's declaration of land reform because he considered that "type of literature" harmful.[13]

As in other political issues, Denikin found most sympathy for his ideas on land reform among the Kadets. The liberals appreciated better than most Russians the importance of foreign public opinion, and they believed that instituting land reform would disprove the prevalent notion abroad that the Volunteer Army was a reactionary organization. Most of them accepted the need for compulsory alienation and were willing to let peasants temporarily retain the lands they had seized in 1917 and 1918, provided that they paid rent. But since Denikin never introduced a land law, even the Kadets disagreed among one another. In May 1919, for example, Rodichev took a position similar to that of the State Unity Council, and argued that the Volunteer Army, which was fighting for the principle of private property, should not introduce compulsory alienation. He believed that since the state did not have the means to provide the new owners with the necessary farm implements, productivity would decline. Instead of compulsory alienation Rodichev advocated a high land tax, graduated according to the size of holdings, which would encourage large landowners to sell some of their land. The tax revenue would also benefit the finances of the state.[14]

Among Denikin's conservative advisers only K. N. Sokolov, a monarchist Kadet, and V. V. Shulgin understood that radical steps were necessary. Sokolov recommended to Denikin the immediate legalization of land seizures. Denikin felt that the proposal would find no support among powerful political groups, and he did not believe he possessed the strength to carry it out.[15] Shulgin wrote already in December, 1918

> It seems to me that without the resolution of the agrarian question nothing is going to happen. Our muzhik, in spite of his barbarism, is healthy in body and soul and extremely obstinate in his fundamental demands. Our landlords are flabby in body and soul and the healthy egotism of ownership, so strong among the English and the French is, to a substantial degree, lost among them. I have the inner conviction that to struggle in this respect is useless. But if we have to

divide the land in any case, the question arises whether we are correct in postponing this issue until the recreation of Russia. Indeed, the main obstacle of reconstruction is this cursed land issue.[16]

The socialists wanted land reform, but no socialist was included in any of the committees working on the plan. The moderate socialists believed that it would have to be the Constituent Assembly which would give land to the peasants, while those further to the left wanted to give all lands immediately to those who cultivated them. These men were completely without influence at the headquarters, and their views were never seriously considered by those who were in positions of authority.

The leadership of the Volunteer Army did not present a consistent agrarian policy, but it repeatedly had to resolve concrete issues affecting the life of the peasants. The most important and difficult issue was what to do with lands which had been seized by peasants before the establishment of the White regime. Members of the Special Council understood that simply taking away the land would fatally alienate the peasants and violently disrupt the economy. On the other hand, an anti-Bolshevik regime could not accept such a flagrant violation of the principle of private property. The dilemma was never resolved; a series of half-measures and compromises allowed the peasants to retain the land temporarily, provided they paid some rent on it. The lack of clarity on the issue of ownership created a great deal of uncertainty, which reduced productivity. The Special Council thus passed new regulations repeatedly, because it was concerned about decreased agricultural production. One might contrast the Special Council in this respect with Kolchak's government, which explicitly allowed the peasants to retain their land until the convocation of the Constituent Assembly.

The Special Council attempted to regulate rents in July 1919, just before the harvest, which created a great deal of confusion. On grass land the peasant could retain half of his harvest; if he had sown grain, he could keep two-thirds, and if he had grown vegetables or other products requiring intensive care, five-sixths of the harvest was his.[17] Concerned about the continuing decline of production, in September the Council further modified the regulations in order to benefit the new owners: the peasants could keep two-thirds of the grain and nine-tenths of the vegetables they produced.[18] In the minds of the peasants, the establishment of rent norms no doubt further identified the Volunteer Army with the landlords who had been chased away.

In order to protect the interests of those peasants who illegally occupied land but lost it when the White armies occupied the province, the Special Council ordered in July that if the person who harvested was not the same as the one who had sown, he had to compensate for seed and labor.[19] How this compensation was to be made was not specified. In any case, it seems rather unlikely that the central authorities could enforce compensation in areas where they had been unable to protect the peasants from being ousted in the first place.

Two regulations of the Volunteer Army especially benefited the well-to-do peasants. The Provisional Government very early had established a bread monopoly which forced the peasants to sell all their surplus grain at fixed prices. To enforce this monopoly it created elected local committees with wide powers. By this means the Government was able to keep the price of bread relatively low. On July 26, 1919, Denikin abolished the bread monopoly and the committees. The only restriction which remained in effect on a harvest was that each producer had to give the army five pounds of grain for each cultivated *desiatina* of land at fixed prices. Obviously, this was a far more burdensome duty for those who had little land than for those who had large holdings.[20] The reestablishment of freedom of trade helped those who produced a sizeable surplus, but it made the life of hired hands who had to buy their food more difficult.

The other regulation concerned land sales. In July 1917 the Provisional Government temporarily forbade these sales because it wanted to avoid speculation and the reduction of the land fund which was available for distribution. In January 1919 Denikin removed this restriction in the name of freedom of trade. The financial speculation which inevitably followed harmed the poor, who could now legally lose their land.[21]

All over Russia, in Bolshevik as well as in White territories, agricultural productivity declined and the acreage under cultivation decreased. This general deterioration of agriculture under the conditions of the Civil War was not surprising. During the World War and in the Civil War peasants were drafted into the army by the millions. The ownership of land was uncertain, and the man who sowed could not be sure that he would reap. Since industry produced very little, the peasant had no incentive to bring his produce to market. In the main agricultural districts under Volunteer rule in the first half of 1919—the Kuban, Don, Terek, Black Sea, and Stavropol provinces—amount of land under cultivation had fallen 36 percent since 1914.[22]

The Special Council was concerned about land left fallow, and in March 1919 it decided to give loans to peasants who could not cultivate their land because they could not afford to buy seed. The Council voted 19 million rubles for this purpose (the budget of the propaganda department at this time was 25 million for three months). The loan had to be repaid from the harvest. Denikin, who usually signed the minutes of the Special Council without comment, this time found it necessary to write in the margin: "I ask the Friday meeting of the Special Council to determine whether the interests of the small and middle farmers are adequately protected in setting up the organs which give out the loans."[23] There is no reason to doubt that Denikin's concern for the poor peasants was genuine, even if ultimately he did little for them.

The weather was favorable, and the 1919 harvest in the South, in spite of the reduced acreage, was good. The relatively bountiful supply of bread in the fall of 1919 was one of the main strengths of the Volunteer Army in its struggle to win over the people.

THE ECONOMY

It is hardly surprising that in the midst of civil strife which followed three years of war, the economy of the country was in great disarray. The Civil War destroyed factories, broke up former economic units, and created a sense of uncertainty among the people. Even the wisest policies could not have prevented privation.

The anti-Bolshevik South suffered all the ill effects of disunity. These were particularly visible in finances. A dozen different types of currency circulated. Monies printed by the tsarist regime, the Provisional Government, the Soviet authorities, the Volunteer Army, various Ukrainian governments, the new Caucasian states, and the Crimea had wildly fluctuating exchange rates. The Volun-

POLICIES   95

teer Army, which failed in the political arena, also failed to have
its claim to leadership recognized in the area of finances.

The ruble issued by the Volunteer Army had no gold backing
and its value constantly fell. M. V. Bernatskii, the head of the department of finances, saw that the only way out of the threatening
financial chaos was to establish ties with Admiral Kolchak and with
his aid issue a currency which would be acceptable everywhere in
anti-Bolshevik Russia. He needed to get Kolchak's cooperation,
because the Admiral was in a strong position; he had in his pos-
ession 652 million gold rubles out of the 1119 million Imperial
treasury.[24] In May 1919 Bernatskii formed a committee to study
the matter and initiated talks with the representatives of the Admiral. However, communications were impossibly difficult; every
message to Siberia had to go through Paris.[25] Inevitably, Bernatskii's efforts failed. The Admiral opened a small credit for the Volunteer Army for foreign purchases, but otherwise he gave no
financial support to Denikin. Bernatskii next attempted to persuade the English and the French to return 320 million gold rubles
in their possession from the Imperial treasury. But since both England and France faced different degrees of financial chaos as a
result of the World War, they were reluctant to part with this gold,
which they held as security for Russia's debts. Nor could they give
financial aid beyond delivering surplus munitions and other war
materiel. In vain Denikin's representatives tried to negotiate private loans from foreign banks.[26] Even at the height of his military
successes, he seemed a poor financial risk.

Under the circumstances inflation was inevitable. The loss of
confidence in the Volunteer ruble was gradual. In the first stages
the army paid for expenses by printing money, and it made up for
the decline in the value of the ruble by printing more. From the
middle of 1919, however, paper currency declined in value so rapidly that printing presses could not keep pace with the depreciation.

Up to October 1919 the Rostov press printed 9 billion rubles,
out of which the Don government kept 4.5 billion and the Volunteer Army took almost 4 billion (small sums were given to the Kuban, Terek, and Crimean governments).[27] In the last months of
1919 the Army established presses in Kiev, Odessa, and Novorossisk. Between October 1919 and March 1920 the Army printed 21
billion rubles. At the same time the department of finances ordered

money printed in England, but by the time it was ready for ship-
ment the army was on the verge of collapse and so it was never delivered.[28] In spite of the uninhibited printing of money, there was
a constant shortage.

This shortage had disastrous economic and political consequences. Factory owners often could not pay their workers. Army
commanders could not compensate the peasants for requisitioned
food; they paid usually in part with rubles and for the rest gave
receipts, which the peasants recognized as worth even less than
the paper money.

One of the most bothersome problems the army faced was what
to do with the Soviet currency in the hands of the population. The
Special Council was worried that the automatic acceptance of Soviet money would make it easier for the Reds to send their agents
South. They also feared that the Soviets might export more and
more worthless currency to the South and thereby further increase
chaos.[29] On the other hand, it was impossible for the government
to exchange all Soviet money immediately, because there was not
enough currency on hand.

For a time the Army would exchange 500 rubles for each individual. At a time when no reliable records were available, cheating
was easy. The exchange of money was carried out at the working
place. Factory owners often drew up false lists which included dead
workers and received money in their name.[30] The brazen corruption created indignation, and the Volunteer Army responded by
discontinuing the exchange. Those workers who had received their
last salary in Soviet rubles now were left penniless. The poorest
were hurt the most. Some had nothing to sell and were condemned
to starvation. This was another reason why the good will which
often existed among the population immediately following the arrival of the Volunteer Army was quickly dissipated.

The tax policy of the Army was regressive. Liberals and conservatives long debated how the burden of supporting the army
should be distributed. Astrov and his comrades wanted to levy
heavy taxes on the rich. The conservatives, on the other hand,
argued that in the prevailing confusion no direct taxes could be
effective. Bernatskii sided with the conservatives and based his
budget on indirect taxes. In the 1920 budget, which he drew up,

the army was to receive 18 times more income from direct than from indirect taxation. Government monopolies on sugar and alcohol, like indirect taxes, hurt the poor the most.[31]

Industry suffered even more from the effects of the Civil War than agriculture did. The effects were cumulative; as industrial production declined further and further, increased shortages in more and more materials caused bottlenecks.

The extent of economic disintegration varied from area to area. The Kuban, which had little industry and experienced relatively little fighting, was the best off. The Terek was in a bad position because of the constant struggle with the insurgent mountain tribes. The northern districts of the Don *Voisko*, which had always been the poorest, was fought over repeatedly with predictable effects. But perhaps the Donets basin and the Ukraine suffered the most. The front line moved back and forth, and partisan warfare made order even for short periods an impossibility. The economy came almost to a standstill.[32]

The collapse of mining, metallurgy, and the transportation system made the reconstruction of other industries impossible. The coal mines of the Donets basin, which had supplied a major portion of the needs of prewar Russia, now could not even provide for the area under White rule. The mines were flooded and to avoid starvation the miners sought refuge in the villages. Out of the 300,000 miners who worked in 1916–1917, only 50,000 were working by the beginning of 1919. The iron mines had 25,000 workers in 1916 and 4,000 in January 1919.[33] As a result of flooded mines, destroyed machinery, and undernourished workers, productivity of the miners fell to 50 percent of the prewar level.[34] The production of the Groznyi oil fields was only 10 percent of what it had been in 1914. The Army needed oil but could not get it from the neighboring oil fields of Baku because of the conflict with Azerbaidzhan.[35] Since there was no coal and iron, metallurgy could not function. Of the 25 iron mills which operated on the Donets basin in the beginning of 1918, 23 were forced to close down in the same year.[36]

The transportation system was in great disarray. By the summer of 1919, 60 percent of prewar rolling stock was out of commission. In January 1919 there were 1049 locomotives, but 357 could not operate. In September of the same year 368 more needed substantial repairs, which left the railroads with only 324 locomotives.[37] Even those in good condition often could not operate because of lack of fuel. Whatever fuel was available was needed by the military. It was a vicious circle: fuel could not be transported because of the collapse of the railroad network, and locomotives could not function because of the lack of fuel. Partisans destroyed tank cars, and oil from the Groznyi fields could not be delivered. The problems of transportation also drastically effected the food supply of the cities. Even when food was available, it could not be distributed to those who were hungry.

The Volunteer Army opposed nationalization in principle and it affirmed the inviolability of private property. When the army occupied a town it annulled all the laws and regulations issued by the Soviet government. This meant that factories were returned to their previous owners. But denationalization did not always bring such a major change as one might expect. Since the Bolsheviks did not have enough technical and business experts to serve them, they often allowed the old owners to continue to run their enterprises. When the capitalists were freed from Soviet control their work did not substantially change or improve. By and large they had little faith in the longevity of the White regime and therefore had no desire to invest in reconstruction. In any case, capital was not available and foreigners would not extend loans. As a result, a paradoxical situation was created in which the factory owners, just freed from the tutelage of the Soviet state, now clamored for state intervention. They wanted subsidies and loans from the treasury, but the treasury was so poor that it could rarely help. The Russian capitalist class did not prove itself capable of directing the reconstruction of the economy.

The selfish behavior of the anti-Bolshevik governments of the South greatly hampered the revival of internal and even foreign trade. V.S. Ivanis, minister of trade and industry of the Kuban, expressed the sentiments which governed the actions of all the new governments: "The basis of my work will be the principle that not one pound of our products will be allowed to leave our district unless we receive in exchange products which are needed by our population."[38] Given this attitude, a rational economic policy was impossible.

The leaders of the Volunteer Army struggled in vain to bring unity to their camp. In negotiating with the representatives of the Cossack governments, however, Special Council had a very weak hand to play. The Cossacks were richer and they had a great deal which the army needed, but the army could give little in exchange. In May 1919 the Special Council concluded an agreement with the Terek, Don, and Kuban about setting up an economic council in order to regulate trade. This very reasonable idea was never realized because both the Don *krug* and the Kuban *rada* refused to ratify the agreement.* Economic relations continued to deteriorate. For example, the Kuban was exporting bread to Georgia at a time when the Volunteer Army was almost at war with the Caucasian state, and districts contiguous to the Kuban, such as the Black Sea province, were threatened with starvation.[39] The Don government sold coal abroad when the Volunteer Army did not have enough for its navy on the Black Sea. Anti-Bolshevik Russia exported and imported coal at the same time at great cost. Denikin plaintively wrote on the margin of the minutes of the Special Council concerning a decision to buy coal abroad: "must we get even coal from foreigners?" (*variag*).[40] The Volunteer Army forbade the export of certain necessary materials, but in vain, because the traders were able to move their merchandise through the Don without interference.

In their frustration, the leaders of the Volunteer Army decided to retaliate, and in the fall of 1919 they set up customs barriers of their own and blockaded the streets of Kerch in order to prevent the export of forbidden merchandise. At a time when the Whites were engaged in crucial battles and the outcome of the Civil War was at stake, the different components of the anti-Bolshevik movement fought a customs war against each other, creating great bitterness.[41]

In spite of its introduction of customs, the Volunteer Army supported the principle of free trade. In the newly liberated territories this was a popular principle, since the people, no doubt wrongly, associated the trade restrictions prevailing in Bolshevik territories with shortages. Free trade meant above all that the peasants were free to sell or not to sell their products. The South enjoyed a rela-

---

rada. Kuban Cossack parliament.

tively good harvest in 1919, but the army still did not succeed in adequately feeding the cities. Since the factories produced next to nothing, the prices of industrial commodities rose rapidly. The peasants who sold their produce on the market soon could not afford to buy anything in the city. As a result, they lost their incentive to sell and agricultural prices also started to rise. This was a politically dangerous development, since it undermined one of the main appeals of the Volunteer Army. Up to the fall of 1919 the entrance of the White troops in a city was immediately followed by a great drop in the price of bread. But the high prices which prevailed at the end of 1919 placed the workers who lived on miserable salaries, and especially the unemployed, in a desperate position.

Since the Army needed much from abroad, and Western powers did not extend credit, foreign trade was essential. With the ruble almost worthless, foreign currency was very attractive to the industrialists and merchants. In fact, everyone who had anything to sell wanted to export, and however much the government disliked controls in principle, it was forced to establish a monopoly over foreign trade. The Special Council hoped to prevent the depletion of strategically important materials and accumulate foreign currency to buy essential products. In February and March 1919 the Special Council established three commissions. One dealt with convertible currency operations, the second with exports, and the third with imports.[42] At the same time it banned the export of certain essential raw materials, such as coal, iron, and leather. It also banned the sale of grain by private individuals. The sale of bread stuff and sunflower seed oil became the main source of foreign currency for the army. For these there was a ready market in war-torn Europe.[43]

The export ban was often circumvented. Since the Don government did not cooperate, anything could be shipped through the Don ports. Through corruption, individuals received export permits to the detriment of the national interest. Upon recognizing that export controls had failed, the Special Council in November 1919 decided to experiment with a new policy. Lebedev, the head of the department of trade, who was responsible for controls, was removed from his post, which was taken over by Fenin. Fenin allowed the export of practically anything, provided that the exporter gave 40 percent of valuta to the treasury and with the rest bought materials abroad, deemed necessary by the department of trade.[44] Fenin's policy might have worked better than Lebedev's, but there was too little time to evaluate it.

The Volunteer Army could have acquired money from abroad by giving concessions to foreign interests for the exploitation of Russia's national wealth. Those who advocated such a policy argued that involving foreign citizens in the Civil War was bound to be politically beneficial. The capitalists who invested in Russia would presumably act as a pressure group on their governments to help the anti-Bolshevik cause. In any case, giving concessions seemed an easy way to acquire foreign currency without any immediate cost. Denikin, however, felt that he had no right to commit the future state in this way, and the idea went against his notion of honor. He remained adamant. Only once did he relent: in December 1919 he gave his permission to a foreign investment group to exploit the forests of the Black Sea province.[45] Since the Army by this time was on the verge of collapse, the work could not even begin.

This short survey of economic life in the South would give a misleading picture unless we pointed out that conditions were even worse in Bolshevik Russia. In comparison, the Whites had a number of advantages. They controlled the most fertile agricultural regions of the country, and at the same time had a smaller urban population to feed. With the occupation of the Donets basin and the Ukraine, they came into possession of areas which were well industrialized, rich in raw materials, and included a well-developed transportation network. (One quarter of the railroad network of Imperial Russia was under Denikin's rule in the middle of 1919).[46] The Bolsheviks had great difficulty attracting managers and engineers, but the Whites had no such problem. But, perhaps most important, when Soviet Russia was so successfully blockaded that neither people nor goods could get through, the Volunteer Army received valuable war materiel from abroad. The Bolsheviks had to use the most draconian methods—at great political cost—in order to mobilize all resources for the needs of war, but the Whites needed no such extraordinary measures; they got most of their weapons as gifts.

White Russia suffered a terrible inflation. In January 1920 the value of the Volunteer ruble was 400 times smaller than the tsarist ruble of 1914 had been, when compared to the greatly depreciated French franc.[47] But the Soviet ruble could not even be exchanged; it was a worthless piece of paper. The shortage of money was so great that workers often received their wages in products made by themselves in the factories. Soviet Russia reverted to a barter economy. No statistics of reduced production, in themselves, can enable us to imagine the sufferings of the Russian people.

LABOR

City dwellers in general and workers in particular suffered cruelly in the Civil War. Factories closed down and thousands upon thousands lost their jobs; neither the Whites nor the Reds could solve the problem of feeding the cities; the workers were badly hurt by inflation. It was increasingly difficult for them to feed their families on the meager wages, and they had little to sell or barter for food. Those who still had ties in the villages returned to live with their relatives. This was a period of de-urbanization.

The workers who lived under the rule of the Volunteer Army faced special problems. The industrialists, freed from Soviet control, abused their position and exploited the workers without restraint. In short-sighted fashion, they wanted to take revenge on the workers for the indignities they had suffered under the Red regime. The leaders of the Volunteer Army did not protect the workers. To the generals the Russian people meant the peasantry, and they believed, however falsely and self-servingly, that they were acting in the best interest of this class. They regarded the peasants as victims of outside agitators and hoped that they would soon see through the propaganda of the Bolsheviks and repudiate them. But they were suspicious of the proletariat. They did not like cities and industry and assumed that the workers were hopelessly corrupted by the alien forces of modernity. This attitude was reflected in the reports of secret agents, who recommended an increase of agitation among the peasants but were willing to concede the workers to the Bolsheviks.

Socialists entirely dominated the Russian labor movement, and among its leaders were a large number of Jews. The generals' vis-

ceral dislike of labor leaders, and vice versa, was so great that collaboration between them was almost impossible.

Land reform was perhaps the most hotly contested issue within
the White movement. Gradually many understood that it was essential to win the good will of the peasantry and that concessions
were necessary, but at the same time powerful landed interests
resisted meaningful reform. It was very different with labor legislation. The industrialists had no organized lobby to defend their
interests. As a result, the Special Council promulgated a number of
laws concerning labor—none of which, however, made much practical difference.

On April 5, 1919, Denikin sent his instructions on land reform
to the Special Council. At the same time, with the aid of N. I
Astrov, he also worked out the principles on which labor legislation
should be based.[48]

1. The lawful rights of owners of industrial establishments must
be reestablished, but at the same time the defense of the professional
interests of the working classes must be guaranteed.

2. In the interests of the national economy, state control is to be
established over industry.

3. The productivity of labor must be raised by all available means.

4. There should be an eight-hour working day in factories and
plants.

5. The interests of the employers and employees should be recon-
ciled dispassionately (arbitration boards and industrial courts).

6. Workers' insurance plans should be developed insofar as
possible.

7. Organized representation of workers and an orderly development of trade unions must be allowed.

8. The workers should receive health protection. Female and
child labor must be protected. The inspection of sanitary conditions
in factories and plants must be organized. The living conditions of
the working classes should be improved.

9. Factories must receive all help in order to recommence work.
The establishment of new factories must be aided in order to prevent unemployment.

The Special Council set up a special commission, under M. M.
Fedorov, the liberal chairman of the National Center, which worked
for several months. In October and November 1919 this commis-

sion presented a series of draft laws and regulations for the consideration of the Special Council, and these were approved.[49]

On November 4 Denikin signed two of the regulations approved by the Special Council. The first established a committee to supervise the work of insurance societies. The committee, whose chairman was named by Denikin, included representatives from the trade unions, employers' organizations, and from the departments of trade, industry, justice, and interior. The second regulation concerned trade unions, and allowed the workers, even those who were employed by the government, to organize in defense of their occupational interests. The union leaders, however, objected to the clause which required them to register at a district court, which involved presenting their union constitution and list of members; unions which did not register within a month were to be outlawed. The regulations remained silent on the question of the right to strike.[50] On December 12 Denikin issued another regulation limiting the working day to eight hours. The force of this regulation was considerably diluted by the right of the employers to demand 400 hours yearly in overtime, and by its selective coverage.[51]

The labor legislation did not gain much popular support for the Army. It could not diminish the long-standing hostility of the proletariat to the generals. In the spring and summer of 1919 the Whites occupied the Donets basin and later the entire Ukraine, and tens of thousands of workers came under their rule. It is unlikely that at this time there were many active partisans of the White cause among organized workers. The majority vacillated between hostility and neutrality. According to the reports of the secret agents who evaluated the mood of the proletariat, time favored the Volunteer Army. It is not that the workers were won over by Denikin's policies, but they were becoming increasingly tired of the Civil War and losing interest in political questions. To many, the Volunteer Army seemed most likely to bring stability. Interestingly, Bolshevik strength remained strongest in areas such as Rostov and Taganrog, which the Reds only held for very brief periods. In the northern districts of the Don and in the Ukraine, Bolshevik strength declined.[52]

Unlike the peasants, who possessed no effective organization of their own, the workers could make their influence felt through the trade unions. Labor's primary weapon, the strike, could threaten the vital interests of the Volunteer Army. Although the Whites never attempted to suppress the unions completely, they harassed organized labor. Reactionary commanders often arrested labor leaders without cause, closed down newspapers, searched union offices, dispersed meetings, and intimidated workers.

On July 21, 1919, the most powerful labor organization, the Council of Southern Trade Unions, Iugprof, sent two delegates to General Lukomskii, the Chairman of the Special Council. In the memorandum which they submitted, they enumerated acts of terror, such as arrests and even murders of trade-union leaders. They pointed out that the behavior of some officers was at variance with Denikin's letter of April 5 to the Special Council. They warned that if the Special Council took no steps to punish the guilty, Iugprof would reconsider its previous decision to cooperate with the Volunteer Army. Lukomskii received the delegates in a haughty and tactless manner. He said that if the statements in the memorandum turned out to be false, the leaders of the Iugprof would be punished. Lukomskii considered it an insult that the unionists did not accept Denikin's word and that they insisted there was a variance between official statements and actual behavior.[53]

Two months later Iugprof addressed another letter of complaint to General Mai-Maevskii, the military governor of Kharkov. The complaints were familiar: local authorities without reason forbade meetings, arrested leaders, and threatened some with execution. In an act of petty tyranny the gendarmerie did not allow the trade unionists to use the word "comrade" in their meetings.[54] Mai-Maevskii did not even bother to respond to Iugprof. The attitude of the leading generals of the Army made it difficult for any unionist to cooperate with the Whites.

The issue of cooperation was debated most sharply in connection with the question whether to accept the invitation of the Special Council to participate in the work of the commission working on labor legislation. In June 1919 Ia. D. Priadkin, a Kadet mine owner and an appointed member of the commission, approached Iugprof in the name of the Special Council and asked that the workers choose delegates. In their conversations with Priadkin, representatives of Iugprof enumerated a number of conditions for their participation.

They wanted strikes removed from the competence of courts-martial, freedom for trade-union meetings and press activities, and a promise of noninterference by the military in the work of unions.[55] Priadkin promised to submit the conditions to the Special Council, and the unionists agreed to submit the question of participation to the local membership. In the following weeks meetings of trade unionists took place in all industrial areas. These meetings revealed the ambivalence of the workers toward the Whites. Although majorities ultimately favored participation, there were significant minorities everywhere which opposed it, and almost everyone had doubts.

The workers realized that now they possessed a bargaining tool. The Army needed their participation in the commission, because their presence would increase the chances that the workers would find the resulting legislation acceptable. The Whites wanted to spread the picture of officers, employers, and employees working together because they wanted to counteract the Army's reactionary image in Russia and abroad. The militant socialists had no desire to give this help to the Volunteer Army, which protected the capitalists and brutally mistreated the workers. On the other hand, the moderates, at this time, expected the ultimate defeat of the Bolsheviks and hoped to maintain good relations with those whom they considered the future rulers of Russia. They wanted to earn the right of the trade unions to exist. Within the Menshevik leadership of the trade union movement, the moderates were in firm control.

On August 20 the delegates of district organizations met in Kharkov to elect 18 representatives (employers were to have the same number) and to agree on a set of principles for the representatives to follow. The composition of the delegation accurately reflected the mood and opinions of the working class. From the composition of the delegation and from the principles the conference adopted, it was clear that cooperation with the representatives of the Army and of industry would not be easy. The conference elected a number of workers who disapproved of collaboration and also adopted a declaration which was bitterly hostile to the policies of the Volunteer Army. This declaration denounced the Volunteer Army, which it said had destroyed the achievements of the March revolution, abolished freedom of press and assembly, instituted terror and executions without trial, and allowed freedom of organization only for reactionary organizations. It further maintained that the Special Council could not represent the interests of the Russian people, and that the workers therefore rejected in advance all responsibility for the resulting legislation.[56]

The commission on labor legislation commenced its work on September 15 in Rostov. After M. M. Fedorov's opening remarks, Labutin, a metal worker, asked for the floor and started to read the Kharkov declaration. When he read that executions had become an everyday occurrence under Volunteer rule, Fedorov interrupted him saying that he would not allow criticism of the Volunteer Army and that the delegates should limit their remarks to issues which were within the competence of the commission. At this point the labor delegates caucused and decided to walk out if they had no opportunity to read their declaration. Fedorov rejected this ultimatum and the workers left Rostov on the same day.[57] Thus ended the cooperation of socialist labor leaders with the Volunteer Army.

Each side, of course, blamed the other. Denikin saw in the behavior of labor leaders the influence of Moscow, which was surely an absurd contention.[58] The Iugprof blamed the Volunteer Army in general and Fedorov in particular. Its resolution of September 18 pointed out that even in tsarist times the workers were allowed to have their say. The representatives of local trade-union organizations approved unanimously the behavior of the delegates.[59]

After the failure of this experiment in collaboration, repression against labor organizations became harsher than ever. Trade-union leaders had to walk a narrow path; they denounced both sides in the Civil War. They fought White repression and at the same time dissociated themselves from the Bolsheviks, whose rule they described as an anti-democratic dictatorship.

While suffering repression and demoralization, the labor movement was also threatened by a split: a movement organized by the engineer K. F. Kirsta attracted a large number of followers.[60] In 1905 Kirsta had been a socialist labor leader, prominent enough to be jailed for his activities. Following his liberation from prison he had retired from politics until 1919, when he began to advocate an ideology radically different from the beliefs of his youth.[61] His message was peace among classes. He repudiated strikes as a weapon and, of course, expressed bitter hostility toward the Bolsheviks. On September 3, 1919, he founded the Organization for the Unification of all Trade Union Workers in Kiev and a week later started to publish a newspaper, *Put' rabochego*.

Volunteer authorities fully appreciated what Kirsta was doing for them. Dragomirov, at that time the Military Governor of Kiev, received him on October 4 and told him that his activities had made a most favorable impression on headquarters.[62] The Army helped him in a number of ways: he received subsidies to publish his newspaper, and his organizational committee was allowed to take over buildings and a printing press confiscated from the socialist workers. Most important, the Army authorized him to exchange Soviet money for the workers.[63] The ability to draw up lists of workers eligible to receive money was a powerful instrument for agitation.

Support of the White authorities partially explains the rapid growth of Kirsta's movement. Within a month of establishing his organizational committee, Kirsta had nine thousand followers in Kiev, which was approximately one-fifth of the entire working population of the city. Soviet historians have maintained that Kirsta found support chiefly in small factories among, in their opinion, the least politically conscious segment of the proletariat.[64] Azbuka agents, on the other hand, reported that Kirsta found most of his followers in the largest enterprises, especially among railroad workers, metal workers, and water-transport workers. Their interesting, and perhaps partially correct, explanation of this phenomenon was that Jews worked in disproportionately large numbers in small establishments and that they were immune to Kirsta's appeal because of their ineradicable hostility to the Volunteer Army.[65] Another Azbuka agent saw the source of Kirsta's appeal in the disillusionment of workers with all ideologies. The Azbuka agents, while recognizing the value of Kirsta's contribution, showed a low regard for his character. They reported their suspicions about shady financial deals, and warned headquarters that the workers might soon be disappointed in such a leader.[66]

Indeed, the collapse of the movement was as sudden as its rise. Kirsta never had significant strength outside of Kiev, perhaps because he had no time to organize it. In the large industrial centers of

Kharkov and the Donets, socialist leaders remained firmly in control of the trade unions. Even in Kiev, Kirsta's strength largely depended on the fortunes of the Volunteer Army. As the workers realized that Volunteer rule would not last long, they left the newly established organization. When the Red Army approached Kiev, Kirsta hoped to mobilize the workers to help to defend the city. This was a singularly unsuccessful attempt. Only a handful answered his call, and he was hardly able to form a company.[67] After the Bolsheviks captured the city, the movement disappeared without a trace. Kirsta escaped to Odessa, where he attempted to repeat his organizational feat. This time, however, the situation did not favor him. The workers no longer believed in the possibility of victory by the Volunteer Army.

CHAPTER 5

The Cossacks

The Civil War in South Russia is usually thought of as a struggle between the rich and the poor, between those who were hostile to the pre-revolutionary regime and those who were basically comfortable in old Russia. This picture is somewhat misleading; reality was more complicated. The Red armies were made up largely of peasants, commanded by ex-tsarist officers, who, in turn, were under the supervision of Bolsheviks. But the White armies, also led by ex-tsarist generals, largely consisted of a special type of Russian and Ukrainian, the Cossack. The significance of the Cossacks' contribution to the White cause cannot be overestimated; at no stage of the conflict could Denikin's armies have long survived without Cossack participation. In the fall of 1919, at a time when the Volunteer Army had drafted thousands of Ukrainian and Russian peasants, it still included between 50 and 65 percent Cossacks.

The Cossacks were excellent fighters and they hated the Bolsheviks, who threatened their age-old privileges. This combination of military skill and political commitment often enabled the Whites to defeat numerically superior forces. However, the Cossacks had a parochial view of the Civil War. From the outbreak of the struggle to its end, the Cossacks and the officers fought for different goals and accepted different ideologies, and therefore their cooperation was always conditional and troubled.

The Whites and the Reds faced dissimilar tasks. The Bolsheviks attempted to impose order on an unwilling population and tried to coerce those who did not want to into fighting. The Whites tried to do these things, too, but they also had to work out compromises between already existing movements. The Bolsheviks formed the Red Army, which consisted of more or less reliable units of varying military value. The Whites, on the other hand, had hardly any forces which they could regard as completely their own. The Don Cossack army was merely an ally, subordinated to Denikin for specific purposes, sometimes carrying out orders, sometimes balking at them. The Kuban did not have an independent army, but politicians demanded it with increasing determination. Denikin's freedom of action was severely circumscribed by what the Cossacks wanted and what they would refuse to do.

The anti-Bolshevik movement among the Cossacks preceded the establishment of the Volunteer Army. Alekseev, Kornilov, and Denikin traveled to Novocherkassk in late 1917 because the Cossacks, who had defied the Provisional Government, had also resisted the Bolsheviks. Nowhere else in Russia could the generals find a safe refuge. When the Red victories forced the young Volunteer Army to leave the Don, it moved to another Cossack Voisko, the Kuban, because it expected a good reception. This unification with the Kuban Cossack army saved the small band of demoralized and defeated officers from annihilation. Soon the military situation improved. But even in May 1918, when Ataman Krasnov, for reasons of his own, tried to persuade Denikin to march on Tsaritsyn and established his base on Russian, as opposed to Cossack territories, Denikin resisted the idea. He feared that his Cossack army would not follow him and realized that he could not form a force of comparable military value from Russian peasants. This was the most serious weakness of the White movement: its leaders did not believe that the Russian people were ready to fight the Soviet regime. This lack of faith, which was probably justified, explains Denikin's overwhelming and debilitating dependence on his Cossack allies.

The Cossacks of the three Southern *Voiska*—the Don, the Kuban, and the Terek—faced different enemies and different economic and political problems. But they had much more to unite than to divide them. They attacked the leadership of the Volunteer Army, especially the Special Council, as reactionary. They denounced Denikin's policies as restorationist and declared that the old regime could not and should not be recreated. It is easy to sympathize with these criticisms. One could also admire the tradition of self-government among Cossacks, and their pride in their way of life. They were also richer and better educated than other Russian peasants. But there was a fatal flaw in their position: their comfortable way of life was based on the exploitation of those peasants who had moved into their districts, relatively speaking, a short time before, the *inogorodnie*. The Cossacks' unwillingness to share their wealth and power with the fellow inhabitants of their rich districts made their protestations of democracy, autonomy, and self-government hollow. In fact, they took arms against the Bolsheviks in order to defend their feudal estate privileges against their neighbors. In order to justify themselves in their own eyes, they created a bogus nationalism based on a mythical past. This combination of nationalism, belief in war-like virtues, and anti-monarchism made them especially susceptible to modern right-wing ideologies. It cannot be an accident that the Germans in the Second World War were more successful in recruiting among the Cossacks than elsewhere in Russia, and that Don Ataman Krasnov and General Shkuro, a hero of the Kuban, both ended their lives fighting for Hitler.

What obscure politicians did in the provincial towns of Ekaterinodar, Novocherkassk, and Vladikavkaz had significance far beyond the borders of the Cossack *voiska*. They largely determined the future of the White movement.

THE KUBAN

The Kuban was the heartland of the anti-Bolshevik South. Kuban Cossacks made up the backbone of the Volunteer Army, and the rich land of the district fed the movement. Although Kornilov and Alekseev established their organization on the Don, it was on the Kuban where it acquired strength, and Ekaterinodar remained the seat of the headquarters or *stavka* until the summer of 1919.

Denikin had a love-hate relationship with the Kuban Cossacks. He fully realized the significance of their contribution and remained faithful to his own conception of the alliance. When Wrangel suggested, during a period of defeats in late 1919, that the army with-draw to the Crimea, Denikin rejected the idea because it implied the abandonment of an ally without a struggle.[1] At the same time, he was bitterly hurt by the activities of some Kuban politicians and took their denunciation of the Volunteer Army personally. To the end of his days he was convinced that the simple Cossacks remained loyal to him, and that the problems with the *Voisko* were merely the result of the work of a few irresponsible politicians.

Even in the context of a complex civil war, the Kuban was excep-tional for the number and severity of the conflicts it harbored. The quarrels between the Army and the *Voisko* were unceasing and loud, but the struggle between the *inogorodnie* and the Cossacks was even more bitter. The *inogorodnie*, who made up 53 percent of the population, owned only 27 percent of the land.[2] Many of them had no land at all, but rented land from the Cossacks. The rich are usually brutal to the poor when the poor threaten their wealth, and the Cossacks, who completely monopolized political power, mistreated and abused their fellow citizens. The *inogorodnie*, for understandable reasons, sympathized with the Bolsheviks, but even those who originally did not were soon driven into the arms of the Reds by the short-sighted and selfish behavior of local poli-ticians. The treatment of the *inogorodnie* was not a subject of politi-cal debate because there was full agreement among all Cossack groups that their demands must be resisted. Nor was this subject an issue between the *Voisko* and headquarters, because the Special Council made no effort to protect the abused Russian peasant.

But Cossacks themselves were not united. The *Voisko* was formed only in the late nineteenth century from two very dissim-ilar groups, the Black Sea Cossacks and the *lineitsy*. Catherine the Great had settled the descendents of the Zaporozhe Sech, a Ukrain-ian Cossack *Voisko*, which existed until the late eighteenth century, on the coast of the Black Sea. Catherine also settled some Don Cos-sacks further inland, in order to defend the newly acquired terri-tories from marauding mountain tribes. Since they had to live on the frontier, or "on the line," they were called *lineitsy*. They culti-vated the rich lands on the banks of the upper Kuban river. The two groups, even after they were amalgamated into one *voisko*, lived separately and there was little contact between them. The Black

Sea Cossacks spoke a Ukrainian dialect, while the *lineitsy* spoke
Russian. The *lineitsy* were wealthier and tended to look down on
their fellow Cossacks.

Denikin found his allies among the *lineitsy*. Their politics were
dominated by liberals who would have been satisfied with a degree
of autonomy for their district. The *lineitsy*, less numerous than their
rivals, needed the help of the Volunteer Army to retain political
power. The Russian generals, however, thoroughly disliked the
political ideas current among the Black Sea Cossacks. These Cossacks retained their consciousness of being Ukrainians and followed with great interest what was happening in their mother
country. Among the numerous factions competing there, they
sympathized with the one led by Petliura, and approved of his combination of nationalism and socialism. Since Denikin and his fellow
generals regarded Petliura as not much better than a Bolshevik, they
suspected the Black Sea Cossacks of treason. The Black Sea Cossacks proclaimed as their goal the reorganization of Russia on a
federal basis. The Russian nationalists could not imagine their
country in any other way than as a centralized state, and to them
federalism simply made no sense. They believed that those who
talked about federalism in fact wanted to destroy the country. The
nationalists, who led the Volunteer Army, thought of themselves as
the defenders of Russia: they opposed the Bolsheviks, who seemed
in a sinister fashion to undermine the values on which their father-
land had existed through the centuries; but at the same time they
felt compelled to struggle against those who threatened the unity
of the state. The bitter and self-destructive feud between the federalist Cossack politicians and the Volunteer Army was merely one
result of the generals' narrow conception of nationalism. The problems were essentially the same ones the Army had with other border nationalities.

In the Kuban political spectrum, conservatives and monarchists
did not exist. It is a remarkable irony that among the Cossacks, who
had for centuries fought for the tsar, the monarchy had no defenders. The *stavka* suspected the Black Sea Cossacks of separatist tendencies, no matter how much the Cossacks protested that they
desired only a federation, and in turn the Cossacks regarded the
Army as monarchist, even though Denikin officially repudiated

monarchism. The gap between some Kuban politicians and the leadership of the Volunteer Army was considerable. The Kuban constitution was complex and cumbersome. The electoral law issued by the *Voisko* government on September 2, 1918, explicitly disenfranchised the *inogorodnie*.[3] Only Cossacks, members of mountain tribes (which included only a small group of people), and the "original inhabitants" (a small minority among the *inogorodnie*, those who came to the district before 1861) had the right to vote. The district *rada* of 500 members elected the Ataman and also a legislative *rada* of 80. The legislative *rada* remained almost constantly in session. Although the Ataman named the government, it was difficult for this body to function if it wanted to pursue policies different from those of the legislative *rada*. This complex system greatly encouraged infighting, and as a consequence the political life of the district was extremely turbulent.

The first Ataman, elected in October 1917, was Colonel and later General A. P. Filimonov, a *lineets*. In the elections of December 1918 Filimonov ran against L. L. Bych, the Premier. Since the Black Sea Cossacks were more numerous in the *rada* and since Bych was a popular leader, he undoubtedly would have become Ataman if the Volunteer Army had not applied pressure. The *stavka* regarded the election of Bych, a federalist, as a great threat and through its agents it let the members of the *rada* know that a vote for Bych was a vote for disunity, and that his election might mean a break with the Volunteer Army. The Cossacks feared this possibility, and their votes gave the election to Filimonov by a narrow margin.[4] The Ataman, instead of reappointing his rival as premier, chose F. S. Sushkov, another *lineets*. This appointment created a difficult political situation: the Black Sea Cossack majority of the legislative *rada* disliked the premier's politics. A bitter political struggle followed. The government's paper, *Vol'naia Kuban;* and the Osvag agitated against the *rada*, while the paper *Kubanskii Krai* expressed the point of view of the federalists and denounced the government.[5] On February 26 Sushkov, realizing that he could not carry out his job, resigned. But Filimonov did not succeed in naming a new premier until May, and consequently Sushkov headed a caretaker government for three months. The Ataman named P. I. Kurganskii, a moderate Black Sea Cossack, as the next premier.[6] The new

government included some of the most vociferous enemies of the
Volunteer Army, and relations between the *stavka* and the Kuban
further deteriorated.

The legislative *rada* published a land law which was most reveal-
ing of the peculiar political philosophy of the Cossacks. The pre-
amble asserted the socialist principle that the land belonged to the
people. But when it came to the practical issue of dividing the land,
it distinguished between two types of citizen: "The right to cultivate the land first of all belongs to all small-holder original inhabitants of the district (Cossacks, mountain people, and peasants who
settled before 1861) and only afterwards to the other inhabitants
of the district engaged in agriculture."[7] Since local government
was entirely in the hands of the Cossacks, the law meant in practice
that the *inogorodnie* did not receive any land at all. It was a peculiar
law which gave land to the rich, withheld it from the poorest, and
did all that in the name of socialism. The law allowed privileged
citizens to retain title to their land even if they had rented it out for
years, but it explicitly took away the property of those few *inogorodnie* who had surplus land to rent out. In some instances, *inogorodnie* had to leave their rented land even if they had built houses
on it, and the land was distributed among the Cossacks and other
"original inhabitants." These provisions did not create a debate.
The *lineets* minority, however, objected to the insistence of the poorer Black Sea Cossacks on establishing rather small maximum holdings. If the law had been fully carried out it would have meant not
only the destruction of large estates on the Kuban, but even the dismemberment of some medium-sized ones. In spite of the objections
of the head of the agriculture department, the *lineets* Skobtsov,
the *rada* passed the law on September 2 and Skobtsov resigned.[8]
In the conditions of the Civil War the law could not be carried out,
but made a great impression everywhere in the anti-Bolshevik
South. Landowners feared the socialist features of the reform and
were concerned that it might serve as a model for other legislatures.

The leaders of the Volunteer Army also disapproved of the land
law, but they did not interfere. They were far more concerned with
two other matters, the question of an independent Kuban army, and
independent foreign relations.

The federalists had wanted to undo the creation of a united
Volunteer-Cossack force from the very beginning. They argued

that the March 1918 Novo-Dmitrievskaia agreement subordinated the Cossacks to the Volunteer leadership only temporarily and only for operational purposes. In fact, the text of the agreement is strangely ambiguous. Although it mentions the unification of two armies, it continues to refer to the "Commander of the Kuban army."[9] After the occupation of Ekaterinodar and the liberation of the entire Kuban, the demands for an independent army grew stronger. The unification with the Don army in January 1919 encouraged the Kuban federalists, for whom the status of the Don army served as a model to strive for.

Ataman Filimonov, a friend of the *stavka*, long resisted the demand of the *rada* for an independent army. However, under mounting pressure and under the threat of losing credibility as a genuine Kuban leader, he decided to accept the point of view of the *rada*. On February 14, 1919, he issued an order which subordinated all Cossack soldiers to the authority of Field Ataman Naumenko, the minister of war. At the same time he ordered the creation of an independent army, which would fight in cooperation with Denikin's other troops. Filimonov wanted to keep at least a portion of his army on the Kuban. Since the Ataman issued his order without consultation with headquarters, Denikin simply disregarded it.[10] Issuing an order which he could not enforce undermined the prestige of the Ataman.

Filimonov tried several times to negotiate with Denikin. He promised that the Kuban army would fight the Bolsheviks shoulder to shoulder with other Russians and march all the way to Moscow. But the generals at the *stavka* did not trust the Cossacks. They believed that the Kuban would not have enough qualified officers, and, more important, in spite of the assurances of the Ataman, they feared that the army would become an instrument of the *rada*. In their opinion, once the influence of Russian officers was removed, the Cossacks would not pursue the Bolsheviks into the Ukraine and into Central Russia. The experience with the Don was not reassuring. The Don army was undoubtedly not as well led as other units, and the fighting value of the troops always perceptibly declined when the soldiers were ordered to march beyond the boundaries of the *voisko*.

Fortunately for the *stavka*, Field Ataman V. G. Naumenko, a Black Sea Cossack, was hostile to the goals of the federalists and a believer in a unified army. In order to buttress his position against the *rada*, he consulted the fourteen senior commanders of the Caucasian army in which most Kuban Cossacks served. As expected, only one, General Geiman, advocated an independent Kuban army. (Shortly after this, General Geiman was removed from his command post. The *stavka* charged him tolerating looting by his soldiers. The Cossacks, however, were very likely correct in believing that this was the price he paid for championing the Kuban cause.)[11] Relations between headquarters and the *rada* deteriorated in September 1919. Naumenko had to resign. The naming of a new war minister did not change the situation; the Volunteer leaders continued to resist the formation of an independent Kuban army.

It was more difficult to prevent the federalists from maintaining relations with foreign countries. The issue came to the fore in connection with the question of Russia's representation at the Paris Peace Conference. Everyone well understood that the interests of anti-Bolshevik Russia would be best protected by sending a united delegation. In December 1918 the Special Council made an unsuccessful attempt to form one. Since it refused to give concessions to the points of view of others, the representatives of the new "states" decided to send their own men to Paris. Anti-Bolshevik Russia did not speak as one: Georgians, Armenians, Azerbaidzhanis, Ukrainians, Crimeans, and Don and Kuban Cossack representatives went to Paris separately, often working at cross purposes.

It was a measure of the confusion of Kuban politics that the district could not agree on a single delegation. L. L. Bych, while still Premier, started to form a delegation. But once Sushkov became Premier, the federalists lost confidence in the government and therefore the *rada* decided to send its own delegation.[12] The government sent two Black Sea Cossacks, L. L. Bych and A. A. Namitokov, and two *lineitsy* autonomists, N. S. Dolgopolov and D. A. Filimonov, a relative of the Ataman. The *rada* delegation consisted of nine men, dominated by federalists. Remarkably, Bych was the leader of both delegations. It was not hard to foresee conflicts.

Dologpolov and Filimonov wanted to cooperate with Russian diplomats in Paris, especially with S. D. Sazonov, the chief representative of the Volunteer Army. The federalists, on the other hand, hoped to gain supporters for their cause in Europe and denounced the very people with whom their fellow delegates wanted to cooperate. Dolgopolov became so frustrated that he resigned, which left the federalist point of view practically unchallenged.

The Kuban "diplomats" hardly made an impression in Paris; the powerful statesmen of the Western world were far too busy to become interested in their cause. Since Bych could not even meet those few men who thought they were deciding the fate of the world, he composed a memorandum for their benefit. This memorandum gave a short and slanted history of the anti-Bolshevik movement on the Kuban. It did not mention the Volunteer Army, but pretended that the Cossacks liberated their district from the Bolsheviks alone. Although it stressed the democratic nature of Kuban politics, and denounced the "danger from the right," nowhere in its eight pages did the word *inogorodnie* appear.[13]

Volunteer agents in Paris reported to headquarters about the behavior of Bych and his comrades. The reports outraged the generals, but there was nothing they could do, which further increased their frustration.

Two unfortunate incidents exacerbated tension between headquarters and the federalists. On May 21 two armed men invaded the apartment of P. L. Makarenko, one of the leaders of the anti-Volunteer faction of the *rada*. The men carried out a search but later apologized and said that they were looking for another apartment in the same building.[14] This rather absurd excuse did not satisfy the *rada*, which ordered an investigation of the incident. The opposition in the *rada* regarded the search as an example of harassment, and its bitterness against the Volunteer Army further increased.[15]

The second incident had more serious consequences. On June 27 N. S. Riabovol, who together with Bych was the most prominent and irreconcilable leader of the Black Sea Cossacks and President of the *rada*, was assassinated. He was in Rostov at the time heading the Kuban delegation to a conference of Cossack *voiska*. The murderer succeeded in escaping and his identity has remained a mystery ever since.[16] There is no reason to believe that the High Command had anything to do with the assassination. Probably the murderer was a Russian officer acting on his own, someone to whom Riabovol's views were repugnant.

Riabovol, an inveterate enemy of the Volunteer Army, never caused as much harm as with his death. The murder had a tremendous effect on Kuban politics and occasioned an orgy of anti-Russian oratory. The *rada* held a hysterical meeting after receiving the news. It decided to hold a memorial service for the martyred leader in every Cossack settlement and military unit, and it ordered a three-day mourning period; it further demanded the expulsion of all Osvag agents from the Kuban and closed down all newspapers which had agitated against the policies of Riabovol. (If the editor was a Cossack he was to be drafted, and if a non-Cossack he was to be expelled.) Foreseeing armed clashes with the Volunteer Army, the *rada* ordered that the command of the Ekaterinodar garrison be given to "reliable" people. The declaration included these sentences: "Neither the monarchists nor the Bolsheviks succeeded in frightening Riabovol. They did not succeed in undermining the faith of the people in him and therefore they treacherously killed him." This accusation was clearly directed at the Volunteer Army.[17]

Riabovol was buried on June 30. On July 1 and 2 special meetings of the district and legislative *radas* took place in his memory. The orators denounced every aspect of the policies of the Volunteer Army. One deputy, Vodopinov, demanded the establishment of an army formed only of Cossacks, in order to resist the hated Special Council. Another deputy, Korbin, denounced the Army as reactionary, pointed out that all important administrative posts were given to those who had served the tsar, and advocated an anti-Volunteer alliance with the Transcaucasian republics.

The situation threatened to get out of hand. Cossacks attacked and killed some Russian officers. It seemed that a new and destructive civil war was about to begin. Denikin, wisely, decided not to respond to the provocations, and instead of sending punishment battalions he ordered the use of prisoners of war in Kuban agriculture. The Kuban government also behaved in a conciliatory fashion. It closed down a newspaper which offended headquarters by writing that only Cossacks did the fighting while Russians stayed behind and received comfortable staff appointments.[18] However, the memory of the July days did not disappear. When the day of reckoning came, it was to be bitter.

During most of the Civil War the Don was a battlefield. Unlike the Kuban Cossacks, who lived in relative security, the Don leaders knew that a break with the Volunteer Army would mean immediate occupation by the enemy, and consequently they moderated their hostility and demands. Also, perhaps because the Don Cossacks and the Russian officers did not become completely interdependent, the Army's relations with the Don were not as tempestuous as its relations with the Kuban.

For example, the Don retained its own army. Although this arrangement removed a source of conflict, it had numerous disadvantages. Denikin had to negotiate crucial strategic decisions with his subordinates, and even so he could not be certain that his orders would be carried out.[19] The Cossacks did not want to go beyond the boundaries of the *Voisko*, which often made it difficult for Denikin to send reinforcements to the sector of the front that needed them most. Cossacks generals did not properly coordinate their plans with the rest of the army. Mamontov, for example, on his famous raid, disobeyed orders, and the High Command in Taganrog did not even know about his movements; for this reason the Whites could not take advantage of the great confusion created by Mamontov's thrust into Soviet territory.

The political orientation of the majority of Don Cossacks was not too uncongenial to the Russian generals. On February 19, 1919, the *krug* elected A. P. Bogaevskii ataman.[20] He had been a participant in the Ice March and was a close friend of many of the leaders of the Volunteer Army. He was devoted to the idea of a united and powerful Russia, and as long as he was in office Denikin did not have to fear the influence of separatists and federalists.[21] Although according to the agreement of January 1919 the Ataman had the right to name the Commander of the Don army, Bogaevskii consulted with Denikin first. He chose General Sidorin, a leader of the anti-Krasnov faction, and General Kel'chevskii, a liberal, as the chief of staff.[22]

The liberals dominated the *krug*. The president of the Assembly, V. A. Kharlamov, had acquired a national reputation while serving in the Imperial Duma. He and his followers desired autonomy for

the Don, but always emphasized their commitment to an indivisible Russia. They were reliable allies of the Volunteer Army.

The Don political spectrum, unlike the Kuban's, included a
strong monarchist-reactionary faction. The popularity of Ataman
Krasnov remained strong. Bogaevskii, realizing that the deposed
Ataman might become a rallying point for his political enemies,
asked Krasnov to leave the district. After offering his services in
vain to General Denikin, Krasnov complied.[23] His followers, however, often retained powerful positions. G. P. Ianov, an enemy of
Denikin, remained the leader of the pro-Krasnov deputies in the
krug. When Allied aid did not arrive soon enough and in large enough
quantities to satisfy the Cossacks, pro-German and therefore pro-
Krasnov sentiment gained further strength. Of course, the expectation of German aid in 1919 was totally unrealistic; nonetheless,
the untutored Cossacks spread fantastic rumors about secret negotiations between Krasnov and Hindenburg, and expected the Germans to come back to fight the Bolsheviks.[24]

The socialist left was considerably weaker than the monarchist
right. The left was fortunate, however, in having an able and attractive leader, P. M. Agaev. Agaev had cooperated with the abortive
efforts of Ataman Kaledin to bring the *inogorodnie* into the government of the *Voisko*. He was among the extremely rare Cossack
politicians who wanted to extend the benefits of citizenship and
socialism to all inhabitants. Agaev attacked the leadership of the
Volunteer Army for its hesitant and conservative attitude in the
question of land reform and denounced the short-sightedness of
Russian nationalists. In February 1919 an attempt was made on
his life, which gave him an aura of martyrdom in leftist circles.[25]
His popularity spread beyond the Don, and especially among the
Black Sea Cossacks he had many followers.[26]

However, Agaev did not greatly influence legislation. The Don
land reform law, published on July 14, differed from the Kuban
program more in rhetoric than in substance. Instead of proclaim-
ing the socialist principle that the land belonged to those who cultivated it, this law reaffirmed the right to hold private property.
However, it established rather modest maximum holdings above
which the land was to be alienated.[27] As in the Kuban reform, the
poorest (those who came to the district after 1861) were excluded

from the benefit of the law. Agaev was shouted down by indignant Cossack deputies as he argued that all inhabitants should receive coveted land.[28] The Don was invaded before the reform could be carried out.

The discussions of the land law reflected the attitudes of the Cossacks toward the *inogorodnie*. The rhetoric was somewhat different after Krasnov's days: Bogaevskii, unlike his predecessor, did not call all Russian peasants of the district enemies, but instead exhorted them to join the anti-Bolshevik army. But the substance did not change. The pent-up hatred of the Cossacks against the peasants was never far below the surface. No troops behaved more cruelly during the Civil War than Don Cossacks occupying *inogorodnie* villages.

The *inogorodnie* and the working class were implacably hostile. The Don, unlike the Kuban, had a sizeable proletariat; according to 1916 figures there were 200,000 workers in the district.[29] Most of these people came from *inogorodnie* families, and so the behavior of the Cossacks toward the peasants also affected the mood of the workers. The *krug* passed a resolution promising liberal labor reforms, but in spite of slogans, the position of workers on the Don was worse than elsewhere on Volunteer-held territories. The largest cities of the *Voisko*, Rostov and Taganrog, became hotbeds of Bolshevik influence.

The Caucasus is like an ethnographic museum. The high mountains and valleys protected a variety of people who would have been doomed to extinction at the hands of their more powerful neighbors if they had lived on the more accessible plains. In this extremely heterogeneous area, the ethnically most mixed part was in the Northeast—the Terek and Dagestan regions.

The Terek, lying east of the Kuban, is a mountainous area with fertile river valleys. Before the Revolution it had a little under a million and a half inhabitants, of which only 40 percent were Russians.[30] But this minority was split in half. The Cossacks, making up 20 percent of the population of the district, were the descendants of warriors brought into this area by the tsars, in order to protect their domain from the warlike people who lived in the mountains.

For their service they had received generous land allotments. The average Cossack holding was 13.5 *desiatina*, (36.45 acres) which was even larger than Cossack farms on the Kuban or on the Don. The Cossacks not only had more land than other inhabitants of the district but also occupied the most fertile areas, the river valleys.[31] The other half of the Russian population, the *inogorodnie*, came in the late nineteenth and early twentieth centuries to rent land from the Cossacks and to work in the developing industrial centers of the regions. The relationship between the Cossacks and *inogorodnie* was no less hostile than in the other two Cossack *voiska*.

The native tribes living in the mountains, called the *gortsy*, consisted of four main ethnographic units, differing from one another in language, in culture, in economic standing, and in religion. They had a long tradition of fighting against each other. The richest of the four were the Kabardians, a Cherkess people, who owned, per capita, even more land than the Cossacks, though the area in which they lived was not nearly as fertile as the river valleys.[32] The Ossetians, an Iranian tribe, engaged in agriculture and were also reasonably well off. They had the highest level of education among all the *gortsy* and a sizeable intelligentsia. The Chechen and the Ingush were much poorer than the other two peoples. They had the smallest land allotment, and they lived in the infertile high mountain ranges. For centuries they had been the terror of the settled farmers, and even at the beginning of the twentieth century they continued to loot and harass their neighbors. With the exception of the Ossetians, who had been converted to Christianity in the fourth century, the *gortsy* were Muslim and welcomed the penetration of Turkish armies in 1918 and the extension of Turkish influence.

The course of the Civil War in the Terek was exceedingly complex. The native tribes, each having a population of not more than a few hundred thousand, not only fought against one another but also killed their own tribesmen. None was united. In the early days of the Revolution, two leaderships competed for influence among the mountain tribes: the native intelligentsia, who led the nationalist movement (which at this time had only modest goals), and the obscurantist clergy, who preached holy war against all Christians and city-dwellers. By the end of 1917 the Chechen and the Ingush had already started an indiscriminate war against all Russians. Under the circumstances, the Russians, even if only temporarily, had to unite. The Cossacks had formed their government following the March revolution and hoped to cooperate with the Don and the Kuban in the defense of their interests. The *inogorodnie* were led by the Bolsheviks. The Russians were helped by the disintegration of the Caucasian front, which freed tens of thousands of soldiers to return to their homes. These men spent substantial periods in the cities of the Terek and participated in the fighting on the side of their fellow Russians.

At the end of 1917, Bolshevik strategy in the Terek was to unite all Russians in defense against the murderous raids of the Chechen and Ingush. In January 1918 they convened a congress in Mozdok in which, aside from the Bolsheviks, the Socialist Revolutionaries, Mensheviks, and Cossacks also participated. Among the *gortsy* only the Ossetians sent representatives.[33] This broad coalition formed the Terek People's Council, which claimed governmental authority in the region. In March 1918 the Council was transformed into the government of the newly proclaimed Terek Soviet Socialist Republic, which established its capital in Vladikavkaz. The head of the government became the Georgian Jewish Bolshevik Noi Buachidze, who hastened to declare the Terek an autonomous part of the Russian Socialist Federal Soviet Republic.[34] Moscow advised moderation, and the Terek Bolsheviks continued to cooperate with other socialists at a time when the coalition broke down in the rest of Russia.

Eventually the alliance floundered on the issue of land reform. The *inogorodnie*, on whose support Bolshevik strength was ultimately based, demanded immediate nationalization of land. The government, fearing the effect of such a move, temporized, but under constant pressure it had to give in. This change of policy led to the immediate withdrawal of the Cossacks from the government and the beginning of anti-Soviet disturbances in Cossack areas. By the end of the summer the Terek was in chaos. The Cossack rising spread. On August 2 a Cossack band killed Buachidze and captured Vladikavkaz.[35] At the same time the Chechen and Ingush renewed their raids.

In August 1918 the Volunteer Army occupied Ekaterinodar and delivered one heavy blow after another to the formerly strong

North Caucasian Soviet forces. The Bolsheviks were suddenly faced with the loss of the entire Northern Caucasus. The Central Committee of the Party sent G. K. Ordzhonikidze to take charge of the deteriorating situation. Ordzhonikidze carried out a basic change in policy: instead of trying to recreate a coalition of all Russians, which had already failed, he attempted to build a front of *inogorodnie* and Chechen and Ingush. The Bolsheviks promised compensation from Cossack estates to the mountain peoples. Now the Civil War reached an especially bitter stage. The Cossacks were expelled from their *stanitsy* by the thousands, and the Muslim warriors distributed the wealth among themselves. The Ingush captured Vladikavkaz and mercilessly looted the city. When Soviet power was reestablished, no one talked any longer of moderation or autonomy: the Terek became an integral part of Soviet Russia.

The reoccupation of Vladikavkaz was followed by five months of fighting. At first it seemed that the Bolsheviks would be victorious: their armies were considerably larger and they maintained ties, however tenuous, with Soviet forces at Tsaritsyn. Their enemies were isolated from other White forces and were not united. The anti-Bolshevik resistance was led by a coalition of Socialist Revolutionaries and Cossacks; the first controlled the government and the second the army. The Cossacks wanted to establish ties with the Volunteer Army, and therefore preferred a strategy of striking west, while the Socialist Revolutionaries, who distrusted Denikin, would have liked to liberate the eastern districts first.[36]

During the fall of 1918 the Soviets organized their forces into armies, of which the Eleventh and Twelfth fought in the Northern Caucasus. In December 1918 it seemed that the Twelfth army would succeed in putting down the rising of the Terek Cossacks; many of the Cossack units dissolved and the Cossacks returned to their native *stanitsy*. But the victories of the Volunteer Army against the Eleventh army suddenly changed the strategic situation. (There had been no ties between the two anti-Bolshevik forces until September 1918, when an agent of Denikin, General Kolesnikov, flew over the Soviet lines and established contact with the Cossacks.) In January 1919 the Twelfth army had to withdraw because Denikin threatened it with encirclement. As a result, shortly after suffering defeat at the hand of the Bolsheviks, the Cossacks were liberated by the advancing Volunteer Army.

Denikin entrusted General V. P. Liakhov, the commander of the forces which liberated the Terek, with helping the Cossacks reestablish their government. The constitution of the Terek was similar to the Kuban's: the Cossacks elected a *krug*, which in turn chose an Ataman and a small *krug*, which remained almost continuously in session. At the same time, each mountain tribe was encouraged to elect a chief. The Terek now recognized the supreme authority of General Denikin and on March 7 the *krug* elected General Vdovenko ataman.

This way a dual power was established. Unfortunately, the Cossacks and the representatives of General Denikin never agreed on a precise delineation of powers. Liakhov, General Denikin's representative in the Terek, like most generals in the army, proved incapable of handling the delicate civilian tasks entrusted to him. Since the Terek was far from the main activities of the Volunteer Army, and since communications in this region remained particularly difficult, Liakhov acted as a viceroy, with practically unlimited powers. He was tactless and had no patience with those who insisted on genuine autonomy for the district. He surrounded himself with men of unsavory character. When his close confidant proved to be a sadistic murderer, involved in sordid extortion schemes, Liakhov himself was so compromised that he had to retire. In April 1919 Denikin replaced him with General Erdeli, perhaps a less capable general, but a more diplomatic man.[37]

Erdeli, in spite of his diplomatic abilities, could not succeed in removing all the sources of discord. To be sure, the Terek Cossacks could not defy the Volunteer Army the way the Kuban did. They were too weak, their enemies too numerous and close, and the memory of Bolshevik rule too fresh. Nevertheless, following the example of the other *voiska*, they demanded a greater degree of self-rule than the army leadership was willing to concede.

Most important, the Cossacks wanted an independent army. Liakhov had incorporated the remnants of the Terek force into his own troops. After the defeat of the Bolsheviks in the Northern Caucasus, Terek Cossacks, together with other soldiers, fought the main Bolshevik forces on the Don and in the Ukraine. In the spring of 1919 Liakhov organized some new units, which had the task of defending the region from the incursions of the hostile mountain tribes. In the summer of 1919 the *krug* repeatedly demanded that all

Cossack soldiers, wherever they fought, must come under the ultimate authority of the Ataman. The Kuban *rada* sent representatives
to Vladikavkaz to encourage the Cossacks and to work out a common position against the Volunteer Army. Headquarters, however,
remained adamant in this matter.

Economic issues also created strong disagreements. The Cossacks
wanted control over the mineral and oil wealth of the districts and
wanted to subordinate the city administrations to the *krug*. But since
the cities were inhabited almost entirely by non-Cossacks, they had
no desire whatever to be ruled by Cossacks; they wanted to elect
their own representatives who could negotiate with the Cossacks
as equals. In September 1919 the cities turned to the Special Council
asking that the laws regulating elections to city dumas be extended
to the Terek, and the Special Council approved the request.[38]

In 1919 the Volunteer Army succeeded in establishing its rule
in areas of the Terek which were inhabited by Russians. To establish control over the mountain tribes was a far more difficult task.
The Chechen and the Ingush were never subdued and their raids
and risings made the Northern Caucasus a festering sore for the
Volunteer Army.

THE SOUTHEAST UNION

The Cossacks very early realized that in order to defend their interests they had to unite. Almost immediately after the March revolution they formed a Council of Cossack *voiska* in Petrograd, in
which Cossack front soldiers played the leading roles. The Council
participated in the turbulent political life of the country, always
supporting conservative, rightist causes.[39]

The victorious Bolsheviks abolished the Council in November
1917, but the de facto independent governments of the Kuban and
the Don made new plans for cooperation against the Red Army and
against the *inogorodnie*. The demise of these governments was so
swift and confusion so great that these plans remained only plans.

Ataman Krasnov enthusiastically advocated bringing all Cossacks
together. The Ataman saw in unity a way to extend his influence
beyond the boundaries of his native Don. As was his wont, he developed ambitious and unrealistic plans. He wanted to build a Cos-

sack state with the participation of the Don, Kuban, Terek, and Astrakhan *voiska* along with Dagestan and the mountain tribes of the Northern Caucasus. In his correspondence with his German mentors he implied that such a state already existed. The Germans approved of the idea, because in the short run they wanted to expand the influence of the pro-German Krasnov, and in the long run they hoped that a Cossack state would be a step toward a radical dismemberment of Russia.[40] However, all the area with the exception of parts of the Don and the Kuban were under Bolshevik rule. The plans developed no further than some noncommittal conversations in June and July 1918 with Kuban delegates. The Kuban Cossacks did not like Krasnov's pro-German orientation and knew of Denikin's bitter opposition to Krasnov's plans. Krasnov's idea remained an ephemeral scheme without practical significance.

The fall of Krasnov and the reestablishment of the Terek *voisko* created conditions in which Cossack cooperation could be discussed meaningfully. In 1919 the Kuban Cossacks took the initiative. Above all, they hoped to gain the support of others in their struggle against the Volunteer Army. The federalist majority in the *rada* wanted to build an organization in which all regional governments would be included. On February 26 the *rada* passed a resolution: "To call a conference not later than March [O.S.] from the representatives of Don, Kuban, Terek, Dagestan, Crimea, Armenia, Azerbaidzhan, and others for the discussion of an alliance and the acceptance of a constitution."[41] The government, acting on this resolution, called a conference for May 18 to which, among others, the representatives of the Volunteer Army were invited.

The conference never took place because the Army headquarters prevented it. Denikin in particular objected to the participation of Georgia, a country with which the Volunteer Army was at war, and to the representatives of Dagestan and the mountain tribes of the Northern Caucasus, regions to which the Army was reluctant to extend autonomy. But the objections of the Russian generals went deeper. They disliked anything that resembled federalism. Conservative and narrow-minded politicians as they were, they could not see that a regional federation was an ephemeral scheme which would have floundered even without the hostility of the *stavka*. Neither the Don nor the Terek was interested in such an ambitious

plan, and the interests of the other "states" varied so much that they
had spent most of their energies in fighting against one another.
The leaders of the Volunteer Army feared experiments and new
ideas, and they were much more likely to see the dangers than the
opportunities.

The Don *krug* hoped to call a meeting of the representatives of
the three *voiska*. It discussed the idea several times during the spring
of 1919, but at the time the meeting seemed premature since the
front line was still so close to Novocherkassk that all energy had to
be concentrated on fighting the enemy. As the situation on the
front improved, interest in the idea of cooperation increased. V. A.
Kharlamov, in the name of the *krug*, issued invitations to the Terek
and the Kuban Cossacks for a conference to be opened in Novocherkassk on June 24.[42]

This time the *stavka* could not object. The Cossacks were clearly
entitled to discuss common problems, and any attempt to prevent
them from meeting would have had serious political repercussions.
In any case, Denikin had full confidence in Kharlamov, a man who
had rebuked the Kuban Cossacks for even thinking of federalism.[43]
Nevertheless, the Russians were full of apprehension. Lukomskii
instructed the Azbuka to send detailed reports on the secret discussions of the conference.[44]

Headquarters had no reason to be concerned. The Don and Terek
representatives took a moderate position, and the Kuban Cossacks
remained isolated. The moderates listened with dismay to Riabovol's blistering attack on the Volunteer Army. He made his usual
criticisms: he denounced the Army as anti-democratic, held it responsible for the terror everywhere, and in particular blamed headquarters for the quarrel with Georgia.[45] His assassination temporarily created sympathy for his point of view, but it did not
change the alignment of forces.

The Kuban delegates went to the funeral in Ekaterinodar and
after a three-day interruption the Don and the Terek Cossacks continued the discussions without them. They quickly agreed on basic
principles and decided to hold a meeting with Denikin. Sakhim-
Girei, the new head of the Kuban delegation from afar, warned
the conference in vain that talks with Denikin were premature.
On July 4 Denikin met Kharlamov and Kakliugin from the Don
and General V. I. Baskakov of the Terek. The discussions were

friendly. The Cossacks unquestionably recognized the supreme authority of Admiral Kolchak and accepted Denikin as his representative in the South.[46] Denikin, in turn, reaffirmed his commitment to Cossack autonomy and accepted the desirability of a legislative body in which Cossacks would participate.

The Cossacks' next task was to work out the details of the constitutional structure which they wanted to present to the Special Council. The work took two and a half months, partly at least because of the disagreements between the three delegations. Following Riabovol's funeral, the Kuban Cossacks did not return, in a show of displeasure at the results of the conversations with Denikin. To break the impasse, the Don *krug* appealed to the *rada* and promised that there would be no discussions with the Volunteer Army until the Cossacks agreed among themselves on a common position.[47] But the disagreements did not disappear; the Kuban federalists periodically walked out of the meetings, and the *rada* again and again instructed them to return, because the Ataman and other moderate *lineitsy* warned that the Kuban might remain completely isolated.

Finally, in September negotiations between the Cossacks and the Special Council began. The Special Council named V. N. Chelishchev, K. N. Sokolov, M. M. Fedorov, N. V. Savich and V. P. Nosovich to represent the Army. These men took an even more uncompromising position than Denikin did, and consequently the fruitless talks dragged on until Rostov had to be evacuated because of the great reverses at the front.[48]

The politicians insisted on two fundamental principles: the unity of Russia, and dictatorship. Within this framework they were willing to concede autonomy and accept a consultative-legislative Assembly.[49] The Cossacks, on the other hand, regarded their autonomy as a starting point, and not as a concession from the Volunteer Army. They argued that the future Russia must be based on the already existing anti-Bolshevik movements, and stated that they could not accept a government in which the role of Cossacks would be purely advisory. Even such pro-Army Cossacks as Ataman Bogaevskii and Kharlamov would not be satisfied with a purely consultative assembly.

Since there was no agreement on the fundamental issues, the delegates spent their time discussing details. The Army and the Cossacks agreed that foreign policy, defense, and finances should be left to the central authorities while matters such as police, local administration, and indirect taxation would be reserved for the *voiska*.[50]

The Volunteer leaders became increasingly frustrated with Kuban politicians. In the summer of 1919 they had to tolerate the immoderate oratory following the murder of Riabovol; they could take no steps against the diplomats in Paris who agitated against the Army; they watched with dismay the negotiations of Cossacks concerning the organization of the movement; and, most important, they listened to the increasingly insistent demands for an independent army.

At the same time, the bitterness against the Army increased in the *rada*. This was not entirely the result of the uncompromisingly centralist policies of the Special Council; Denikin's tactlessness was also a factor. When Ataman Filimonov reminisced in exile about the events of the autumn of 1919, he blamed not so much Denikin's acts as his insensitivity to the feelings of the Cossacks. It is hard to see the significance of Filimonov's examples, but we must take his word and accept the fact that Denikin's behavior incensed the Cossacks. For example, on June 19 Denikin met Cossack representatives in Ekaterinodar and asked them to state whether "they were for Russia or against it." Since many Cossacks regarded themselves as good Russians, this formulation disturbed and insulted them. On the same evening, in the course of a dinner given in honor of the visiting atamans, Denikin spoke of "terrible yesterday, strange today, and beautiful tomorrow." The Cossacks interpreted Denikin's words about the "strangeness of today," rightly or wrongly, as an attack on their autonomy. According to Filimonov, Denikin also betrayed his irritation at seeing the Kuban flag.[51]

The increasing hostility between headquarters and the *rada* made the position of the moderates untenable. Filimonov's influence in the *rada* continuously diminished. Most important, the *rada* removed Naumenko from his post of minister of war, because he did not work for the creation of an independent army.

A number of people at headquarters had recommended the use

of force. General Pokrovskii, the last commander of the Kuban army, and a political primitive, repeatedly offered his troops for use against the *rada*. In November 1918, when the *rada* accepted Bych's program which the generals regarded as offensive, Denikin for a while considered accepting Pokrovskii's offer. He finally decided against intervention and the incident was smoothed over by a compromise.[52] The Commander-in-Chief would have approved a coup d'etat carried out by the Ataman, but Pokrovskii offered his services to Filimonov in vain.

September and October 1919, a period of great victories against the Red Army, seemed a convenient moment to take care of internal disputes and strengthen the rear. At the end of September, a mysterious Colonel N. appeared at the *stavka* and suggested organizing the *lineitsy* in support of a constitutional reform which would make the Ataman stronger against the *rada*. He asked for 600,000 rubles for agitational work. The frugal Denikin would not give such a large sum, but he did not repudiate the idea. Colonel N. received some money, which indicated that the headquarters were now ready to intervene;[53] but he accomplished nothing and the money was wasted.

In the course of his discussions with Wrangel, Denikin decided to carry out a more ambitious plan. Wrangel, who at the time headed the Caucasian army, made up almost entirely by Kuban Cossacks, was especially concerned about political life of the Cossack district. He found that morale among his soldiers had declined, and he blamed separatist agitation. Since his army depended on the Kuban for food, he was concerned that political instability might also disrupt the supply system. Denikin and Wrangel understood that in the district *rada*, which was scheduled to meet within a short time, the Black Sea Cossacks would have a greater majority than ever. There were rumors that the new *rada* would demand the resignation of Filimonov and elect Bych in his place.[54] Neither Wrangel nor Denikin thought highly of Filimonov; they considered him indecisive and lost confidence in him. But the election of Bych would have been a direct challenge to the Army.

The military plan was simple. Pokrovskii would assemble reliable soldiers in Ekaterinodar on November 6, the day of the opening of the *rada*. Wrangel would arrive and in his speech to the *rada* would support a constitutional reform project, already submitted by a pro-army deputy. If the *rada* would bow to this pressure then the problem was easily resolved, but if the *rada* balked then Wrangel would turn to his troops "and explain matters to them."[55]

The first task was to produce a constitutional reform plan to be submitted to the *rada*. On October 22 Denikin instructed K. N. Sokolov to work out such a plan in consultation with Wrangel. Sokolov, a determined centralist and a man with experience in drawing up constitutions under the pressure of time, was the obvious choice for the job.

The Sokolov-Wrangel draft included these points: (1) The legislative *rada* was to be abolished and its functions distributed between the district *rada* and the Ataman. (2) When the district *rada* was in session it possessed supreme authority. The Ataman alone had the right to convene the *rada*, but he had to do so at least once a year. (3) The Ataman was responsible to the *rada*, but the government was responsible to the Ataman alone. (4) There was to be no independent army. However, the Volunteer Army would pay for everything taken from the Kuban; the Kuban would receive a share of the booty taken by the Caucasian army; the Kuban government could draft *inogorodnie* to serve in Cossack units; and Kuban Cossacks would be obliged to serve in an army other than the Caucasian only with the permission of the *Voisko*.[56] Denikin introduced two changes. He did not accept the recommendation that the Kuban could take a share of the booty, because it would have encouraged looting. He also rejected the idea of *inogorodnie* serving in Cossack units, because he understood better than Wrangel the bitterness which separated the two groups.[57]

When the *rada* opened on November 6 its composition and first acts surpassed the worst fears of Denikin and Wrangel. Not only a larger number of federalists were elected than ever before, but many *lineitsy*, recognizing their impotence, decided to stay away. The *rada* elected I. Makarenko president against the candidate of the *lineitsy*, Sushkov, and decided to devote an entire session to the memory of Riabovol, which predictably occasioned a number of anti-Volunteer Army speeches. The report of Sakhim-Girei on the Southeast Union and of Ivanis, the minister of trade, on the "blockade" of the Kuban further increased hostility to the Army.[58]

For once, Wrangel was indecisive. In his letter to Lukomskii he reported that he was uncertain about the reliability of his troops. His forces contained a large percentage of new recruits, and he did not know about the attitude of these men who had only recently joined the army. He hoped that military confrontation could be avoided because of the possibly disastrous effects not only on the Kuban, but also on other Cossack districts.[59]

In this tense situation, a new element was introduced which acted as a spark. A. I. Kalabukhov, a member of the *rada* delegation in Paris, returned to give a report. Just at this time it became public knowledge (it had only been rumored before) that Bych, Namitokov, Savitskii, and Kalabukhov had concluded a treaty of friendship in July with the Medzhilis, the government of the Chechen and Ingush, who had been fighting against the Volunteer Army for months.[60]

The representatives of the *rada* clearly had no right to conclude any treaty in the name of their government. That the delegates understood this is shown by the fact that they decided to keep the treaty secret. Of course a secret treaty of friendship was pointless and had no practical significance. The Kuban delegates acted irresponsibly and impulsively in order to express their dislike of the Volunteer Army. The Georgians exploited the situation. They had supported the Chechen and Ingush against the Volunteer Army, and had learned about the treaty from Medzhilis representatives. In October 1919 the Georgians decided to publish it, presumably to raise the prestige of their protégés and to further poison the relationship of the Cossacks with the Volunteer Army. The Russian press took over the news from the Georgian papers and the Georgians succeeded better than they had expected.[61]

For Denikin this was the last straw. He sent a telegram to Filimonov, demanding an explanation. The Ataman knew nothing about it, and he consulted with Sakhim-Girei, the president of the legislative *rada*. Sakhim-Girei did not deny the treaty, but came up with an ingenuous explanation. He maintained that the agreement was concluded against the Bolsheviks, in case the Volunteer Army was defeated and the Kuban had to face the Red Army alone. It was hard to take this explanation seriously, for it was unlikely that an independent Kuban could survive the defeat of the Volunteer Army.[62] Upon receiving this explanation from Filimonov, Denikin

decided to take immediate and energetic steps. On November 7 he
ordered the arrest and court martial for high treason of those who
had signed the treaty.

Denikin's impetuous act made the peaceful resolution of the conflict impossible. Wrangel and Sokolov, planning their next move,
were taken completely by surprise. Wrangel was dismayed that
Denikin had forced his hand instead of waiting for the appropriate
moment to act. More than ever he worried about the reliability of
his own troops. Vain man that he was, he feared losing his popularity among the Cossacks. He confided to Sokolov that carrying out
Denikin's order might force him to resign.[63]

But Wrangel exaggerated the dangers. After all, the advantage
of overwhelming force was on his side. Denikin declared martial
law on the Kuban, which suspended the organs of self-government,
and conferred the authority of military governor on General Pokrovskii. Pokrovskii had a long wait for this opportunity. He anticipated
armed resistance and prepared for battle. He cleared the district
surrounding the building of the *rada* and was ready to move.[64] Even
at this late hour the Ataman hoped to avoid confrontation. On the
one hand, he fired the head of the local militia, Tsibulskii, because
he expected him to fight for the *rada;* and, on the other, together
with premier Kurganskii, he wrote Denikin imploring him to withdraw his order. He argued that the Paris representatives did not
really commit treason, and even if they had, only the *rada* had the
right to judge its own representatives.[65] But neither the *rada* nor
Denikin was interested in conciliation. The *rada* countermanded
Filimonov's order to fire Tsibulskii and turned down the Ataman's
suggestion about sending a peacemaking delegation to Denikin.[66]
Denikin's response to the request was to telegraph Wrangel and
instruct him to disregard the Ataman.[67]

Wrangel did not himself go to Ekaterinodar. He stayed in Kislo-
vodsk and used Pokrovskii to do his dirty work. Pokrovskii gave
an ultimatum to the *rada*, demanding the handing over of 33 leading members of the opposition, including Kalabukhov. The Ataman
and some of the moderates tried to persuade Pokrovskii to give them
more time, and to consult with Denikin once more before the ultimatum expired. Pokrovskii refused to extend the time period, but
reduced his demand from 33 members to 11 leaders. He instructed

his troops to disarm the Taman Cossack troops, who defended the
rada. At this point the *rada* understood that resistance was useless, and the leaders of the opposition, with the exception of I.
Makarenko, who went into hiding, gave themselves up. The next
morning Kalabukhov was court martialed, found guilty of high
treason, and immediately hanged.[68]

When Wrangel learned of this he sent a telegram to Pokrovskii:
"I warmly thank you for the brilliant and decisive solution of a difficult task."[69] Now Wrangel was ready to enter Ekaterinodar, address the *rada*, and be magnanimous. He promised to spare the lives
of those who had been arrested, if the *rada* "behaved." Resistance
had collapsed. While Pokrovskii's soldiers surrounded the building,
the *rada* without debate deprived the Paris delegation of its credentials; passed a resolution which stressed unity with the Volunteer
Army; elected Skobtsov president in place of I. Makarenko; and
modified the Kuban constitution. These modifications did not go as
far as Sokolov had wished, but they went far enough to satisfy Denikin and Wrangel. The main points in Sokolov's plan, such as the
abolition of the legislative *rada*, the strengthening of the power of
the ataman by enabling him to dissolve the *rada*, and having the
government responsible to him alone, were now realized. Wrangel
used the opportunity to resolve two other matters. He had the op-
positionist paper, *Kubanskaia Volia*, which had been frequently a
thorn in the side of the Army, closed down. He bombarded headquarters with telegrams about the necessity of getting rid of Filimonov, who in his opinion, proved weak in the crisis.[70] Filimonov,
who realized that his policy of conciliation had failed, was ready
to go in any case.[71]

The *rada* elected a new ataman on November 24. Pokrovskii very
much wanted the job and now counted on the support of the Volunteer Army as a reward for his accomplishment. He asked Wrangel to support his candidacy, but neither Wrangel nor anyone at
headquarters considered it necessary to interfere, for every candidate was acceptable to the Army.[72] It shows Pokrovskii's lack of
understanding of Kuban politics that he even asked K. N. Sokolov
to stay in Ekaterinodar, to help him compose manifestoes and by
his presence indicate the support of headquarters. Sokolov explained to him that there was no politician more unpopular in Eka-

terinodar than himself, and that his presence would only hurt his chances.[73] Indeed, Pokrovskii had no support in the *rada*, which elected N. M. Uspenskii, a friend of the Volunteer Army but one uninvolved in the previous events. When after the election Wrangel asked Pokrovskii to describe what happened, Pokrovskii responded by saying he did not want to talk about it because the wound was still fresh and hurt too much.[74]

For a short time, it seemed that the Army had successfully solved the Kuban problem. The *lineitsy* held all the responsible positions. The new government of Sushkov and the *rada* modified the Kuban's economic policies, and the Army responded by removing the blockade. The Volunteers felt so secure that they could free all the arrested politicians, on condition that they left the district. I. Makarenko came out of hiding and promised to retire from politics.

However, the improved atmosphere lasted only for a month. Military defeats undermined the strength and prestige of the Army and its enemies came to the fore once again. Ataman Uspenskii contracted typhus and died after a brief illness. In December the federalists in the *rada* expressed their hatred of the Volunteer Army by electing as ataman a man who had no qualification for the job other than a history of quarrels with Denikin: Ataman Bukretov had an undistinguished military record and a reputation for shady financial deals.[75] The Black Sea Cossacks recaptured the government. But by this time nothing seemed to matter; the White cause was lost.

In reviewing the history of the relations between the Volunteer Army and the Kuban Cossacks, one is struck by the intensity of feeling on both sides. Why did the antagonists hate one another so much? One can only speculate. The generals felt particularly threatened by Cossack federalism because the federalists attacked the concept of a united and great Russia, which for them had become a magic slogan, one which justified their struggle. The pseudo-socialism of the Cossacks made their eclectic ideology all the more repugnant. The Cossacks, on the other hand, disliked their dependence on the reactionary officers. They were threatened by the Bolsheviks who wanted to take away their privileges, but at the same time they fancied themselves democrats, socialists, and progressives. Under the circumstances their inevitable alliance with reactionary officers was a source of embarrassment.

Intervention did not benefit the Volunteer Army. The morale of the Kuban troops had begun to decline in the second half of 1919, and as a result of the destruction of the *rada* it accelerated. Denikin's decision to court martial Kalabukhov was dictated more by anger than by considerations of political benefits and costs. His armies suffered decisive defeats and Denikin struck back against those whom he considered his enemies and responsible for the failures. Wrangel was very likely correct in arguing that without the execution of Kalabukhov the use of force could have been avoided, and the political costs minimized. The leader of a national movement could not afford the luxury of acting on his feelings. Wrangel, on the other hand, acted with remarkable skill. After some initial hesitation he took full advantage of the situation and at the same time managed to avoid direct involvement in the most unpleasant tasks. He was fortunate in having a perfect tool, Pokrovskii, who was so naive he did not even realize he was being used. Wrangel had only contempt for Pokrovskii and dropped him immediately when he promised to be an embarrassment. The Kuban federalists showed themselves once more for what they were: provincial men who played in politics, who had no sense of responsibility, who could not evaluate their forces, who could not distinguish the important from the trivial.

CHAPTER 6

The Ukraine

Imperial Russia was a multinational empire, in which Russians, according to the census of 1897, made up less than half of the population. The other half had little in common. On the one extreme there were the Poles, who had a memory of their own independent state, possessed rich cultural traditions, and benefited from a relatively modern economy; on the other, there were dozens of small Asiatic tribes, who had no written languages, whose economies remained almost unchanged through the centuries, and who had never demonstrated any desire for self-government. The tsarist regime had no consistent policy toward nationalities which differed from one another so much.

In the nineteenth century, in an age of nationalism, the Ukrainians, the Belorussians, the Finns, the Baltic peoples, and some of the nations living in the Caucasus became increasingly conscious of their national identity. Yet, up to the revolutions of 1917, with the exception of the Poles, none of the minorities living under Russian rule seemed a serious danger to the unity of the empire.

The disintegration of the once mighty state occurred remarkably quickly. The war demonstrated that the country could not be ruled by the old system of government. In the course of 1917 it became clear that liberal democrats also could not keep the empire together. The best argument for the existence of Imperial Russia had always been its power and success. When the government had obviously failed, when the power of the state had crumbled, it was not surprising that among the subject peoples aspiring leaders emerged who wanted to use the opportunity to attain independence or at least greater autonomy. Some politicians organized governments in outlying regions simply because Moscow and Petrograd were no longer capable of enforcing Russian rule. Many of these politicians in the past had shown little interest in nationalism, but once they acquired governmental portfolios they went through a remarkable transformation. Socialists, who had rejected nationalism on ideological grounds, now came to define their success in terms of the national interests of their "countries." "Internationalist" politicians became embroiled in territorial disputes with rival "internationalists" and soon behaved like ministers of imperialist empires. Russia fell apart. Not only did class struggle against class and ideology against ideology, but the country fell victim to the conflicting territorial demands of newly developed nationalisms.

This sudden flowering of nationalism hurt the White cause far more than it hurt the Bolsheviks. The Bolsheviks, flexible politicians, were much better prepared to give concessions. The Whites, on the other hand, fighters without clear goals, fastened to Russian nationalism as a unifying idea. Their obsession had disastrous consequences. On the one hand, the appeal to "a Russia great, united, and indivisible" had little attraction to the peasants, who wanted social reforms and tangible benefits. On the other hand, it made it almost impossible to come to terms with those who might have been allies against the new regime in Moscow.

The Reds occupied Russian populated areas, and their enemies, by and large, established themselves in non-Russian regions. This was not an accident. Generals Alekseev and Kornilov chose the Don as a place to organize their army because the Don Cossacks had already defied the Bolsheviks and therefore could offer a sanctuary. In the summer of 1918 Denikin would not move his headquarters to Saratov province, because he consciously or subconsciously realized that the Russian peasants would not follow him on a march on Moscow and so continued to base his movement on Cossack anti-Bolshevism. A year later he decided to invade the Ukraine because nationalist resistance to Bolshevik rule made the Soviet hold on this strategically and economically important region weak.

The Whites faced a dilemma. The most successful opposition to

Bolshevik rule came from a variety of national minorities and the Whites could not win without their help. At the same time ideological commitment made it difficult to give concessions which would win allies. The anti-Bolshevik movement had to be a coalition and to organize and hold together such a movement, the leaders needed flexibility, tact and skill. Even to the most superficial observer it is clear that the leaders of the Volunteer Army lacked all three.

THE CIVIL WAR IN THE UKRAINE

Denikin lost the Civil War in the second half of 1919 in the Ukraine. He allowed himself to be drawn into a morass.[1] Instead of gaining strength by attracting new soldiers and exploiting the valuable natual resources of the country, his administration could not overcome anarchy and his army was fatally weakened by an ever-increasing partisan movement. The Ukraine was a test case, and the Whites failed the test.

The Ukrainian peasants were not like the Russians. During the time of serfdom, *barshchina* or service obligation had never developed there, and another characteristic Russian institution, the peasant commune, was not at all widespread. Those who cultivated the land were poor according to European standards, but well off compared to their Russian brothers. Their relative wealth and individualism made the Ukrainian peasants more like Cossacks than like the ex-serfs in the heartland of the empire.

The peasant movement which developed in the years of chaos was stronger in the Ukraine than elsewhere in the country. None of the governments, which changed with great rapidity, was able to extend its rule over the countryside. The peasants rebelled against the cities, which were inhabited by Jews and Russians, and which only wanted to take and were unable to give. The anti-urban ideology of the peasantry was utopian and bound to be defeated, but it made the task of those who hoped to govern the country very difficult.

The country was rich in mineral wealth. Although it remained overwhelmingly agricultural, in 1913 it still provided 76.5 percent of the coal and 57 percent of the iron ore of the empire.[2] However, because of the nature of the industry, the working class remained relatively small and industry was concentrated in the southeast corner of the Ukraine, the Donets basin. The Donets provided Russia with raw materials, and in this sense the Ukraine was exploited. The permanent loss of this region would have been a tremendous blow to Russia.

Paradoxically, the wealth of the country contributed to its misery during the Civil War. Whites, Reds, and foreigners all wanted to get control of the agricultural and mineral resources. The starving European and Russian cities hoped to feed themselves at the expense of Ukrainians.

Its strategic location also made the Ukraine a coveted prize. The Germans, who found it impossible to conquer and hold the vast expanses of Russia, hoped to exercise control in the east by occupying the Ukraine. After the end of World War I the Allies wanted to contain Bolshevism by separating it from Europe, and they were therefore vitally interested in this region. The Poles and the Rumanians also planned to exploit the weakness of their eastern neighbor and expand into the Ukraine. The Bolsheviks regarded the region as a bridge to European revolution. When in March 1919 a semi-Communist regime was established in Hungary, they redoubled their efforts to defeat their enemies in the Ukraine, because only in this way could they hope to send help to their besieged comrades in Central Europe.

In the period following the abdication of Nicholas II, in Kiev, as elsewhere, a number of political groups competed for attention, yet it seemed that there was national unity in favor of a new and democratic society. The Ukrainian Central *Rada*, which had been created by moderate politicians, without qualification recognized the authority of the Provisional Government in Petrograd, and the interests of the nationalists were limited to cultural issues.

Nationalism, however, took a remarkably quick hold on the people. Soldiers on the front started to demand the establishment of Ukrainian units, and the peasants, who feared that in a general land reform they might lose their wealth to the poorer Russians, wanted the establishment of a land fund under exclusive Ukrainian control.[3] The dominant mood in the *rada* changed accordingly. Socialists who combined nationalism with social radicalism gained positions of leadership. And V. Vinnichenko and S. V. Petliura, the leaders of the Ukrainian cause, acquired prominence during the Civil War.

As a result of this evolution, the concerns of the nationalist movement turned from cultural to political. In June the *rada* demanded
from the Provisional Government recognition of Ukrainian autonomy, establishment of a separate administrative area, and the formation of a Ukrainian army. The Provisional Government, which in
principle favored regional autonomy, could not accept these demands because it feared that a large-scale reorganization in the
middle of a bitter war would lead to disaster. It wanted to avoid
major decisions affecting the future of Russia until the convocation
of the Constituent Assembly.

However, Petrograd lacked the force to impose its authority, and
it rapidly lost control over events. The *rada*, claiming to speak for
the Ukrainian people, formed a government which challenged the
Russians. As the extremists among the nationalists gained influence,
the people became increasingly polarized. The Russian and Jewish
minorities wanted to preserve the unity of the state, and feared that
in the Ukraine of the future they would be mistreated.

The Provisional Government accepted the fait accompli: it recognized the right of the *rada* to speak for the population of the Ukraine
and thereby the region achieved de facto autonomy.[4] However,
the nationalist politicians found it a great deal easier to oppose the
weak central authority than to establish order in the country. In
the second half of 1917 the Ukraine, like the rest of the Russian empire, suffered increasing chaos. The soldiers, like their Russian comrades, grew tired of the war and the poor peasants became dissatisfied
with the nationalists who did not give them land. The struggle within
the nationalist camp and the futile discussions with the Provisional
Government over the limits of autonomy seemed increasingly irrel-
evant to the majority of the people. Thus the nationalists failed to
gain grassroots support, and also failed to create a network of organizations on which they could base themselves during future battles.

When the Provisional Government collapsed in November 1917,
the position of the *rada* did not improve but deteriorated. In September and October the nationalists and the Bolsheviks worked
together against the Provisional Government, but Lenin's victory
ended this brief cooperation. The *rada* and the Bolsheviks now
competed for power.

The majority of the people, no doubt, would have preferred to be ruled by the *rada* rather than by the Bolsheviks, but the Bolsheviks had strength where it counted—among the workers, who organized themselves into soviets. By contrast, the nationalists had no organization and proved themselves incapable of forming a strong military force. After a short struggle, the Red Army took Kiev on February 8, and Bolshevik rule would have been established here, as elsewhere, if the Germans had not decided to intervene. The Germans concluded a separate peace with the Ukraine, and in a short time sent an occupying army. After three weeks of Soviet rule in Kiev, the Germans marched in and the Bolsheviks were in no position to resist.

The *rada's* victory, however, was short-lived. The Germans intervened because they wanted the resources of the Ukraine. Since the *rada* could not provide order, which was necessary for requisitioning, the Germans unceremoniously disbanded it. They entrusted the government to Lieutenant General P. Skoropadskii, a rich Ukrainian landowner, who assumed the historic title of Hetman. The new regime was openly reactionary. The Hetman repudiated the entire legislation of the Provisional Government, aided the landlords in their efforts to reclaim their lands, and rejected all "socialist experiments."

In order to increase his popularity, the Hetman came to endorse Ukrainian nationalism. However, this old officer of the Imperial Army visibly lacked a commitment to the Ukrainian cause, and there was never any doubt that he held his office only with German help. The Germans, with Skoropadskii's assistance, established a degree of order and took grain from the peasants. Their policy of brutal and naked exploitation created conditions for the growth of both nationalist and Bolshevik oppositions.

The defeat of the Germans in the World War and their concomitant withdrawal from the Ukraine plunged the country into the depths of chaos. In the course of 1919 a three-cornered struggle took place between Denikin's Russian nationalist Volunteers, the Bolsheviks, and the Ukrainian nationalists. The three antagonists shared a great deal: they were weak, they were rent by dissension, they could not control their followers, and they could not extend their rule to the countryside.

At the end of 1918 the Ukrainian nationalists appeared to be the strongest. When German defeat was imminent, and the collapse of

Skoropadskii's government therefore inevitable, the members of the dispersed *rada* formed a Ukrainian National Union, headed by a five-man Directorate. The leader of the Directorate was V. Vinnichenko, and the commander of its armed forces S. Petliura. The Directorate established its headquarters at Belaia Tserkov, only fifty miles from Kiev. The Hetman frantically tried to enlist the help of Russian conservative forces, but the Russians did not trust him. His army disintegrated; regiment after regiment went over to the side of the nationalists, and the Directorate's campaign turned into a triumphant march on Kiev. On December 14, 1918, Skoropadskii escaped to Germany.

The nationalists held Kiev for less than two months. When the Bolsheviks invaded the country, their advance was as rapid as the Directorate's had been a short time before. The peasants who had fought against the Hetman with enthusiasm now had little interest in the continued struggle, and the non-Ukrainian workers of the cities joined the invaders. The partisan groups which had been formed in the previous year to defend the people from foreign requisitioners, and who had sided with Petliura against Skoropadskii, deserted to the Bolsheviks. On January 3 the Reds took Kharkov and on February 5 Kiev.[5]

This remarkably swift defeat was a consequence of the character of the nationalist movement. Nationalism was the primary concern only for a group of intellectuals and semi-intellectuals, such as village teachers, minor bureaucrats, and journalists. Since the cities were Russianized, the movement had to find a base among the peasants. But it was more difficult to organize the countryside than the cities, and the commitment of the peasants to nationalism was dubious. In the beginning of 1919 the peasants did not care enough to defend a Ukrainian government in Kiev.

Furthermore, the Directorate was weakened by dissension. Those who were committed above all to nationalism gathered around Petliura, and those who took socialist reform plans seriously saw their leader in Vinnichenko. The split between the two wings became increasingly wide. Ironically, as the army suffered one defeat after another, its commander gained dominance within the movement.

No doubt the Directorate would have been eliminated in the spring of 1919 had it not been saved by developments beyond the borders, in neighboring Galicia. Galicia was the easternmost province of the Austro-Hungarian Monarchy, which the Habsburgs had acquired during the eighteenth century as a result of the divisions of Poland. Eastern Galicia had a Ukrainian majority and a Polish landed upper class. The Ukrainians there used the opportunity created by the dissolution of the monarchy to achieve independence, and formed a People's Council, which assumed authority in Lvov. From the beginning, the position of the People's Council was precarious. The Poles had designs on this region, and they possessed a strong army. Within three weeks the Council had to evacuate the capital. Galicians requested help from their eastern brothers.

The eastern and western Ukrainians obviously needed one another. However, cooperation between them was bound to be difficult, not only because they had been separated for a century and a half and had therefore developed traditions, but because different enemies threatened the survival of each. Petliura wanted to avoid a clash with the Poles and considered Denikin a friend rather than an opponent.

In the spring of 1919 Petliura's army retreated to a small strip of Galician territory which was still free from Polish occupation. In these difficult circumstances the nationalist leaders believed that the survival of their movement depended on foreign help. The idea of an independent Ukraine was alive not so much in the Ukraine itself as in foreign capitals, where delegations lobbied for their cause. Ironically, the nationalists counted on foreign help while the internationalist Bolsheviks became the defenders of national honor.

The French, who in December 1918 landed troops in Odessa, seemed the most promising patrons. However, they were ignorant of Russian circumstances and lacked the will to make sacrifices; their policy confounded friends and encouraged enemies. In turn, they lectured and humiliated each anti-Bolshevik faction and provided real help to none.

The nationalists were saved not by the French, but remarkably, by Denikin's advance into the Ukraine. The Reds had to concentrate their troops in the East and this enabled Petliura in the beginning of June 1919 to return from his Galician "exile." The change in the military situation occurred just in time, for the Poles now advanced successfully against the Galicians. On June 16 it was the Galicians' turn to lose the last strip of their homeland. Petliura gained forty thousand able and relatively disciplined fighters.

The Bolsheviks found ruling the Ukraine a very difficult task. Their problem was complicated by a deep division within their own ranks. This division had existed since the birth of Ukrainian communism, and was the result of ethnographic and social peculiarities of the country.

One faction, based in Kiev and in the western agricultural provinces, was led by two Ukrainians, G. L. Piatakov and V. P. Zatonskii. These men believed that they understood the particular local situation better than their comrades in Moscow, and they wanted to pursue an independent policy. Through their insistence, at the Taganrog Congress in April 1918 a separate Ukrainian Party was formed. They well understood the weakness of the Ukrainian working classes, and in order to carry out a revolution they wanted to gain the support of the peasantry. They planned to take advantage of the anti-German sentiment which existed in the villages and wanted the Party to take a leading role in the guerrilla movement. Their policy prevailed and it led to a fiasco. The Party participated in the anti-German rising in August 1918, which was easily suppressed.[6] This failure undermined the strength of the Kiev faction, the left wing within the Party. The right was influential in the industrial eastern provinces of the country. In Ekaterinoslav and Kharkov provinces and in the Donets basin the workers were Russians, Jews, and thoroughly Russianized Ukrainians, who had no interest in nationalism. The leaders of the right, F. A. Artem and E. I. Kviring, disapproved of participating in an ill-prepared resistance movement against the Germans. They regarded not the foreigners but the Volunteer Army as the most dangerous enemy. Following the August fiasco, the rightists won in the intra-party struggle and when the Second Congress met in October in Moscow, they dominated the highest party organs.

The withdrawal of the Germans from the Ukraine presented the Bolsheviks with a strategic choice. The rightist faction argued that since the proletariat was weak, the country was not yet ready for revolution. To these men it seemed that Soviet Russia must not be enticed into a dangerous adventure, but must concentrate on defeating its internal enemies. They would have been willing to continue cooperation with the forces of the Directorate, on the basis of allowing the nationalists to rule and the communists to organize.

The left, however, prevailed once more. While the communists negotiated with the Directorate, the leftists regarded the opportunity as too favorable to wait, and from the defeated partisan detachments formed an army at the northern boundaries of the Ukraine. Lenin and the Central Committee hesitated for awhile before approving plans for opening a new front. When they finally did, the triumphant march of the Red Army into the Ukraine seemed to have justified the policy of the left.

The Bolsheviks, like the nationalists before and the Volunteers later, found the country easy to conquer and difficult to rule. As the rightists had feared, the Party sank into the Ukrainian morass. The communists behaved tactlessly: Moscow removed the indigenous leadership and the new men had no understanding of local circumstances and needlessly violated national pride. The local communists also pursued a more radical policy than the Russians did at home.[7] Instead of dividing the land, many large estates were saved for state farms and collectives and the peasants were coerced into joining.

But most of the problems of the communists were not of their own making. The cities of Soviet Russia desperately needed food, and it was understandable that the communists, whose survival depended on it, made every effort to get grain. Since they could offer little in exchange, they were bound to alienate the peasants.[8]

As the peasants' hostility to the new regime increased, the partisan bands defected from the Bolsheviks and harassed their rear and communications. Perhaps nowhere did the Bolsheviks suffer as much at the hands of peasant guerrillas as in the Ukraine. The countryside was plunged in anarchy and the villages were ruled by no one. The Volunteer agents reported with obvious glee about peasant bands burning bridges, destroying railroad lines, attacking convoys, and cutting off the cities from the outside world.[9] Ironically, within a short time the same agents reported on the activities of the same bands, except at this time the partisans were fighting Denikin's regime.

The Volunteer Army from its inception had close ties with the Ukraine. Many of its leading figures had lived there and continued to maintain contacts with local politicians. In 1918 Kiev was the seat of both the Azbuka and the Army's most successful recruitment center. At first sight, it might appear strange that a Russian nationalist movement had such strong support in a non-Russian region. The explanation of the seeming paradox is that those who felt threatened by the unexpected force of Ukrainian nationalism saw their savior in the Volunteer Army; none were more rabid nationalists than those who felt their previous privileged position endangered.

In the first half of 1918 Kiev became the political capital of anti-Bolshevik Russia. Those who had escaped from the North found Kiev preferable to Ekaterinodar. Denikin did not welcome politicians, and in any case life in Kiev was far more interesting than in the provincial Kuban city. Socialists and monarchists, pro-Germans and anti-Germans, the friends and the enemies of the Volunteer Army held meetings, worked out projects, planned political combinations, and drew up more or less impractical plans for the future. The White leaders were kept informed by their friends.

The partisans of the Volunteer Army could work freely in Kiev because Skoropadskii protected them. He, of course, had to pursue a pro-German policy and pay lip service to the cause of Ukrainian nationalism, but in background and ideology he was so close to the generals in Ekaterinodar that under somewhat different circumstances he would have been one of them.

Denikin did not see it this way; he was not a man who thought in terms of the lesser evil. To him, Skoropadskii's espousal of Ukrainian nationalism and cooperation with Germany were examples of treason, and the fact that any conceivable alternative to the Hetman's rule would have been worse for the Volunteer Army made no difference.

In the fall of 1918 the Volunteers suddenly acquired a role in Ukrainian affairs. Realizing that he would soon be losing German support, Skoropadskii was frantically searching for new allies. He dismissed his pro-German cabinet and approached General Denikin for help. A small force of a few thousand Russian officers, organized by the local Volunteer recruiting center, acquired great importance, because only these men were willing to fight against Petliura. Thus the first "independent" government of the Ukraine could be defended from its own people only by men who passionately hated the idea of Ukrainian independence. But Skoropadskii's maneuver failed. Denikin at the time was fighting the Bolsheviks in the Northern Caucasus and on the Don, and he was not in a position to extend serious help even if he wanted to. The number of Russian officers in Kiev was far too small to stop Petliura's march on the capital.[10]

The late spring of 1919 was an optimistic period in the history of the Volunteer Army. The Whites advanced on every front and Denikin, of course, knew about the fragility of Bolshevik rule beyond the front lines. It was at this time that the Commander-in-Chief decided to invade the Ukraine. He wanted to gain control of the shortest route to Moscow and acquire economically valuable territories. He well understood that the loss of the grain-producing region would be a major blow to Soviet Russia. But once again, the Ukraine was easy to conquer and difficult to hold.

Of all the contenders for power in the Ukraine, Denikin was the only one who made no concessions to nationalism. He even went so far as to deny the existence of a separate Ukrainian people. In his formulation, the Russian people were made up of three components: Great Russians, Little Russians (Ukrainians), and White Russians. He saw no reason why the "Little Russian" provinces should be administered separately, or why they should be administered as a unit.

As his agents reported, the people found the term "Little Russian" insulting. One of them, writing from Kiev in November 1919, suggested a compromise, "Ukrainian Russia," but Denikin, even at this late date, remained inflexible.[11] In his opinion Ukrainian nationalism was not a genuine movement, but merely the result of the work of domestic and foreign subversives.[12] Among the foreigners he blamed the Germans, and at home the intelligentsia. He, and his advisers, deluded themselves with the belief that once the small group of subversives was isolated, the problem would simply disappear. It is a common failing among nationalists to be unwilling or unable to take the aspirations of others as seriously as their own.

An Azbuka representative wrote from Kiev: "Ukrainian nationalism opened up new perspectives for the half-intelligentsia: priests, village teachers, petty bureaucrats, medics—people who could speak Ukrainian. The victory of the Volunteery Army threatens them with a return to their former status."[13] This analysis is not without merit. The semi-intelligentsia indeed played a major role in the development of national consciousness (though not necessarily from self-interested motives), and the peasants and the workers had other concerns, such as land reform, inflation, unemployment, and the reestablishment of order. However, the Ukrainians, or, for that matter, the Russians, preferred to be ruled by their own government and had a profound allegiance to their language. To deny the appeal of nationalism was to delude oneself.

Denikin's attitude to the Ukrainian question was most concisely expressed in his proclamation to the "Little Russian" people, printed in August 1919. The proclamation, which was prepared with the assistance of the Kadet lawyer Professor P. I. Novgorodtsev, included these sentences:[14]

> Wishing to weaken the Russian state before declaring war against it, the Germans long before 1914 tried to destroy the unity of the Russian tribe, which had been forged in hard struggle. For this goal they supported and fanned a movement in South Russia which aimed at separating from Russia its ten Southern provinces under the name "Ukrainian state." The attempt to deprive Russia of its Little Russian branch even today has not been abandoned. Past associates of the Germans, such as Petliura and his aides, who began the dismemberment of Russia, continue their wicked work of attempting to form an independent "Ukrainian state" and fight against the recreation of united Russia.

This was bad history and even worse propaganda. The Germans obviously did not create Ukrainian national consciousness, and the way to win over waverers was not to call them foreign agents.

Denikin's arrogant denial of the authenticity of Ukrainian nationalism had fateful consequences. He made no efforts to win over the moderates and thereby divide the camp of his enemies; and more important, he would not temper his hostility to Petliura in order to achieve a temporary modus vivendi. He underestimated Petliura's strength. He could not see that the nationalist ideology had an appeal to the peasantry, and he, as a soldier, had only contempt for the irregular Ukrainian army.[15] While it is true that Petliura's subordinates often did not carry out his orders and that his army ran away from serious resistance, the Ukrainian nationalist partisans were adept at harassing the rear of the enemy. Petliura was a formidable opponent.

In the summer of 1919 the Ukrainians engaged the Red Army from the West and the Volunteers from the East; the benefits of cooperation between the two anti-Bolshevik forces were too obvious to miss. The Allies pressured Denikin and Petliura to patch up their differences. Churchill, whose prestige was enormous at White headquarters, sent a telegram to Denikin in August 1919 saying, "in the critical circumstances it would be reasonable to go as far as possible to meet the demands of the Ukrainian nationalists."[16] The Americans, through their representative in Warsaw, General Jadwin, made the same suggestion. Petain, the French military agent in Bucharest, brought Petliura's and Denikin's representatives together in the Rumanian capital.[17]

The nationalists seemed willing. In July 1919, Colonel Strizhevskii, the Ukrainian representative in Bucharest, made a sensible proposal to General Gerua, the Volunteer representative. He said that the Ukrainians would cooperate with anyone, "even with the Chinese," against the Bolsheviks. Of course the nationalists could not renounce the idea of independence, since that would be self-denial, but for the time being the question of the future form of the Russian state could be postponed. Petliura was willing not only to form a common front but even to accept Denikin's operational command. After the victory over the Bolsheviks, the struggle between the "allies" could be resumed. It is hard to see how the nationalists could have offered more, but Denikin still was not interested.[18]

There were some further diplomatic contacts between the Volunteer Army and the Petliurists. A Ukrainian general, Omelianovich-Pavlenko, headed a delegation to Volynsk in mid-September. The Ukrainians were friendly, and admitted that they came because of Allied pressure and because of the influence of some Russian commanders in their army. They hoped that it would be possible to establish a demarcation line, and perhaps to coordinate the struggle against the Bolsheviks.[19] Denikin once again turned down the offer.

The three-cornered struggle between the Whites, the nationalists, and the Bolsheviks created strange situations. For example, at the end of August 1919 a Volunteer unit under General Bredov and a Ukrainian Army under General Tarnovskii approached Kiev almost simultaneously. The Bolsheviks retreated and on the morning of August 31 Tarnovskii took the city. The population greeted the Ukrainians with enthusiasm and celebrated the occasion by murdering a large number of Jews. A few hours later the Volunteers entered the city, and they too received a warm welcome. At the center of the town on the Kreshchatik, there was some shooting between the two occupation armies. Bredov gave an ultimatum to the Ukrainians. Tarnovskii, whose troops were made up mostly of Galicians, had no desire to fight and evacuated the town within 24 hours.[20]

During the fall of 1919, when Denikin fought the crucial battles against the Bolsheviks, he had to use eight to ten thousand soldiers against Petliura.[21] In October the Whites dealt a series of blows to the Petliurists and their army fell apart. Some of the soldiers returned to their villages, many were captured, and others escaped to Poland. In the beginning of November the White troops reached the Zbruch river, the Polish border.

Denikin benefited from the fact that Petliura had shamelessly betrayed his Galician allies: in secret, he had concluded a treaty with Poland in which he recognized the Polish occupation of Galicia. The Galicians were put in a difficult position. Petliura became the puppet of their enemy, Pilsudski, but they could not return to their homeland and had no alternative to coming to terms with Denikin. On November 16 the Galicians and the Volunteer Army concluded an agreement, according to which they would join the Volunteer Army and be allowed to retain their own military organization. By this time these troops possessed slight military value: typhus had decimated their ranks, their morale was broken, and they were exhausted. Denikin withdrew them from the front lines and kept them in reserve.[22]

It is impossible to guess how much difference it would have made if the Petliurists had fought on Denikin's side, rather than against him. At least arguably, their help might have been decisive. In fairness to Denikin, it must be pointed out that Petliura's policy was so devious that it bordered on being dishonest. For example, shortly before receiving Gerua's report from Bucharest, Denikin had learned that Strizhevskii had suggested cooperation to the Rumanians against all Russians, White and Red, and warned them that a White victory in the Civil War would endanger their newly won province of Bessarabia.[23] Denikin, of course, also knew about Petliura's past contacts with Germany and his current relations with the Allies. He remembered the cooperation between the nationalists and the Bolsheviks both before the November revolution and during the days of the Hetman.

However understandable Denikin's revulsion to Petliura's diplomacy, he could not afford the pose of moral superiority. At times a statesman must conclude temporary alliances with those whom he cannot trust. Denikin had to establish priorities. He should have seen the overwhelming need to concentrate all energies on defeating the one enemy with whom there could be no compromise, the Bolsheviks.

Denikin's real failure was not military but administrative. Nowhere were the failures of Volunteer administration clearer than in the Ukraine. Here the army encountered a troublesome nationalist movement, a turbulent peasantry, which was disappointed in the reactionary agrarian policies, and an organized and hostile working class. The Volunteers, for the first time, also faced the uncongenial task of administering large cities.

Denikin usually gave administrative posts to Ukrainian Russians, who knew the local environment. Leaning on local people turned out to be not an advantage, but a source of weakness. The Army proclaimed a short-sighted and chauvinistic policy; the embittered Russian nationalists, however, went even beyond Denikin's goals and used their positions for petty revenge. Shulgin had a decisive influence in personnel matters. On his recommendation, for example, A. I. Savenko became the head of the Kiev propaganda bureau. This man was a notorious anti-Semite, a member of the reactionary Black Hundreds and such a fanatic hater of Ukrainian nationalists that even Dragomirov, Shulgin's friend, had to complain about him in a letter to Denikin.[24] The population formed their image of the Volunteer Army on the basis of their knowledge of men like Savenko.

Under the guidance of such politicians, the Whites attacked two institutions which they regarded as the mainstays of the nationalist movement, the cooperatives and the schools. An Azbuka agent wrote from Kiev in September: "The cooperative movement is the citadel of separatism where business is carried out in Ukrainian and you cannot hear any Russian at all. The cooperative movement as a whole is in the hands of separatists and is hostile to the Volunteer Army and to the idea of a united Russia."[25] The Volunteers disliked cooperatives everywhere, because they regarded them as socialist dominated, but in the Ukraine they tried to suppress them. They passed regulations which discriminated against them and closed down a number of them, often without ostensible cause.

The issue of Ukrainian schools was even more explosive. Denikin in his proclamation said this about the teaching of Ukrainian:

> While maintaining Russian as the state language of entire Russia, I consider completely unacceptable and forbid the persecution of the Little Russian national language. Everyone may speak in local establishments, *zemstva* offices, and in court the Little Russian language. Private schools, maintained by private means, may choose the language of instruction. In state schools, if the students so desire, classes teaching the Little Russian language in its classic form may be held.[26]

As Denikin must have realized, making Russian the language of instruction in state-supported schools effectively ended the teaching of Ukrainian. He knew that the teachers were nationalists and wanted to undermine their influence. His entire proclamation was received with great hostility by the Ukrainians, but the clause about the schools created the most indignation. The authorities responded by closing down those newspapers which complained.[27]

The Ukraine was a heterogeneous country in which the strength of the nationalists varied from region to region. The Volunteers in different sections of the country encountered different problems. In the west, especially in Poltava province, the peasants followed Petliura. By contrast, the rich peasantry of the north was relatively friendly. Here the peasants had rebelled against the Bolsheviks and welcomed the Volunteer Army. Since they feared that the Reds might return, many of them volunteered to fight for Denikin. The southeast, which was dominated by anarchist bands, was the most troublesome and most difficult to administer.[28]

Denikin, instead of setting up an administrative machinery to administer the country as a whole, created three military governorships: The first was for Kiev (including Kiev, Volynsk, and most of Podolsk, Poltava, and Chernigov provinces). The first military governor was General N. Bredov, who was later replaced by General A. M. Dragomirov. The second was for Kharkov (parts of Kursk, Voronezh, Poltava, Kherson, and Ekaterinoslav provinces). General Mai-Maevskii was Kharkov's military governor. The third was for Novorossiia (Kherson, part of Podolsk province, and the Crimea). Here the military governor was General Shilling.[29]

The two main centers of Volunteer rule were Kiev and Kharkov. It is worthwhile to examine these two cities in some detail, for each represented a different Ukraine. The history of these two cities during the autumn of 1919 was, to a large extent, the history of the Volunteer Army in the Ukraine.

Kharkov was held longer. The Whites took the city on June 24 and lost it only on December 12. By reading intelligence reports we can follow the gradual but constant worsening of living conditions, demoralization, and disorganization. In June the population greeted the Volunteer Army with great enthusiasm. The Bolsheviks had carried out more than a thousand bloody murders during the last days of their rule.[30] Also, the Reds could not provide the city with food and during the beginning of June the people suffered great privation. A report sent in the first days quotes a worker as saying: "that power is good which gives us bread."[31]

Since the great majority of the people was Russian, Ukrainian nationalism was not a problem here, and Kharkov received Denikin's declaration to the "Little Russian people" without objections. Volunteer representatives worried about the strength of organized labor, not about the nationalists. But in the first days even the workers put aside their hostility. In their eyes the most positive feature of the new regime was its ability to provide cheap bread. Immediately after the occupation, the price of bread fell to one tenth its previous level. In these enthusiastic first days the recruitment drive progressed successfully; five thousand men volunteered in the first three days.[32] Political life in the city also had a promising beginning. The city duma reassembled and elected a council consisting of five

Kadets and one National Socialist.[33] The duma took responsibility
for the reorganization of economic life not only in the city, but also
in the province.

Disenchantment with the army began among the workers. The
annulment of Soviet money was a great blow to them. Then they
found that the Whites could not reconstruct economic life and the
factories remained idle. Although food prices were lower than in
Soviet Russia, the unemployed workers could hardly feed their
families.

In August the agents complained about a general apathy. As one
of them who reported from the province rather than from the city
put it: "among the peasants a feeling of uplift is missing." He continued: "The peasants are passive and not willing to participate in
the struggle against Bolshevism though Bolshevism is alien to their
nature. But they refer to the Cossacks as 'yours' and not 'ours.'
They are merely observers. There are instances when they do not
respond to mobilization."[34]

After a momentary burst of enthusiasm, the apathy spread to
political life. Experienced local leaders had disappeared in the confusion and their place was taken by newcomers who had no strong
local ties. At the same time, because of the difficulties of communications, the organizations which operated in Kharkov had little contact with nationwide centers or parties.[35] In any case, the population
was visibly uninterested and the "leaders" were moving in a vacuum.

Even the most active group in Kharkov, the Union for Regeneration, which brought together leftist Kadets, Socialist Revolutionaries, and some Mensheviks, had only twenty-five members. The
Union enjoyed the support of the leftist intelligentsia and of the two
major papers of the town, *Novoe Slovo* and *Iuzhnyi Krai*. It organized
meetings in support of the policy of the army, and its behavior was
unfailingly loyal. The National Center was made up largely of rightist Kadets and it expressed the point of view of the local bourgeoisie.
It had only nineteen members.[36] The third major national organization, the Council for State Unity, was not represented in Kharkov.

Two months later, the agents reported not apathy, but active
hostility on the part of the population. The peasants had come under
the influence of the anarchists, and their bands threatened White
rule in the entire region. The workers struck increasingly often.

The capitalists speculated by buying up Soviet money. According to the opinion of one reporter, they purposely provoked their workers into strikes, in the hope that the Volunteer Army would interfere and suppress the trade-union movement.[37]

At a time when the Volunteer Army ruled over a large part of the former Russian Empire and threatened Moscow, the population of Kharkov lost faith in the ability of the Whites to survive. Rumors were rife. Some people claimed to know that Denikin was planning to name Shkuro "Dictator of the Ukraine," and since Shkuro had the reputation of a lawless marauder, the "news" created fear. Bolshevik agitators among the workers, and nationalists among the peasants, operated with increasing freedom. Whenever the authorities arrested subversives, there were others to take their places.[38]

A Volunteer Army agent, a certain Lieutenant Fedorov, wrote: "The Jews are playing a most negative role. They spread rumors and insinuations about the Volunteer Army. It must be said that not one class, not one political group, acts responsibly and can be trusted. In the present situation compromises are not enough and palliatives are futile. The extraordinary situation requires extraordinary measures."[39] The Lieutenant recommended the intensification of terror. Kharkov had come full circle; the population was now ready to welcome the Bolsheviks as liberators.

The Volunteer Army held Kiev from August 31 to December 16. Privation and the atrocities of the Cheka had united the population against the Bolsheviks. At the end of August bread cost 120 to 140 rubles a pound, which meant that it was out of reach for many. The Reds stepped up executions before they were forced to flee. On the day of the arrival of the Volunteer Army, the populace broke into Cheka headquarters and found dozens of corpses which the executioners had had no time to dispose of.[40]

During Bolshevik rule the Whites successfully prepared the soil by operating an underground organization, which informed headquarters about enemy strength and intentions, drew up a list of Bolshevik collaborators, and even published an illegal paper printed on the Communist Party's press.[41] The work of the underground enabled the Whites to arrest some of their enemies immediately. The greatest trump card of the Whites was cheap bread: in the first days of September bread cost only 7 rubles a pound.[42]

However, the Volunteer Army had made no preparation for taking over the city administration, and during the first days complete
confusion prevailed. The Bolsheviks had destroyed everything they
could; they left the offices not only without typewriters, but also
without tables or chairs.[43] The Whites punished everyone who had
worked under the Bolsheviks no matter in what capacity, and as
a result there were not enough experienced bureaucrats to take care
of day-to-day business. Embittered men used the opportunity for
petty vengeance and there was no defense against false denunciations. Perhaps worst of all, the Army could not guarantee public
safety: armed bands roamed with impunity, looting and murdering.[44] General Bredov, the military commander, proved to be
unequal to his task. He tried to resolve all issues by himself and
therefore thousands of people stood in line waiting to be received
by him. Of course, in the confusion he accomplished little.[45]

Kiev's political life was more conservative than Kharkov's. The
Kadets, in spite of having been compromised by previous association with the Hetman and the Germans, dominated the town. Their
leader, Grigorovich-Barskii, returned with the Volunteer Army
and placed his followers in the town administration.

The crucial issue for the Volunteer Army in Kiev was what attitude to take toward the Ukrainian nationalists. Political life was
polarized. Although the moderate nationalists first played down
their commitment to the Ukrainian cause, they received Denikin's
proclamation with consternation and hostility. Shulgin and his
friends, on the other hand, refused to make distinctions between
the various shades of nationalists and advocated an unyielding policy toward all of them. His paper, *Kievlianin*, was an influential
organ which disseminated hate propaganda against all non-Russians.

The Army acted in Shulgin's spirit: it suppressed those who advocated even modest concessions to the Ukrainians. When a newspaper, for example, recommended the resumption of post and
telegraph contacts with the parts of the country still under Petliura's
rule, the authorities closed down the paper.[46]

The apathy toward political organizations was even greater in
Kiev than in Kharkov. The Kadets organized some meetings and
lectures, but these were poorly attended and made little impact on
the population. "Leaders" were left without followers. As time went

on the people increasingly realized that the Whites were about to lose the Civil War, and as a result they tried to avoid identification with the regime. In the beginning of October a small band of Bolsheviks managed to break into the city and occupy it for a few days. This episode revealed the fragility of the Volunteer Army rule. The Whites tried to counteract the sense of impending doom and helplessness by an increase of terror. They brutally repressed those whom they suspected of sympathy toward the Bolsheviks or the Petliurists.

ANARCHISTS

During the summer and fall of 1919 the Volunteer Army captured the major cities of the Ukraine, and it controlled the railroad lines. But in the rest of the country, in the faraway villages, the Army usually made its presence felt only as long as its troops marched through. On other occasions chaos prevailed: peasants took the law into their own hands and small bands harassed the representatives of authority. For most of the inhabitants of the Ukraine, Denikin's conquest of the country made little difference.

At the time of the Civil War, the word anarchy had a double meaning. It denoted a condition of lawlessness and confusion, and also an ideology of the peasant movement. Obviously it would be misleading to describe the peasant fighters as conscious anarchists. The average peasant knew no more of Bakunin and Kropotkin than the average Red Army soldier knew of Marx. However, the peasants' violent rejection of governments was very much in the spirit of Bakunin, and therefore they can be fairly described as instinctive anarchists.

It is hard to characterize this movement. Hundreds of bands existed in the course of 1919, many of them only accidental gatherings of a dozen or so people who carried out raids against their enemies. The authorities did not know the names of the leaders, and at times they were not even aware of the existence of the bands themselves. Furthermore, it is impossible to draw a line between peasant bands and regular armies. All too often commanders fighting in the "regular" armies of the nationalists, the Bolsheviks, or the Whites did not differ in ideology and fighting methods from the anarchist chiefs. The most famous, or notorious, Ataman G. Grigorev, fought in turn for the Hetman, for Petliura, and for the Bolsheviks, then finally ended his career fighting for himself.[47] Obviously it would be misleading to describe him in the last weeks of his life as a changed man. The Volunteer leader Shkuro, the Don Cossack Mamontov, and the Red Army commander Budennyi shared much with Ataman Grigorev, although none of them defected. *Partizan-shchina*, as it was called, was in the temper of the times, and it thoroughly infected all the protagonists.

The origin of the anarchist bands goes back to the violent agricultural revolution of 1917. Peasants organized in order to dispossess the landowners, and the authorities did not have the power to stop them. During the era of the Hetman, the peasants banded together in order to resist German requisitioners. After the withdrawal of the Germans many of the groups did not disperse but continued to fight the Bolsheviks. By the summer of 1919 the Bolshevik hold on the Ukraine had become tenuous, largely because the Reds could not check the spread of the anarchist movement. However, the greatest flourishing of partisan activities occurred during Denikin's rule. On the one hand, the Whites had the misfortune of facing peasants who already had months of organizing and fighting experience; on the other, White ideology and practice were especially obnoxious to many peasants.

The anarchists had more success in the Ukraine than elsewhere because the tradition of rebelliousness was still alive there. Also, no other region had so many successive governments. The frequent changes of regime in Kiev made the peasants lose respect for authority and encouraged them to settle matters themselves.

The peasant bands to a large extent shared a common world view. Of all the participants in the Civil War, they were both the most radical and the most obscurantist; they rebelled not only against a social system, but also against urban civilization. As they cut telephone lines and blew up railroad tracks they were not only trying to harm their enemies but also expressing a deeply felt hatred. Ataman Zelennyi articulated this feeling when he said: "under no circumstances will we allow [that] a group of men, who do not want to work, to rule over us." In his opinion, none of the city dwellers wanted to work.[48]

The utopian character of their ideology and their inability to organize large armies condemned the peasants to ultimate defeat. However, the poorly equipped and ill-disciplined bands could inflict a great deal of harm on their enemies. Wily peasant leaders quickly learned how to take advantage of the assets of the partisans: a familiarity with the terrain and support from the population. Small armies assembled to carry out a particular military task, and when confronted by a well-organized regular force, they dispersed. When circumstances changed, the leaders reassembled their troops and struck at the enemy. The partisans often captured towns of considerable size, but they made no attempts to hold them.

Zelennyi, Struk, Angel, and Sokolovskii were among the best-known leaders. Zelennyi was a peasant with only two years of schooling, who operated in Kiev province. His real name was Danil Terpilo. The *nom de guerre* Zelennyi, meaning Green, was chosen to symbolize the peasant cause. He was a Ukrainian nationalist who fought against the Bolsheviks with great success.[49] After the retreat of the Reds, Zelennyi's representatives negotiated with the Volunteer Army, but no agreement was reached, and the partisans went on fighting.[50] Struk, who had dealt severe blows to the Bolsheviks in Chernigov province, did join the Volunteer Army. But according to Dragomirov, his ill-disciplined, marauding troops only brought harm to the White cause.[51]

The most able and successful of the peasant leaders was Nestor I. Makhno. In 1919 he was only 29 years old. He was addicted to alcohol, and had received very little formal education. At the same time he was the most colorful, talented, and charismatic peasant leader brought forth by the revolutionary upheaval.[52] He first became involved in politics during the 1905 revolution. In 1908, for participating in the murder of a police officer, he received a death sentence which was later commuted to life imprisonment. He spent nine years in jail, where he acquired all the education which he was to have.[53] He never learned to speak Russian well.[54] He was anything but an intellectual, yet he had a passionate interest in anarchist theory, which distinguished him from his fellow peasant leaders. When the March revolution freed him, he returned to his native village, Guliai Pole, in the Southeastern Ukraine. As one of the few martyrs from the village, he received a hero's welcome and was elected president of the District Land Committee of the Peasant-Workers Soviet and of the Peasant Union.[55]

At the time of the Hetman, he formed a sizable band which attacked German and Austro-Hungarian requisitioning detachments, burned down manors, and took revenge on those whom he considered enemies of social revolution. Though his fighting style was similar to that of the other peasant leaders, he was more daring, more imaginative, and more resourceful. Taking advantage of the element of surprise, his forces appeared where they were least expected and then disappeared before the enemy could organize. He won the respect and affection of the peasants. Legends spread about him. The peasants believed that he knew everything and could not be defeated.

Of the three forces fighting for the Ukraine in 1919, Makhno found the Bolsheviks the least objectionable. Unlike other peasant leaders, he had no interest in Ukrainian nationalism and therefore was never attracted to Petliura. To him nationalism was a bourgeois phenomenon, not the proper concern for the revolutionary peasantry.[56] In his opinion, the Volunteer Army was fighting for the interests of the landlords and therefore it was the most irreconcilable enemy of the peasants. He would not consider even a temporary alliance with such a force.

Makhno disliked cities, Marxism, and Bolshevism. Nevertheless he regarded the Bolsheviks as revolutionaries and therefore was willing to collaborate with them. In the early months of 1919 the Soviet hold on the north shores of the Azov sea was tenuous, and Makhno became the de facto ruler of the region. When during the spring of 1919 the Volunteer Army was approaching the Ukraine, he subordinated his rapidly growing army to the Bolshevik High Command. He received munitions and supplies and was allowed autonomous control of his forces.

Communists and anarchists did not work well together. Red agricultural policies, especially requisitions, alienated the peasants, and Makhno felt duty-bound to protest. On the other hand, Makhno's troops did not give a good account of themselves in conventional battles. Time and again their disobedience endangered the stability of the entire Red front. Trotskii, who had fought against partisan-type warfare for a year, was especially hostile to everything Makhno stood for. He blamed all the failures of the Red Army in the Ukraine on the anarchists. Since the Red High Command came to believe that Makhno caused more harm than good, it stopped delivering supplies and munitions, and finally removed him from his command. Makhno, who retained the fierce loyalty of his followers, could have easily defied the Reds. But he did not want to endanger the anti-Denikin front, and therefore retreated westward with a small group, occasionally fighting a small Bolshevik unit and "liberating" towns and villages.

At this time, when his military fortunes were at their lowest, Ataman Grigorev suggested cooperation. Makhno, however, regarded Grigorev as unprincipled and not a fitting partner. When he learned of the Ataman's plans for offering his forces to the Whites, Makhno had him killed. He then incorporated Grigorev's troops into his own army.

Makhno achieved his greatest successes during the second half of 1919, at the time of Denikin's occupation of the Ukraine. In July and August he retreated under the pressure of the advancing White armies. Although he suffered several defeats and was forced to leave his native region, he succeeded in building an army of about fifteen thousand.[57] On September 26 he decided to take a stand at Peregonovka, and in one of the crucial battles of the Civil War he defeated the Whites.[58] The Whites had concentrated their strength against the Bolsheviks and consequently denuded their rear. After Makhno defeated the only units in the rear, there was nothing to stop him. The consequences of this victory were enormous: in the following weeks the anarchists advanced hundreds of miles eastward, capturing some of the largest cities of the Ukraine, disrupting communications, creating havoc, and undermining the faith of the population in the ability of the Whites to impose order. For some time the anarchists held Krivoi Reg, Nikolpol, Aleksandrovsk, Melitpol, Berdiansk, and Mariupol. On October 20 Makhno took Ekaterinoslav and occupied the city for several weeks. The anarchists everywhere freed prisoners and burned down the jails. Predictably, however, they made no serious attempts to build an administrative structure and rule the territories which they had so easily conquered.

Makhno made an immense contribution to the defeat of the Whites. He was far more helpful to the Bolsheviks in the second half of 1919, when he was not an ally but operated on his own. At a time when the Whites hoped to capture Moscow, Makhno threatened Taganrog, Denikin's headquarters. The threat was so serious that in November even the British military mission was put in a state of defense and the British formed a fighting unit from thirty-two officers.[59] Denikin had to withdraw troops just at the time he needed them most. When the Whites retreated along the entire front, they found no secure bases. The rear was disorganized, largely thanks to Makhno's achievement. Denikin could not rebuild a stable front for months.

POGROMS

Before the advent of Hitler, the greatest modern mass murder of Jews occurred in the Ukraine, in the course of the Civil War. All participants in the conflict were guilty of murdering Jews, even the Bolsheviks; however, the Volunteer Army had the largest number of victims. Its pogroms differed from mass killings carried out by its competitors: they were the most thorough, they had the most elaborate superstructure, or to put it differently, they were the most modern. A brief examination of these pogroms may shed some light on the circumstances in which mass murders can take place and also contribute to our understanding of the character of the White movement.

The Russian empire, and especially the Ukraine, had a long tradition of pogroms. Times of social upheaval were usually accompanied by large-scale attacks on an innocent and seemingly unassimilable minority. The seventeenth-century Cossacks of Ataman Bogdan Khmelnitskii, when rising against Polish rule, carried out massacres of Jews which would have no parallel until our own times. While nineteenth-century Western Europe rapidly progressed toward emancipation, in Russia this progress was not only limited but also met by reaction. The last tsars had a peculiar mixture of anti-Semitism, which combined the ignorant xenophobia of the peasant with the shrewd calculations of a politician looking for scapegoats. The partisans of the regime always depicted the revolutionary movement as the work of aliens and grossly exaggerated the significance of Jews in it. It was anti-Semitism in high places which allowed the pogroms to occur following the assassination of Alexander II in 1881 and, on a larger scale, again in 1905. In fact, pogrom is among the very few words in the English language which is taken from Russian.

On the basis of Russia's past history, it was sadly predictable that the people would punish the Jews for the miseries of the World War. In 1914–1915 the High Command of the Imperial Army imposed further restrictions on Jews. Soldiers, on the ridiculous pretext that the Jews were helping the Germans, abused those who lived near the front line. Newly established Poland, which had acquired a large Jewish minority, was the first country in the postwar world to allow its citizens to carry out raids against this abused minority.

The majority of Jews who remained in the territory of what was to become the Soviet Union lived in the Ukraine (1.6 out of 2.6 million). In 1918 anti-Semitic agitation in German-occupied territories gathered force. However, compared to what followed, the Jews survived the first stages of the Civil War well. But the withdrawal of the occupation army, following the Armistice, plunged the country into unparalleled anarchy and rather suddenly, pogroms began. The first murders occurred in January 1919 in areas under Petliura's control, as his army was retreating under the pressure of the Bolshevik advance.[60] Petliura, who based his hope on foreign recognition and help, had to repudiate pogroms and he even named a Jew "minister of Jewish affairs." However, he did little to prevent anti-Semitic outbreaks, and his followers well understood that his injunctions against "excesses" were meant exclusively for foreign audiences. The nationalists habitually depicted their enemies as Jewish and thereby did a great deal to prepare the soil for what was to come.

The anarchist bands, unlike Petliura and the leaders of the Volunteer Army, did not have to worry about foreign public opinion and they engaged in the most unrestrained verbal violence against the Jews. However, because they were ill-organized and controlled only small strips of territory, they were not in a position to murder many, whatever their intention. For the violence to reach an even higher level of intensity, a larger and better organized army was necessary.

Up to June 1919 the Volunteer Army occupied areas which had only very small Jewish communities. These communities did suffer.

For example, in the summer of 1918, Shkuro herded the Jews of
Stavropol together in a synagogue and threatened them with burning unless they paid an exorbitant ransom.[61] But the number of victims was small until the invasion of the Ukraine brought the Whites
into an area with a large Jewish minority. Then mass killings immediately began.

N. I. Shtif, on the basis of material collected by a Jewish committee in 1922, distinguished three periods in Volunteer Army
pogroms. The first period he named "quiet pogroms." These occurred mostly in June and July 1919 in areas which had just come
under White rule. Cossacks attacked individual Jews, looted some
houses, and raped some women. In August, at a time when the
Volunteer Army was advancing most rapidly, "quiet pogroms"
turned into mass pogroms. At this time the Cossacks looted on a
large scale. Everything which could be taken was removed and the
immovable was often burned. Many Jews were murdered, but at
this time it was still possible to buy off the murderers. The third
period, the time of retreats and repeated changes in possession of
individual towns, was a time of mass murders. The defeated took
revenge on the defenseless.[62]

From the accounts of survivors we can reconstruct a typical
pogrom. Volunteer troops, usually Cossacks, entered a little town.
They immediately divided themselves into small groups of five or
ten, which often included officers. These groups attacked Jews on
the street, beat them, and at times took their clothes. Then they
entered the houses in which Jews lived, demanding money and other
valuables. The frightened victims handed over everything they
owned without the slightest sign of resistance. The pogromists then
searched and destroyed the inside of the house. The destruction
was frequently followed by rapes. At times the Cossacks forced
the women to follow them; those who resisted were murdered. The
local population, often but not always, joined the looting once the
violence began. After several days of unrestrained murder and looting the local commander would issue an order in which he would
blame the Jews for Russia's troubles and therefore for their own
misfortune, but promise that measures would be taken to preserve
order. Since the soldiers knew the attitude of their commanders
by experience, at this point the pogrom would either stop or turn

into "quiet pogrom" of chronic violence, depending on the soldiers' perceptions of the attitude of their officers.[63]

Methods of murder varied greatly. Most often the Cossacks shot or bayonetted their victims to death, but there were instances of hanging, burning, drowning in wells, and live burials. There were recorded instances of men buried in the sand up to their necks and then killed by having horses driven over them.[64] Many victims were not killed but were wounded and abandoned to die. Thousands died of hunger, disease, and exposure. There was nowhere to escape to. In the very same town, the appearance of fresh troops might start the wave of killings and looting once again.

Ironically and tragically, the Jews had awaited the coming of the Volunteer Army with high hopes. Although they were represented in the Bolshevik leadership disproportionately, the overwhelming majority of Jews, artisans and tradesmen, suffered as a result of Soviet economic policies, such as restrictions on free trade. The Jewish minority was one section of the population which had little interest in Ukrainian nationalism and therefore was unlikely to sympathize with Petliura. The Jews expected the return of law and order after White victory, and they hoped to be able to resume their normal lives. Soviet agitators and publications did not play up the anti-Semitic exploits of the Whites; then, as in the Second World War, this was not considered good propaganda.[65] Even after the bloody wave of Volunteer pogroms began, every little Jewish settlement had to learn for itself.

In any case, the exhibition of a friendly attitude on the part of the victims toward their tormentors did not help. Often the pogroms began by killing those Jews who participated in a good will delegation approaching the entering army. In Korsun', for example, the town sent a mixed Jewish and Christian delegation led by the rabbi to the Volunteer Army. Next day the Bolsheviks retook the town and the rabbi went into hiding. The Bolsheviks captured two Jewish members of the delegation, who were killed. The following day the Volunteers chased out the Bolsheviks and immediately started a vicious pogrom, killing the rabbi as he came out of hiding.[66]

Self-defense against the Petliurists and anarchists was successful at times; against the Volunteer Army it was hopeless. Anti-Semitic propaganda often described Jews firing from windows on retreating

White soldiers. It even talked about imaginary Jewish detachments fighting against the Volunteer Army, but these were pure fabrications. In Kiev, for example, after the Bolsheviks managed to occupy the city for a few days in October 1919, anti-Semitic papers started a campaign charging the Jews with responsibility. The anti-Semitic *Vechernie ogni* published detailed charges of Jews firing from windows, but the liberal organ, *Kievskaia zhizn'*, decided to investigate and found all the accusations false. As one would expect, such an investigation made no impression on the pogromist press.[67]

Ultimately the Jews did learn. It was Soviet rule, which in spite of its economic policies, in spite of occasional pogroms carried out by some ill-disciplined Red troops, offered the best chance of survival. On occasion, an entire Jewish settlement would follow the retreating Red soldiers.[68] White memoirists, such as General Denikin, wrote with great glee that anti-Semitism was rife even under Soviet rule.[69] While this is true, at the same time it was clear to everyone that Soviet leaders were willing to fight against pogroms and punish the offenders. As a result, the number of victims of the Red Army was only a few hundred compared to the thousands who were slaughtered by the Whites.

Because of the very nature of the pogroms, it is impossible to establish the exact number of victims. Gusev-Orenburgskii, a Kiev researcher, collected materials soon after the events and on the basis of his findings reported thirty-five thousand deaths. He estimated that since his material came only from some parts of the Ukraine, and that since entire families disappeared without a trace, the actual number of murdered was likely to be in excess of a hundred thousand.[70] According to others, the number was considerably higher. Ilya Trotzky writes about a million pogrom victims, in which he includes not only those killed, but also those who were raped, wounded, and orphaned.[71] Heifets, the chairman of the Relief Committee for pogrom victims, estimated about half of those murdered fell the victim to the soldiers of the Volunteer Army.[72]

The Volunteer Army succeeded in murdering as many Jews as all the other armies put together because its pogroms were more systematic, often leading to the elimination of entire settlements.[73] The nature of the Volunteer Army pogroms differed from the others. Other pogroms were the work of the peasants, whether belonging to an armed band or not. The pogroms of the Volunteer Army, on the other hand, had three different participants: the peasant, the Cossack, and the Russian Officer. The anti-Semitism of these three participants was not the same; they had different methods, goals, and ideologies. The particularly bloody nature of these massacres can be explained by the fact that these three types of murderers reinforced one another.

The anti-Semitism of the Ukrainian peasant has been frequently analyzed, and of the three it is the easiest to understand. The breakdown of order allowed the people to exhibit their centuries-old hatred. The senseless and brutal killings, so characteristic of the Russian Civil War, cheapened human life. The Ukrainian peasant, too, often became the victim of the Cheka punishment battalions, murderous lootings of White soldiers, and the vengeful hatred of the landlord who now reclaimed his land. When Ukrainian peasants died on the battlefront and in their villages, it was tempting to massacre the defenseless Jews. However wretchedly poor the Jews were, from the point of view of the Ukrainian peasants, they were still exploiters. They made up a petit bourgeoisie, precisely that element in the exploiting class with which the peasants came most often in contact. At a time of economic chaos, the peasants turned against those whom they considered responsible. Among other things, the Civil War was a struggle of the village against the city, and for the ignorant peasant the Jew epitomized the hated city. Petliurist and Volunteer propaganda always identified the Soviet regime with the Jews, and thereby succeeded in harming both. The peasants, who had just been exposed to brutal Bolshevik requisition policies, often did not repudiate the Bolshevik regime as a whole, but blamed only the Jews.

However, in Volunteer-occupied areas most of the murders were committed not by peasants but by Cossacks. The "contribution" of the peasants was nevertheless crucial: their traditional anti-Semitism legitimized the murder carried out by others. The Cossack murderers encountered moral revulsion neither in the peasants nor in their commanders: after leveling a Jewish settlement they could believe that they had just contributed to the anti-Bolshevik cause.

The majority of the Cossacks fighting in the Ukraine came from the Kuban. The Don Cossack army at this time was engaged in the defense of the northern boundaries of their own district against the Bolsheviks. Of all the Cossacks, however, the Terek Cossacks had the reputation of being the most bloodthirsty. Since the Kuban, but especially the Terek, had an extremely small Jewish population, these Cossacks could not have had a great accumulated hatred. It is therefore something of an irony that those who did most of the killings had been traditionally the least concerned with the "Jewish question." The Cossacks, above all, wanted to loot, and anti-Semitism, fanned by official propaganda, justified the looting. The killing came as a justification for looting: the murderers convinced themselves that the Jews were vicious enemies and therefore it was not wrong to take their property. Many succeeded in convincing themselves so well about the Jewish danger that it became natural to kill. It was so much easier to face the "enemy" in a Jewish settlement than on the battlefield.

The officers of the Volunteer Army were obsessed with anti-Semitism. Reading secret reports which were obviously not meant as propaganda, it is clear that this anti-Semitism, full of paranoid delusions, bordered on the pathological. In the thousands of reports and documents in the Volunteer archives, one cannot find a single denunciation of pogroms. The agents sending reports to their headquarters simply assumed that Jews were responsible for all miseries, Bolshevism, inflation, and lost battles.[74]

The language and imagery of the reports can only be compared to Nazi tracts. For example, an agent of the White Secret Service, describing the political situation from the Ukraine, spent as much space on the discussion of the activities of the Jews as on all other subjects together. He wrote: "No administrative step would help; it is necessary to make harmless the microbe—the Jews." "As long as the Jews will be allowed to do their harmful work, the front will always be in danger." "The Jew is not satisfied with corrupting the soldier. Lately he pays even greater attention to officers. But he is most interested in youth. Clever [Jewish] agents under the cover of patriotism and monarchism mix with military youth and with the help of cards, women, and wine they attract the debauched youth into their nets." The Jews are always blamed in particular for economic problems and inflation. "We must not forget that the entire industry and above all trade is in the hands of the Jews; enor-

1. General Denikin.

2. Rostov on the Don.
Departure of a student
detachment to the front.

3. Rostov on the Don. Armoured car.

4. Parade after the capture of Karkov by the Whites.

5. Bolshevik prisoners.

6. From left to right: Prime minister Krivoshein, General Wrangel and
Chief of Staff, General Shatilov.

mous supplies of all kinds of materials are hidden by them. They do not take these materials to the market, but on the contrary, spare no effort to buy more and hide them." The recommendation of this agent is that no humanity should be shown to these enemies because they exploit it, and because such humane treatment would alienate the population.[75] The same motives appear in dozens of other reports.

The Orthodox Church contributed a great deal to the pogrom atmosphere. An extremist priest, Father Vostokov, established a conspiratorial monarchist organization, The Brotherhood of the Life-Giving Cross, whose goal was to fight "Jewish masonry." On one occasion he proposed to lead a crusade of priests armed with holy icons against Jewish Bolsheviks.[76] Vostokov's pogrom agitation was so violent that in September 1920 General Wrangel finally restrained him. His demagoguery fired the crowds, who, after listening to him, chanted hysterically "Beat the Jews, Save Russia."[77] Vostokov was an extreme case, but hundreds of priests elsewhere called Jews Christ-killers and blamed the misfortunes of the Church at the time of Civil War on Jews. The Church repudiated neither Vostokov in particular nor pogrom agitation in general. A Jewish delegation turned to Metropolitan Antony of Kiev for help. On November 10, 1919, the Metropolitan wrote in *Kievskoe ekho*, "In answer to a request of Jewish representatives [to denounce pogroms] I suggested to them that first they should turn to their coreligionists and ask them to leave immediately the Bolshevik establishments."[78]

None of the major political groups which was important at Denikin's headquarters came out in defense of the persecuted. It was not surprising that such veteran anti-Semites as V. V. Shulgin contributed to pogrom agitation. His paper, *Kievlianin*, was among the most rabid. In the first issue after the Volunteer Army occupied Kiev he wrote: "The south west district [the Ukraine] is Russian, Russian, Russian . . . we will give it neither to Ukrainian traitors, nor to Jewish executioners."[79] His only worry about pogroms was that they might create too much sympathy for the Jews.[80]

The Russian liberals, the Kadets, who had been in the forefront of the struggle for Jewish emancipation, and who had repeatedly condemned tsarist authorities for organizing and allowing pogroms,

now remained silent. The last conference of the Kadet party in
Russia, in November 1919 in Kharkov, refused to condemn the
Volunteer Army for the massacres. The Party resolution called on
the Jews to repudiate Bolshevism in order to save themselves. The
same resolution disingenuously blamed the Bolsheviks for organizing pogroms in the rear of the Volunteer Army in order to create
confusion.[81] As if the Cossacks needed help! The resolution of the
Party on the Jewish question was another sign of the bankruptcy of
liberalism during the Civil War.

Denikin and his closest associates were anti-Semites. Denikin
admitted this himself. When he was visited by a Jewish delegation
which complained about "excesses" he told them: "Gentlemen, I
will be honest with you. I don't like you, Jews. But my attitude toward you is based on humanity. I, as Commander-in-Chief, will
take steps to prevent pogroms and other acts of lawlessness and
will punish severely those who are guilty. But I cannot guarantee
that in the future there will be no excesses."[82]

He held all of Jewry responsible for the "crimes" of those who
fought on the Bolshevik side. He believed and proclaimed that Bolshevism and Judaism were almost the same. If these two were re-
lated, then how could the people be asked to fight against one without
the other? Denikin privately deplored the pogroms, which seemed
to him manifestations of barbarism. He disapproved of the "excesses," but his belief in collective responsibility, and his conviction
that the people's hatred of the Jews was justified, made those "excesses" possible.

His official acts were based on the assumption that all Jews were
enemies of his regime. He forbade Jews buying land on the Black
Sea Coast, hoping to combat speculation.[83] The propaganda agency,
the Osvag, under the brief tenure of the liberal Kadet politician
Paramonov, acquired a number of Jews as associates. This was one
of the reasons for removing Paramonov. The new leader, Sokolov,
on Denikin's instructions, fired all Jews. Soon the Osvag was transformed into a bastion of anti-Semitism, which tolerated extremists
guilty of the most rabid pogrom agitation.

The saddest incident concerned the few Jewish officers in the
Volunteer Army. During the time of the Provisional Government
a number of them became officers and a few of those joined the

Volunteer Army at its inception. These men participated in the first bloody battles and in the very difficult Ice March. Denikin, under the pressure of anti-Semitic officers, removed them from active service. The Jewish delegation, which visited Denikin in July 1919, requested him to reinstate the officers, arguing that their very presence in the army would show the population that not all Jews sided with the Bolsheviks and therefore would undermine pogrom propaganda.[84] Denikin refused the request. If he would not protect those who joined his army in the most difficult period, how could other Jews expect help from him?

Denikin's were crimes of omission. He allowed the Osvag to spread the most vicious anti-Semitic propaganda. Osvag posters always portrayed Bolsheviks as Jews. The agency fabricated stories about Jews shooting from windows on retreating White soldiers, about Jews forming anti-Volunteer Army detachments. Denikin allowed his subordinates, for example General Mamontov, to issue proclamations such as: "Arm yourself and rise against the common enemy of our Russian land, against the Jewish Bolshevik communists. . . . The evil force which lives in the hearts of Jews-communists will be eliminated."[85]

The Jews in vain asked Denikin to condemn pogroms. He refused, saying that such a proclamation would only increase hostility against his regime and support suspicions that he had sold out to the Jews. He told the delegation that the only solution was a general improvement of the moral climate and the repudiation of all forms of lawlessness. Finally, in October 1919, he relented and denounced pogroms. He addressed his troops in Kiev: "I have received reports on the use of force by the Army against Jews. I demand you take energetic measures to stop these and take harsh measures against those found guilty."[86] This proclamation was followed by the bloodiest progroms in the history of Kiev.

It is not surprising that a condemnation of pogroms was not taken seriously by anyone. The soldiers and the officers would assume that it was issued to appease foreign public opinion. Most important, the high command did not punish the guilty. Official "investigating commissions" were farcical: Jews were coerced to testify that no pogroms had occurred at all. The government forbade the newspapers to report on pogroms. General Dragomirov, the military governor of

Kiev, pardoned those who were found guilty of mass murder after the Metropolitan interceded on their behalf. When a Kiev trade-union delegation protested the arrest of four Jews, Dragomirov threatened the workers with court martial for impudence.[87]

The anti-Bolsheviks' obsessive anti-Semitism often amazed foreign observers. An English journalist, John Hodgson, who stayed for some time at Denikin's headquarters, wrote: "The officers and the men of the army laid practically all the blame for their country's trouble on the Hebrew. Many held that the whole cataclysm had been engineered by some great and mysterious society of international Jews, who in the pay and at the order of Germany, had seized the psychological moment and snatched the reins of government."[88] He wrote elsewhere: "When America showed herself decidedly against any kind of interference in Russia the idea soon gained wide credence that President Woodrow Wilson was a Jew, while Mr. Lloyd George was referred to as a Jew whenever a cable from England appeared to show him as lukewarm in support of the anti-Bolsheviks."[89]

Secret reports and contemporary correspondence of participants of the White movement make it clear that anti-Semitism was neither a peripheral nor an accidental aspect of White ideology; it was a focal point of their world view. How can we explain this obsession? Of course, the Russian officer corps had long been anti-Semitic in Imperial Russia. Jews could not become officers. Even at the time of the First World War, when the army desperately needed more officers, some candidates for officers' schools found it necessary to show that neither their parents nor even their grandparents were Jewish.[90] The officers looked down on Jewish soldiers and mistreated them. They identified Jews with liberalism and socialism, ideologies which they loathed. The great majority of them had no trouble at all condoning tsarist policy, which regarded Jews as a hostile and alien minority, whose very existence was somehow threatening to the Russian people.

Yet their "normal" anti-Semitism was mild compared to the murderous obsession which they developed in the course of the Civil War. Seeing Jews in important positions in the Soviet regime no doubt contributed to their hatred, but this cannot be the full explanation, for obviously most of the Soviet leaders and most of the workers of the Cheka were as Russian as themselves.

One fatal weakness of the White movement was its lack of ideology, a lack of clearly defined goals. The Russian officers, who proudly regarded themselves as apolitical, accepted without thinking the Imperial regime as the best for their country. When the Revolution and the Civil War destroyed the Russia they loved, they were equipped neither emotionally nor intellectually to search for the causes of the collapse of the empire. It was too painful to contemplate that the Bolsheviks were in Moscow because the Russian people did not object as strenuously to their presence as to the idea of reconstructing old Russia. The officers lacked the emotional strength and the intellectual courage to recognize that tsarist Russia collapsed because it was anachronistic, corrupt, and, most important, inefficient.

Anti-Semitism allowed them to explain the failure of their Russia without asking too many searching questions. As they murdered more Jews, they needed increasingly fanciful explanations, and their picture of the sinsister power of the Jews became more and more like paranoid delusions. One can follow the progression: as the pogroms in the fall of 1919 turned increasingly bloody, the language of secret reports became increasingly shrill.

Denikin believed that the pogroms hurt the White cause, because they undermined the discipline of the army. One would like to believe that he was right, and that the Whites were punished in this way for their crimes, but such was not the case. Anti-Semitism was one of the trump cards of the Whites. No theme of White propaganda hurt the enemy more than the association of Jews and Bolsheviks. Their natural anti-Semitism, fanned by White propaganda, made many Russian and especially Ukrainian peasants choose the Whites. Ultimately the Bolsheviks did win, but in spite of the anti-Semitism of the people.

CHAPTER 7

Intervention

The most remarkable feature of Allied intervention in the Civil War—led by the British and the French—was its extreme ineptness. The French embarked on the venture without thinking through their goals and without understanding the difficulties. Incredibly enough, they imagined that their very presence would inspire the anti-Bolshevik forces in Russia to march victoriously on Moscow. The French often remarked that a few good regiments could overthrow Lenin's government. In that case, those who landed in Odessa and in the Crimea certainly were not such regiments. In the entire course of the Civil War, there were no more ill-disciplined soldiers than the French, Greek, Algerian, and Senegalese troops commanded by French officers; these soldiers simply did not want to fight, and were useless.

The British were not much better. They allowed their local representatives to make policy, and therefore—as in Ekaterinodar and in Tbilisi, for example—they made mutually contradictory promises, confusing and ultimately alienating everyone. The British "instructors" who at times fought side by side with the Whites took little care to hide their contempt for their hosts and thereby created ill will.

Why did the Allies bungle intervention so badly? First, they grossly underestimated the difficulty of their task. They were tempted by the obvious weakness of the revolutionary regime, and could not see that their "friends" were even weaker. They did not realize that victory would go to the side which could impose order on the Russian peoples, and that in this crucial task foreigners could provide no help. Second, they were woefully ignorant of the enormously complex situation. Lloyd George thought Kharkov was a general; General Borius led the intervening French troops into the confusion of Odessa with no more precise instructions than "to make common cause with the patriotically thinking Russians."[1] Third, and this was perhaps the most reprehensible, British and French statesmen did not see the constraints under which they had to operate. It was not enough to hate the Bolsheviks; it was necessary to have the force to suppress them. The British and French soldiers, after the horrifying experience of the First World War, had no desire whatever to fight in Russia for the Whites, whom they perceived as restorationists. Statesmen who do not know that there must be a congruence between their goals and the means to achieve them are not worthy of the name.

It is hard to establish how much difference Allied intervention made in the Civil War. Soviet historians have always grossly over-emphasized the role of foreigners. It served their nationalistic pur-poses to portray the struggle as one in which the Russian people fought against a few reactionary generals who were supported by the entire world capitalist system. Of course, the accomplishment of the Red Army would seem much greater if we believed that it had defeated the combined forces of the Western world. Soviet his-torians have manipulated the record shamelessly, choosing as their chief villain the country which happened to be the most dangerous adversary at the moment, first the British, then the Germans, and finally the Americans. They have created fanciful scenarios in which the entire history of the Civil War is organized according to mythical campaigns of the Entente.

After we dismiss the obviously exaggerated claims, there can still be legitimate disagreements about the significance of intervention. On the one hand, one may argue that however much Allied weap-ons helped the Whites, this contribution was counterbalanced by the harm they did in allowing the Bolsheviks to depict themselves as defenders of the national cause. On the other hand, it is safe to say that without foreign help the Whites would have had to make difficult adjustments in their economic system in order to produce much-needed weapons; it is likely that this additional strain would have broken the White regimes earlier.

However we resolve this controversy we must remember that the Civil War was indeed a civil war: fought by the peoples of the defunct empire, an outgrowth of Russian circumstances, and ultimately resolved by the relation of internal forces.

Intervention of foreigners in Russia started in the context of the First World War. British and French politicians despised everything the Bolsheviks stood for, but as long as the war in Europe continued, their primary interest was the defeat of Germany. Their policy toward Russia was based on the illusory hope that the second front could be reconstructed. For that purpose they would have been willing to cooperate even with Lenin's government. Allied troops came to Russia at first to prevent the munitions they had delivered during the war from falling into German hands. Foreigners, however, landed in small numbers and they remained in outlying areas where their influence on the course of the Civil War was limited.

The end of the war in Europe was a turning point in the history of the intervention. On the one hand, it could no longer be defended as a part of the anti-German effort; on the other, the Allies for the first time possessed the means to send substantial help to their friends. The statesmen in Paris and London did not hesitate long: the French landed troops in the Crimea and in Odessa and the British sent their men into the Caucasus within a month of the Armistice. It was in these three areas that the Volunteer Army was in direct contact with the interventionists.

ODESSA

In the first months of 1919 the Volunteer Army became involved in a complex series of events which took place in Odessa. By studying this involvement—the White generals' relations with French interventionists and local politicians—we may gain additional insights into the Whites' conception of the Civil War.

Odessa, one of the largest cities in the Ukraine, was not a typical Ukrainian city. Only 17 percent of its population was Ukrainian; 36 percent were Jewish, 39 percent were Russian, and there were small minorities of Greeks, Armenians, and Poles.[2] Ukrainian nationalism had only a limited appeal here, and the nationalists regarded the town as an alien entity. Odessa was established only in the late eighteenth century, but it grew quickly and by the time of the Revolution it was not only one of the largest ports of the country, with almost a million inhabitants, but also a center of industry with a sizable working class.

In the beginning of December 1918, the Austrians and Germans withdrew from Odessa and it seemed the pattern of events would be similar here to developments in Kiev.[3] The authority of Mustafin, the Hetmanite governor, disintegrated as the foreigners departed.[4] Skoropadskii named General Biskupskii commander of the small and demoralized Ukrainian forces, and he hoped to save the city from Petliura by enlisting the aid of the organization of Russian officers. The Volunteer Army center, which had been operating under the command of Admiral Neniukov in semi-clandestine circumstances, had only 1500 men.[5] As in Kiev, the Russians had to make the unpalatable choice between fighting for Skoropadskii, whom they disliked, or coming under the occupation of Petliura, whom they hated. They chose to fight.

Politicians of various persuasions, from radical socialists to monarchists, tried to fill the power vacuum. The situation became further complicated when most of the delegates to the ill-fated Jassy conference came to Odessa. This conference had been organized to unify the White camp and to coordinate the actions of the anti-Bolshevik movement with the plans of the Allies. The delegates moved to Odessa because they wanted to be on hand when the intervention actually began. The two representatives of the Volunteer Army, V. V. Shulgin and A. N. Grishin-Almazov, soon found themselves deeply involved in the local situation. The energetic Shulgin took charge. He persuaded Admiral Neniukov to hand over command to the 32-year-old General Grishin-Almazov. The change in command made little difference: the Russian forces were obviously not strong enough to stop the nationalists, and Denikin was not in a position to give assistance. The Petliurists entered the city on December 11, and the Russians were saved from complete defeat and humiliation only by the help of a remarkable French diplomat, Emile Henno.

Henno had been a low-ranking member of the French mission to the short-lived Ukrainian *rada* at the end of 1917 and later worked on the staff of the French Embassy at Jassy. The confused circumstances and the lack of clarity in French policy made it possible for a junior diplomat to take important initiatives. He had excellent contacts with Russian politicians, and perhaps under their influence, he became a partisan of the Great Russian cause.[6] He was instrumental in calling the Jassy conference, and played a role in the preparation of French intervention. Since Henno gave his backing to the Russian forces in Odessa, the Ukrainians, who understood that their future depended on Allied good will, did not dare to drive them out. The Petliurists occupied only a part of the city and left free a "French" zone, which in fact remained under the control of the Russians.

The situation completely changed with the arrival of the long-awaited French forces in Odessa harbor on December 17. General Borius, the commanding officer, demanded that the Ukrainians withdraw from the city, which they refused to do. Grishin-Almazov offered his services and after a seven-hour battle in which he was aided by French naval guns he cleared the city of Petliurists, who, it seems, put up only token resistance.[7]

From Denikin's point of view, French intervention started in a most promising way. He assumed that the landing was only the first step in a large-scale effort. He hoped that the French would take the place of the Germans and soon occupy the entire Ukraine, thereby allowing the Whites to organize behind their shield of protection. He took it for granted that the foreigners had no other goal than to support his movement. Since it was Grishin-Almazov who cleared the city of Ukrainians, the French came not as conquerors, but as guests. One of Borius' first acts was to name Grishin-Almazov military governor. The young General immediately notified Denikin and said that he considered himself an officer of the Volunteer Army and therefore under no circumstances would he act contrary to the orders of his superior.[8]

As elsewhere in Russia, local administration in Odessa had almost ceased to function. The city duma, which was elected in the summer of 1917, was dominated by socialists. The mayor, M. V. Braikevich, was a liberal Kadet and a member of the Union for Regeneration. Although the liberals and socialists did not have enough strength to administer the city, they were strong enough to object to Grishin-Almazov's policies. With the hope of French help, they increasingly defied the representative of the Volunteer Army.[9]

The cards were stacked against Grishin-Almazov from the very beginning. He was an inexperienced and tactless man, not qualified for his complex assignment. Soon complaints against him started to pour in to the headquarters in Ekaterinodar. Among the senior leaders of the Army, Grishin-Almazov was hardly known. He had just returned from Siberia, and the Volunteer Army chose him as a delegate to Jassy, because he was able to give a first-hand account to the conference of the coup d'etat of Admiral Kolchak. It was, of course, totally unforeseen that this young and unknown person would soon occupy such a sensitive position.

Grishin-Almazov formed a civil administration (which he rather pompously called a cabinet) under A. I. Pil'ts, rather than attempting to revive local organs of self government.[10] He removed elected officials, took control of the city treasury, and arrested some men whom he suspected of Bolshevik sympathies. These steps united liberal and democratic opinion against him. Denikin did not object to these moves per se, but he was concerned that Grishin-Almazov showed too much independence. He did not like the new civil administration because it reminded him too much of the "governments" of the newly established "states." Although it was obviously impossible to administer Odessa from Ekaterinodar, Denikin feared that Grishin-Almazov's independence might establish a precedent and would be a step toward a federal Russia.

On January 9 Denikin sent a telegram to the young officer in which he severely criticized his policies. He ordered him to abolish his "cabinet" and base his administration on the already existing city organs. The frugal Denikin especially objected to the amount of money Grishin was spending.[11] The source of the disagreement was that Odessa was especially hard hit by inflation. A dinner which in January 1919 cost five rubles in Ekaterinodar, cost thirty in Odessa.[12] Although the officers of the Volunteer Army were so poor that they could hardly afford to eat, Denikin was unwilling to give them special consideration. He forbade his subordinate to spend money without authorization.

Perhaps as a result of Shulgin's and Henno's pleading, Denikin softened his stance somewhat. On January 14 he allowed Grishin to spend money from an emergency fund. But he still intended to hold a tight rein. In his telegram he promised that members of the Special Council would periodically travel to Odessa to acquaint themselves with the situation.[13]

From the point of view of the Volunteer Army, the situation greatly deteriorated in the middle of January, when the new commander of the French forces, General Phillipe d'Anselme, and his chief of staff, Colonel Friedenberg, arrived. Henno's attempts to base French policy on the exclusive support of the Volunteer Army no longer reflected the views of the French government. Paris decided to regard the Volunteer Army as only one of the forces involved in the struggle, and to deal with all those anti-Bolsheviks who possessed de facto authority. In the French capital it seemed sensible to bring together all anti-Bolshevik factions. The French leaders obviously did not understand how wide a gap separated the various protagonists and how strong the enmities were. Nor was it easy to find out who had the support of the population. The French no doubt overestimated the strength of Petliura and of the local democratic politicians.

General d'Anselme, a military man, had no taste for politics and gave a free hand to his chief of staff, Colonel Friedenberg, an Alsatian Jew. Friedenberg had previously served in the colonies and treated Russians and Ukrainians in a most imperious manner. Predictably, he only made enemies for himself and for the policies of his country.[14]

The most pressing task was the solution of the supply problem. The French either had to occupy the hinterland or come to terms with those who controlled it. Grishin-Almazov had several times proposed to Borius that his small army occupy the surrounding villages. He wanted to do this because he expected a good reception and recruits from the German colonist population. However, Borius was afraid that the French might become involved in a war and vetoed the plan.

Friedenberg immediately initiated negotiations with the Directorate. The Ukrainians, who had fallen back under the pressure of the advancing Bolsheviks, were willing to give concessions in the hope of foreign help. Therefore an agreement was quickly reached which allowed the French to occupy a large area from the Bessarabian border to Kherson and Nikolaev. The Russians watched French-Ukrainian negotiations with helpless dismay.[15]

Although the lifting of the blockade improved the supply of the city, economic conditions remained chaotic. The factories did not resume work and the great majority of workers remained unemployed. While some lived well, the poor starved.[16] The city could not support the influx of refugees from the north. Grishin-Almazov's administration did not succeed in reorganizing the police, and there was no public safety; people were killed on the streets for their overcoats, and bands of hungry men raided shops and the apartments of the rich with impunity.[17] Odessa under French occupation was a hellhole of misery, starvation, and confusion.

In order to improve the situation, Friedenberg tried to deal directly with local Russian politicians, which further undermined Grishin-Almazov's position. It was ironic that the vocally nationalist right was the most willing to compromise with the foreigners, even to the extent of accepting cooperation with such enemies of the Russian cause as the Ukrainian nationalists. The conservatives lost faith in the Russian people and pinned their hopes on the interventionists. However, to further heighten the irony, Friedenberg, who preferred the rightists, nevertheless needed the cooperation of the socialists in order to convince French public opinion that the adventure in South Russia was not a reactionary undertaking.[18] While on the one hand he denounced the Volunteer Army as restorationist, he derived support precisely ·from those political circles in Odessa which regarded the Volunteer Army as far too liberal.

Russian politicians with the encouragement of Friedenberg drew up a number of plans for the reorganization of the political structure of the anti-Bolshevik South. One, sponsored by the State Unity Council, envisaged the formation of a South Russian regional government. Since Denikin opposed such a project, the Council thought up a more modest proposal. Two representatives, S. N. Maslov and Prince E. N. Trubetskoi, traveled to Ekaterinodar in order to discuss with Denikin the formation of an administrative council which would aid the work of the military governor in

Odessa. Maslov and Trubetskoi pointed out that it was impossible to administer a large and distant city from Ekaterinodar, and warned that if the Russians could not create a functioning administration, the French would disregard them and take matters into their own hands. Denikin was hostile to this plan, as he was to all others in which he saw germs of federalism and decentralization.[19]

Instead of accepting local autonomy, Denikin hoped to improve the situation with the appointment of a new military governor. Grishin-Almazov was useful as long as he had the support of Henno, but now there was no longer any reason to keep him in office. When Grishin-Almazov closed down the city duma at the end of January for being "obstructionist," the local politicians protested so vehemently that Denikin considered it necessary not only to countermand the order, but also to dismiss his subordinate.[20]

Denikin named A. S. Sannikov military governor. General Sannikov had served on the Rumanian front during the war and had been military governor of Odessa for some time. As a result he had good contacts with local politicians. However, during the war he had a serious quarrel with General Berthelot, who now commanded the Allied forces in Rumania. Since Berthelot was one of the highest-ranking officers concerned with the organization of the intervention in South Russia, the choice of Sannikov was extremely undiplomatic.[21]

He never assumed his duties. He learned during his audience with General d'Anselme that the French did not recognize Denikin's right to name a military governor, and would accept him only as Denikin's personal representative.[22] Under the circumstances Sannikov asked Ekaterinodar not to issue an announcement of his appointment.

The arrival of Sannikov, besides failing to improve the position of the Volunteer Army, further contributed to confusion. In February the political crisis deepened and the hostility within the anti-Bolshevik camp increased. Sannikov occupied himself with the building of a Volunteer force which could eventually be used against the Bolsheviks. Grishin-Almazov tried to attract Russian officers who had remained in Kiev after Petliura's victory, but the response was minimal.[23] When Sannikov arrived in Odessa on January 26 the Russians had only five thousand soldiers, including 1600 cavalry.[24]

French policy made further expansion difficult, for they forbade mobilization within Odessa and recruitment outside of the city. Presumably they feared that mobilization within Odessa would lead to resistance and disturbances, while recruitment beyond the boundaries of the city might provoke the Directorate.[25]

Equipping and supplying the army was a difficult task. Boots and uniforms were not available, and the volunteers often had to wear their own tattered clothes. It was especially difficult to provide the cavalry with horses, since the Whites could not go beyond the city limits. On one occasion, Sannikov approached d'Anselme for permission to take weapons from the large stores which were left from the war at Nikolaev and Tiraspol; d'Anselme refused the request and when a month later the Bolsheviks took these cities and captured the stores intact, the Whites felt great bitterness.[26] They were not even allowed to fight the enemy. When a Bolshevik band threatened the water supplies of the city, the French, who had absolutely no taste for fighting, instructed the Whites to combat the enemy. The Volunteers defeated the Reds easily, but the French did not allow them to pursue.[27]

The French, who prevented the Russians from building an army of their own, did not bring enough of their own men to South Russia. General Borius had landed with only 1800 soldiers and in the following months the occupying force expanded to only 12,000 men. Only about half of these were French; the rest were Greek, Polish, and in the last days of the occupation, Algerian.[28] Although the troops were far better supplied and equipped than the Russians, their morale was extremely low.

The French, instead of bringing more soldiers to Russia, decided to build "mixed" brigades.[29] General d'Anselme informed Sannikov on February 23 that he planned to organize an army commanded largely but not exclusively by French officers. Some of the non-commissioned officers would also be French, and these would act as instructors. The foreigners would supply the army and pay the soldiers, who would be wearing French uniforms. Sannikov, anticipating Denikin's response, forbade Russian officers to join. When Denikin's response came, it was unequivocal: he threatened to court-martial those who obeyed an illegal order. Under the circumstances, d'Anselme's efforts were condemned to failure.

In March the Bolsheviks advanced southward against the crumbling armies of the Directorate, and this deterioration of the military situation exacerbated the political crisis in Odessa. Ataman
Grigor'ev, at the time an ally of the Bolsheviks, first confronted
"French" troops in the middle of March. The foreign occupation
troops fought very poorly, and two important towns, Kherson on
March 10 and Nikolaev on March 12, fell to the enemy after brief
resistance.[30] The French, Greek, and Polish soldiers discovered
with dismay, that the population which they were supposed to protect actually sided with the Bolsheviks during the battle.

These defeats greatly undermined French prestige. The Russians
saw that "the Army which had defeated the Germans" could not
stop a disorderly and poorly equipped partisan band. Understandably, their confidence in the permanence of the regime in Odessa
was shaken. At the same time the morale of the occupation troops
fell disastrously as it became clear that they might have to fight.
Bolshevik agitators carried out skillful propaganda among the
French troops. (It was somewhat more difficult to work among the
Greeks, for the Reds could not find enough agitators who could
speak the language.)

Now Odessa was blockaded once again, this time by the Bolsheviks. Aside from the shortage of food, the lack of coal was more
debilitating. Supplies were depleted to such an extent that ships
could not sail and ties with the outside world were endangered.[31]

In the deepening crisis and confusion, facing possible military
defeat, the French decided after weeks of futile negotiations to disregard the Volunteer Army. On March 15 d'Anselme declared
martial law and appointed a new government headed by D. F.
Andro de Langeron, a Ukrainian politician of French descent.
Andro, a conservative, had served under Skoropadskii and was
close to the Council for State Unity. Denikin predictably objected
both to the person of the governor and to the principle which allowed the French to interfere in the administration of a Russian
city. He immediately sent a telegram to Sannikov (with copies to
d'Anselme and Berthelot) in which he forbade his representative
to have any dealings with the new "government." Denikin allowed
Sannikov to obey operational directions from the French military,
but Russians could cooperate with the foreign occupiers only
through Sannikov.[32]

Although not as a result of Denikin's protest, the French changed their scheme a few days later. On March 20 Franchet d'Esperey came to Odessa and participated in the formation of a new authority. On Friedenberg's recommendation, he chose a Russian general, A. V. Shvarts, as military governor, and Andro de Langeron's government became only a civilian advisory council. Shvarts was hesitant to accept his new responsibilities, but Franchet d'Esperey succeeded in persuading him by promising increased Allied aid in men and supplies, general mobilization (which would make the formation of a real army possible), and his intercession with General Denikin to gain approval of the arrangement.[33] Shvarts was anxious to reconcile the differences between the Volunteer Army and his foreign patrons. After assuming his job he reported to Denikin about his work and intentions, but Denikin did not deign to answer.[34] To him, Shvarts was no more acceptable than Andro de Langeron. Because Shvarts had served briefly under the Bolsheviks, when he applied to join the Volunteer Army Denikin turned him down. To improve Shvarts' position, the French decided to expel both Generals Sannikov and Grishin-Almazov, and Denikin was insulted once again. The break between the Volunteer Army and the French was complete.

But this time Denikin was not alone in his opposition to French policies. All political groups in Odessa, with the exception of the extreme right, deplored French actions. The representatives of the city duma, the city *zemstvo* union, the Union for Regeneration, the National Center, and even the Socialist Revolutionaries and Mensheviks protested the violation of Russia's sovereignty. Even the opponents of the Volunteer Army preferred to live under Russian rule rather than under what seemed to them a colonial regime.[35] The French, who had hoped to create a united front, finally succeeded: the Russians were united against the interventionists.

The Russians faced an uncomfortable dilemma. On the one hand, it was painful to acquiesce in French actions which seemed a violation of national honor; on the other, it was clear that an open break with the French would strengthen the Bolsheviks. By and large they accepted the fait accompli. Before his departure from Odessa, Sannikov instructed his subordinates to carry out the orders of the French command. General Timanovskii, who possessed Denikin's full confidence, took command of the Volunteer brigade.

His relations with the French remained frustrating. For example, d'Anselme ordered him to guard the approach to the city by occupying Ochakov. But after the Russians carried out the assignment, on March 29, they were commanded to withdraw as the enemy approached. This precipitous retreat further undermined morale.[36]

French policy remained confused to the very end. Privately and publicly, the generals assured the inhabitants that the city would be held. Indeed, on March 26 and March 30 fresh French, Greek, and Algerian troops arrived and the fortifications were repaired. Then suddenly, on April 2, General Franchet d'Esperey ordered d'Anselme to evacuate Odessa within 72 hours, and d'Anselme, for some unknown reason, decided that 48 hours would be enough to carry out the task.[37]

It is clear in perspective, as it was clear to contemporaries, that Odessa could have been defended. The anti-Bolsheviks had numerical superiority, and they were incomparably better armed than their enemies. It is true that it was difficult to supply the blockaded city, but certainly the French navy could have solved the problem. The French withdrew not in order to avoid defeat, but in order to avoid fighting.

They had made no plans for evacuation. The thousands of refugees who had come to Odessa to escape Bolshevik rule now all wanted to leave the city, but there were not enough ships. Only the rich managed to bribe the authorities and secure passage. The French left behind enormous stores of military materiel. They had assumed responsibility for the Volunteer Army detachment by removing its commander, General Sannikov, but in the crucial moment they betrayed the Russians. They found places on their ships for pro-French politicians, but not for the Russian troops. General d'Anselme ordered Timanovskii to leave Odessa through Akerman to Bessarabia overland. Since the soldiers had not been paid, Shvarts allowed them to take 75 million rubles from the state bank, but it was already too late. Even before the French left the city, local Bolsheviks seized the bank and the French did not restrain them. At this point, d'Anselme promised 10 to 20 million rubles in foreign currency to finance the evacuation, but he did not keep his promise. Consequently, the indigent Russians suffered terrible privations on their long walk to the Rumanian border. The Rumanians were hostile: they disarmed the refugees and detained them for a month before they allowed them to leave on ships in order to rejoin the main forces. Approximately six thousand men arrived in Novocherkassk.[38]

In the course of the Civil War there were numerous instances of panic and confusion when the responsible authorities mismanaged their tasks. None was worse than the French organization of the evacuation of Odessa. On the basis of this performance, the French certainly had no right to feel superior to their Russian hosts.

Primary responsibility for the Odessa debacle belongs to the French. They embarked on an ambitious scheme without clear goals, without an understanding of the consequences and with insufficient forces. Their combination of ignorance, arrogance, and cowardice made their policies extremely unattractive. In contrast, the leaders of the Volunteer Army became involved in the Odessa adventure against their will. They fully realized that Russian forces on their own could not defend the city from the Bolsheviks. They always remained conscious of their role as defenders of Russia's honor, and Denikin, especially, behaved with great dignity during his dealings with the foreigners. At the same time, many of the weaknesses of Denikin's leadership were in evidence. He was concerned with matters of form rather than substance, and unreasonably jealous of local initiative and authority. He was afraid of even a taint of federalism, and tried to impose central supervision in circumstances where this was clearly impossible. He made the task of those who wanted to work with him extremely difficult. In brief, Volunteer policies in Odessa were no wiser than elsewhere.

THE CRIMEA

Although the French landed in the Crimea before they had occupied Odessa and stayed three weeks longer, their role here was much smaller. While in Odessa the Volunteer Army had to find a modus vivendi with the foreigners; in the Crimea its main task was to establish good relations with a liberal Russian government.[39]

In the Crimea the social revolution of 1917 was less violent than in the rest of the country. The peasants were relatively well-to-do and there was little land hunger. The peninsula had almost no industry, and in the absence of a proletariat the Bolsheviks could find support only among the sailors of the Black Sea fleet. The situation, however, was complicated by national antagonisms. The Tatars, who made up only a quarter of the population, possessed a highly developed sense of national consciousness, and used the opportunity first to demand autonomy and later to agitate for restoring the peninsula to Muslim Turkey.[40]

Following the November Revolution the Bolsheviks and the Tatars struggled for power. The Tatars convened a Constituent Assembly, the Kurultai, which established a government in Simferopol. The Bolsheviks initially controlled only Sevastopol, the home base of the Black Sea fleet, but they gradually expanded their rule over the northern half of the peninsula. On January 26 a Bolshevik force made up by sailors defeated a Tatar army and dispersed the Kurultai and the Simferopol government.[41]

The Bolshevik regime, which lasted for three months, was remarkable only for its senseless cruelty. No one could control the looting and sadism of the sailors.[42] The population suffered so much that they greeted the Germans in April with relief. The occupiers entrusted civil administration to General S. Sulkevich, a Lithuanian Muslim, who had fought against the Allies on the Rumanian front as commander of a special Muslim army. Like Skoropadskii, Sul'kevich established a reactionary regime, which tried to undo as many of the achievements of the Revolution as possible. He alienated all groups of the population. The liberal politicians refused to cooperate when they understood that the ultimate goal of German policy was the dismemberment of Russia; the peasants became increasingly hostile because they had to bear the heavy burden of German requisitioning; and the Tatars were disappointed by the limited autonomy conceded to them. As the German defeat in the World War became evident, Sulkevich well understood that he could not stay in power without outside help and therefore approached Denikin.[43] Denikin neither could nor wanted to give assistance. On the one hand he would never have supported a general who had fought on the side of the Germans during the war, and on the other, he was well informed about the political situation in the Crimea and knew that the Russian liberals were ready to assume the government.

Indeed, even before the Germans withdrew in the beginning of November 1918, the Crimean Kadets were ready to take power.

The regional *zemstvo* elected S. S. Krym—a Karaite Jew, a landowner, and a former member of the state senate—head of the government. Krym was an appropriate choice for the job, for he had been active in the *zemstvo* movement, where he was regarded as a friend of the poor, and he was generally well-liked, even by the Tatars, who appreciated the fact that he had learned their language.[44] Although Krym created a predominantly Kadet government, he gave the portfolios of trade, education, and controller to the socialists. Two Kadets who had been well known in national politics, M. M. Vinaver and V. Nabokov, took the important portfolios of foreign affairs and justice.

The new government embarked on one of the most remarkable undertakings in the history of the Civil War: an experiment in liberal democracy in a war-torn country. The ministers took their liberal principles seriously: they allowed the Tatars to reconvene the Kurultai and to publish their separatist newspapers; they encouraged organs of self-government to take the burden of responsibility on themselves; and perhaps most important, they were determined not to violate civil liberties and to observe the rule of law. Although most of the ministers had experience in national politics and were committed to the idea of a united Russia, they understood that a successful anti-Bolshevik movement must be built from below. They had no desire whatever for a permanently independent Crimea, but they understood that temporarily autonomous governments had to be organized in order to overcome chaos.[45]

The liberal regime failed, chiefly because the Kadets had no indigenous support. In the election to the Constituent Assembly in November 1917, they had received only 7 percent of the vote.[46] They could take power at the end of 1918 only because their competitors, the Bolsheviks and the Tatars, were weak and because they controlled the *zemstva*. Their government did not attempt to solve social problems and it took no position on land reform. They lacked both the experience and the ideology to mobilize the people. As a result, the government could not defend itself. It did not even consider building an armed force, but instead counted on the Volunteer Army for defense.

Ekaterinodar was in close touch with developments in the nearby

Crimea. The peninsula under German occupation had attracted many refugees from the north, including officers, among whom a secret Volunteer recruiting center operated under General Baron de Bode. In October 1918 N. N. Bogdanov, the future minister of the interior, and Vinaver visited headquarters.[47] Bogdanov requested the dispatch of a Volunteer detachment and Denikin consented. Vinaver had extensive talks with Dragomirov and Lukomskii and agreed with them on the principles of future cooperation.[48] The two generals drew up a letter, later signed by Denikin, which they addressed to de Bode, giving a copy to Vinaver. The letter included these three important points:

1. The Volunteer Army troops will be in the Crimea entirely for the preservation of order and will not interfere in internal matters. 2. The Volunteer Army does not pursue reactionary goals. It wants to recreate Russia. Now and in the future, it recognizes the need for broad autonomy. The Volunteer Army does not prejudge the future form of state or even the means with which the Russian people can express its will concerning the form of state. 3. The Volunteer Army disapproves of any attempt to set nationality against nationality and class against class.[49]

In spite of its promising beginnings, Volunteer-Crimean relations were stormy from the beginning, causing great harm to both sides. The headquarters sent General Korvin-Krukovskii with a small force to the Crimea, and a few days after his arrival, on November 27, he issued an order to mobilize doctors and officers. The government, which learned of the order only from reading the posters on the streets of Simferopol and Yalta, was indignant. It telegrammed Denikin asking him to withdraw the order of his subordinate. Denikin complied and the crisis was averted, but the consequences of the misunderstanding were profound and each side blamed the other.[50] The quarrel was the result of a misunderstanding. The government interpreted noninterference in internal matters as precluding mobilization, while the representatives of the Army assumed that they had the right to organize defense any way they saw fit, and therefore thought they were acting within the terms of the agreement.

The government did not object to mobilization in principle; it merely insisted that such a step could not be taken without its participation. On December 12 the representatives of the army and of the government published an order that all officers under forty years of age living in the Crimea appear for duty by December 20.[51] The move was regarded as a step toward general mobilization. Within a short time the Whites succeeded in organizing a force of four to five thousand.

During the first days of the Volunteers in the Crimea, the army was popular and an impressive number of people volunteered, but the popularity did not last long. The soldiers, as elsewhere, behaved poorly and the population increasingly resented the army for behaving like an occupation force. The Whites, stung by the hostility, sought a scapegoat. They were convinced that socialist and communist agitators misled the people, and they believed that the only way to combat their enemies was to close down newspapers which offended them, to disband organizations which did not support them, and to arrest those who seemed suspicious.

As elsewhere, Denikin's subordinates were even more conservative and intolerant than he was. Korvin-Krukovskii was an intelligent officer, but one without political sense, who constantly advocated declaring martial law and doing away with legal niceties. General de Bode allowed his reactionary chief of staff, Colonel Dorofeev, to handle matters in his name.[52] In the middle of January Denikin sent Korvin-Krukovskii to the front and entrusted General Borovskii with the command of a newly formed Crimean-Azov army.[53] Borovskii's Chief of Staff, General Parkhomov, handled relations with the government. Parkhomov's politics were similar to Dorofeev's and Korvin-Krukovskii's. Denikin formed his views on Crimean affairs largely on the basis of reports from these reactionary subordinates, who constantly bombarded him with telegrams complaining about subversion and about the "weakness" of the government.

The White soldiers committed numerous atrocities. On one occasion soldiers killed a boy for his bicycle. When the government attempted to prosecute the guilty ones, the military authorities simply transferred them out of the Crimea.[54] Soldiers of the Volunteer Army also killed two prominent anti-Bolshevik socialist leaders, Aliasov and Markovich. When Bogdanov complained to Denikin about the matter, Denikin was visibly upset but then said: "What do you want? I know the degree of disorganization and lack of discipline in the Army. I am satisfied when my military orders are carried out."[55] This was a terrible confession of failure.

The worst offender was a guard regiment assigned to protect the members of the Imperial family in Yalta. The officers openly showed their disdain for the liberal government. In December soldiers murdered a certain Guzhon, an industrialist and a French citizen. He was killed not because he was suspected of Bolshevik sympathies, but because in the first year of the war he had some sort of disagreement with Grand Duke Nikolai Nikolaevich.[56] The affair made a painful impression in the Crimea and further undermined the prestige of the government, which protested in vain. The Volunteer High Command once again made no attempt to punish the guilty.

As the Red Army approached and the political situation deteriorated, relations between the liberals and the army became increasingly bitter. The officers believed that political disintegration was the consequence of the failure of the government to take drastic measures against subversives. The government faced a difficult dilemma. The politicians recognized that they could not stay in power if the Volunteers withdrew; on the other hand, the behavior of the White soldiers made a mockery of their protestations of legality. The population looked to them for protection in vain, because they had no authority over the soldiers. Under the circumstances the position of the liberals became increasingly weak, and the prestige of the government fell.

There were close contacts between the leaderships at Ekaterinodar and Simferopol. At the end of December Astrov, Stepanov, and Lukomskii went to the Crimea for talks, and a month later Krym, Bogdanov, and P. S. Bobrovskii (a Socialist Revolutionary member of the government) traveled to Ekaterinodar to smooth over difficulties.[57] These attempts failed because the points of view of the two groups differed profoundly. The Crimeans vainly tried to allay Denikin's fear about subversion and Tatar separatism. The Commander-in-Chief obviously had no confidence in the politicians. When they requested that the newly captured three northern districts of the province, Melitopol, Berdiansk, and Dneprovskaia, be placed under civilian rule, Denikin refused. Conversely, when

Denikin informed his guests that he was considering moving his headquarters to the Crimea, the politicians rather candidly revealed that they did not look forward to such a development.[58]

Indeed, by the end of January 1919 the population of the Crimea was so hostile to the Volunteer Army that the news of the possible moving of the *stavka* to Simferopol almost created panic. In order to allay the fears of the people, Krym published a manifesto saying that the move would not occur before the end of February.[59] When the military situation changed and the idea of moving had to be dropped, the Crimeans were relieved.

During the last few weeks of the government's tenure, the Crimea plunged into chaos. Bolshevik advances into the Tauride meant that the invasion of the peninsula was only a matter of time. The loss of the northern districts, only recently captured by the Whites, was not only a military setback but also a serious blow to the economy of the district. The government found it increasingly difficult to feed the population; the economy was in ruins; 80 percent of the workers were unemployed.[60]

The deteriorating military situation undermined the faith of the population in the ability of the regime to survive, and the economic collapse, which caused great suffering, added to the political instability. The Tatars and the socialists, who in the past had taken a relatively friendly attitude toward the government, now denounced the liberals together with the officers. The suffering population increasingly associated the government with the army. As a result of unceasing attacks, the government abandoned much of its liberalism: it closed down newspapers, outlawed meetings, and disbanded unfriendly organizations.

A particularly serious incident occurred on March 17 in Sevastopol. A meeting of the metal workers passed resolutions demanding the withdrawal of the Volunteer Army, the freeing of political prisoners, and a transfer of power to the Soviet of Workers and Peasants' deputies. The government arrested the organizers of the meeting.[61] As they were transported to prison, a detachment of Volunteer soldiers attacked and killed them. As a result of this incident the Mensheviks and the Socialist Revolutionaries threatened to withdraw from the government, and the workers called a strike which was cripplingly effective.

The strongarm methods of the government and the increased danger did not bring the liberals and officers together. The government had requested that the isthmus of Perekop, the gateway to the Crimea, should be fortified, but the army did nothing. The ministers suspected treason.[62] In this emergency, the government, which had lost faith in the army, decided to participate in the organization of defense. It appointed an engineer, S. N. Chaev, chief of self-defense, and provided him with money. Since both Borovskii and Parkhomov participated in the meeting at which the appointment was made and offered no objections, it came as a great surprise that on March 28 Borovskii sent a letter to Krym in which he protested the interference of the government in military matters.[63]

Denikin, who was kept informed by Borovskii, sent a telegram the next day in which he expressed his accumulated bitterness. He not only accused the government of violating a previous agreement but blamed it for the strength of the Bolsheviks. He threatened retaliation against those who dared to interfere in the work of the army, and warned that all Volunteer troops would be immediately withdrawn unless the government backed down.[64]

Understandably, the Crimeans were not in a position to defy Denikin. On April 3 the Red Army broke through at Perekop and entered the peninsula. There was no force to stop the advance. At this point the government and the army established a Committee of Defense, consisting of Krym, Chaev, and Bogdanov and headed by Borovskii. But it was too late: the days of the anti-Bolshevik regime in the Crimea were numbered.

The failure of the Crimean experiment had a significance for the course of the Civil War, for it discredited the idea of dividing military and civilian authority. Had the liberals succeeded in winning public confidence, and had the officers and politicians been able to work together, the arrangement, advocated by many politicians, might have been tried elsewhere.

The liberals were not particularly able politicians. They quarrelled among themselves over relatively unimportant issues, and did not succeed in winning over and organizing even a segment of the population. Yet the main responsibility for the failure of the experiment belongs to the generals. They had no comprehension of the problems the politicians faced and of the importance of the work they were trying to do. As a result, instead of supporting them, they undercut their influence. The leaders in Ekaterinodar did not realize that the Crimean government extended the authority of the Volunteer Army; on the contrary, they saw politicians merely as troublesome meddlers and resented any manifestation of independence.

The army-government relations repeated the pattern established in 1917. The officers, seeing general disintegration around them, blamed the politicians for not taking energetic measures against subversives. They advocated strongarm methods, not realizing that these could not work, for no one had a strong arm. Repression was bound to be ineffective because it could not be complete.

The liberals hoped that the foreign interventionists would support them in their quarrel with the Russian generals. The first Allied ships arrived in Sevastopol already in November 25, 1918. The Kadet government, which was founded on hope, assumed that democratic countries such as England and France would throw their full weight behind a just cause.

V. Obolenskii, a liberal Crimean politician, described in his memoirs a poignant episode.[65] The population of Sevastopol planned a great reception for the Allied navy. The entire government appeared, the Volunteer Army sent a representative, and Obolenskii headed a *zemstvo* delegation, consisting aside from himself of two simple peasants. The Russians, of course, had prepared formal speeches. But the occasion did not turn out to be a festive affirmation of Allied-Russian friendship. When the Russians were allowed to board the English flagship, they were made to wait for hours without even being able to sit down. The British Admiral Calthorpe, who finally received them, knew nothing about the political situation in the Crimea and had not even heard about the existence of a government. The two peasants of the *zemstvo* delegation asked Calthorpe to come ashore in order to receive the traditional bread and salt, but the Admiral refused; he had no instructions for such an eventuality.

The British-French agreement of December 1917, which divided Russia into zones and about which the Russians knew nothing, placed the Crimea in the French sphere of interest. Accordingly, the British ships soon left Sevastopol and sailed to the Caucasus. At the end of December 1918 the French had only one regiment in Sevastopol, a force obviously much too small to make an impact on the course of the Civil War.[66]

However, hope long persisted. The liberals continued to believe that the regiment was merely a token of more to come, and therefore nothing seemed more important to them than winning the good will of the foreigners. Vinaver even moved his office from Simferopol to Sevastopol in order to be closer to the French. He made every effort to gain the support of Colonel Ruillier, the commander of the Sevastopol garrison, not recognizing that the low-ranking French officer was not in a position to influence the policy of his government.[67]

As the Crimeans' relations with the Volunteer Army became increasingly strained, the government became more and more anxious to exchange Volunteer occupation for French rule. If the French could be induced to send more men, the White army could go to the front and fight the Bolsheviks. However, all efforts were in vain: the French would go no further than setting control over the city of Sevastopol, and they were emphatically not interested in coordinated action with the Volunteer Army, even in the case of Bolshevik attack.

The fact that they made only a modest investment in men and supplies did not prevent them from telling the Russians what to do. As a consequence of his disagreements with Bethelot and d'Anselme, Denikin planned to move Timanovskii's troops from Odessa to the Crimea, but the French forbade the move. It is possible that the additional six thousand men might have saved the Crimea. The abandonment of Odessa, for which the Volunteer Army was entirely unprepared, opened up the left flank of the White front and doomed the Crimea.

When Denikin planned to transfer his headquarters to the Crimea, Franchet d'Esperey presumed to advise him: "I believe that General Denikin should be with the Volunteer Army and not in Sevastopol, where there are French troops whom he does not command."[68] On March 25 Franchet d'Esperey came to Sevastopol. He lectured the government and the Volunteer naval command. He denounced as shameful the behavior of Russian officers, intelligentsia, and bourgeoisie in trying to hide behind the back of the

Allies, expecting others to do the fighting.[69] Since at this point it was clear that the Volunteer Army could not stop the advance of the Bolsheviks, the survival of the anti-Bolshevik Crimea depended on French help. Under the circumstances, the Russians listened meekly. The General promised help: if the Russians could hold the enemy for two weeks, reinforcements would be sent. Once again, the Allies did not keep their promise.

The Bolsheviks broke into the peninsula and advanced almost without resistance. On April 8 the government had to evacuate Simferopol and place themselves under French protection in Sevastopol.[70] Colonel Trousson, whom Franchet d'Esperey had just appointed in place of Ruillier, had completely disregarded the existence of the government. He declared martial law and a state of siege. He declared himself to be military governor and took all authority into his own hands. He appointed General Subbotin, the commander of the Volunteer forces in Sevastopol, his assistant and thereby subordinated the Russian troops to himself.

It seemed that Sevastopol might be held. On April 12 and 14 Senegalese and Algerian troops, which had been too late to disembark in Odessa, landed in the Crimea.[71] Trousson now had seven thousand men under his command and a crushing superiority in firepower over the enemy. He planned to base the defense of the city on the naval guns of the ships in the harbor.

During these days the Russians had to suffer one last indignity.[72] Since the troops had not been paid, the Volunteer command, with the knowledge of the government, took money from the city treasury. This act incensed Colonel Trousson. On April 11, when the government was already on a Greek ship, ready to leave the Crimea, he forbade the ship to leave and ordered the politicians to disembark and appear in front of him. He demanded the money taken by the Volunteer soldiers. The Russians in vain tried to explain that taking the money was perfectly legal, that the troops had to be paid and the evacuation had to be financed. Trousson ordered the arrest of Subbotin and Admiral Sablin, the Volunteer Naval Commander, and threatened the arrest of the entire government unless the money was returned to him the next day. The Russians tried to complain to Admiral Amet, the Commander of French naval forces in Sevastopol, but the Admiral would not even receive them.

The ministers found themselves in a profoundly humiliating
position from which there was no escape. When they met Trousson
next day, the Colonel received them: "Where is the money? Give
me the money or you will not leave. I need the money and not your
explanations." The ministers drew up a declaration which gave
control over all assets to the French, but stipulated that what was
left over after financing the defense of the city and evacuation would
be handed over to Russian representatives abroad and not allowed
to fall into the hands of the Bolsheviks. Even at this point, the ministers were not allowed to leave the Crimea. The Greek ship had
already sailed for Constantinople and the Russians boarded a Russian vessel called *Nadezhda* (hope). Trousson's agents followed them
on the ship and confiscated everything they could lay their hands on.
The Crimean minister of finance, A. P. Bart, meanwhile collected
all the money and short-term notes he could find and handed them
over to the French. Only then, on April 15, was the *Nadezhda* allowed to sail.[73]

The Volunteer detachment took up a defensive position on the
Kerch peninsula and the defense of Sevastopol was left entirely to
the French. Their efforts were as feeble as they had been at Odessa.
The largest French ship, the *Mirabeau*, ran aground, which made it
impossible to use its guns properly. After a brief exchange of fire,
the French and Bolshevik negotiators came to an agreement. The
local Soviet would govern the city from April 19, but the Red Army
would not enter until the French evacuation was complete. The
last French ship left Sevastopol on April 30.

THE CAUCASUS

The Volunteer Army, in attempting to impose its authority over
Odessa and the Crimea, had come into conflict with local politicians
and French interventionists. In contrast, there could have been
no question of extending White rule over the Caucasus. During the
Civil War this region was governed by three de facto independent
governments, and Denikin obviously was not in a position to overthrow them. It should have been a primary goal of Volunteer diplomacy to establish good relations with the Caucasian states,
thereby achieving a secure rear, but the Whites could not acquiesce
in the dismemberment of the Russian empire and consequently

their relations with Georgia and Azerbaidzhan remained strained. According to the British-French agreement of December 1917, the Caucasus fell into the British zone of interest. The British gave most valuable materiel and diplomatic support to the Volunteer Army. They were not as crude and self-righteous as the French. They sent high-ranking officers to Ekaterinodar with whom Denikin established warm personal relations based on mutual respect.[74] Nevertheless, largely as a result of British support to the Caucasian states, relations between London and Ekaterinodar were often troubled. British officers-diplomats came to identify with the interests of the governments to whom they were accredited. As a result, British officers in Ekaterinodar on the one hand, and in Tbilisi and Baku on the other, pursued contradictory policies and made contradictory promises. London's policy, which lacked clarity, appeared to Denikin as two-faced.

Georgia was the most powerful of the new countries and caused by far the most trouble to the Volunteer Army.[75] The Menshevik government in 1918 received help from the Germans. From the point of view of the Volunteer leadership the combination of socialism, separatism, and German orientation was most unattractive. Nevertheless in the summer of 1918 it seemed that the two anti-Bolshevik powers might cooperate against the common enemy. This did not happen. Negotiations in Ekaterinodar between the leaders of the army and a high-level Georgian delegation, headed by foreign minister Gegechkori, broke down because of a disagreement over the silly issue of who should occupy the strategically insignificant resort town of Sochi. Relations soon deteriorated to such an extent that the two armies fought small battles against one another.

The end of the World War and the arrival of British troops in the Caucasus were interpreted by both the Georgians and the Volunteers as favorable developments. The White Russians believed that the British would support the principle of United Russia and resist separatist tendencies, while the Georgians based their hopes on Wilson's principle of national self-determination. It was impossible for the interventionists to please everyone.

Denikin, who had always remained fiercely loyal to the Allies, was disappointed to find that the British soon forgave the Georgians for their earlier cooperation with Germany. London's policy toward the Caucasus was based on the desire to maintain the existing governments, without predetermining the future of Russia, until the Peace Conference. The British rather naively believed that the struggle against Bolshevism would be perceived as so important that all anti-Bolshevik forces would unite for this cause. They made vain efforts to bring together the Georgians and the White Russians.

As the Turks withdrew from the Caucasus at the end of the World War, the Georgians and the Armenians began to fight one another for the territories just freed. This struggle made the Georgians withdraw troops from the Sochi district. Denikin immediately took advantage of the opportunity and occupied some of the disputed territory. To his intense disappointment, the British guaranteed the territorial status quo.

Denikin was insulted that the British disposed of a bit of territory which he considered a part of Russia without even consulting him, and he protested to General Poole, the British representative in Ekaterinodar. Poole was not in a position to change high policy, and had to submit to the decision of the Transcaucasian command, according to which Great Britain supported the status quo, and therefore Denikin should not move further South.[76]

Denikin had no intention of obeying. When he learned of an Armenian rebellion in the district, he decided to interfere. On February 6 his troops crossed the River Loo and in the course of four days of fighting occupied the entire district. The Commander of the Georgian forces, General Konev, his Chief of Staff, 43 officers, and 700 soldiers were captured.[77]

The episode lowered British prestige. Denikin did not forgive them for taking the side of his enemies, and the Georgians blamed them for allowing the Russians to take the district. Both sides understood that the British wanted to preserve the status quo; however, if that status quo was challenged by force, the British were unwilling or unable to reestablish it. The lesson was that the advice of the foreigners could safely be disregarded.

The Georgians acted accordingly. Contrary to explicit British orders and in the presence of British observers, on April 17 they attacked Volunteer positions. The attack coincided with the harassment of the Whites by peasant partisans and therefore the Russians were forced to retire to the Mekhadyr' river. Only a few miles of seacoast and the town of Gagra changed hands.[78] In retaliation Denikin was ready to order an attack all along the Georgian border and not only to take back the lost territories but also to "liberate" the district of Sukhum, where according to his information the Abkhaz minority was dissatisfied with Georgian rule. This time, however, General Briggs, who had replaced Poole in Ekaterinodar, succeeded in dissuading the Commander-in-Chief with a promise of maximum British pressure in getting the Georgians peacefully back to the previous Bzyb' frontier.[79]

Briggs traveled to Tbilisi, but there he was regarded more as a representative of Denikin than of London. In vain did he point out to the Georgian ministers that Allied troops would sooner or later be withdrawn, and then Georgia would have to face Russia alone.[80] He conveyed Denikin's offer of economic cooperation in exchange for territorial concessions, but this was futile; the Georgians were unwilling to give up a single square foot of conquered territory. The Georgian view was that there could be no discussions over an agreement until Denikin unconditionally recognized existing frontiers.

The momentous victories of the Volunteer Army against the Bolsheviks, which brought it close to Moscow, influenced Denikin's attitude toward Transcaucasia, as well as the attitude of the Transcaucasian governments toward the Whites. Denikin, believing that victory was near, revealed his ultimate aim, the unification of all Russia, even more explicitly than he had done before. The Georgians regarded the Whites as an increasing threat to their independence. Not daring to challenge Denikin openly, the Georgian government adopted a slightly more friendly stance, but at the same time it redoubled its secret work against him.

In the first half of 1919 there was no direct contact between the Volunteer Army and the Georgian republic; relations were handled entirely through the British. In the middle of July, however, Denikin felt that the time had come "to prepare the painless reunification" of Transcaucasia with Russia, and for this purpose he sent a permanent representative to Tbilisi. This post was given to General N. N. Baratov, a man who had fought on the Caucasian front in the war, and who had many Georgian officer friends and a Georgian wife.[81]

The secret instructions Baratov received upon his departure reveal that Denikin had learned nothing from the experiences of the previous year: "Having it in view that all Transcaucasia within the border existing before the 1914 war should be regarded as an inseparable part of the Russian state, you are entrusted to prepare the ground for the painless reunification of these districts into one whole with Russia, under the supreme government of an all-Russian state authority."[82] Denikin was willing to grant self-government only until the reestablishment of central power. He himself put it succinctly in his memoirs:[83] "In the final analysis, the chief, the real, and the only cause of the struggle in the Caucasus was the contradiction of the idea of a united Russia with the idea of complete independence of the new Caucasian states. All the rest, small or large, important or insignificant, were only derivatives." It can hardly be questioned that the Georgians had reason to fear for their independence in the event of a White victory in the Civil War.

Aside from Baratov's chief task, he had other aims: he was to help those Russian officers still in the Caucasus to join the Volunteer Army, and try to obtain the munitions left behind in the area after the war. He could promise trade relations to the Georgians only if they recognized that their independence was temporary and only if they immediately retired to the Bzyb' River—conditions which were unlikely to be accepted.

Baratov's presence in Tbilisi helped to crystallize the differences in the Georgian leadership's attitude toward the White Russians. His General's good reception by the Georgians was perhaps due more to his personal qualities than to the power he represented. It seems that Zhordania, the premier, and Gegechkori, the foreign minister, were more inclined to compromise, while Ramishvili, the minister of interior, and Khomeriki, the minister of trade, communications, and industry, took an inflexible position. The further to the left a politician stood in the Georgian political spectrum, the more likely he was to oppose any concession to the White Russians. The most Russophile element at the time in Georgia was the officer corps, while the National Guard, formed and dominated by socialists, was implacably hostile to Denikin.[84] Every significant political force in Georgia insisted on an independent Georgia within the existing frontiers as a precondition for further agreements. Thus,

Baratov's conditions could not be met and his mission achieved nothing; he left Tbilisi in November.

With the failure of this mission the leaders of both sides imagined that they now had the advantage over their opponents. Denikin believed that the economic blockade he imposed would force Georgia to give in. The Georgians were, in fact, seriously affected by this measure, but they were able to retaliate: they seized trains carrying supplies to Denikin from the British, while the suppliers vainly protested, and they allowed some Red units pursued by the Whites to enter Georgian territory.

But the Georgians harmed the Whites most by fomenting rebellion in the rear of the Volunteer Army. The partisans tied down a substantial portion of Denikin's army just when the crucial battles for Moscow were being fought. The Georgians supplied the insurgents with weapons, financial aid, and at times even sent them instructors. It is impossible to document Georgian involvement in every uprising, in every partisan movement, but there is no doubt that without Georgian encouragement the Volunteer Army would have had much less trouble in suppressing dissidence.

The Chechens were the Georgians' most able pupils. Their uprising in March 1919 threatened the important town of Groznyi and the Volunteer commander, General Dratsenko, put down the rebellion with difficulty. In May, fighting with the Chechens was renewed. Then, in June, the Ingush joined the Chechens and the fighting spread to all Dagestan, which at one time was completely in the hands of the rebels. Denikin's entire Caucasian army could not cope with the rebellion and had to ask for reinforcements from headquarters. As Denikin's position deteriorated in the North, the partisans, knowing of the Whites' weakness, attacked with renewed force. White domination of the Caucasus was endangered.[85]

Of all the partisan movements which plagued the Volunteer Army, the most threatening was a rising on the Black Sea coast in January 1920. This movement was led by Social Revolutionaries, who asked their followers to fight Red and White alike. At one time the insurgents controlled the entire coast from the Georgian border to Novorossisk, and they interfered with the evacuation of the defeated White armies. This movement started on Georgian territory and received Georgian aid.

The White generals identified the partisans with the Georgians to such an extent that when the attack started, General Cherepov, who was in command of the Volunteer forces of the area, simply notified headquarters that the Georgians had attacked. Denikin, with characteristic impetuousness, immediately declared war on Georgia.[86] The declaration was a pure formality: the Whites were no longer in a position to fight either Reds or partisans, to say nothing of starting another war. The misunderstanding was soon cleared up and Denikin retracted his unfortunate declaration of war, but the experience did not make negotiations easier at a time when the Volunteer Army very much needed Georgian good will.

In January and February 1920 the Whites still had substantial territory and possessed sizable forces, but their fighting spirit was broken, and friend and foe alike sensed that the end of the Volunteer Army's struggle was near. The Georgians no longer had any reason to fear for their independence from Denikin, but, on the contrary, they became increasingly aware of the more serious threat— occupation by the Red Army. The nearness of the common enemy accomplished what could not be achieved in better times: English diplomacy helped to bring the Georgian government and the White movement together.

On January 14 Denikin, at the prompting of the English representative at his headquarters, Sir Halford Mackinder, issued a statement in which he recognized the de facto independence of the Georgian republic.[87] Denikin still insisted that border questions could be resolved only after the creation of an all-Russian government; however, for the first time he did not make cooperation conditional on a Georgian withdrawal to the Bzyb' River. This concession made possible more substantive agreements.

In February Denikin named General Baratov his foreign minister.[88] Presumably Denikin chose him because he was the man most likely to achieve an accommodation with the Caucasian states. Indeed, Baratov immediately started to work on bettering relations with Georgia, and entrusted Colonel Den, his representative in Tbilisi, to make far-reaching agreements with the government.[89] The Georgians were still not eager to cooperate. They no longer had any reason to fear the Whites, but the other side of the coin was that the alliance with the Whites was now less valuable. Denikin could not provide protection and therefore it did not seem worthwhile to provoke the victorious Red Army by open collaboration with its enemies. The Georgians stopped far short of Baratov's suggestion of a military alliance, but they definitely abandoned their previous hostile attitude. They allowed British war materiel to pass through their territory, concluded some trade agreements, and, most important, allowed White troops, pursued by the Reds, to enter their territory.

When the Reds succeeded in cutting off the Caucasian army from the main White forces, for the soldiers the only alternative to capture was asylum in Georgia. The Commander of the Army, General Erdeli, and his chief of staff, E. V. Maslovskii, entered direct negotiations with Tbilisi.[90] These negotiations were briefly interrupted by Denikin's declaration of war, but were later carried to a successful conclusion. The Whites were allowed to enter the republic, though they were disarmed at the border. Some of the officers and soldiers must have felt the indignity of being disarmed by the Georgians.

Georgia preserved the appearance of neutrality by not allowing refugees to go openly to the Crimea for the purpose of continuing the struggle. In fact, the Georgian authorities were well aware that the English ships, full of Russian refugees supposed to be on their way to Constantinople, were headed for the Crimea. While Georgia wanted to avoid war with the Soviets, it was not in her interest that the Russian Civil War should end quickly. Indeed, the Georgian regime survived Denikin's by only a year.

Azerbaidzhan is a poor and mountainous region on the shore of the Caspian Sea. It became an independent country in May 1918 when the short-lived Transcaucasian Federation collapsed. The country had a Muslim majority and its politics were dominated by the Mussavat, a socialist and nationalist party. The people hoped for a Turkish victory in the World War, for they expected that their coreligionists would support them against both the Russians and the neighboring states with which Azerbaidzhan had territorial quarrels. However, the Turks soon disappointed the people. Conservative officers disliked the social racialism of the Mussavat, stopped land reform projects, and removed the socialist politicians from office.

The British landed in Baku soon after the Armistice.[91] They removed from power those who had cooperated with the Turks and reinstated the socialist politicians. They did not, however, help in the reconstruction of the country, which suffered economic hardships and political disintegration. The region was cut off from its traditional supplier of bread, the Northern Caucasus, and from markets for its oil. Partly because of the privations the people had to endure, the Bolshevik underground acquired substantial strength among the workers of Baku. The country had no experienced administrators or officers. When the Azerbaidzhani formed a small army, they entrusted command to General Sul'kevich, the one-time dictator of the Crimea, because there were no capable native candidates.

During 1918 the Volunteer Army had little reliable information about events in Azerbaidzhan, but after White victories in November and December in the Northern Caucasus and the arrival of the British, it seemed necessary to establish contacts. In January 1919 Denikin sent General Erdeli to Baku.[92] The British commander, General Thomson, did not receive him well. He would not allow the Russian officers living in the country to organize military units. He ordered the removal of a unit which already existed under General Bicherakhov. He demanded the disarming of the Caspian fleet because he suspected it to be under Bolshevik influence. Erdeli in vain asked for British help in recovering Russian property left in the county. Thomson sent him to the Azerbaidzhani government, which was tantamount to refusal.

In May 1919 the Volunteer Army and Azerbaidzhan came close to fighting one another. Denikin decided to occupy Dagestan, an area north of Azerbaidzhan on the coast of the Caspian Sea, because he considered the territory strategically important. As long as the Bolsheviks retained their hold on Astrakhan, there was always a danger that they would try to reestablish themselves in the Northern Caucasus. Dagestan, one of the poorest and most backward regions of the former Russian empire, was inhabited by a Muslim people. The Azerbaidzhani government would have liked to incorporate this area, but it was concerned that the Russians would not stop at the border but proceed southward. Denikin, in order to allay the fears of the Azerbaidzhanis, stated that he temporarily recognized the independence of the country.[93] The government in Baku, however, did not accept his word. On June 16 it concluded an alliance with Georgia against the Russians and started to organize the defense of the frontiers.[94]

The quarrel greatly harmed the White Russian cause. In June and July 1919 the people of Dagestan, sparked by Denikin's order of mobilization, rebelled against the Volunteer Army and the rebellion spread to the district inhabited by the Chechens. Azerbaidzhan gave complete support to the partisans, even to the extent of sending volunteers.[95] The fighting went on for several months, tieing down 15 thousand White soldiers.[96] Some White officers believed that the rising could be suppressed only if the sanctuaries of the rebels in Azerbaidzhan were eliminated, and therefore suggested the occupation of Baku.[97] Although Denikin had a low opinion of the fighting capabilities of the Azerbaidzhani army, he wisely refrained from extending the war.

At the end of December 1919 the Baku government realized that the Whites had ceased to be a threat to the independence of the country, but the Red Army seemed increasingly dangerous. It was clearly in Azerbaidzhan's interest that the Russian Civil War should continue. Mussavat politicians approached the Volunteer Army and proposed a renewal of trade in exchange for permitting the Whites to use harbor facilities.[98]

Denikin, in response, recognized the *de facto* independence of Azerbaidzhan on January 14. The Whites greatly profited from improved relations. In March and April the Volunteer Army was forced to evacuate the northern Caucasus and many of its soldiers escaped to Azerbaidzhan. The authorities there disarmed the soldiers, but allowed them to proceed to Georgia. Most went on to the Crimea in order to continue the struggle to the bitter end.

The third Caucasian state, Armenia, separated from White territories by Georgia and Azerbaidzhan, was in a difficult position. The country was so miserably poor that it was constantly on the verge of famine; it was inundated by refugees from Turkey, who had survived the massacres of 1915; and every neighboring country was hostile.

Armenia and the Volunteer Army had some of the same enemies. Ekaterinodar and Erevan quickly realized that it was in their inter-

est to support one another. Simon Vratzian, an Armenian representative, traveled to Ekaterinodar in the summer of 1918 and had
cordial talks with General Alekseev. Alekseev gave his permission
to Russian officers to help in the defense of the beleaguered country and promised to send food to alleviate famine. Through no
fault of the White leaders, little of the promised grain arrived. The
Georgians interfered successfully.[99]

In December 1918 Denikin sent Colonel Lesli to Erevan as his
permanent representative. The Armenians recognized that the survival of their state depended not so much on the White Russians as
on the good will of the Allies. They were somewhat concerned that
overly friendly relations with the Volunteer Army might compromise them in the eyes of the British, who were the defenders of
Georgia and Azerbaidzhan.[100] Nevertheless, relations remained
cordial. The Volunteer Army treated the Armenians who lived
in their territories as a friendly minority and allowed them to organize military units which went to fight for the young republic.[101]

CHAPTER 8

Disintegration and Defeat

Fortunes can change quickly in a civil war. The White armies, which had fought victoriously during the summer and early fall, fell back in disorder in November and December. The months of defeat were a period of distintegration: soldiers and officers increasingly often refused to carry out orders; the alliance of officers and Cossacks, which had always been tenuous, broke down amidst angry shouts of recrimination; the governmental structure, designed during the fall of 1918, fell apart. Denikin desperately tried new political combinations, creating and dissolving institutions with increasing frequency, but nothing seemed to help. The methods with which the Whites attempted to restore order in the country did not work. The social forces which had allied themselves against the Bolsheviks were insufficient to defeat the enemy. The principles and goals which were vaguely called the "White cause" went down in defeat.

DECISIVE BATTLES

During the fall of 1919 the mood in the White camp was strangely ambivalent. In October Denikin ruled more than forty million people and controlled the economically most valuable parts of the Russian empire. The speed of the advance of the armies had convinced many that victory was near, and it seemed that one more great exertion of strength would bring the fall of Moscow.

At the same time, not far below the surface, there was a feeling of doom. As victory seemed closer, it also seemed more distant. Even the politically unsophisticated could see that the administrative structure barely functioned and that the population was plagued by anarchy and anarchists. Contrary to expectations, capturing provinces did not make the movement stronger, but weakened it. The front line became dangerously long; the new recruits did not want to fight; and the population became increasingly hostile and restless. Under the circumstances the capture of Moscow acquired an almost mystical significance. Even some clear-sighted men believed that only the occupation of the ancient capital could cure the ailments of the movement. The conquest of Moscow became not a well-planned military objective but a *deus ex machina*, something essential for the survival of the Army. When, after the defeats of November, the goal was not clearly immediately attainable, many lost faith in the movement altogether.

The Bolsheviks did not know how weak their enemies really were. Understandably, Denikin at Orel created an atmosphere of crisis in Moscow, worse than anything the Reds had experienced since the spring of 1918. Fortunately for the Bolsheviks, Kolchak's army had ceased to be a serious danger. In the east, the Whites had been retreating almost continuously already since May 1919. At the end of August they had achieved some local successes, and for awhile it seemed that the front might be revitalized. This did not happen. In October the Reds won decisive victories and in the beginning of November they occupied Kolchak's capital, Omsk. Although a large number of Red soldiers continued to be tied down in the east, the High Command did not have to worry about a new White offensive.

However, another danger appeared at the crucial moment. An army under General N. N. Iudenich crossed the Estonian border and within a short time threatened Petrograd. Iudenich had organized his "Northwestern army" with British and Estonian aid. In May and June he carried out his first attack with the support of Estonian forces, but he was beaten back. Since his soldiers were growing restless in inactivity, and since he feared that Estonia might conclude a peace treaty with the Soviets at his expense, in September he decided to try again. This was a desperate venture. His poorly organized force had only twenty thousand men, while the enemy which faced him, the Seventh Soviet army, was twenty-five thousand strong. Also, he could not expect a friendly reception from the population of Petrograd, where the working class supported the Communists. Iudenich had made no attempt whatever to coordinate his moves with Denikin's, and it was purely an accident that the two White armies approached the capitals at the same time.

Largely because of the element of surprise, Iudenich achieved major successes. He sent an army directly eastward which captured Luga and threatened to cut the Moscow-Petrograd railroad line, while the main forces moved against the old capital. On October 11 the Whites took Iamburg and on October 16 Gatchina, a town only thirty miles from Petrograd.

The Bolsheviks faced a cruel dilemma. Abandoning Petrograd, the "birthplace of the revolution," would have been a psychological blow with incalculable consequences. On the other hand, weakening the southern front seemed much too dangerous. Lenin was inclined to retreat from Petrograd in order to concentrate all available forces against the greater danger, Denikin, but Trotskii disagreed and on this occasion prevailed. The Commissar for War went to Petrograd to direct the defense of the city. His resolute acts created confidence. He sent new working-class recruits to the front, he organized partisan detachments to fight in the city if necessary, and ordered the workers to raise barricades. In the battles of October 21–23 at the outskirts of Petrograd, Iudenich was stopped. The Whites did not have the strength to organize a protracted siege and fell back quickly. On November 3 they evacuated Gatchina and ten days later retreated into Estonia, where they were interned. Now Estonia was ready to conclude peace with the Soviet government.

The Red Army had won decisive victories in the east and in the west, but it was clear that the most difficult would have to be fought in the south. In September and October the Bolshevik leaders organized feverishly for the battles which they expected to be decisive. The party was able to mobilize new soldiers to meet the crisis, for, unlike their enemies, the Reds were capable of an extra exertion when it was most necessary. Between September 1 and November 15 the Reds sent over one hundred thousand new soldiers to the

Southern front.[1] In the first two weeks of October Moscow alone sent 13,600 new recruits against the Volunteer Army.[2] At the same time the Red High Command reconsidered its strategy, formed new units, and placed new commanders in responsible positions.

In the middle of October, at the time of the crucial battles, the Bolshevik forces were superior to the Whites in manpower and supply. The Reds had 160,000 infantry, 26,000 cavalry, and 4,500 machine guns, and their enemies had 63,000 infantry, 48,000 cavalry, and 2,300 machine guns.[3] The Red Army's strength in machine guns shows that the Soviet war industry had made a great contribution to eventual victory.

The Whites' chief advantage had always been their excellent cavalry, but by the second half of 1919 this superiority lost some of its significance. The remarkably successful Don Cossack cavalry of General Mamontov, which had carried out devastating raids in the rear of the Bolsheviks only a short time before, was greatly weakened by constant fighting. The Reds, on the other hand, became aware of the importance of the cavalry and made great efforts to match their enemies. The Party promulgated the slogan: "proletarians, to the horse!" This was a fine slogan, but not surprisingly only a few workers in fact learned the difficult art of horsemanship. The Red cavalrymen came largely from among the *inogorodnie* of the Don district. Many Cossacks from the poorer, northern areas of the Don *Voisko* also preferred the Reds over the Whites.[4]

In August and September the two sides followed the military plans which they had worked out months before. Bolshevik strategy had been designed by Commander-in-Chief S. S. Kamenev, who wanted to deal the main blow through the Don in order to reach the enemy's home base. In the course of August the weakness of this plan became abundantly clear: the Red offensive against the Don Cossacks, who were defending their homeland, bogged down, while the best White units advanced through the Ukraine and threatened Moscow. The blindness with which the Reds stuck to this mistaken plan can be explained only by pointing to the strength of the anti-Trotskii element within the army. The Commissar for War had always seen the dangers inherent in Kamenev's strategy and advocated an offensive through the Donets basin.

Only the extreme danger, which the Bolsheviks began to perceive at the end of September, forced them to initiate a large-scale reorganization. On September 27 the High Command divided the anti-Denikin front into two sectors: the Ninth and Tenth armies, holding the front from Tsaritsyn to Bobrov, were formed into the Southeastern Front, under the command of V. I. Shorin; and the Eighth, Twelfth, Thirteenth, and Fourteenth armies, fighting between Zhitomir and Bobrov, were formed into the Southern front under General A. I. Egorov. S. S. Kamenev was responsible for the coordination of the two fronts. This reorganization greatly strengthened the central sector. Now the best Bolshevik troops faced the best White units; the excellent Latvian sharpshooter division fought against these White troops which had advanced furthest.[5] The Reds now followed the early Trotskii-Vatsetis strategy.

White strategy was based on the "Moscow directive," which called for advance along the entire, enormously long front from the Caspian Sea to the Polish frontier. Although Denikin had envisaged a three-pronged attack on Moscow, his deployment of troops made the front in the Ukraine the most mobile. In the middle of October the White front consisted of four main groups. On the extreme left, defending Kiev against the Twelfth Red Army, General Dragomirov had nine thousand soldiers. In the center the Volunteer Army, 20,500 strong, fought under General Mai-Maevskii. This was the best unit, which contained the largest percentage of veterans of the early campaigns. Further east, fifty thousand Don Cossacks under General Sidorin faced the Reds, and General Wrangel's Caucasian army with 14,500 men defended Tsaritsyn.[6] Separated from the main forces in the Northern Caucasus, three to five thousand White soldiers fought in the hope of capturing Astrakhan and finally dislodging the Reds from the Caspian.

Though Denikin was well aware of the regrouping of the enemy, a combination of weakness and optimism restrained him from responding. All his reserves were tied down fighting Makhno and other insurgents in the Ukraine, so he could not strengthen the now exposed Volunteer Army. Makhno, who had captured major cities and threatened even the headquarters at Taganrog, proved to be a far more dangerous enemy than the Whites had first thought. The partisan chief made his greatest contribution to eventual Bolshevik victory in the Civil War by tieing down Denikin's reserves at this crucial moment. Under the circumstances Denikin, a normally cautious man, should have shortened the front and withdrawn from the most exposed positions. The foolhardy strategy which the Whites adopted was the result of an unrealistic optimism which still prevailed at the *Stavka*. Denikin believed that his troops had faced uneven odds in the past and won, and therefore would so do again.

The Bolshevik counteroffensive began in the second half of October at two different points. A newly formed shock group, made up of a Ukrainian cavalry brigade under V. M. Primakov and the Latvian infantry division, attacked the enemy at Orel from the West, forcing Mai-Maevskii to evacuate Orel on October 20 in order to avoid being cut off. The Whites withdrew in good fighting order to Kursk in the face of a numerically much stronger enemy.

Almost at the same time the Reds won an even more significant victory against the Don Cossacks. It is characteristic of the conditions in the Civil War, that this victory, which turned out to have far-reaching consequences, came about as a result of disobedience and lack of military discipline. Front Commander Shorin ordered S. M. Budennyi's cavalry to move Southwest. Budennyi, however, learning that the famous White cavalry leaders Mamontov and Shkuro were fighting around Voronezh, decided to try his luck. He won a brilliant victory and on October 24 he occupied Voronezh.[7] The Reds were now able to cross the Don River, which had great strategic importance, since they could threaten separating the Don and Volunteer Armies. The Whites, aware of the danger, resisted with determination. The battle went on for thirty days for the important railroad junction of Kastornoe. On November 15 the Reds took the little town and two days later occupied Kursk. (See Map 3.)

After the defeats at Orel and Voronezh, the Whites ceased to be a direct threat to Moscow and to the survival of the Soviet regime. They had lost the initiative. However, the battles of Kastornoe and Kursk were the turning points in the Civil War. At the end of November the spirit of the White armies was broken and they could no longer resist the enemy in a sustained battle. They constantly retreated without being able to form a stable front once again.

Denikin feverishly tried to stop the impending disaster. In the beginning of December he worked out a new strategy.[8] He wanted to concentrate his strength in the center, hold Tsaritsyn and Kiev,

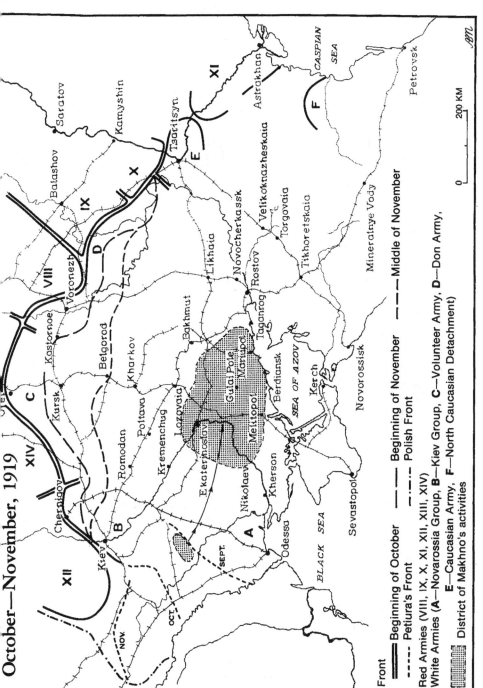

October—November, 1919

XII
XIV
VIII
IX
X
XI
C
B
A
D
E
F

Chernigov
Kiev
Kursk
Kastornoe
Voronezh
Saratov
Balashov
Kamyshin
Tsaritsyn
Astrakhan
CASPIAN SEA
Petrovsk

Belgorod
Kharkov
Poltava
Romodan
Kremenchug
Lozovaia
Ekaterinoslav
Nikolaev
Kherson
Odessa

Bakhmut
Gulai Pole
Mariupol
Melitopol
Berdiansk
SEA OF AZOV
Kerch
Likhaia
Novocherkassk
Rostov
Taganrog
Velikoknazheskaia
Torgovaia
Tikhoretskaia
Mineralnye Vody
Novorossisk
Sevastopol

BLACK SEA

SEPT.
OCT.
NOV.

0   200 KM

MAP 3

Front

Beginning of October ——— Beginning of November ——— Middle of November
Petlura's Front ——— Polish Front

Red Armies (VIII, IX, X, XI, XII, XIII, XIV)
White Armies (A—Novarossia Group, B—Kiev Group, C—Volunteer Army, D—Don Army,
E—Caucasian Army, F—North Caucasian Detachment)

District of Makhno's activities

and take advantage of the Don and Dnepr rivers for protecting the two flanks. Seeing Budennyi's successes, Denikin decided to concentrate his own cavalry. In order to carry out this plan, Denikin dismissed Mai-Maevskii and gave command of the enlarged Volunteer Army to General Wrangel. Since the new cavalry force would come under the command of the Commander of the Volunteer Army, it seemed appropriate to select a cavalry officer for the post.

Wrangel, who assumed his new responsibilities on December 8, turned out to be a disastrous choice. A vain man, he would not take responsibility for defeats. Instead of trying to save the situation by patient work, he used his considerable energies to denounce the deplorable conditions which he had found. Of course many of Wrangel's criticisms of Mai-Maevskii (and by implication of Denikin) were justified; however, at a time of defeats and confusion, the bitter denunciation of his fellow officers and his superior merely added to the general demoralization. In his very first report to Denikin, on December 1, he rather prematurely declared that the Volunteer Army had ceased to exist.[9] Wrangel was more interested in saving his reputation than in helping the cause he served.

The plans for concentrating the cavalry did not succeed. Wrangel would have neither Shkuro nor Mamontov serve under him, and he named General Kuchuk Ulagai Commander of the new force. The removal of Mamontov led to trouble. (Shkuro at the time was ill and therefore readily acquiesced.) General Sidorin, the Commander of the Don army, and Ataman Bogaevskii backed Mamontov and gave him a command post in the Don army. The firing of the popular commander further depressed the morale of the Cossack cavalry. Demoralization and disorganization went so far that the once brilliant cavalry refused to face Budennyi's horsemen.[10] (See Map 4.)

Soon Denikin and Wrangel once again became embroiled in a furious debate over strategy. In case of need, Wrangel wanted to withdraw his army to the Crimea, because, he argued, the geography of the peninsula aided the defender and the population was friendly.[11] Denikin, however, would not even consider such a move. Whatever the strategic advantages of retreating westward, he would not let down his Cossack allies. To him it was a question

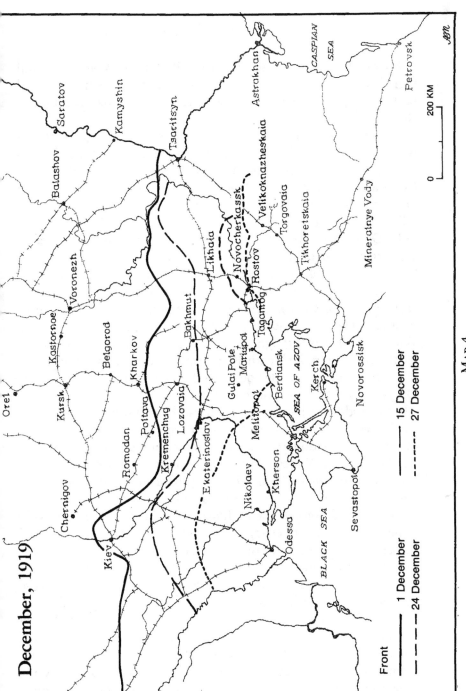

December, 1919

Orel
Chernigov
Kiev
Romodan
Kursk
Kastornoe
Belgorod
Kharkov
Poltava
Kremenchug
Ekaterinoslav
Lozovaia
Bakhmut
Gulai Pole
Mariupol
Melitopol
Nikolaev
Kherson
Odessa
Berdiansk
SEA OF AZOV
Kerch
Sevastopol
BLACK SEA
Novorossisk
Likhaia
Novocherkassk
Rostov
Taganrog
Velikoknazheskaia
Torgovaia
Tikhoretskaia
Mineralnye Vody
Astrakhan
Tsaritsyn
Kamyshin
Saratov
Balashov
Voronezh
CASPIAN SEA
Petrovsk

0   200 KM

Front

1 December
24 December
15 December
27 December

MAP 4

of honor: the Cossacks had fought loyally for the White cause and therefore abandoning their native land without a struggle would be treachery. The Whites retreated eastward, in the direction of Rostov.

As a result of constant disagreements and of the great defeats which reduced the size of his army, on December 24 Denikin removed Wrangel, renamed the Volunteer Army the Volunteer Corps and attached it to the Don army. Wrangel went to the Kuban to try to raise new cavalry, and A. P. Kutepov took command of the Volunteer Corps.

In December and January the speed of the Bolshevik advance accelerated. On January 6 the Red Army reached the Black Sea Coast at Mariupol and Taganrog and thereby cut the White forces in two.[12] General Shilling defended Odessa and the Taurida, the entrance to the Crimea, in almost complete isolation from headquarters. The only tenuous link which remained between the two White groups was through the Taman peninsula and Novorossisk. At the same time the Tenth Red Army succeeded in driving back the enemy and cut a wedge between the Caucasian and Don armies. On January 9 they occupied Rostov.

In the middle of January Denikin had 81,000 soliders, 54,000 of which were concentrated in the main Don-Sal' theater.[13] He established his headquarters at the remote railroad junction of Tikhoretskaia. The Whites had now lost all the territories which they had conquered in 1919, and held approximately the same area in which they had started two years before.

Denikin did not yet lose all hope. He believed that a successful stand anywhere might change the course of the war once more, and he based his optimism on the weakness of the enemy. Indeed, the Soviet troops were extremely tired: between October 20, when Orel fell, and January 9 they advanced 500 miles. They moved so fast that in the beginning of January they were 250 miles from their headquarters. At a time when the railroad network hardly functioned, this headlong rush forward meant that the troops could not receive reinforcements and supplies. They had to fend for themselves and live at the expense of the population.[14] At the same time the army was decimated by a terrible typhus epidemic.

In many ways, the fast advance was just as risky as Denikin's strategy, which took him to the heart of Russia, and then to ultimate defeat.

The basic causes of White defeats were political. The Whites could not mobilize enough soldiers; many of those who fought did so without enthusiasm; because of the disorder in the rear, the anarchists with minimal forces could capture enormous territories and disrupt communications; and the defeats coincided with an exacerbation of the disagreements with the Cossacks.

Other causes were inherent in the nature of the White army. Denikin could not always deploy his troops as he wanted them. For example, the leadership of the Don army insisted on reconquering and then holding the entire *Voisko*. Denikin in vain ordered Sidorin to strengthen his left flank and protect his ties with the Volunteer Army. As a result, the Whites suffered the disastrous defeat at Voronezh, while they continued to advance in the east and occupy some strategically unimportant Cossack territory.[15] Wrangel was no more obedient than Sidorin. At the end of October he refused to send reinforcements to Mai-Maevskii. He threatened resignation if Denikin insisted.[16]

After the initial reverses the Whites lost their morale. Not only the soldiers, but even the majority of the officers lost faith in victory. The Whites, in the moment of crisis, were not capable of taking a stand which might conceivably have saved them.

THE ABOLITION OF THE SPECIAL COUNCIL

The series of defeats further contributed to the disintegration of the White administrative structure. At the same time, the generals began to understand the political causes of military reverses. Only days after the defeats at Orel and Voronezh, Denikin entrusted N. I. Astrov to improve the situation.[17] On November 19 Astrov delivered a deeply pessimistic report to the Special Council, in which he described vividly the depth of disorganization but did not offer realistic remedies. He wanted the movement to project an image of strength and convince the population that the army stood for democracy and not for the reestablishment of the old order. He criticized marauding soldiers for alienating the people. Astrov, however, did not ask the difficult questions: How to project an image of strength and resolution? How to insure that the soldiers would not loot? How to make the local commanders carry out Denikin's policies? How to keep the local commanders from supporting the landlords against the peasants? Denikin remarked after listening to the report: "Nothing else remains for me to do but to put a bullet into my forehead. But let us try once again."[18]

The only concrete result of Astrov's presentation was that Lukomskii, the Chairman of the Special Council, asked Astrov, K. N. Sokolov, and N. V. Savich to prepare another report. Since Sokolov and Savich were occupied with other matters and since the political views of the three men diverged greatly, they did not agree on a plan. On December 9 Denikin and Chief of Staff Romanovskii invited the three politicians to Taganrog to make their recommendations.

They presented three differing points of view. Savich, a monarchist, used the opportunity to plead the cause of Grand Duke Nikolai Nikolaevich once again. In a moment of crisis, he argued, only some sort of psychological lift could help. The people wanted a savior, a man not compromised by politics, but one who stood above class and political interests. Only the Grand Duke was such a person. Sokolov, on the contrary, reasoned that the Army needed firm support and it was realistic to expect such support only from conservatives.[19] He wanted a government of intelligent conservatives, people who recognized that it was necessary to accept the agrarian revolution which had taken place in 1917–1918. Romanovskii, after listening to Sokolov, pointed out that the flaw in this line of reasoning was that Russia possessed no enlightened conservatives to carry out sensible policies.[20]

Astrov's memorandum advocated the reorganization of the Special Council and called not for a new political program, but for enforcing previous decisions.[21] He complained that the conservative generals sitting on the Special Council did not carry out Denikin's policies. Astrov's remarks undoubtedly helped Denikin make up his mind to abolish the Council.

This step had been discussed for months, but since negotiations with representatives of the Cossack *Voiska* about the reorganization of the governmental structure dragged on, the time never seemed to be right. Finally, the defeats and demoralization made it impossible to wait any longer. The Special Council had never been popular. It seemed wise to try to remedy the situation by creating a new institution and giving responsibility to those who had not yet been discredited.

The final stimulus came from further reverses at the front. On December 19 Denikin informed the Special Council that Rostov would soon have to be evacuated.[22] This would be extremely difficult: the city, which had 200,000 inhabitants before the war, now housed a million and a half. Many refugees had no permanent shelter and suffered terrible privations. Thousands died in a raging typhus epidemic.[23] The refugees lived in panic. They realized that there were no safe places left for them in Russia. The members of the Special Council had not understood the seriousness of the situation, and thus were unprepared for the difficult task of evacuation. The Kuban government was so hostile to the Special Council that it would not allow it to return to Ekaterinodar. Under the circumstances, Denikin instructed department heads to reduce their staffs drastically and move temporarily to the port of Novorossisk.[24]

On December 29 prominent Kadets Astrov, Fedorov, V. P. Iurchenko, Stepanov, and V. N. Chelishchev wrote Denikin and recommended the immediate abolition of the Special Council. The politicians argued that it was useless to try any more to design a grand policy. What was needed for the present was to have men around Denikin who could help in the day-to-day problems of administration and in organizing the supply of the army. They proposed a cabinet of experts, rather than of politicians, headed by someone who possessed Denikin's full confidence.[25] Prominent conservatives such as Savich and Lukomskii expressed agreement with the content of the letter. On the next day, Denikin issued an order abolishing the Special Council and setting up a government consisting of seven departments: military, interior, finance, supply, communications, trade and industry, and justice. The departments of foreign affairs and control came under Denikin's direct authority. Conspicuously missing was the department of propaganda. The Osvag's unpopularity was so great that it seemed better to Denikin to be without an independent propaganda department. Denikin chose Lukomskii as president of the government. Among the new faces the only significant one was the ex-tsarist minister of agriculture, A. V. Krivoshein, the leader of the conservative wing in the White camp. Interestingly, Krivoshein was recommended by the Kadets, because they hoped that his presence would broaden the appeal of the government. In any case, the liberals did not want to assume new responsibilities in the rapidly deteriorating situation. With the exception of S. N. Chaev, a man who had helped to organize the defense of the Crimea in April 1919 and now became chief of the department of communications, the members of the government were holdovers from the Special Council.[26]

If Denikin hoped that his reorganization would make a favorable impression on public opinion, he was soon disappointed. In the confusion the population barely noticed the changes.[27] Indeed, the changes were hardly significant. The reorganization was purely formal: the size of the government was reduced, its name changed, but its character remained the same.

The most immediate task was to complete the evacuation of offices from Rostov, to Novorossisk. At this time Denikin had his headquarters in Tikhoretskaia, and the Cossack governments and assemblies functioned in Ekaterinodar. The geographical separation added to the confusion. The character of the political life in the three towns differed. Ekaterinodar was dominated by separatist and "democratic" Cossack politicians, Novorossisk by conservatives, who were increasingly skeptical about collaborating with the Cossacks successfully and hostile to the idea of giving new concessions to them. The *stavka* in Tikhoretskaia tried to moderate between the two groups. Denikin, in order to overcome this impasse, decided to replace Lukomskii with Ataman Bogaevskii. Bogaevskii could not come to Novorossisk to assume his duties, so Lukomskii continued as chairman of council of ministers.

During its short life the restructured government governed only in name. It was clear even to the ministers that their work no longer had significance. They met every day in Lukomskii's residence, more from a sense of loyalty and solidarity than because of pressing business.[28]

THE COSSACKS AND THE FORMATION
OF THE SOUTH RUSSIAN GOVERNMENT

From its establishment, the anti-Bolshevik movement in the South depended on the ability and willingness of the Cossacks to fight. In periods when the Cossacks were determined to win, White armies advanced, but when their morale fell, the entire movement suffered. In the course of the Civil War the mood of the Cossacks changed several times. Usually when their native *stanitsy* were occupied by the enemy their willingness to continue the war was rekindled. This fact gave hope to Denikin, who believed that a new turn in the struggle was still possible. Denikin, unlike some White politicians and generals, fully understood his dependence on the Cossacks. He never envisaged continuing the struggle without them.

This time, however, there was no revival of spirit. The mortal danger to their way of life did not bring the various warring Cossack factions together. The desire to find scapegoats was even stronger than the will to survive. Cossack politics had never been more confused and bitter than in this last stage. Although the left wing gained strength, this development did not lead to a reconciliation with the *inogorodnie*. As before, aside from a rich minority (the so-called original population), the peasants had no representatives in the self-governing voisko institutions.[29] Many *inogorodnie* joined the Bolsheviks or the increasingly numerous guerrilla bands.

When the Bolsheviks occupied the Don and the Terek, parliaments, governments, and armies took refuge in the Kuban. The guests did not behave well and they were received with hostility not only in *inogorodnie* villages but also in Cossack *stanitsy*.[30] The Don army retained its discipline better than the Kuban units, and consequently the *stavka* used these troops to put down risings and organize punitive expeditions against those who did not want to fight. The Don leadership was anxious to resume the offensive in order to liberate their native territory as soon as possible. In contrast, the Kuban Cossacks grew increasingly tired of war and wanted to limit their activities to purely defensive actions.

There was also a great deal of friction between Terek and Kuban politicians, largely as a result of the Kalabukhov affair. Kalabukhov had been executed for concluding a treaty with the representatives of the mountain republic, which had been in a stage of war with the Terek. Consequently the Terek Cossacks approved the harsh retribution carried out by the Volunteer Army, which Kuban politicians regarded the hanging as a gross violation of their sovereignty. When the Kuban politicians looked for a united Cossack front against Denikin, they did not always find support.[31]

The Kuban Cossacks no longer believed in the possibility of victory. Many of them, instead of joining the army, preferred to go into hiding. The already existing units refused to fight. Discipline was especially low and the desertion rate especially high among the Black Sea Cossacks, but conditions among the *lineitsy* were not much better.[32] General Zabrzhitskii, the head of the department of supplies, wrote about them: "The Cossacks do not engage in fighting. When they hear the sound of guns, they saddle their horses and retreat. There is no panic and there is no disorder. This is the worst. They simply do not want to fight."[33]

Kuban politics reflected the war-weariness and hostility to the Volunteer Army. The elections which were held in December, following the humiliation of the *rada*, returned the most uncompromising group of delegates. For the first time the Black Sea Cossacks dominated *voisko* politics completely. When Ataman Uspenskii unexpectedly died of typhus, the Black Sea Cossacks succeeded in electing their candidate, General Bukretov, as his successor. This election contradicted Kuban law, which required that the Ataman be a Cossack or have fifteen years' service in the *voisko*. However, the radicals were anxious to elect him and therefore willing to overlook his lack of legal qualifications. His main appeal was his well-known hostility to the *stavka* and the fact that Denikin despised him. Interestingly, Denikin's low opinion of the new Ataman had nothing to do with political differences. The Commander-in Chief regarded him as a dishonest speculator and suspected him of embezzlement.

Bukretov disappointed the separatists. As a Russian officer, he had little interest in the independence of the Kuban. After General Denikin's resignation he had no trouble at all in cooperating with General Wrangel, the new Commander-in-Chief. He worked well with the moderate *lineitsy* politicians.

The *rada* elected V. N. Ivanis, a Black Sea Cossack, premier. Ivanis, as minister of trade in a previous government, had established export controls and tariffs on exports and imports, which led to an economic war with the Volunteer Army. Understandably, Ivanis' election was another disturbing development from the point of view of the *stavka*.

But the most powerful Kuban politician of the period was I. P. Timoshenko, the newly elected president of the *rada*. The 32-year-old Timoshenko, a Social Democrat, was the leader of the left wing. He was irreconcilably hostile to the Volunteer Army.[34] He hoped to create a third force between Reds and Whites, and to that end he initiated contacts with Menshevik Georgia and with Petliura. When the Kuban had to be evacuated, Timoshenko did not follow the Army to the Crimea, but escaped to Georgia.

Ivanis, Timoshenko, and Bukretov shared a hostility to the Volunteer Army, but they disliked one another and often worked at cross purposes.[35] Had Denikin been a skillful politician he could have taken advantage of the disagreements between his enemies, but from his point of view all three were so evil that even a pretense of temporary cooperation or small concessions to them were simply out of the question.

On January 18 the Supreme Krug met in Ekaterinodar.[36] Each *voisko* sent 50 representatives. The Terek Cossacks, who understood that their native territory could be retaken only with Russian aid, were the least hostile to the Volunteer Army. Aside from a small left wing, which voted with radicals from the Kuban, the Terek delegates acted as intermediaries between the Krug and the headquarters.

The Don delegates, as representatives of the largest *voisko* and strongest army, played a crucial role. Three quarters of the Don delegates were moderates, led by such reliable friends of the Volunteer Army as Kharlamov and Paramonov, and, of course, Ataman Bogaevskii, one of Denikin's oldest comrades-in-arms. General Sidorin, the Commander of the Don army, who had become increasingly critical of Denikin's leadership, nevertheless remained convinced that a break with the Volunteer Army would be disastrous. The strength of the moderates, however, was seriously undermined by vocal left and right wings. The left was led by P. M. Agaev, a socialist, who had a strong following among soldiers. By and large the soldiers were more radical than the *stariki* (the old ones) who stayed at home. Ianov retained the leadership of the pro-German, pro-Krasnov, and monarchist right. Although the left and right were weak, they often successfully cooperated in opposition to the *stavka*. In general, under the impact of continuous defeats, Don politics became more radical and hostile to the Volunteer Army. Old methods did not work; many were ready to experiment with new ones.

The Krug elected Timoshenko as its president. This was a great blow to the *stavka*, which expected Kharlamov's election. But Kharlamov, the head of the Don delegation, could not be elected simply because he was regarded as too good a friend of General Denikin.[37]

Since the summer of 1919 representatives of the Volunteer Army and of the Cossacks negotiated about how the governmental structure of South Russia should be reorganized. The defeats radically changed the relative bargaining strengths of the two sides. The Volunteer Army, which had always been the best fighting unit of the Armed Forces of South Russia, suffered the heaviest casualties. In the beginning of 1920, this unit, now called the Volunteer Corps, still retained its discipline and morale, but it was so small that it could not possibly stand on its own. The Cossacks, who now more than ever made up the great majority of the fighting men, demanded a greater share in the decision-making process.

Both Wrangel and Denikin had foreseen the possibility of such a development in December 1919. One of the reasons for Wrangel's desire not to retreat to Cossack territories was his profound dislike of Cossack "leftism."[38] Wrangel and his political friends would rather have written off the Cossacks than give them political concessions. Denikin also must have realized that retreating eastward meant an increased reliance on the Cossacks and therefore a turn toward a more leftist political orientation. Strategic and political considerations were clearly intertwined.

Denikin had frequently said that he wanted to find a balance between the right and left of the political spectrum. (He had a rather narrow definition of left and right: the socialists and the Black Hundred elements were beyond the pale for him.) In the traumatic days of the winter of 1920 he found that he could no longer maintain what had seemed to him a centrist position. Under the pressure of events he made significant concessions to the left.

As he put it in his memoirs: "The issue was clear to me. No sacrifice in the sphere of limitation of civil authority was too great, if thanks to that sacrifice the Cossacks would regain their health and the Bolsheviks would be defeated."[39]

The removal of Lukomskii was his first concession. Lukomskii had been especially disliked by the great majority of the Cossacks, who blamed him for the uncompromisingly centralist policies of the Special Council. The General alienated many Cossack politicians by his insulting behaviour and brusque manner during the long months of negotiations concerning Cossack autonomy. Denikin chose Bogaevskii as Lukomskii's successor to win Cossack support but he only partially achieved his goal. Although the appointment was regarded favorably by moderates, it did not mollify the separatists, who disliked Bogaevskii for his close relations with the leaders of the Volunteer Army.

From Denikin's point of view, a far greater concession was his permission for a separate Kuban army. The issue had been bitterly debated for months, but the *stavka* had always successfully resisted. Now it seemed to Denikin that an independent army might be able to attract more volunteers and therefore it had to be tried. The large majority of Kuban Cossacks had fought in the Caucasian army, which in January 1920 had the lowest fighting value and worst discipline among all the units of the anti-Bolshevik army. This unit, which was falling apart, was to become the nucleus of the Kuban army.

After Wrangel's transfer to the Volunteer Army, General Pokrovskii took command of the Caucasian army. Pokrovskii, who in 1918 had a great role in forming the first Kuban force and had remained an important participant in Kuban events ever since, became odious to Cossack politicians because of his role in the Ekaterinodar events of November 1919.[40] Denikin chose General Ulagai, a fine officer and a man of integrity, as Pokrovskii's successor. However, Ulagai was ill with typhus and therefore the Commander-in-Chief named Shkuro instead. This appointment did not satisfy the radicals. Shkuro had never supported the separatist movement and had collaborated too closely with the *stavka* in the past. In general, the separatists did not recognize Denikin's right to name the Commander of their army. They further objected to the arrangement according to which in matters of supply the Kuban army remained dependent on the *stavka*.

As another concession, Denikin was ready to renounce the cherished principle of military dictatorship. On January 25 the atamans, the heads of Cossack governments, and senior Cossack military leaders visited the Commander-in-Chief at his headquarters.[41] The Cossacks agreed to continue the fight and recognized that a break between themselves and the Russian officers would be suicidal. Denikin, in turn, conceded that civil authority had to be immediately and radically reorganized.

On January 29 Denikin traveled to Ekaterinodar to address the Supreme Krug.[42] He obviously attributed great importance to his speech, which he wrote out and showed to some senior military leaders beforehand. It was one of Denikin's best speeches, and it impressed many in his audience. As usual, he avoided histrionics and spoke simply, with obvious sincerity.

First he described the military situation, which he saw as grave. But he had not lost hope, he said, because he believed that the Bolsheviks had overextended themselves, were poorly supplied, and suffered from weak discipline. Then he discussed the reorganization of political institutions. He warned his listeners that if they decided to form an independent state he would leave the area, along with the remnants of the Volunteer Corps, the Russian officers, and many Cossacks. He predicted that such a move would lead to the immediate collapse of the front and victory for the Red Army. In conclusion, he summarized his program:

1. A great and indivisible Russia.
2. The Don and Kuban armies form parts of a united Russian army. All units of the army were governed by the same laws and come under the same ultimate authority.
3. Continued struggle against the Bolsheviks.
4. The Cossack *voiska* will receive broad autonomy. This autonomy is justified by the historical contributions of the Cossacks to the Russian cause. All provinces and districts will receive broad autonomy.
5. A government will be formed from persons who hold moderate views and are honest and effective. This government will deal with all matters concerning the state. The entrance of Cossack represen-

tatives into this government will guarantee the defense of Cossack interests.

6. A representative assembly will be called which will have legislative and consultative functions.

7. The land will be given to the peasants and working Cossacks.

8. The professional interests of the workers will be protected.

9. An All-Russian Constituent Assembly will be called to determine the future form of state.[43]

This was one of Denikin's most leftist statements. He once again reiterated his commmitment to land reform, and after a year of vacillation he promised a Constituent Assembly. On these matters and also on the immediate problems of building a governmental structure, little now separated Denikin from the majority Cossack opinion. However, the memories of past struggles were still fresh and many of his listeners did not trust Denikin. As Timoshenko pointed out in his reply, struggle for a Constituent Assembly and land reform were good slogans, but they should have been presented earlier.[44]

Negotiations for forming a new government immediately began. Savich and Chelishchev bargained in Denikin's name with Cossack representatives. The dispute centered on Denikin's sixth point, concerning a legislative assembly.[45] The Cossacks wanted the government to be responsible to the assembly and temporarily wanted the Supreme Krug to play the role of this assembly. A compromise was worked out which allowed Denikin to veto the decisions of the assembly, but the representatives could override the veto after the passage of four months if they had a two-thirds majority. Temporarily a newly formed commission would play the role of the legislature. The Krug would elect half of the members of the commission and Denikin was to name the others. Military decisions and communication remained under Denikin's exclusive authority. Now Denikin ceased to be a "dictator" and became a "constitutional monarch."[46]

On February 4 the Krug accepted the project against only two negative votes, and the difficult task of building a government began. Denikin chose N. M. Mel'nikov, a prime minister of the Don, as the head of his government. In order to gain the confidence of the Cossacks, the cabinet was made up almost entirely of local figures. The era of the Special Council was now definitely over. Some of the politicians suggested by Mel'nikov were difficult for Denikin to accept. The Commander-in-Chief found especially odious P. M. Agaev, the Don socialist, as minister of agriculture. But Mel'nikov argued that Agaev participation would gain the support of the left, and Denikin gave in. Perhaps the most important post in the cabinet, the war ministry, went to General Kel'chevskii, who had been chief of staff of the Don army. General Baratov, who had lost both of his legs in an assassination attempt in Tbilisi, became minister of foreign affairs. This appointment shows that Denikin finally understood the significance of good relations with the Caucasian states. Baratov's main qualification for the post was his good connections in Georgia and Azerbaidzhan. Denikin considered it very important that the portfolio of finances should remain in the hands of a man in whom he had full confidence, and so M. V. Bernatskii became the only holdover from the Special Council. The most remarkable choice was that of N. V. Chaikovskii, a veteran socialist and revolutionary, active in underground activities since the 1860s.[47] Chaikovskii became a member of the government without portfolio, and a little later he assumed direction of propaganda work. The old man had already played a significant role in the anti-Bolshevik movement in North Russia. After the defeat in the North he went to Poland. He returned to Russia to join Denikin, whom he obviously did not fully trust or like, at a time when the Volunteer Army was near collapse. Chaikovskii hated the Bolsheviks so much that he was willing to make any sacrifice.

The Mel'nikov government was largely made up of moderate Don Cossacks and Kuban *lineitsy* politicians. Denikin would not tolerate the appointment of a separatist Black Sea Cossack. Consequently, the Kuban separatists refused to have anything to do with the new cabinet, which created a paradoxical situation.[48] The Whites occupied only one province, but even this province refused to recognize the authority of the White government. At the same time, Russian politicians looked down on the Mel'nikov cabinet, which was composed of what they contemptuously called "local talents." Only the Kadets, ever loyal to Denikin, expressed approval of Denikin's compromises and concessions.[49]

The government began to function only in the beginning of March. It was clear even to the ministers that they could not play an active role and that their task was limited to preparing manifestos and working out projects which could be realized only after a change in military fortunes. These proclamations show that Denikin's last government, with the exception of the Socialist Revolutionary groups of 1918, was the most leftist and liberal section within the anti-Bolshevik movement. Mel'nikov proclaimed:

> The South Russian government regards its task as the reestablishment of the Russian state through the Constituent Assembly. It will work on the basis of all-national representation and representative government. It aims to use the democratic state for introducing radical economic and social reforms, in the interests of the people, above all, the working peasants, Cossacks, and workers. Small property belonging to communes or to individuals will remain inviolable. All land, no matter to whom it belongs, above a certain legal norm will be distributed among the needy by government organs which will also provide the new owners with legal papers proving ownership. Soon a provisional land law will be published which will regulate land relations until the convocation of the Constituent Assembly. The owners of the alienated lands will be forbidden to negotiate or to draw up accounts with the new owners. Accounts and negotiations will be handled by the proper agencies of the government constituted on democratic principles.[50]

Mel'nikov also promised protection of cooperative institutions, honest local administration, defense of religion, and support of the legitimate economic interests of the workers.

Would the outcome of the Civil War have been different if the White movement had announced such progressive and democratic principles at an earlier date? It was not an accident that the Whites waited until the last moment. They gave concessions out of desperation, at a time when the chances of victory seemed remote. But even assuming that the officers, who made up the leadership of the movement, would have accepted policies and principles which went contrary to their beliefs at an earlier date, the Whites still would have faced great difficulties. It was far easier to promise reforms than to introduce them in reality. The Socialist Revolutionaries promised in 1918 everything which the Mel'nikov government came to advocate almost two years later, and still they never came close to victory.

Denikin and his friends certainly erred in not introducing progressive slogans, but their far more significant failure lay in not building a functioning administration. Officers, who represented the movement to the peasants, did not carry out Denikin's policies or the decisions of the Special Council. Contrary to decisions made in Ekaterinodar, reactionary and vengeful landlords returned with the White troops and reclaimed their land. Nothing in the political changes of early 1920 indicate that the Whites learned from their failures. In all probability, had the fortunes of war changed once again and anti-Bolshevik armies reached the neighborhood of Moscow, the unreconstructed reactionary officers would have cheerfully disregarded the promises of the Mel'nikov government. In Russia those who wanted to fight the Bolsheviks did not want reforms, and those who were genuinely committed to change by and large lacked the determination to continue the struggle against the new leaders in Moscow. Those socialists who hated the Bolsheviks remained leaders without followers.

FURTHER DEFEATS

At the beginning of 1920 Denikin's troops fought in three separate theaters: in Novorossia, at the entrance to the Crimean peninsula, and in the Northern Caucasus. General Shilling commanded White forces in the two theaters in the Ukraine. He had planned to withdraw all his troops to the Crimea; however, British and French representatives convinced Denikin that Odessa must be held at all cost. General Holman argued that the loss of this city would have a profound effect on Western public opinion.[51] He promised aid and help with evacuation should that prove necessary. He also suggested an idea which the British had opposed in the past, that the German colonists in the Novorossia district should be organized. Under this pressure Denikin instructed Shilling on December 31 to try to hold both Odessa and the Crimea. Shilling divided his forces: he sent his best troops under General Slashchev to defend the entrance to the Crimea while he took charge of the troops in

Novorossia. He had under his command the remnants of the troops of the ex-Kiev district and the Galician soldiers. The efforts to mobilize German colonists or officers who had been living in Odessa did not succeed. Shilling's position was further undermined by attacks on his troops by Ukrainian partisan bands. He was forced to withdraw constantly as the Twelfth and Thirteenth Red Armies advanced.

At the end of January the Whites held only Odessa and its environs. The situation became catastrophic: the British did not provide enough ships for evacuation, and Denikin in vain ordered his naval command in Sevastopol to help. The Whites could not use their fleet because they did not have enough coal. Odessa once again had to face a tragic, poorly organized evacuation accompanied by panic. The British ferried some soldiers to the Crimea, and others under General Bredov started a march to Bessarabia. However, the Rumanians did not allow the Russians to enter their country, and therefore the tired soldiers had to fight their way northward to Poland, where they were interned. On February 7 the Bolsheviks entered Odessa.

Slashchev was more successful. He was a young officer, a narcotic addict, insubordinate and unreliable, but a man with considerable military ability. He concentrated his troops beyond the narrow strip of land connecting the peninsula with the mainland. He allowed the Bolsheviks to occupy the isthmus and then counterattacked. The Bolsheviks had no room for manuevering and had to withdraw. It was not, however, this clever strategy alone which saved the Whites. Makhno now turned against the Bolsheviks and consequently the Fourteenth Red Army had to fight the anarchists and the Whites at the same time.

While Slashchev was defending the Crimea successfully, the rear was in complete disorder. It seemed that the White movement might disintegrate on its own. The crucial theater was in the Northern Caucasus. Here Denikin still had forty to fifty thousand men against fifty to sixty thousand Red soldiers. The Whites had usually fought against worse odds and won, but this time their morale was broken.

In the middle of January the front line stretched from the Azov Sea to the steppes of the Sal' River. In the crucial central sector of the front, the Don River separated the enemies. Kutepov's Volunteer Corps protected the left flank, the most numerous and powerful Don army tried to prevent the enemy from crossing the Don at the center, while Pokrovskii's Caucasian army fought in the Kalmyk steppes by the river Sal'.[52] The Red Eighth army under Voroshilov, the Ninth under Stepin, and the Tenth under Kliuev engaged Denikin's forces, and the most valuable Red unit, Budennyi's first cavalry army, was kept in reserve in the area between Rostov and Novocherkassk. A great weakness in Denikin's strategic position was that he had no forces to defend himself against an outflanking movement from the east. Here there was no stable front. The Whites could field only a small force under General Erdeli to oppose the rapidly advancing Eleventh army.

The Bolsheviks experimented with a strategy which had worked before: they directed their main blow at the junction of the Volunteer and Don armies. This time, however, the Whites successfully resisted. The Bolshevik high command added Budennyi's cavalry to Voroshilov's army, yet it could not achieve its objective. The Reds succeeded in crossing the river, but they were beaten back on January 19 and had to retreat to the northern side. Meanwhile the Ninth and Tenth armies advanced successfully. The Caucasian army was so demoralized that it could not hold the front. On January 26 it retreated beyond the Manych River.

In the middle of February the Volunteer Corps and the Don Cossacks not only held the enemy, but on occasion even went on the offensive. Units of the Don army crossed the river and cut communications between Rostov and Novocherkassk. On February 20 Kutepov achieved a great victory against the Eighth army and succeeded in capturing Rostov. These victories made a great impact on public opinion, and people in Ekaterinodar and Novorossisk attributed greater significance to them than was warranted. In fact, these were Denikin's last victories.

The successes on the western end of the front were more than cancelled out by the great defeats in the east. The Bolsheviks, after their failure in the central sector of the front, decided to concentrate against the weakest troops of the enemy. Denikin received intelligence reports that Budennyi's cavalry was marching east. At the same time the Tenth army broke through the front and threatened communications between Tikhoretskaia and Torgovaia. On February 12 Denikin learned that Budennyi in a great outflanking movement from the east was moving against Tikhoretskaia, the site of his headquarters. In order to meet the threat, Sidorin, sent his best cavalry ten to twelve thousand strong, under General Pavlov to bolster the front held by the Kuban Cossacks. This forced march had tragic results for the Whites. The cavalry had to cross uninhabited steppes which provided no shelter. The weather suddenly and unexpectedly turned very cold and the tired and weakened soliders froze. Many had to be left behind to die. By the time Pavlov reached his goal his soliders were not in any condition to fight. The Whites never recovered from this catastrophe.[53]

On February 23 Denikin had to move his *stavka* from Tikhoretskaia to Ekaterinodar. The Volunteer Corps, which still held Rostov, had to evacuate the city and withdraw because it was in danger of being cut off from the rest of the army. In the beginning of March Denikin's only hope was that his armies could hold the enemy at the Kuban river long enough to give him time to organize the evacuation to the Crimea.

THE GREENS

In a period of defeats and disintegration the Whites had to face yet another enemy. In the first months of 1920 all over the Northern Caucasus partisan bands appeared, harassing retreating White troops, capturing supplies and munitions, and in general contesting White control of the countryside. They called themselves Greens because this was the color of agriculturalists and it denoted opposition to both sides in the war. The partisans differed from one another: some were principled opponents of Whites and Reds; others were prisoners of war from the Red Army who had been forced to fight against their comrades, but then managed to escape; still others were peasants and Cossacks who above all wanted to escape the draft, but when compelled to take weapons, preferred to use them against Denikin; and also there were bandits. From the point of view of the White authorities, the ideology of their opponents did not matter much for they all presented the same problem. At a time when the Whites could least afford it, they had to use their troops for pacification.

By far the strongest and best organized insurgent army came into being in the Black Sea province, in the area of Sochi. Only half of the population of this district was Russian; the rest were Armenians, Georgians, Greeks, and Estonians.[54] This relatively well-to-do area had a highly intensive agriculture, but the peasants never grew their own bread. In normal times the district exported its products, above all, tobacco, through the Black Sea and received grain from the Kuban. As a consequence of the interruption of trade relations and the imposition of artificial economic barriers, the population suffered great hardships during the Civil War.

In 1918 Georgia administered this district and it came under Volunteer rule only in the beginning of 1919. The Armenians, who were the traditional enemies of the Georgians, welcomed Denikin's soldiers, but the Russian peasantry watched the change with indifference. Soon the Whites turned the peasants against them: the troops behaved badly; the administration was made up of reactionaries. Here, too, returning landlords punished the peasants who had occupied land in their absence. Even those who had received their land from land committees set up at the time of the Provisional Government, and who therefore believed themselves to be legal owners, found that the White officers and administrators did not discriminate. They too were evicted.

The partisan movement started on a small scale immediately after the beginning of the Volunteer occupation. Those politicians who for ideological or other reasons had cooperated with the Georgians now found it necessary to escape into the mountains. Soon they were joined by peasants who wanted to avoid service in the Volunteer Army. The first attempt to organize a movement took place in August 1919, when partisan representatives held a secret meeting in the village of Vorontsovka. White counterintelligence discovered this meeting and arrested and immediately executed E. B. Spivak, a Socialist Revolutionary peasant leader. The Whites also jailed a number of peasants. Those who managed to escape vowed to continue the struggle and elected an executive committee.[55]

The movement grew quickly during the fall of 1919. In November the executive committee called a meeting in the Georgian coastal town of Gagry. The organizers first wanted to hold this meeting in secret on White territory, but experience convinced them that this would be too dangerous. The Georgians gave hospitality. As socialists they sympathized with the ideology of the incipient peasant movement. They regarded the Socialist Revolutionaries as comrades in arms and considered Denikin the common enemy. The Volunteer Army was now paying for its previous short-sighted policy toward the Menshevik Republic. However, the Tbilisi government feared that any open support of the Green movement might provoke the British, and therefore insisted that the meeting be conducted in secrecy. The prudent Georgians also refused to give arms and military experts to the partisans. Nevertheless, the Greens greatly benefited from Georgian friendship: they had a secure rear and a sanctuary. Without this help the partisans could have never become a major danger to Denikin's rule.

The conference adopted a platform which expressed hostility toward both Reds and Whites. The delegates denounced not only the Communists but also cities in general as exploitative. In their plan for the revolution, the proletariat had no place. Not only the peasants' ideology but also their strategy was utopian. They decided that the immediate task was to defeat the Whites ("Kadets" as they called them). They wanted to conquer the district before the arrival of the Bolsheviks because they believed that the Red Army, made up of peasants, would not fight against them. They imagined that when the Reds learned about the establishment of peasant power, they would return home to establish similar regimes.[56]

The delegates elected a Committee of Liberation, headed by the veteran Socialist Revolutionary V. A. Filipovskii, who had been the leader of the Samara government in 1918. N. Voronovich was elected deputy leader and commander of the army.

Voronovich immediately started to organize a military force. There was no shortage of volunteers, but the peasants did not have enough weapons. The first two thousand men had only three hundred rifles. They also lacked trained officers and communication experts, and therefore Voronovich could never properly coordinate the action of units under his command. Even when the peasants fought with determination and courage, the quality of leadership was so poor that they often suffered defeat at the hands of numerically much smaller enemies.

Voronovich divided the small Sochi district into nine regions from which his representatives reported on the mood of the peasants, on the availability of horses, and on the number of new recruits.[57] This well-functioning grassroots organization was the strength of the partisan movement. The Whites could never organize anything similar.

The peasants flocked into the insurgent army. Denikin had issued an order of general mobilization and the young men had to go into hiding. Since they had to fight, they preferred to use their guns against Denikin rather than for him. The Whites' situation was paradoxical: the worse their armies fared on the major battlefields, the more they needed reinforcements, but the less they were able to enforce a mobilization order. As they became weaker the peasants dared to defy them. Denikin needed new fighting men, but in the process of trying to assemble them, he alienated the population even more. Defeat in a civil war is a self-reinforcing process.

The peasants had to appear at Volunteer recruiting stations no later than January 26; the rising which engulfed the entire Sochi district started on January 28. Voronovich lacked confidence in the ability of his army to win even when he gave the order which started the rising. He feared that because his soldiers did not have enough weapons, small but organized and well-equipped units could disperse them. However, the enthusiasm of his new recruits carried him away. What happened then cannot be described purely in military terms: in a matter of days, Denikin's shaky chain of authority collapsed and the Greens were completely victorious. The demoralized White troops left the district in such a hurry that they did not even carry their weapons with them. Many switched sides and joined the rebels. For the first time, the Green movement acquired a large store of arms. From the point of view of Denikin, this defeat was a disaster of the first magnitude. Not only did he lose a bit of valuable territory and many fighting men, but now the peasants threatened his control of the vitally important port of Novorossisk. Losing this port would have meant that Denikin's army could not escape and would fall to the Reds.

The speed of victory surprised even the Green leaders. The Committee of Liberation had to assume authority in the Black Sea province. Most of the leaders were aliens in the district, without knowledge of local circumstances, and they found it easier to direct an army than to govern. They could not find enough men who could write and carry out official business.[58] The population was deeply divided. The Russians resented the support which the Armenians had given to Denikin and wanted to take revenge. The first task of the government was to establish a truce and prevent bloodshed. By skillful appeals they won over the Armenians and at the same time directed the hostility of the rest of the population against the Whites.

In order to develop their victory further, the Socialist Revolutionaries wanted to gain the good will of the radical Kuban Cossacks. An agreement with the *rada* would have been a diplomatic coup. However, the Kuban Cossacks still fought in Denikin's army, which was the Greens' main enemy. Only a complete break between Denikin and the *rada* would have made peace with the Kuban possible. Although the Socialist Revolutionaries were ultimately disappointed, they were well informed about developments in Ekaterinodar and had justifiable hopes.

The attitude of the British was crucially important for the survival of the peasant regime. Voronovich traveled to Gagry in order to discuss with the Georgian authorities some frontier matters, and there he met General Keyes, the Acting British High Commissioner for South Russia. The British, who wanted to arrest the disintegration of the anti-Bolshevik movement, wished to make every effort to achieve peace between Denikin and the Greens. Keyes persuaded Voronovich to travel with him to Novorossisk in order to talk with the White leaders. This effort proved to be a complete fiasco. General Lukomskii, the commander in Novorossisk, would not even allow Voronovich to disembark.[59] Voronovich had to return without accomplishments to Sochi. Since the Committee of Liberation had not empowered him to enter into negotiations with the enemy, his comrades accused him of treason.

The British made one more attempt to mediate between the Whites and the Greens. General Cotton came to Sochi on February 24 and was allowed to address the congress of peasant delegates.[60] Since the Green Army at the time was on the verge of capturing Tuapse, the peasant leaders saw no need to negotiate and turned down the British offer.

The demise of the Greens was not caused by the strength of their enemies, but by internal disintegration. After the great victories the army came to be dominated by soldiers who had first fought in the Red Army and then were coerced to fight for Denikin, from whom they defected at the first opportunity. Members of the original peasant army disagreed with these newcomers on strategy. The soldiers, supported by the small proletariat of Sochi, looked forward to meeting the approaching Red Army, while the peasants remained hostile. At the district meeting, which opened in Sochi on February 21, a split between the two groups was barely avoided.

When the Greens occupied the important coastal town of Tuapse, the pro-Bolsheviks carried out a coup d'etat. They established a "revolutionary soviet" and renamed their army the "Black Sea Red Army." The leaders established contact with the approaching Bolsheviks. These men were not satisfied with Voronovich's passive strategy. They wanted to participate in the defeat of Denikin and decided to advance into the Kuban. Since the Black Sea Red Army took all the weapons, its departure meant that Voronovich was left once again with an inadequately equipped small peasant band.

Soon after the pro-Bolshevik force entered the Kuban, it encountered the retreating Cossacks of General Shkuro. The Cossacks, even in their demoralized state, easily defeated the enemy. Now not only was Denikin freed from the threat to Novorossisk, but the Greens could not even hold their liberated territory. Voronovich had to evacuate Tuapse. He called on his peasant insurgents, but they were no match for Shkuro's Cossacks. The Committee of Liberation, together with partisan bands which continued to support it, had to leave Sochi and go into hiding in the mountains.

The Green strategy of receiving the Bolsheviks in a liberated district failed. The Black Sea province was the last area which the Bolsheviks conquered in the Northern Caucasus, and when the Red Army arrived it came in pursuit of the Whites. The Bolsheviks captured Sochi at the end of April.[61] Some of Shkuro's Cossacks escaped to Georgia, some proceeded into the Crimea on British boats and joined Wrangel, but many were left behind and captured by the Reds.

The peasants could harm their enemies, but could not establish a government capable of defending their interests. Peasant risings in the Ukraine in the fall of 1919 and in the Black Sea province in the winter of 1920 ultimately helped only the Bolsheviks. The peasants achieved quick victories because the Whites had been unable to establish a functioning administration in the villages, but then they lost power for the same reason: they, too, had no remedy for disorganization. Of course the sources of White and Green administrative failures were different: the Whites failed to penetrate the villages; the Greens did have grassroots support, but they had neither the personnel nor the ideology necessary for administering the territory under their rule.

Although Makhno was an anarchist and the Black Sea peasant leaders were Socialist Revolutionaries, the similarities between the two movements were striking. The rejection of cities and the repudiation of discipline and organization made both movements hopelessly utopian. The most significant difference between them was that the Ukrainian peasants possessed in Makhno a charismatic leader with uncommon military ability.

DENIKIN'S LAST WEEKS IN POWER

In February 1920 chaos engulfed all territories still under Denikin's nominal control. The Crimea suffered from what was called "Orlovshchina." A Captain Orlov, a hitherto obscure officer, was sent by General Slashchev from the front to Simferopol in order to organize new units.[62] Instead of fulfilling his mission, Orlov embarked on a mutiny. He completely lacked conspiratorial finesse and acted quite openly and carelessly, but he could organize with impunity because White authority was inept and weak.

Orlov had no coherent political program. When he negotiated with the representatives of the Communist underground and was asked about his political philosophy, he could not be more precise than to say that he "stood a bit to the right of the Left SR's and a bit to the left of the Right SR's."[63] At the same time he considered subordinating himself to General Wrangel, a man identified with the right wing of the anti-Bolshevik movement. Orlov above all appealed to the junior officers, who had carried a large share of the burden of fighting. The success of the mutiny can be explained by the frustration of many young men, who had sacrificed themselves and now saw only confusion, bungling, and disorder. Their past sacrifices seemed in vain. Orlov's message, that first of all it was necessary to clean up the mess in the rear, found willing listeners. Of course he had no recipe for creating order; instead of arresting disorganization, his abortive movement greatly contributed to it.

Orlov wanted to have at least a thousand followers before he proclaimed his rising. Once he had his army, he planned to break through the Bolshevik front and join Makhno in the Ukraine. This was a totally unrealistic strategy, for Makhno would have never cooperated with a man such as Orlov. In any case, the strategy was never tried. On February 2 Slashchev ordered Orlov to proceed to the front immediately, and Orlov was forced to act prematurely. He had only two hundred men. However, Volunteer authority was so weak in Simferopol that such a force was sufficient for taking power. On February 4 the rebels occupied government offices, arrested Count Tatishchev, the Governor of Tavrida province, General Subbotin, the Commander of the Sevastopol fortress, and General Cherniavin, Shilling's chief of staff. Orlov issued a proclamation in which he professed to act in the name of the Volunteer Army and in the name of Slashchev. He negotiated with the city duma and addressed a meeting of workers and peasants. He asked his listeners to join his army and help him to create order.[64]

His rule in Simferopol lasted only two days. Slashchev sent against him reliable units from the front, and Orlov, who wanted to avoid fighting, freed his prisoners, and with about seventy to ninety men and ten million rubles from the city treasury he retreated into the neighboring hills.[65] On February 19, in a surprise move, he captured Yalta. He issued a new proclamation in which he denounced General Shilling as responsible for the ill-fated evacuation of Odessa, but he spoke with great admiration about General Wrangel. Evidently Wrangel was embarrassed by such support and advised him to submit to his superiors. Wrangel, who had only contempt for the plebeian ways of the young captain, did not see that both of them had been working for the same end: undermining Denikin's authority.

Slashchev sent troops against the rebels a second time and Orlov decided to capitulate. Slashchev was inexplicably careless; instead of disbanding the unit, he sent it to the front.[66] On March 20 Orlov's detachment mutinied once more. Orlov retreated with his men to Simferopol, and Slashchev again had to send troops against him. This time bloodletting could not be avoided. Orlov managed to escape into the hills with a few of his followers, but the movement was destroyed forever.

A more sustained and serious challenge to Denikin's authority came from General Wrangel. Wrangel was a difficult and demanding subordinate from the moment he joined the army, but during the first few months of his service he did not seek to undermine Denikin's authority and supplant him. He was simply an extraordinarily vain man, who could not see another man's point of view, and was convinced that his strategy was in every respect superior to Denikin's.

As the army suffered defeat after defeat, the quarrel between the two generals became increasingly bitter. Wrangel sought to escape responsibility for failures by blaming others. He denounced the *stavka's* decisions in letters to Denikin, and then widely publicized his complaints. Denikin greatly erred in not removing his subordinate. He admired the dashing aristocrat, obviously an able officer, and feared the charge that he was not using Wrangel's talent because of personal considerations. A better politician would have realized that as head of the movement, he could not afford to be modest and had to resist those who wanted to take away his authority.

Wrangel was a dangerous opponent: he believed in himself and he had a charismatic personality. He delighted in theatrical gestures. Since he consistently opposed the main elements of Denikin's policies and strategies, and made his opposition widely known, now that the movement was in trouble he became the obvious candidate to succeed. Many conservative politicians, who considered

Denikin too liberal and disliked his concessions to the Cossacks, saw their savior in Wrangel.[67] Wrangel was not a reluctant candidate. From the time he gave up the command of the Volunteer Army, he made conspiratorial moves. On December 24 he met General Sidorin, the Commander of the Don Army, and openly broached the subject of Denikin's removal. Sidorin, who understood that Wrangel wanted the job for himself, rejected these overtures. He told Wrangel that in a revolutionary period the people would not follow an aristocrat.[68] A few days later Wrangel tried again to consult with Sidorin and General Pokrovskii, the Commander of the Caucasian army. Although Denikin did not know the nature of the discussions, he was incensed when he learned that commanders of his armies wanted to carry out consultations without representatives of the headquarters. He forbade the meeting as contrary to military practice.

Wrangel's next assignment was to build a cavalry force in the Kuban. In this he failed; no one could make the Cossacks fight. The political situation here had changed greatly since November 1919. Now the radical Cossacks, who had regained their positions of power, blamed Wrangel for the suppression of the *rada*. Wrangel gave up trying to organize the Cossacks in disgust. Since Denikin gave him no new task, he settled down in Novorossisk and devoted all his energies to intrigues. Novorossisk was the headquarter of the pro-Wrangel forces. Here gathered all the conservative politicians who had lost their positions because of Denikin's compromise with the Cossacks. The military governor of the town, General Lukomskii, was a conservative man who sympathized with Wrangel's efforts.

At the end of January, on Lukomskii's suggestion, Denikin named Wrangel chief of staff to General Shilling, who at this time still held Odessa.[69] Although Wrangel recognized the situation as hopeless, he did not refuse. By the time he was ready to take up his post it was too late; the Whites meanwhile had to evacuate Odessa.[70] On February 9 Wrangel and his close friend General Shatilov left Novorossisk for Yalta.[71] This was a moment of great confusion in the Crimea. Orlov was operating in the hills. The authority of the Commander of the White forces in the Crimea, General Shilling, was greatly undermined as a result of the disastrous evacuation from the Odessa. He was opposed with special bitterness by naval circles with which he had a series of disagreements concerning the organization of the evacuation of the city. Worst of all, Shilling lost self-confidence. When he was approached by Admiral Neniukov, the Commander of the Fleet, and Admiral Bubnov, his deputy, who asked him to hand over his powers to General Wrangel, Shilling was willing to agree. Before this change in command could take place, it was necessary to secure Denikin's agreement.

General Lukomskii had arrived in the Crimea a few days before in order to attend the funeral of his mother. Seeing the disorganization and confusion, he came to believe that only Wrangel could save the situation. He wrote Denikin warning of dire consequences if the appointment was not soon made.[72] This time, however, Denikin remained firm. Under no circumstances would he again cooperate with Wrangel or ask his services. In his order, dated February 21, Denikin removed from service Admirals Neniukov and Bubnov and "accepted the requests of Generals Lukomskii, Wrangel, and Shatilov to retire."[73]

Denikin should have removed Shilling. A man who had lost the respect of his subordinates and also his self-confidence was not in any position to create order in a difficult situation. Denikin believed that Shilling could not be blamed for the Odessa misfortune and he did not want to give satisfaction to his enemies. Also, he thought that he soon would move his entire army into the Crimea, and then he himself would assume command.[74]

General Holman, realizing the harm which an open split between the leaders would cause to the White movement, wanted to arrange an interview between Wrangel and Denikin.[75] Wrangel, however, refused to go to see Denikin. He would only agree to send Shatilov. Under the circumstances Holman suggested to his friend Denikin that the best thing would be to ask Wrangel to leave the Crimea. With Denikin's concurrence, Holman composed a tactful letter in which he appealed to Wrangel's patriotism in asking him to leave the country.[76]

Wrangel decided to obey, but before leaving for Constantinople he wrote a brutally insulting letter to Denikin. He wrote about himself as a man "who invariably led his troops to victory" and "saved the general situation." He accused Denikin of not giving him important posts, in spite of the fact that army and society saw in him the only person able to save the situation, because of jealousy. He again criticized Denikin's compromise with the Cossacks. He attributed self-serving motives to his commander's decisions. He repeated his baseless accusation that Denikin did not choose Tsaritsyn as his primary objective in the summer of 1919 because he wanted Kolchak to fail. "The troops of Admiral Kolchak, treacherously abandoned by us to their fate, were defeated." Wrangel's final and most gratuitous insult was: "the poison of ambition entered your soul, and drunk with power, surrounded by dishonest flatterers, you thought more of safeguarding your power and authority than saving your country."[77]

Wrangel sent copies of this letter to Holman, Neniukov, Bubnov, and Lukomskii, and it quickly appeared not only in Russian papers, but also in the foreign press, undoubtedly causing great harm to the cause Wrangel had served. Even Wrangel was soon sorry for his outburst.[78]

Denikin was deeply hurt. Perhaps these accusations achieved their purpose and helped Denikin to make up his mind to retire. In these days of defeat, when control was rapidly slipping from his hands, Denikin showed himself for the decent man he was. He answered Wrangel briefly and calmly. He rejected Wrangel's accusations as lies and asked God to forgive Wrangel for the harm he had done to the Russian cause.[79]

Denikin had one more task to carry out before he could think of abandoning his post. By the middle of March it was obvious that the front in the Northern Caucasus could not be long held. Denikin planned to evacuate to the Crimea at the moment when he could no longer prevent the Reds from crossing the Kuban river. He hoped to move his artillery and cavalry through the Taman peninsula, a narrow strip of land only a few miles away from Kerch, in the Crimea, but because of the unwillingness of the Cossacks to fight and because of the insubordination of officers who did not carry out orders, the Bolsheviks easily crossed the Kuban and succeeded in cutting off retreat through the Taman.[80] This development had momentous consequences, for it was impossible to evacuate all the civilian refugees and the war materiel through the only remaining port, Novorossisk.

The bulk of the Kuban army at this time fought the Greens and was cut off from the main forces. Only a few thousand Kuban Cossacks under Ulagai managed to retreat to Novorossisk. Until the very last days, Denikin did not know whether the Don Army would follow him to the Crimea.[81] In view of the fact that he did not have enough ships available, it is not certain that he was glad when he learned of Sidorin's decision to go along. Tens of thousands of refugees waited in Novorossisk for evacuation. This was a mixed group: entire Cossack villages decided to escape Bolshevik retribution; anti-Bolshevik Russians, landlords, politicians, and simple people who had served the White movement often only in humble positions, all clamored for passage.

Denikin's task of organizing an orderly evacuation was made especially difficult by the bitter hostility which flared up between Cossacks and non-Cossacks. Since among the Don soldiers discipline had broken down to such an extent that they did not carry out the orders of their officers, the Volunteer Corps remained the only unit still capable of performing military tasks.[82] Sidorin, who was Kutepov's superior, wanted to use the Volunteers to cover the retreat of the Cossacks. The Russians greatly resented this, and in any case they did not want to allow the Cossacks to get to Novorossisk first. At Kutepov's request, Denikin removed the Volunteers from Sidorin's command and subordinated the troops directly to himself.

The Volunteers and the Cossacks struggled to get on the few boats in Novorossisk harbor. Denikin did not have nearly enough ships. On March 24 General Milne, the Commander of British forces in the east, and Admiral Seymour came to Novorossisk to consult with him. Denikin asked for help and the British officers promised that they would do everything within their power. They could take five to six thousand men on their ships.[83] They would send more boats, if the Whites could hold back the enemy for awhile. Denikin had dispatched several telegrams to his naval command in Sevastopol ordering them to send all available vessels, but at this crucial time the White fleet proved nearly useless.[84] Most of the ships were in foreign ports, especially in Constantinople, where they had carried the sick, the wounded, and the families of officers and soldiers. Allied quarantine regulations held up the boats for long periods. Many of the White ships were not seaworthy, and since there were not enough mechanics they could not be repaired. In any case, the Whites could not even use their available ships, because they did not have enough coal.

Nevertheless, if the Whites could have held back the enemy for four or five days it would have been possible to evacuate nearly everyone. Ships were arriving in Novorossisk, and Denikin remained hopeful until the last day. Since the port was protected by hills, the defenders had a natural advantage. But now even the Volunteers were too demoralized to fight. The soldiers did not want to go to battle because they feared that they would be sacrificed and left behind. Everyone wanted to get on a boat and escape as soon as possible. The last two days, March 25 and 26, were a time of nightmarish confusion. Sidorin and Kel'chevskii visited Denikin repeatedly at his headquarters, a railroad carriage at the harbor, and demanded ships for their soldiers. Denikin promised ships if the Cossacks slowed down the advance of the army. Sidorin, in the presence of General Holman, burst out: "You have ships for the Volunteer Corps. This is treachery and meanness! You have always misled me and betrayed the Don Cossacks."[85] Denikin must have been deeply humiliated.

In fact, Denikin did discriminate in favor of his Volunteers. The soldiers guarded their ships and embarked with weapons in hand. They were ready to shoot at the Cossacks. The Cossacks did receive some ships, and so many men boarded them that they almost capsized. There could be no question of taking horses or artillery; those had to be abandoned.[86]

Kutepov reported to Denikin on March 26 that he could not defend the city any longer and everyone who could leave should do so immediately. Denikin and his staff were among the last to embark. The Bolsheviks entered the city in the evening. The ships, as they were still being boarded, fired ineffectually on the enemy. The Reds captured twenty-two thousand soldiers, large quantities of horses, and munitions.[87]

Denikin's decision to resign matured gradually. Ultimately he acted not only because staying in office brought great pain and frustration, but also because he saw with increasing clarity that the defeats undermined his authority and that holding on to power only harmed the cause he hoped to serve. In a letter to his wife, written while still in Novorossisk, he intimated that he would not long stay on his post and that he looked forward to resignation as deliverance.[88]

The mismanaged evacuation was a further blow to his prestige. The leader of the Don army accused him of treason with impunity, and General Kutepov, the trusted commander of his beloved Volunteers, sent him unsought advice, recommending that the *stavka* should not be evacuated before the troops. Denikin recalled in his memoirs that Kutepov's letter hurt him more than all the other insults he had to suffer. If even Kutepov lacked faith in him, he did not want to remain Commander-in-Chief.[89]

On arriving in the Crimea, Denikin set up his headquarters at Feodosiia. He consulted with his senior commanders about the military situation. The Don Cossacks managed to bring 10,000 men to the Crimea. Kutepov had 25,000 men under him. Slashchev continued to fight at Perekop with 5000.[90] The Whites had 100 cannons and 500 machine guns. While the Volunteers were relatively well equipped, the Don Cossacks had to leave almost everything behind. Fortunately for the Whites, the Bolsheviks made no attempt to pursue them. Had the Red commanders decided to cross the Kerch straits, the demoralized and disorganized Whites could not have resisted. The Bolsheviks missed a good opportunity to end the Civil War.

The Whites used the valuable time to rest and reorganize. On March 29 Denikin dismissed the South Russian Government. This organ had been formed as a concession to the Cossacks, and in the drastically changed circumstances there was no need for it. The government had been so bitterly unpopular among the officers that Denikin feared for the safety of its ministers. Nevertheless the members of the dismissed cabinet were indignant at what they saw as a high-handed action. Chaikovskii, who had come back to Russia only a short time before, asked Denikin why he had decided to carry out what amounted to a coup d'etat. Denikin was too tired to argue. He simply told the ministers that they did not understand what was happening around them.[91] Denikin entrusted Bernatskii with forming a small civilian council to help him resolve immediate issues.

On the same day Denikin greatly reduced the size of his *stavka*, dismissing 60 percent of the staff.[92] The Commander-in-Chief removed Romanovskii from his post as chief of staff. Denikin had resisted the insistent demands for Romanovskii's dismissal for months, because he felt he needed the help of the one person whom he completely trusted and who shared his political and military views. But the hostility toward Romanovskii was so great that while in Novocherkassk his safety was in danger.[93] In the confused days of the evacuation it was impossible to give the job to someone else. Now, at the first opportunity, Denikin named General P. S. Makhrov, the ex-Quartermaster General, as his new chief of staff. This appointment indicates that Denikin must have decided by this time that he himself would not long stay in his post, for while he knew Makhrov as a competent and liberal officer, he had not been particularly close to him.

Four days later, on April 2, Denikin made his decision. He handed Makhrov an order calling the Military Council together in Sevastopol for the next day for the purpose of electing a new Commander-in-Chief. Makhrov tried to dissuade him, but in vain. Denikin admitted: "I am broken spiritually and I am physically ill. The army lost faith in its leader and I lost faith in the army."[94]

The meeting of the senior commanders opened under General Dragomirov's chairmanship. The tone of the discussions reflected the confusion and demoralization within the movement. General Sidorin protested the inadequate representation of the Don Cossacks. Slashchev expressed his disapproval of the entire procedure. He, who had planned to remove Denikin by force only a few days before,[95] now said: "We are not Bolsheviks. We do not elect. Let Denikin name his successor."[96] Following this statement, he walked out of the meeting and returned to his troops. Many other officers disliked the principle of election and worried about establishing a precedent. The representatives of the Volunteer Corps wanted Denikin to reconsider his decision. As a result of the disagreements, Dragomirov reached Denikin by telegraph and asked him not to resign. Denikin, however, remained firm. Next day the Council reconvened, and at the suggestion of the representatives of the

Fleet it chose General Wrangel to be recommended to Denikin as Commander-in-Chief.

Denikin must have known that the Council would elect Wrangel. Indeed, there were no other serious candidates. He could have prevented Wrangel from getting the post only by appointing someone else, for example General Kutepov. Although Denikin never revealed his thoughts on the matter, it seems he believed that Wrangel would be more capable of preserving the army than anyone else. At the same time he could not bring himself to appoint his adversary. He wanted the senior commanders to share the responsibility. He immediately accepted the recommendations and named Wrangel his successor. On the same day in great haste, together with Generals Holman and Romanovskii, he left for Constantinople on a British ship.

A. I. DENIKIN

Denikin's departure ended the decisive stage of the Civil War in South Russia. From April 1918 to April 1920 his biography and the history of the White movement were inseparable; he single-mindedly devoted all his time and energy to his enormous task, and his personality made a profound mark on the movement he led. How are we to evaluate his performance?

He was a man of many appealing qualities. He was kind and considerate to his subordinates, and in a corrupt era possessed a degree of personal integrity which raised the prestige of his cause. No one could ever accuse Denikin of seeking his private interest and living well while his country suffered. He received such a small salary that he had to wear boots with holes in them. He insisted that his salary should not be raised at a time of great inflation.[97]

He regarded his task, above all, as a military one. Indeed, the immediate cause of the collapse of the White movement was the defeat of the anti-Bolshevik forces on the battlefield. The Volunteer Army under Denikin's leadership performed some amazing feats: the retreat from Ekaterinodar, in the spring of 1918, the Second Kuban campaign, the fighting in the Northern Caucasus during the fall of 1918 and the winter of 1919—all can be regarded as major accomplishments. During 1919, when the armies were

much larger and the front line longer, he frequently appeared on a
section of the front, took charge, and usually made his subordinates
perform better. Undoubtedly, he was an able tactician.

It is harder to evaluate him as a strategist. His armies were ultimately defeated, and his major decision, the attack on Moscow,
has been criticized ever since. His opponents have argued that to
attack on all fronts was no strategy at all, and that Denikin's decision contradicted the age-old military principle which calls for
concentration of strength. Denikin replied that in the conditions of
Civil War, other principles must apply; maintaining momentum,
faith in victory, and hope of gaining followers in the newly conquered territories dictated his decision. He may have been correct.
The strategic plans of his opponents were never tried, and therefore
had no chance of failing.

He failed as a politician. His failure, however, must be put in perspective. He succeeded in establishing a more orderly administration than any other White leader—with the exception of Wrangel,
who learned from Denikin's mistakes and built on his achievements.
He avoided fanciful schemes of the type which Kornilov, his predecessor, liked very much.

However, his attractive qualities and his sobriety did not make
him into a leader of a divided nation. How could he be an effective
leader when he rejected the very notion of politics? The idea that
he should appeal to his followers, or that he should promise something to the uncommitted, was alien to his whole way of thinking.
He naively and at the same time arrogantly believed that he was
called on to lead, and that the people's duty was to follow. He would
have considered it slightly dishonest to tell his listeners what they
wanted to hear. He did not have the ability to evaluate the strength
of the opposing sides, to decide what was attainable and what was
not, to separate the important from the ephemeral. He could not
bring together the competing anti-Bolshevik forces because he rejected the idea of compromise. To those who criticized his policies,
however mildly, whether from the left or the right, Denikin responded with bitter hostility. He was not a man to appreciate another's point of view. At the same time, we should remember that
Denikin had the misfortune to confront skilled opponents who
possessed precisely those abilities which he lacked.

Denikin was not a charismatic leader. He was an able speaker, but he did not inspire the same degree of enthusiasm and loyalty in people who came into contact with him briefly, as did Wrangel and Kornilov. He was too private a person; historic poses did not come naturally to him.

Many of the qualities which made Denikin a decent human being hindered him from becoming an effective leader. Wrangel (or, for that matter, Trotskii) would appear on the front, shoot some captured enemies, and if need be even shoot some of his own men, and reestablish discipline. Wrangel boasted that on one occasion he lined up 370 Bolshevik officers and NCO's and had them all killed on the spot.[98] One cannot picture Denikin behaving this way. Many cruelties were committed by Denikin's army, for which he was ultimately responsible, but Denikin was not the person to order massacres.

He lacked that will to power which makes some men take an interest in every question of detail. He recognized his ineptitude for politics, and was happiest when he was away from headquarters at the front. His closest aides, Generals Dragomirov and Lukomskii, pursued a policy which differed from his own and Wrangel openly organized the discontented, yet Denikin tolerated them. Only when the movement was in ruin and defeat near did Denikin lash out in anger.

His fate was a tragic one. Circumstances conspired to make him a leader of the anti-Bolshevik movement. It was a role he did not seek. In 1917 he did not participate in the ill-fated Kornilov mutiny, but he expressed his approval of the goals of his Commander-in-Chief. For his outspokenness he was arrested, and at the time of the Bolshevik Revolution he was the second highest-ranking officer in prison. The prisoners used the confusion created by the Bolshevik rising to escape and join General M. V. Alekseev, who was organizing an anti-Bolshevik army in Novocherkassk. Kornilov was the charismatic leader whose name attracted the anti-Bolshevik officers, and Alekseev's political contacts and organization skills made the formation of the small army possible. At first Denikin remained in the background. But when in April 1918 Kornilov was killed by a stray shell, it was Denikin who assumed command of an army, which he himself could never have organized. General Alekseev was in poor health; moreover, because of his cautious attitude toward the mutiny in 1917, he was unacceptable to the followers of Kornilov. Later Denikin could say with justice that he assumed command because there were no other candidates. He was a man with a high sense of duty, and he believed he must carry out his task. An essentially decent man, a capable officer, one of the better products of the Imperial officer corps, he was confronted with tasks which were beyond his abilities and alien to his personality. The Whites lost the Civil War for reasons far more important than Denikin's inadequate leadership, but it is clear that his errors contributed to the defeat.

The spring of 1920 was the worst period of Denikin's life. He was bitterly hurt by mounting criticism of his leadership and by disloyalty, but he suffered his greatest blow after leaving Russia. He traveled together with his only true friend and confidant, General Romanovskii. Because of his liberalism, Romanovskii had inspired great hatred among the officers; they regarded him as the evil genius of the movement. Many blamed him, wrongly, for the policies of his superior, and those who did not dare to attack the Commander-in-Chief attacked instead his chief of staff. Romanovskii was assassinated in the Russian Embassy in Constantinople by a man in the garb of a Russian officer. Denikin broke down under the impact of this tragedy. He understood that the bullet, in a sense, was meant for him. This leader of the anti-Bolshevik movement, a career officer in the Imperial Army, could not go to the funeral of his beloved friend, because, as he confessed, he could not bear to look at the uniforms of Russian officers.[99]

Denikin spent the rest of his days in exile. After a short stay in London he moved to Hungary, because he believed that life would be cheaper there.[100] From 1926 to 1945 he lived in France. He never learned any major European language except Russian, and made a precarious living by writing and lecturing. Not for a moment was he attracted by Hitler. After the Second World War he moved to America. The last defender of the old order in Russia had nine dollars in his pocket when he came to the New World. He died in 1947 in Ann Arbor, Michigan.

CHAPTER 9

Wrangel

General Baron P. N. Wrangel succeeded in reorganizing the White fighting force in the Crimea and thereby postponed final defeat for seven months. This last stage of the Civil War differed from the rest. Wrangel's base was so small that he could never hope to raise an army which would rival the Bolsheviks forces, and therefore his chances for success depended on circumstances outside of his control. Undoubtedly the Red Army would have broken the last resistance of the Whites much sooner had it not been forced to combat the Poles, who coveted Ukrainian and Belorussian territories.

In some ways, Wrangel was a more able leader than his predecessor: he had charisma and he introduced new policies which were a novel mixture of liberalism and conservatism. It would be wrong, however, to attribute the differences between the two regimes entirely to the talents and personalities of the two leaders. They operated in different environments and worked under different constraints. The very lack of chances for success made Wrangel's task easier. Had Denikin died in the spring of 1919, we might remember him now for his inspired leadership at the time of the two Kuban campaigns, and for the strategic and tactical abilities he displayed in the battles for the Northern Caucasus. Only the disappointed hopes of 1919 turned many of his followers against him. Denikin attempted but failed to keep together an enormously diverse coalition; Wrangel ruled a relatively homogeneous Crimea. He had an easier task in persuading his conservative supporters to give concessions, because these men regarded him as one of them, because the chances of victory seemed remote in any case, and because the lessons of the previous year were too obvious to disregard.

THE ARMY

The Bolsheviks did not pursue Denikin's demoralized forces. They made no attempts to cross the Kerch straits and used only small forces against Slashchev, who was guarding the entrance to the peninsula at Perekop. They were well-informed about the extent of disorganization in the camp of their enemies, and hoped the White army would fall apart on its own. Instead of delivering a coup de grâce to the South Russian counterrevolution, Red strategists used the opportunity to move troops to the Ukraine, where a Polish attack seemed imminent. Later, the Bolsheviks had to pay dearly for this mistake.[1]

When Wrangel assumed power he fully realized the weakness of his army and the demoralization of his soldiers, but his most immediate concern was the British threat to end all support. The London government was ready to accept the fait accompli of Bolshevik victory in the Civil War and disengage from Russian affairs. In order to do so, foreign secretary Lord Curzon proposed to his Russian allies that he would intercede with the Bolsheviks in their behalf. He hoped that if the Whites put down their arms, the Bolsheviks would offer amnesty to members of the defeated army and to the entire population of the Crimea. While negotiations progressed he offered the use of the British navy in order to maintain the status quo. The British backed up this suggestion with a threat that if the Whites did not accept these conditions they would disinterest themselves in the fate of the army.

Curzon made these proposals while Denikin was still in office. The British High Commissioner in Constantinople, Admiral de Robeck, however, delivered the note to Wrangel. Apparently it was such a foregone conclusion that Wrangel would inherit Denikin's post that the Admiral had no hesitation in dealing with him even before he was elected.[2]

Wrangel had a more realistic understanding of Bolshevik policies than Curzon. He realized that the Bolsheviks would not accept the proposed terms, and that the British would therefore find it more difficult to extricate themselves than they hoped. Also, he saw that the coming Bolshevik-Polish war would bring important benefits, and that it was therefore essential to gain time. It is unclear how much Wrangel knew about the state of Russian-Polish negotiations and whether he understood how near war was, but he obviously knew that the Reds were not using their best troops in the South, but were trying to protect their Western borders. Even before he assumed office, the new Commander-in-Chief may have realized that the protectors of Poland, the French, might be more suitable allies than the increasingly recalcitrant British.

Wrangel was in a difficult position. On the one hand an admission by the leader of the anti-Bolshevik movement that the fight was lost would further undermine morale and would make the task of reconstruction almost hopeless. On the other hand, a clear defiance of the British warning would risk the loss of aid at a time when the Whites needed it most. Wrangel handled the problem with skill: he ordered his chief of staff General Makhrov to draw up plans for the evacuation of the Crimea, but at the same time strengthened his forces in a clear anticipation of further battles with the enemy.

He revealed this thinking to the War Council which had just elected him: "The English have decided to withdraw from the game. If we reject their mediation, our refusal will give them a pretext for washing their hands of us and withdrawing altogether. I will most certainly never countenance negotiations between ourselves and the Bolsheviks. But I think the most important thing is to avoid giving England an opportunity to leave us in the lurch. We must throw the odium of these negotiations upon England, and prolong them until we have attended to our fortifications, put the army and the rear in order and secured coal and oil for the fleet in case of evacuation."[3] Like a good politician, he tried to keep his options open as long as possible.

Accordingly, on the day of his election, April 4, he sent a telegram to Admiral de Robeck, officially notifying him about the change in command. He disingenuously blamed the English for his inability to continue the struggle, but at the same time asked them to use their good offices for negotiating an amnesty. He wanted two months before the evacuation of those who decided not to accept amnesty and a place of refuge for these men.[4] Although he was trying to keep his options open as long as possible, in perspective we know that his task was hopeless; the Whites had already lost the war. However, it was not entirely unrealistic to want to continue. The Bolsheviks might still suffer a defeat at the hand of foreign enemies; their government might be overthrown by a disillusioned population; circumstances might force Moscow to accept something less than a total victory. It is not surprising that the Whites, whose only alternative was miserable exile, wanted to fight as long as there was a glimmer of hope. Lenin would not have acted differently.

A curious incident during the meeting of the War Council revealed Wrangel's thinking and character. He wanted and received from his colleagues a written understanding that his task was not to lead the army to victory, but merely to negotiate through Allied mediation the best possible terms with the Bolsheviks. He made his assumption of command conditional on such a note. In this critical moment of his country's history, this extremely vain man wanted to escape responsibility and blame for defeat, and rather childishly believed that his place in history books could be protected by a few signatures. He explained to the assembled officers that he needed their signatures not for himself but for his eight-year-old son. He wanted his son when he grew up to be proud of his father.[5] Some of the senior officers regarded Wrangel's request as a sign of lack of confidence in them, and therefore for awhile they demurred, but ultimately they all gave in.

Wrangel's first task was the reorganization of the army. Considering that he bitterly attacked Denikin's personnel policies, he introduced surprisingly few changes in the high command. He even retained for several months General P. S. Makhrov as chief of staff. It was ironic that the General, who received his post in the last days of the Denikin regime because the conservatives had succeeded in getting rid of his predecessor, General Romanovskii, turned out to be an even more liberal man. Wrangel respected Makhrov's abilities, but the political philosophies and backgrounds of the two men were so different that they could never cooperate closely. Makhrov submitted to his new chief a political program which was the most enlightened and radical ever produced by a White military leader

in the course of the Civil War.[6] At the end of June, Wrangel named
Makhrov his representative in Warsaw.

As expected, Wrangel chose his closest friend, General P. Shatilov, to succeed Makhrov as chief of staff. Shatilov, a relatively
young man, had little prestige and he soon came to be greatly disliked by officers. Shatilov did not deserve this dislike any more
than Romanovskii had deserved the hatred of the conservatives.
The two chiefs of staff were the victims of the same psychological mechanism: those who disliked some aspects of the policies of
the commanders-in-chief did not directly blame the leader, but
blamed his closest advisers. Shatilov, a guard officer, a son of a
general, shared a personal style and outlook on life with Wrangel.
Because Wrangel often listened to his friend's advice, Shatilov soon
became the second most powerful man in the army.

General A. P. Kutepov retained the command of the Volunteer
Army, the best fighting unit. Kutepov, a guard officer, had served
in the White army from its earliest days and had managed to keep
the confidence of both Generals Denikin and Wrangel. He was a
good line officer and a very brave man, but completely without
appreciation of political issues and needlessly cruel.[7]

Wrangel also retained General Ia. A. Slashchev as head of the old
Crimean army, now the second most important fighting force. Of
all the strange figures brought to the surface by the trauma of the
Civil War, none was stranger than General Slashchev. He, too, had
served in the guards and during the fighting of the early months of
1920 he proved himself an imaginative and capable leader. Wrangel
bestowed on him the title "Krymskii" (Crimean), for stopping the
Bolsheviks at the entrance of the Crimea. Even at the time of his
important victories, his behavior was often odd. For example he
always had a caged crow carried after him, for he believed that the
animal would bring him luck. He would have people hanged unsere-
moniously just because they aroused his ire. In the spring of 1920
the strain of the war showed on him increasingly: he drank heavily
and became dependent on morphine.[8] He had himself surrounded
with more and more birds, laughed at inappropriate moments,
and unexpectedly burst into tears.[9] His behavior became so erratic
that he obviously endangered the men under his command. Yet
Wrangel, who had criticized Denikin sharply for tolerating Mai-

Maevskii, did not remove Slashchev until it became crystal clear that he was dealing with a sick man.

Wrangel regarded the main task of his reorganization efforts to be reducing the swollen staffs and sending more soldiers to the depleted fighting units. The small proportion of fighting men in the White army was a constant problem, but the situation deteriorated even further in March 1920. Of the 150 thousand people supported by the army, only about one-sixth fought. Although the front-line units lost thousands of soldiers, the size of the staffs remained constant. It was clear that radical measures were needed to redress the balance. Wrangel and Makhrov believed that having fewer people at the headquarters and army staffs would actually improve efficiency.[10] However resolutely the leaders acted in this instance, the remedy turned out to be temporary. Within a short time the staffs and various other institutions and offices situated in the rear started to grow once again. As a contemporary observer remarked, a colonel was far more likely to be found in an office than on the battlefield.[11]

In the middle of April Wrangel had approximately twelve thousand men in the front and ten thousand in reserves. Fortunately for him, the enemy, the Thirteenth Red Army, was no stronger. In fact the Whites, who had 24 tanks and the same number of airplanes, had the military advantage.[12] When the Reds started a small-scale and ill-planned offensive on April 13, the Whites not only held the front but even improved their defensive position by occupying some of the strategically important passes between the mainland and the Crimean peninsula.

Wrangel used the ensuing period of relative quiet to reorganize his troops into four units: (1) Kutepov commanded the First army corps. This force was made up of the remnants of the Volunteer Army and included the famous Kornilov, Drozdovskii, and Markov divisions. The corps also included a small cavalry unit. This was the best corps. (2) The Second army corps was commanded by Slashchev. This unit was the successor to the Crimean army and it included the Thirteenth and Fourteenth divisions and two cavalry brigades of Astrakhan and Terek Cossacks. (3) General Sidorin and later General Abramov headed the three-division strong Don corps. In spite of leaving thousands of Cossacks in Novocherkassk,

this unit remained a substantial force. (4) General Pisarev commanded a mixed corps which was made up largely by Kuban Cossacks. The great bulk of Kuban Cossacks remained in the Northern
Caucasus, and uniting them with the main forces remained one of
Wrangel's main tasks. Pisarev's corps was by far the weakest of the
four.[13]

In the beginning of May the Whites requisitioned horses which
enabled the Don Cossacks to function as a cavalry force once again.
On May 28 Wrangel mobilized two classes of recruits (those born
in 1900 and 1901).[14] He also tried to encourage defection from the
enemy. Denikin had made the mistake of promising punishment to
those officers who had served the Reds. Although few offenders
were in fact punished, White leaflets and newspapers in Denikin's
period restrained rather than encouraged defection from the enemy.
Wrangel reversed his predecessor's policy. He published a series
of edicts and proclamations promising forgiveness. Under the conditions of the Civil War it was easy to change sides and Wrangel
successfully expanded his army at the expense of the enemy.[15]

As a result of mobilization and recruitment, in the beginning of
June Wrangel had forty thousand fighting men. Since the main
armies of the Bolsheviks were tied down by the Poles, the Reds
could not increase their strength in the south and Wrangel soon
achieved a substantial superiority. An important element in White
military strength was the ever-improving navy. In April and May
Wrangel received coal shipments from Constantinople which enabled the ships to function.[16] The Whites created an impressive
Black Sea fleet and an Azov sea flotilla. They had a battleship,
three cruisers, ten minesweepers and eight gunboats on the Black
Sea, and fifteen boats in the Azov sea which were capable of operating in shallow waters.[17]

In morale and fighting ability, Wrangel's army at the end of May
surpassed anything the Whites had possessed since the first months
of the Volunteer Army. For the first time since the spring of 1918,
the Cossacks did not dominate the South Russian anti-Bolshevik
movement. It is true that as a consequence the previous White superiority in cavalry was lost; however, the army now contained a
larger percentage than before of men who were determined to fight
the enemy. Lenin paid this compliment: "In the Crimea Wrangel

gathered more and more strength. His troops consisted almost
entirely of officers in the hope that in the first possible moment the
army would be expanded by entrance of peasants. Wrangel's army
was equipped with tanks, cannons, and airplanes better than all
the other armies which had fought in Russia. While we fought the
Poles, Wrangel gathered his forces."[18]

The decisive change in Wrangel's strategic position resulted not
so much from the improvement of his army as from the outbreak
of the Russo-Polish war. The Bolshevik government, recognizing
its own weakness, wanted to avoid this war. Marshal Pilsudski,
however, the Polish head of state, was determined to regain the territories his country had lost in 1772. He planned to incorporate into
Poland Ukrainian and White Russian provinces and, perhaps most
important, weaken Russia, Communist or anti-Communist. Negotiations between the Russians and the Poles broke down because
Pilsudski absurdly insisted that the talks take place in the small
town of Borisov in the middle of the battle zone. He refused to
accede to the Soviet request for an armistice for the duration of
the negotiations.[19]

Pilsudski prepared for the war by coming to terms with the
Ukrainian leader Petliura. Petliura, who realized that he could
regain his country only through Polish aid, had a weak hand to
play. He renounced Galicia in favor of the Polish state in exchange
for military help. The Polish attack started on April 25 and soon
the invaders achieved major successes. On May 6 Kiev fell.

The involvement of the Red Army in a major new war was, of
course, welcome news at Wrangel's headquarters. It meant that the
Bolsheviks would be tied down and forced to take a defensive posture against the Whites. Soon after the outbreak of the fighting,
Budennyi's famous calvary army moved from the Rostov area into
the Ukraine.

The war also greatly improved Wrangel's diplomatic position.
The French, committed to Polish victory, fully realized that Wrangel's small but good army could make a great contribution to the defeat of the Bolsheviks. The prospect of French aid enabled Wrangel
to be less concerned about British warnings and to shape his military strategy as he saw fit.[20]

Wrangel was ready to take the offensive. To avoid alienating the British more than necessary, he announced that he wanted to conquer only the Northern Tauride, in order to improve the defensive posture of the army, and in order to acquire an agriculturally rich province capable of feeding his increasingly large movement. He argued that his victories would only help British efforts to bring peace because they would persuade Moscow to give concessions. The Whites carried out their offensive with skill. On June 6 General Slashchev achieved complete surprise as he landed his troops at Kirilovka, south of Melitopol, at the rear of the Thirteenth army.[21] When Pisarev attacked at Chongar and Kutepov engaged the main enemy forces at Perekop, the Reds were caught off balance and had to withdraw in order to escape being surrounded.[22] Within a few days the Whites captured Melitopol and soon afterward the entire province. The victory doubled the territory under Wrangel's control. Now he was able to requisition enough horses for his cavalry and enough grain to feed the Crimea, enough even to send a substantial amount abroad. The fine performance of his army raised the prestige of his movement and made it easier to gain financial and diplomatic support in Europe.

In spite of his success, Wrangel decided not to continue the offensive. Although the Thirteenth Red army suffered heavy losses, it was far from eliminated. Wrangel, who had criticized Denikin harshly for over-optimism, did not want to advance further and lengthen the front line. He knew that his army was far too small to carry the war into central Russia. In order to defeat the Bolsheviks he needed a much larger army—which he never succeeded in building.

RIGHTIST HANDS

P. B. Struve, Wrangel's foreign minister, described the task of the anti-Bolsheviks as being "to make leftist policy with rightist hands."[23] The phrase was new, but the idea was not. K. N. Sokolov, Denikin's adviser, suggested something similar in the fall of 1919, but Denikin was not the person to act on this advice. On the one hand, he distrusted those who had been closely identified with the defunct imperial regime; on the other, he could not pursue a policy which was contrary to his own deepest beliefs.

It is debatable whether there was anything leftist about Wrangel's policies, but it is clear that his government was made up of "rightist hands." His victory over Denikin was a victory of the conservative wing within the White movement. In this last period of the Civil War the guard officers and the ex-imperial officials came to the fore. Denikin, the son of a poor man, who made his career in the tsarist army while suffering from the snobbery of the guard officers, resented them. Baron Wrangel, however, was so proud to be a member of the guards that after his graduation from the Academy of the General Staff he turned down a staff appointment which would have meant quick advance, in order to return to his old regiment. Not surprisingly, as Commander-in-Chief he surrounded himself with his old comrades. Generals Shatilov, Kutepov, Slashchev, Dragomirov, and Iuzefovich had all served in the guards.[24] Wrangel promoted those colonels who had supported him.[25] All these younger men had been opponents of Denikin's "liberalism." Denikin had hesitated to give responsible posts to those who had achieved their reputation in serving the tsarist government, but Wrangel had no such scruples. He filled his administration with important functionaries of the old regime.

Wrangel retained the lion's share of the power for himself. The aristocrat and proud guard officer remained faithful to his background and upbringing. He saw nothing whatever good in the March Revolution, and would have liked to reconstruct pre-revolutionary Russia. However, he was an intelligent man and a pragmatist who recognized that for the time being the only task which mattered was the defeat of the Bolshevik enemy. He described his own political philosophy concisely: "even with the devil, but against the Bolsheviks."[26] Only occasionally did he allow himself to be carried away by his own rhetoric, and then we can catch a glimpse of the unreconstructed monarchist. For example, on June 2, before embarking on his offensive, he published the "goals" of the movement. Most of these were neither new nor surprising, and with the exception of one, Denikin could have announced them. It is impossible to render in English the quaint yet powerful phrasing of his short manifesto:

Hear, Russian people for what we are fighting:
For outraged faith and desecrated shrines.
For the liberation of the Russian people from the yoke of communists,
  tramps, and criminals who in the end would ruin Holy Russia.
For the end of civil strife.
For the right of the peasant—after acquiring the land to cultivate
  as his property—to engage in peaceful labor.
For the honest worker to be provided with bread in his old age.
For the rule of genuine freedom and law in Holy Russia.
For circumstances in which the Russian people could choose its
  own MASTER.
Help me, Russian people. Save the Motherland.[27]

"Master" (*khoziain*), a word printed in capitals, could mean only monarchist restoration. At a time when monarchism was highly disreputable, Wrangel's statement was a great political error. Indeed, it created a furor. Wrangel soon saw his mistake and decided to back down, offering an unusually disingenuous and inept explanation: he told journalists that he meant by "Master" the Russian people themselves.[28]

Wrangel by and large restrained himself from making declarations. General Makhrov recommended the publication of the goals of the movement for domestic and foreign audiences, but Wrangel did not accept the suggestion. He said that he wanted people to judge his movement on the basis of policies rather than words, and that issuing a manifesto would be superfluous.[29]

Wrangel's background enabled his opponents to describe him plausibly as an arch-reactionary. Soviet propagandists often referred to him as the Black Baron, and identified him with the old regime. His impeccable conservative credentials brought harm but also some benefits to his movement. The reactionary image of his government made it difficult to generate public enthusiasm, but since his right flank was protected he could initiate some liberal policies. Reactionary officers and conservative landowners, who would have violently objected to a policy introduced by Denikin, accepted the same measure from Wrangel without protest.

Even Wrangel, however, could not take the support of the extreme right for granted. On one occasion the monarchists orga-

nized a conspiracy. On June 14 the counterintelligence service discovered that a group of officers had held conspiratorial meetings
discussing the substitution of Prince Leuchtenbergskii for General
Wrangel. The participants were remarkably irresponsible and unrealistic people without a sense of politics, who had no chance of
success, but Wrangel did not dismiss the incident lightly. He returned from the front and personally interrogated more than twenty
people. He sent some of the participants to the front and excluded
others from service. Although the Prince had participated in the
conspiracy, Wrangel tactfully did not arrest him.[30]

Although Wrangel hesitated to identify himself as a monarchist,
he proudly declared himself a dictator. In an interview given to a
journalist, he once again harshly criticized Denikin for allowing
the Special Council to tie his hands.[31] This was an unfair criticism,
for Denikin's power was limited not by the decisions of the Special
Council but by the lack of a functioning administration. In fact,
Wrangel and Denikin held similar views about the necessity of dictatorship and both assumed that it was a matter of declaration.
On April 11, a few days after his election, Wrangel took the title
"Ruler" and announced that he would concentrate in his hands all
civil and military authority. He subordinated to his command all
Cossack troops, which meant that for the first time in the course
of the Civil War the leader of the Southern anti-Bolshevik movement could command his entire army as he saw fit.[32] He promised full autonomy to Cossack territories, but autonomy remained
purely a theoretical issue as long as there were no Cossack areas
under White rule.

On April 11 Wrangel also announced the formation of his cabinet. He wanted to name A. V. Krivoshein the head of civil administration. Krivoshein, who had been a close associate of Prime Minister Stolypin and minister of agriculture in his government, was
one of the most enlightened and able statesmen of Imperial Russia.
Wrangel got to know him well in the fall and winter of 1919 when
they cooperated in undermining Denikin's authority. After the
evacuation of Novorossisk, Krivoshein went to Constantinople,
where he met Wrangel once again, and from there he proceeded
to Belgrade and later to Paris. On April 7 Wrangel sent Shatilov to
Constantinople to consult with the British representatives and to

find Krivoshein and induce him to return. Krivoshein hesitated. His friends considered Wrangel's cause hopeless and advised him against associating his name with the General's, but ultimately he decided that it was his duty to do everything within his power to defeat the Bolsheviks, and that therefore he must help Wrangel. However, it took almost two months for him to arrive in the Crimea. Meanwhile, he carried out important negotiations with French politicians, among whom he had excellent contacts dating back from his service in the Imperial government. His presence in the Crimea was greatly missed. Wrangel had so much confidence in him that he postponed decisions on many crucial issues until his arrival.[33]

D. D. Perlik temporarily assumed Krivoshein's responsibilities. Perlik had served as governor of the Taurida and of the Crimea during the Denikin regime, and presumably Wrangel chose him for this important position because Perlik knew the special problems of the Crimea. M. V. Bernatskii retained responsibility for finances. Bernatskii had started work for the army almost at the moment of its inception and served under various regimes. He was regarded as an expert rather than as a politician. A crucially important figure in the new cabinet was the foreign minister, P. B. Struve. A socialist as a young man, he had gradually moved to the right and by the time of the Civil War was an ideological comrade of ex-tsarist minister Krivoshein. Struve, however, spent most of his time in Paris and his place was taken by Prince Trubetskoi, who was generally regarded as a competent man. Lieutenant General Viazmitinov, an ex-member of the Special Council, became minister of war and Admiral Gerasimov Commander of the Fleet. Gerasimov, however, was mortally ill and within a few weeks had to resign. Admiral Sablin took his post. Nalbandov, a Crimean politician and an Armenian by nationality, took the portfolio of commerce, and ex-senator Glinka, an associate of Krivoshein became minister of agriculture.[34]

The first meeting of the Cabinet took place on April 22. In the following six and a half months the group met 54 times, approximately twice a week. The responsibilities of this body were similar to those of the Special Council. The heads of departments discussed most of the important questions of the day. Generals Wrangel, Shatilov, and Makhrov frequently participated in the deliberations and the Commander-in-Chief himself often reported

on the military situation.[35] Wrangel, a man far more interested
in the reality of power than Denikin, took an interest in details
which Denikin gladly delegated to others. The cabinet did not
make the crucial decisions. Wrangel consulted on controversial
issues with two or three trusted men and made the decisions himself. As a consequence, aside from Wrangel, the only two genuinely
powerful men in the Crimea in 1920 were Shatilov and Krivoshein.

Wrangel, like his predecessor, found it much more difficult to
organize a functioning local administration than to set up a central
government. Local government, as before, was a mixture of appointed agents and of organs of self-government.

Wrangel and his conservative advisers handled self-government
with even greater suspicion than Denikin had. Shortly after Wrangel's assumption of power, V. Obolenskii, a Kadet *zemstvo* leader,
consulted with the Commander-in-Chief and suggested calling a
congress of representatives of *zemstvo* and city organizations. He
argued that such a forum would enable the local population, and
especially the intelligentsia, to express support for Wrangel. Since
the *zemstvo* movement was especially strong in the Crimea, such
a congress promised to be successful. Although Wrangel respected
and trusted Obolenskii, he was evasive. He evidently feared that
the *zemstva* might become a hotbed of anti-government and socialist agitation.[36] Since the cabinet refused to appropriate money, the
organs of self-government in the first few months of the regime
could hardly function.[37]

The reorganization of the *zemstva* began only after Krivoshein's
arrival. He drew up a new electoral law which limited the right to
vote to those who owned property.[38] This was a new departure:
Denikin's election laws for *zemstva* and city councils included no
such restrictions. Krivoshein wanted to exclude the poor peasants
and the village intelligentsia from the organs of self-government.
In spite of this restricted suffrage he continued to regard the *zemstva*
with some suspicion: in order not to give a forum to potentially
hostile elements, he forbade the creation of a provincial assembly.[39]

Obolenskii and his liberal colleagues, who had been active in
the *zemstva*, were horrified by the Krivoshein project. Traditionally, the village intelligentsia—teachers, doctors, and notaries—
played leading roles in local government, but now these people were

excluded. When Obolenskii failed to persuade the Premier to give the vote to every citizen, he, as a compromise, urged extension of the vote to those who had received secondary education.[40] Krivoshein remained unyielding. As an able student of Stolypin he believed that a stable conservative regime could be based only on the support of the relatively well-to-do. The conservative bureaucrats and army officers distrusted the intelligentsia.

Wrangel published the law concerning *zemsto* elections on July 28. During the following months in many localities the new organs of self-government came into being. The population remained apathetic. Many of the most able men did not want to compromise themselves by cooperating with a government whose survival seemed doubtful. The *zemstva* never acquired much authority during this last phase of the Civil War.

It was not the locally elected representatives who held the real power, but the military commander. Perhaps it could not have been otherwise at a time of a bitter civil conflict, when the front line was never very far. The corps commanders acted as military governors. They were assisted by civilian councils in which the departments of finance, justice, and agriculture had representatives. The elected heads of the *zemstva* were subordinate to the military governors. This arrangement further undermined the independence of self-government because the generals would always put pressure on *zemstva* leaders. The local police and gendarmarie came under the exclusive authority of the military governor.[41]

Most of the peasants did not care about self-government. They were much more interested in protection from marauding soldiers and in relief from the burden of requisitioning. On May 23 Wrangel issued regulations on requisitioning. These regulations only allowed taking food and supplies from the peasants in the case of demonstrable need and with the permission of the department of supplies. When a military unit could not buy necessary supplies, its commander had to turn to the village elder, who was obliged to take what was necessary from the population. The army had to pay for everything at pre-established prices. In the absence of such prices a commission had to be formed, made up of the representatives of the army, the department of supplies and of the local population.[42]

WRANGEL

The revitalized military-judicial department performed an essential service in protecting the population. In Denikin's army only military commanders had the right to initiate judicial proceedings against their subordinates. This system often did not work, either because the commanders themselves had participated in looting or because they chose not to notice the wrongdoings of their soldiers.[43] Denikin had set up field courts martial to deal with crimes of soldiers against the population. These institutions could decide cases speedily, but their capricious functioning and the participation in them of men without judicial education reduced respect for the law.

On April 19, only two weeks after assuming command, Wrangel empowered the military-judicial department to initiate legal proceedings. On April 27 he set up military judicial commissions in the four army corps and in fortresses. Later several dozen commissions were created, each division receiving one. The commissions came not under the authority of the local commander, but under the Chief Prosecutor. The competence of these commissions covered all illegal acts committed by soldiers against the population.[44] If a sentence was not confirmed by the local commander, the case was not dropped but transferred to an appeal court.[45]

Wrangel further improved this system by his order of June 20, which called for the inclusion on the commission of two representatives of the local *zemstvo*. These representatives gave their views on the guilt or innocence of the accused, but had no vote.[46] Since local government barely functioned, these commissions were often the only governmental institutions in the villages. Under the circumstances they increasingly took upon themselves tasks which were not directly connected with the administration of justice. For example, they mediated between the army and the population on issues such as requisitioning. Often their work had to take place under difficult circumstances. There were instances when battles were raging so near that business had to be postponed while soldiers and officers went to fight.[47]

Perhaps even more important than his efforts to produce a functioning military-judicial department was Wrangel's willingness to mete out punishment. He believed that the reputation of the White army as a bunch of marauders was one of the most important causes of past failures. He ordered his commanders to shoot looters on

sight, and he was willing to dismiss and punish some popular officers who had tolerated looting. His vigorous struggle against marauders was one of his most important accomplishments, one
which made the difficult life of the peasants somewhat easier to bear.
Wrangel reduced lawlessness, but he could not eliminate it.[48]
Peasant delegates continued to come to his office and complain
about unlawful requisitions and every other form of injustice suffered by them. Even in 1920 the peasants had good reason for calling the army not Dobrarmiia (Volunteer Army) but Grabarmiia
(Looting Army).[49]

Wrangel, who was determined to stamp out looting among his
soldiers, did not disapprove of all acts of terror. He continued to
support General Kutepov, who was becoming increasingly notorious. Kutepov, an able officer and a favorite of both General
Denikin and Wrangel, was brutal and had only the most primitive
understanding of politics. In 1918, as military governor of Novorossisk, he established a bloody and reactionary regime which
greatly alienated the population. In 1920, as Commander of the
First Corps, he became military governor of Sevastopol. In this
capacity he surpassed everyone in his cruelty and frequency of executions. Complaints poured in to the office of the Chief of Staff
and to Wrangel himself.[50] The town council sent a delegation to
Wrangel in April complaining that the parents would not send their
children to school because the children were terrified by seeing so
many people hanged on the streets. The mayor of Simferopol,
Usov, protested against Kutepov's high-handed behavior. But
Wrangel, instead of restraining the General, ordered Usov to come
to see him. In his memoirs he recalled his reprimand.

> I know all about your disagreement with General Kutepov, who is
> merely carrying out my orders. I am not going to discuss with you
> who is right, or which of us two has given orders. I am responsible to
> the Army and to the people, and I follow the dictates of my con-
> science. I am quite sure that were you in my place you would act
> differently; but as it happens destiny has given me and not you the
> direction of the Russian Cause, and I will do my duty as I see it.
> Furthermore I will stop at nothing in the accomplishment of my
> duty, and will not hesitate to cut down anyone who tries to stop me.
> You protest because General Kutepov has hanged a score or so of

men who were a danger to the Army and to the Cause. I warn you
that should the necessity arise I would not hesitate to increase the
number by one, and that one would be yourself.[51]

It is not surprising that Usov resigned. General Wrangel recalled
the incident years later and quoted his speech because he was proud
of himself. He had no reason to be. He was wrong in this particular
instance, and he was wrong in believing that terror was efficacious.
Several independent witnesses agree that Kutepov executed perfectly innocent people. The inhabitants of Simferopol were particularly aroused by the hanging of a young and popular Tatar poet
accused of nothing but vague Bolshevik sympathies. Leading citizens of the town tried to save him in vain.[52] Kutepov and Wrangel
in particular, but other White generals also (and, one must add,
many Bolshevik leaders) acquired a predeliction for summary
execution. The cruelties of the Civil War taught these men the
wrong lesson: they came to believe in violence for the sake
of violence. They always wanted to show their firmness and determination and frighten the enemy. It is very likely that terror was
usually counterproductive: it frightened the peaceful citizens and
only made the enemy more determined.

Slashchev's case was somewhat analogous to Kutepov's. He, too,
executed people without trial, very often without a serious cause.
But Slashchev, unlike Kutepov, also looted the population. His
friend and chief of counterintelligence, Sharov, was a common
bandit and murderer. Again, the population complained in vain.
However, Sharov overplayed his hand. On one occasion he hanged
not a defenseless peasant but a colonel of the army, a certain Pro-
topopov. The military judicial department initiated an investigation which revealed that Sharov had committed dozens of similar
murders.[53] The court martial sentenced him to death. In wake of
the scandal Wrangel finally removed Sharov's protector Slashchev,
who was by this time clearly out of his mind.

To Wrangel, the need to fight subversives and the partisan movement justified terror. He appointed Major General E. K. Klimovich
head of counterintelligence, and of all his appointments this one
provoked liberal public opinion the most. Klimovich, an ex-general
of the gendarmarie, made his reputation in 1907, when he sup-

pressed the disorders in Vilna with great brutality. Subsequently he became a department head in the ministry of the interior. In 1917 he was jailed by the Provisional Government, an incident which fueled his obsessive hatred of socialists and liberals.[54] He refused to make distinctions among socialists, and considered Socialist Revolutionaries, Mensheviks, and Bolsheviks alike his enemies.[55]

He was a capable man, experienced in his business. He knew the methods of revolutionary underground activities and successfully ferreted out secret cells. He always preferred to err on the side of caution and arrested everyone who was even slightly suspicious. He encouraged denunciations, which inevitably led to the settling of personal scores and acts of revenge. He executed suspected Bolsheviks on capture. The jails were filled with innocent people. He had some socialist honorary justices of the peace removed and arrested, even some who had refused to serve the Bolsheviks.[56]

Perhaps as a result of Klimovich's work, the Bolshevik underground, never very strong in the Crimea, accomplished very little in 1920. Counterintelligence was much less successful against the Green partisan movement. The peasants, who knew the terrain well, established themselves in the hills and tied down a relatively large number of soldiers. Klimovich successfully dug out the links between the Reds and the Greens, but he did not succeed in eliminating the partisans.[57]

Whatever mistakes Wrangel may have committed in building his administration, he was a master in dealing with public opinion. He had a flair for the theatrical. He cut an imposing figure: he was extremely tall and slender and exuded self-confidence. Even on occasions when the news from the front was bad, his words could calm an audience and avert panic.[58] He expressed himself simply and he was talented in coining phrases ready-made for the use of agitators. For example, General Makhrov in his memorandum suggested dropping the name Volunteer Army, since it neither had a good reputation nor corresponded to reality. He proposed the cumbersome title, Crimean-Russian Army.[59] Wrangel improved on the idea and on May 11 published an edict changing the name of his force to "Russian Army."[60] This was a clever choice, for the new title implied that the enemy was somehow less Russian.

Wrangel did not revive the thoroughly discredited propaganda agency, the Osvag. Instead, he made the political department of the General Staff responsible for propaganda matters. Makhrov's Quartermaster General, Colonel Dorman, was a liberal who selected enlightened censors and maintained good relations with most newspaper editors.[61] However, Dorman's liberalism soon aroused General Klimovich's suspicions, and Dorman not only lost his job but also was forced to leave Russia.[62] When Krivoshein arrived in the Crimea he insisted that press matters be transferred from the General Staff to the Ministry of the Interior.

In June 1920 a monarchist journalist, G. V. Nemirovich-Danchenko, took charge of the press department. Even within the Ministry of Interior, Nemirovich-Danchenko found that most of his subordinates were young General Staff officers. At a time when the army needed all the available fighting men, officers held jobs which civilians could have filled better. The young men, who obviously did not want to risk their lives at the front, at the same time intensely resented working for a civilian and made their new superior's life extremely difficult.[63] On September 30 Nemirovich Danchenko resigned and Professor G. G. Vernadskii was appointed in his place, with a tenure in office too short to accomplish much.[64] Later in America he acquired a great reputation as a leading historian of Russia.

The press department did not publish its own newspapers, but subsidized existing ones. Since paper on the open market was almost unavailable, all newspapers depended on free paper from the press department. The government expended valuable foreign currency to import paper. Under these circumstances it was an easy task to control newspapers; the government granted or withheld paper, depending on the behavior of the editors.[65] In spite of the extremely difficult circumstances in which papers were published, their numbers for some reason multiplied.

Wrangel was extremely interested in the newspapers. As a vain man he wanted to know everything the domestic and foreign press wrote about him and his regime. He read most of the important domestic papers and directly intervened when he found something not to his liking. He believed that newspapers should report only favorable news and tolerated no signs of dissatisfaction.[66] Even those newspapers which most loyally supported his government's point of view often suffered from censorship. They frequently appeared with white columns of empty space, the tell-tale signs of the work of military censors.

Wrangel paid special attention to the foreign press. The political department of the General Staff continued to be responsible for liaison with the foreign journalists. The department prepared news stories from local papers for foreign correspondents.[67] It also subsidized Russian papers abroad and maintained press agents in important European capitals. Wrangel's close associate A. A. Von Lampe worked in Constantinople and Von Dreier in Berlin. Burtsev's paper, *Obshchee delo*, published in Paris, received support from the Crimea.[68] The press agents responded quickly to articles which they considered unfavorable to the White movement. In this way they succeeded in counteracting damaging publicity and in creating a relatively positive image for Wrangel.

In the middle of the summer the government set up schools for agitators. After two weeks of training, the students went to the villages to acquaint the population with the new land law and speak on a variety of issues. They also addressed audiences of soldiers.[69] The point of view expressed by the agitators was uncompromisingly reactionary. They did not disdain the simple yet powerful weapon of anti-Semitism.[70]

White propaganda was not particularly successful in reaching the enemy. The government on occasion sent airplanes over Bolshevik territory dropping leaflets. It also used the tactic, first developed by the Bolsheviks, of spreading fake proclamations. The forged documents purported to show that the Bolsheviks were near panic and considered Wrangel their most dangerous enemy. Although the forgers committed some silly mistakes, such as calling Savinkov a revolutionary, the documents were rather skillfully composed.[71]

"LEFTIST POLICIES"

Those who describe Wrangel's policies as leftist base their evaluation largely on the land reform law of 1920. The attitude of the White leaders toward land reform went through a remarkable change. While in 1918 at Denikin's headquarters hardly anyone raised the subject, by 1919 it became a bitterly divisive issue. During the last phase of the struggle, most of Wrangel's advisers agreed that some landlords' land must be divided among the peasants. Wrangel, who had criticized almost every aspect of Denikin's policies, never advocated land reform in 1919; instead, he seemed to have opposed the idea.[72] Krivoshein had disapproved of the feeble attempts of Denikin's government to legalize previous land seizures, and as the leader of the State Unity Council he had agitated against land reform.[73] But the lessons of the great defeats of 1919 were too clear to disregard. Even the conservative landlords moderated their opposition at a time when the White cause seemed almost hopeless in any case.

An indication of the change in attitude was the memorandum which General P. S. Makhrov, the chief of staff, handed to Wrangel on his assumption of power. This document included some of the most radical proposals ever conceived by a White leader. On the matter of land reform, Makhrov suggested that a 100-*desiatina* maximum (270 acres) should be established in the Crimea, and that all lands in excess of that be subject to immediate and compulsory alienation. The land would then be distributed free among the peasants. Makhrov wrote that the promises made by both sides in the Civil War had made the peasants understandably skeptical, and that therefore only quick and decisive action could restore their faith and assure the success of White mobilization efforts. Wrangel was willing to ally with the devil, but he was not ready to go so far as to give land to the peasants without payment. He wrote on the margin of Makhrov's memorandum: "This is true. But it is impossible to carry out the proposal, because there is no money available to compensate the landlords. The first step in improving the agricultural situation must be the parcelization of state lands and the compulsory cultivation of all suitable lands."[74]

Although Wrangel did not accept Makhrov's radical proposal, he was determined not to follow Denikin's example of procrastination. He not only wanted to develop a land policy, but wanted to do so quickly. After only a few days in office he entrusted G. V. Glinka with putting together a committee to work out a reform project; he gave Glinka three days to choose his associates. Ex-senator Glinka had worked in the tsarist ministry of agriculture under

Krivoshein as a department head, and most of the other members of the committee had impeccable conservative credentials. General Levashov, a friend of Wrangel, had been a president of the union of landowners in South Russia; Count Apraksin had been a governor of the Taurida province; V. S. Nalbandov had served in the reactionary cabinet of General Sul'kevich; and P. P. Zubovskii had been an assistant minister of agriculture. There were only two men committed to reform: V. A. Obolenskii, a Crimean *zemstvo* leader, and K. O. Zaitsev, a young economist. When the newspapers published the list of members, rumors spread that Wrangel did not really want to divide the land, but had created this committee only to allay criticism.[75] The truth was less sinister. Wrangel approved this conservative committee for the same reason he chose men of the old regime as his associates: he had confidence only in these "rightist hands."

On April 20 the committee commenced its work in Yalta. Soon Wrangel decided to broaden discussions. He called a special conference in Simferopol on May 4 to discuss the land question. In the six-day conference, aside from the members of the Glinka committee, a few elected peasant delegates participated. Wrangel wanted each of the four districts (*uezd*) to send two representatives, but only three peasants arrived in Simferopol. It never became clear who selected them. In any case, these men kept almost completely silent during the discussions.[76] The Simferopol conferences dispersed without tangible accomplishments.

However, the Yalta committee continued to meet for over a month. The Commander-in-Chief sent a memorandum to Glinka in order to guide the work. The main points of the memorandum were similar to the ideas Denikin had expressed a year earlier in his letter to the Special Council:

1. Land, on the basis of private property, should belong to those who work on it. It must not be subject of renting or speculation.

2. The state must have the obligation to assure that the land is cultivated properly and is neither exhausted nor left unused.

3. Depending on the availability of land, on density of population, and on the prevailing type of agriculture, norms should be established in such a way as to suit different circumstances (in districts and in provinces).

4. All lands, state, church, and private, which exceed a certain norm to be established for the locality (districts and provinces) must become subject to alienation. From these lands a land fund should be created from which those who have little or no land would receive some for a price.

5. Intensively cultivated estates and special farms should be protected by the establishment of higher maximum norms for them, depending on local conditions.

6. The right to ownership should be officially affirmed.

7. Compensation for the land should be paid on the basis of prices prevailing in the locality.

8. Everybody who receives land should be obligated to give part of the harvest to the state, in proportion to be established by local committees.

9. The state should create a fund from the monies received from the peasants and from it compensate the landowners.[77]

The reform plans received great publicity. Wrangel published his memorandum in the newspapers, and the papers also reported in detail on the debates taking place in Yalta and in Simferopol. The government even advised its representatives abroad about the project. From the outset it was evident that the chief goal of the regime was to gain foreign and domestic support.

Debates of the Glinka committee were heated. A substantial minority continued to oppose any land reform; the majority realized that something must be done, and after numerous warnings from Wrangel, very grudgingly accepted the principle of compulsory alienation; a few believed that immediate and radical measures must be taken in order to win the sympathy of the peasants. Wrangel repeatedly had to apply pressure to prevent a breakdown.[78]

The conservatives repeated the arguments of the past: the present period of turmoil was inappropriate for tinkering with agrarian relations; at this time of inflation, credit was unavailable and the value of the land impossible to determine; in Russia it was dangerous to violate the principle of private property, because people in a short time might demand the division of gardens, factories, and even buildings; the army must not risk losing the support of the landowning class; land reform would create economic chaos. Although the conservatives were outvoted in the major issues, their views influenced the final project.[79]

The committee tackled the most crucial matter first. It agreed that the peasants should retain illegally occupied land and promised compensation to the landowners. The issue over which the Whites had hesitated for years was finally resolved.

When the committee turned to the question of providing land to the landless, it decided first of all that the project would be applied only in the Crimea, and the measures to be taken elsewhere would be decided at a later date. This decision very much simplified work, for the Crimea was a province with little land hunger. In fact, in the northern half of the province land lay fallow. As a consequence, during the Revolution and Civil War there were very few instances of land seizures.[80] Indeed, it was questionable whether the lessons of land reform in the Crimea would be applicable to the country as a whole. Wrangel and his advisers worked hard to realize some sort of reform, but under the difficult circumstances of the Civil War the task was almost insurmountable. One is entitled to wonder how the Whites would have solved the issue in provinces where agrarian relations were much more embittered.

After some debate the participants agreed on the necessity of creating four county (*uezd*) committees and one provincial committee to carry out the work. Representatives of the Land Bank argued that the Bank had experience in similar work and therefore should be responsible for the land reform. The majority turned down the suggestion, fearing that the Bank would inevitably look at the problem from a purely commercial point of view. The committees as planned were to include representatives of the *zemstvo* organization, representatives of the Departments of Justice, Interior, and Finance, as well as elected representatives, but only people who themselves owned land. The chief task of the committees would be to sell land and to mediate between landlord and peasant. All sales would have to go through the committees. The framers of the law wanted to keep contact between peasant and landlord to a minimum, for it seemed that this would be the best way to lessen class hostility. A provincial committee would supervise the work of district organizations.[81]

Which lands would become subject to compulsory alienation caused some disagreements. Except for representatives of the Land Bank, everyone agreed that uncultivated land and lands belonging to the Land Bank should be divided.[82] Similarly, it was assumed that lands which had been given out for rent in the past would now be divided. Some members of the committee believed that three years of renting would be a proper time limit, but the majority decided on six.[83] The committee made no attempt to define maximum holdings and left this task to the future district committees. Those who had rented land in the past would have preference in buying it, for it was assumed that they possessed the necessary implements for cultivation. Interestingly, the district committees were instructed to discriminate in favor of individual ownership. Communes would be allowed to buy land only with the stipulation that they must dissolve themselves within five years.[84] This anticollectivist bias shows that the ideological origins of the project go back to the Stolypin years. Also, it may be that the Whites were influenced by Bolshevik propaganda and assumed that communal form of landholding would inevitably lead to socialism.

The members of the committee hoped to use as little force against the landlords as possible, and therefore they decided that compulsory alienation would not begin before March 1, 1921, hoping that the landlords would use this time to sell their land freely. The conservatives wanted to gain time. They assumed that in case of Wrangel's victory there would be no need to divide lands. The survey of lands to be subject for compulsory sale would begin only on January 1, 1921. Of all the provisions of the land reform plan, this one was the most unreasonable.

V. A. Obolenskii, the most liberal member of the committee, attacked the point bitterly. He wrote a separate opinion in which he pointed out that since the peasants had experienced several governments in the past years, they had no confidence at all that the present regime would last longer than the previous ones. They would receive the news of postponement as a sign that the government lacked commitment to a serious land reform. He argued that it was wrong to expect many voluntary sales: both sides would wait for favorable circumstances. When the front was near, the peasants would not buy, thinking that the Bolsheviks would either give them land free or would not recognize the validity of the transaction carried out by their enemies. When the front was at some distance, the landlords would have no incentive to sell, since money was almost useless.

Obolenskii insisted that the chief goal of the reform must be to gain peasant support rather than economic improvement. He believed that the collapse of 1919 occurred because of the inability of the Denikin government to satisfy the desire of the peasants for land. Land reform was now essential, and the survival of the regime depended on the good will of the peasantry. The landowners would suffer, of course, from the introduction of a radical plan, but other segments of the population had already suffered more in the Civil War. If the considerations were to be purely economic, the best course would be to have no reform at all. Under the circumstances, the main economic task of the committee must be to reduce inevitable disorder to a minimum. He feared that the peasants who had rented land in the past, having no money now to buy land, would be forced off the land with their animals and would have nowhere to go. Obolenskii wanted some protective measures to avoid chaos. In his view the project, as it was worked out by the Glinka committee, failed both from an economic and from a political point of view. Although he did not convince the majority, his opinion obviously influenced the thinking of General Wrangel.[85]

Wrangel was appalled by the reactionary character of the project. He well appreciated Obolenskii's opinion about the error of waiting for another year. Instead of accepting the work of the committee, he instructed Glinka to form a new committee and introduce fundamental modifications.[86] The final project, which Wrangel published on June 7, differed in some important ways from the plan originally developed by Glinka's committee.

Wrangel published two laws. The first dealt with the substance of the reform and the second with the machinery to carry it out. The land law contained these points:

1. Land is protected from seizures, except in line with regulations introduced here.

2. These lands are protected: peasant allotment, lands bought with the help of the state bank, church lands, lands belonging to scientific establishments, intensively cultivated special estates, private agricultural lands in quantities to be determined by district committees.

3. All lands with the exception of those mentioned in point two
. . . will be distributed among the peasants and become their private
property after they have paid compensation.
    4. District [*volost'*] and county [*uezd*] committees will carry out
the reforms. . . .
    9. District committees will establish the value of the land on the
basis of past productivity. (Value is equivalent to five times the average harvest. The price must be paid in 25 years. This means that
the peasant must pay in produce or in money one fifth of his harvest
to the state)

The second law ordered the establishment of district (*volost'*),
county (*uezd*), and provincial committees. A noteworthy feature
of this law was the provision that landless peasants and members
of village communes were not allowed to serve on the committees.[87]
Wrangel's land law was hardly a radical one. It was certainly not
the "total redistribution" of which populists had been dreaming. It
did not promise equalized holdings or something for every landless
peasant. The land law's provisions were directed against communes, and in its rather explicit favoring of rich peasant over poor,
the law was in the Stolypin tradition. Not only were the poor peasants excluded but obviously those who lacked agricultural implements and animal draft power would hardly be able to cultivate
more land without financial aid, which was not forthcoming. The
landlords were certainly to be compensated generously. At a time
when land prices were low, calculating the value of the land on the
basis of past harvests benefited the landlords.[88] It is possible to
maintain that the provisions of the law served the interests of the
landlords at least as much as the interests of the peasants. But perhaps worst of all, the law was enormously complicated. Such a complex piece of legislation might have been justified in peacetime, but
under the circumstances of a civil war the complexity was certainly
a strategic error. Yet, in spite of all the deficiencies of the law, Wrangel deserves credit for resisting the temptation to postpone or avoid
the issue. Unlike all other leaders of the White movement, he fully
appreciated the significance of land reform and as long as he remained in power he devoted a considerable amount of energy to
the project. It is clear that without his great determination the reform plans would have been scuttled by his conservative advisers.

It was Wrangel who was responsible for embarking on the division of land immediately. It seems that it was also his idea to create over one hundred district committees instead of the four county committees envisaged by the Glinka committee. These committees had great autonomy: they alone established how much land the landlords could retain and the value of the land. By bringing land reform closer to the village level, Wrangel hoped to speed the work.

The realization of the land reform proved to be extremely difficult. The complexity of the law meant that the peasants did not understand many of its features. Therefore the most immediate task was to acquaint the population with the new law. It took a long time for the cumbersome propaganda machinery even to print and distribute the land law in pamphlet form. Stupidly, in the first few weeks the authorities charged 100 rubles for the little brochure (half the price of a box of matches).[89] The incompetent propaganda work angered Wrangel, who urged his subordinates again and again to remedy the situation. In July the government started a major propaganda drive: leaflets were dropped from airplanes in the Crimea and also over Soviet territory; the propaganda bureau prepared a simplified version of the land law; the government also entitled the services of teachers, village elders, and surveyors to help popularize the reform.[90]

The creation of the machinery to carry out the redistribution of land inevitably took time. As an agent of the department of agriculture reported in September, it was difficult to establish committees because the most trusted and prominent people did not want to participate. They expected the Bolsheviks to arrive soon and did not want to compromise themselves. This agent recommended that in areas near the front the reform should be postponed until some degree of stability was established.[91] The first district (*volost'*) committees were formed in July. By mid-September out of the 140 districts under the rule of the Russian Army, 86 had formed committees. The four county (*uezd*) committees had also started their work.[92]

The local committees had complicated and difficult tasks. First, they had to establish how much land was available in the community. Second, they had to survey the need of the population for land. Third, they had to establish norms which would apply in the district. Fourth, they had to collect data about past harvests in order to determine the value of the land. In the few months that the district committees existed, it is unlikely that many did more than survey the available land and establish the size of maximum holdings. Understandably, how much land a landowner could retain varied greatly from district to district. While in some districts it was as much as 600 *desiatina* (1620 acres), in others it was only 100 (270 acres). Plots assigned to the peasants correspondingly varied between 10 and 150 *desiatina*.[93] Actual transfers of land directly resulting from the land law must have been extremely rare.

Wrangel received reports that some landlords tried to sabotage the law by denying to the peasants that such a law existed. Others told the peasants that the existing regime would not last long enough to carry out the reform. But the apathy of the peasants was perhaps a more serious obstacle than the resistance of the landowners. The peasants did not believe that Wrangel's regime would last. They also considered the price of the land too high and hoped that they would get it free from the Bolsheviks.[94] The Bolsheviks spared no effort in undermining peasant confidence in Wrangel's land reform. They, too, used airplanes to drop leaflets telling the peasants that the law served only the interests of the landlords and that it was no reform at all. The Bolsheviks also spread among the peasants forged documents which purported to be secret instructions from Wrangel to the committees instructing them not to carry out the reform. Wrangel feared that the slow work of the committees might convince people that the documents were genuine.[95]

The main goal of Wrangel's land reform was to gain the support of the peasantry. It is difficult to establish the degree of its success; the opinions of contemporary observers are contradictory. It seems that the peasants had already formed a picture of the two opposing sides in the Civil War, and a hesitant land reform was not enough to change the minds of many. Probably the successful effort to curb lawlessness made a greater difference in the life of the villages and therefore did more to increase the popularity of the White Army than the abortive land reform.

Wrangel's industrial, financial, and labor policies were even less "leftist" than his land law. The economy of the Crimea was in shambles. The breakdown of the transportation system destroyed internal trade; the war cut off the peninsula from its normal supply of raw materials and markets; inflation and lack of faith in the ability of the regime to survive discouraged industrialists from reopening their factories. In 1920 industrial production declined from the already dismal standards of the traumatic year of 1919. The regime could not long survive without external trade and foreign economic support.

The Whites needed a great deal from abroad. Without coal the navy could not operate. The population completely lacked meat and animal fats. The headquarters constantly bombarded General Lukomskii, its representative in Constantinople, with requests for goods which could not be obtained in Russia.[96]

The Whites, however, did not have enough funds. They hoped to get a share of German war indemnities; they attempted to sell a part of the Russian commercial fleet; and they wanted to get recognition as rightful owners of Russia's national property abroad.[97] None of these attempts succeeded. Under the circumstances it was essential to export as much as possible and to get credits abroad.

In the first few weeks of its existence the government sold abroad wine, fruits, leather, tobacco, and salt,[98] but the sale of these goods did not bring in nearly enough revenue. It would have been tempting to export grain, but the army did not have enough. In April General Vil'chevskii, the head of the department of supply, reported to the cabinet that it was necessary to take stringent conservation measures to assure the supply of the army until the next harvest.[99] When Wrangel decided to invade the Tauride in June, one of his chief aims was to acquire grain. Luckily, in the newly occupied territories the harvest of 1919 had been excellent and the peasants possessed considerable reserves of food.

The speculators were quick to take advantage of the situation. Since the ruble was practically worthless, the best way to save one's wealth was to buy goods, especially grain, for export and then retain the foreign currency. Many businessmen who went to Europe, ostensibly to conclude trade transactions, never returned to Russia. The government soon faced the danger of losing its valuable grain reserves without acquiring essential materials from abroad. The Whites, who posed as defenders of private property and freedom of enterprise, had to adopt monopoly of foreign trade. This pro-

cedure, which clearly resembled communist methods, was somewhat embarrassing. White trade representatives abroad always
emphasized that the monopoly was extraordinary and a temporary
measure.[100]

Grain exports (mostly barley) could not pay for everything the
Whites needed; it was essential to get credits. Wrangel had the misfortune of having to deal with the French rather than with the considerably more generous British. Although they were interested in
his good military performance, they drove a hard bargain and
wanted to be paid for everything they delivered. Wrangel had to
accept humiliating conditions in exchange for aid. In return for at
least a part of what they had requested, the Whites had to agree to
recognize Russia's debt to France and promise to pay her first after
victory at 6.5 percent interest in 35 years. As a guarantee on the loan,
the French had the right to exploit Russia's European railroads, to
control customs and duties at the ports of the Black and Azov seas,
and to dispose of all exportable grain from the Ukraine and from the
Kuban. In addition, the Whites mortgaged three-fourths of the oil
and one-fourth of the coal production of the Donets basin.[101] Denikin would have never accepted such terms. Admittedly, Wrangel's
position was far worse; for him, the withdrawal of support would
have meant almost immediate collapse.

Economic recovery was retarded by a severe financial crisis.
Since the Allies did not support their Russian friends generously,
the only source of money for the war was the people of the Crimea.
Bernatskii, the minister of finance, wanted to tax the population
and introduced a sales tax. This form of indirect taxation hurt the
poor the most. However, the sales tax did not provide nearly enough
revenues and monopoly such as that on the sale of salt did not help
much.[102] The government had no alternative but to turn to the
promiscuous use of the printing press. Inflation ran rampant. Prices
rose so fast that there was a constant shortage of money, even though
the printing presses worked continuously. In the course of 1920
the White regime printed 176 billion rubles.[103] (In tsarist Russia
in 1914 there were 1.6 billion rubles in circulation.)[104] Bernatskii
ordered the printing of 22 billion rubles in England and made plans
for devaluation, but the regime did not survive long enough to carry
out these projects.[105]

The consequences of the financial collapse were far-reaching. Just as in Soviet Russia, money lost its value and various products took its place. In the Crimea tobacco, wine, and barley were used. The peasants did not want to sell their products to the government for worthless money. In circumstances in which money was almost useless, orderly economic planning was impossible.

Inflation was both the cause and the effect of rampant speculation. Everyone tried to protect himself by selling on the black market, by hoarding valuable goods, and in general circumventing regulations. The government passed increasingly severe laws against speculators in vain. Even the promise of capital punishment was no deterrent. The regime promised first 5 and then 10 percent of the confiscated property to those who denounced speculators.[106] The newspapers were full of reports of guilty ones captured and sentenced. But nothing seemed to help.

It was the urban poor, the workers, who suffered the most. The Crimea, which did not have a well-developed industry, had only twelve thousand workers in 1920.[107] Wrangel was ready to concede this small working class to the enemy. His regime made no efforts to ameliorate their problems and win them over. Makhrov devoted little space in his remarkable memorandum to the workers' question.[108] His recommendations merely reiterated Denikin's labor laws. He wanted Wrangel to reaffirm the eight-hour working day, allow the workers to organize insurance and pension societies, and pass legislation limiting female and child labor. He further recommended that the Whites not alienate the unions. Wrangel wrote on the margin of the memorandum: "Correct, but we cannot do everything, considering the state of our finances." It is hard to guess what he had in mind, for none of these recommendations implied a large financial outlay.

Inflation hit the workers very hard. From January to October 1920 the price of bread increased 80 times, the price of sugar 220 times, and the price of potatoes more than a hundred times.[109] Wages, of course, also increased, but not nearly enough to keep up with the prices. Since most of the workers in the Crimea were in small shops, there were few organized strike movements. The dock workers of Sevastopol stopped work in June demanding higher wages. Since the strike endangered the fleet, the authorities reacted energetically: the police arrested the leaders and mobilized the workers. Such measures broke the strike, and after this episode the workers made no further organized opposition to the Wrangel regime.[110]

Wrangel rarely addressed himself to the worker question. On one occasion, on July 9, he had this to say to his cabinet: "The peasantry is with us, and so is a large part of the intelligentsia, but it is different with the workers, who make up the most hostile part of the population. We must take urgent measures: we should give everything to the workers compatible with state interest, but the other side of the coin is that we must fight against strikes in the most determined fashion."[111]

Wrangel had learned from Denikin's mistakes. He saw that Denikin's shortsighted and inflexible policies toward the national minorities had brought the movement close to disaster and therefore was prepared to make concessions. However, his greater flexibility could no longer make a difference.

In 1918–1919 Denikin had to deal with a great variety of well-organized movements which presented far-reaching demands. In 1920 in the Crimea, the Tatars, who made up approximately a quarter of the population, represented the only sizable minority. By this time the Tatars had come to distrust both sides in the Civil War. In January 1918 the Bolsheviks had dispersed their assembly, the Kurultai. In the second half of 1919 Denikin took a blindly hostile attitude toward their nationalist aspirations: he suppressed all Tatar organizations and reinstated the Tsar-appointed Mufti, the Muslim religious leader who had been dismissed by the Tatars themselves in 1917.[112]

Wrangel not only allowed the Tatars to organize, but in May 1920 he addressed their assembly and promised them far-reaching autonomy after victory.[113] But in view of the quiescence of the Tatars, the issue of autonomy did not have immediate and practical importance and Wrangel paid little attention to it. His bureaucracy labored for months in order to prepare legislation which would define the limits of autonomy. This project was completed only in October, but the cabinet had no time to discuss it and therefore it was never promulgated.[114] In June the Mufti decided to resign, and it was Wrangel's responsibility as Commander-in-Chief to name a

successor. He never did so.[115] Wrangel's land law and *zemstvo* law
did not consider the special needs of the Tatars. The land reform
project protected the large holdings of the Muslim Church as it
protected the property of all churches.

COSSACKS

Wrangel had criticized Denikin repeatedly for giving in to the
demands of the Cossacks; now it was his task to find a modus vivendi
with them. The Cossacks remembered Wrangel as the man who
had destroyed the Kuban *rada* in November 1919, and this memory
militated against easy cooperation, but in many ways he was in a
better position to deal with them than Denikin had been. Now the
Cossacks financially depended entirely on the High Command.
The most radical politicians never came to the Crimea and therefore the legislative assemblies were less militant than before; in any
case, these assemblies lost much of their power and therefore the
Commander-in-Chief worked mostly with the atamans rather than
with unruly politicians. Shortly after coming to power he consulted
with Bogaevskii of the Don, Vdovenko of the Terek, and Bukretov
of the Kuban, who without protest accepted his proclamation of
April 11 in which he claimed direct leadership of all armies and
reserved for himself the conduct of foreign relations. He promised
to the atamans that he would consult with them periodically and
reestablish the autonomy of the *voiska* as soon as possible.[116]

In spite of this promising beginning, problems soon emerged.
Although Wrangel considered Bogaevskii a close comrade, his relations with the leaders of the Don army, Generals Sidorin and
Kel'chevskii, were tense. Wrangel's predecessor, General Denikin,
had already realized at the end of March that he should remove
General Sidorin following the bitter exchanges at Novorossisk, but
he did not do so because he assumed that his own resignation would
alleviate the difficult situation. He was wrong. Sidorin now found
it difficult to cooperate with any Russian general. He wanted to
lead his army in an attempt to liberate the Don, and would have
liked to break all relations with the Volunteers. The march never
took place because Bogaevskii insisted that such a venture would be
suicidal, and argued that in the prevailing circumstances coopera-

tion with the Russian officers was more important than ever before. Sidorin planned to reorganize his forces and then resign.[117]

It is not surprising that the disagreements between Wrangel and Sidorin soon came into the open. The two generals stood at the opposite end of the political spectrum within the anti-Bolshevik movement. Wrangel was a leader of the right and Sidorin, partly under the influence of his chief-of-staff, General Kel'chevskii, increasingly moved to the left. Also, Wrangel's attempt to get Sidorin's help in his intrigues against Denikin in December 1919 backfired, and the memory of that event added to their mutual hostility.

The spark which ignited the struggle was the editorial policy of the *Donskii vestnik*, a newspaper published by the Don command. The editor of the paper, Count du Chayla, was the chief of the political section of the staff of the Don army. Articles in the paper extolled the achievements of the March Revolution, denounced the Whites for not bringing freedom to the people, advocated building a federal and democratic Russia, and proposed the creation of a Cossack state with the participation of the Don, the Kuban, and the Terek.[118] *Donskii vestnik*, because it was the official paper of the Don army, was not carefully examined by the censors, and Wrangel for some time did not learn of its political orientation. It came to his attention because the editor of the competing paper in Evpatoria, *Evpatoriiskii kur'er*, a certain Ratimov, complained to Kutepov, who immediately notified the Commander-in-Chief. On April 19, Wrangel closed down *Donskii vestnik*, ordered the arrest of du Chayla, and asked Sidorin, Kel'chevskii, and Quartermaster General Kislov to come to Simferopol at once. Bogaevskii in vain tried to intervene. Wrangel had decided to take the opportunity to crush the opposition. He had the officers arrested and handed them over to a court martial. He appointed General Abramov as Commander-in-Chief of the Don Corps.

Since it seemed possible that the Cossacks would resist, the arrest of the leaders was a dangerous move. Indeed, Sidorin did not accept Wrangel's right to arrest him and considered calling on his followers to protect him. Ataman Bogaevskii, however, pointed out that a confrontation, which would inevitably have disastrous consequences, must be avoided at all cost and persuaded Sidorin to submit. Wrangel fully realized that there was a possibility of an armed clash and ordered his troops to be ready for such an eventuality.[119]

General Dragomirov was a member of the court martial, headed by military judge Seletskii. The Cossacks considered Dragomirov's participation particularly unfair, since the *Donskii vestnik* had personally attacked him for his leadership of the Special Council. Count du Chayla, remembering the fate of Kalabukhov, hanged by Wrangel in November 1919, attempted suicide. He succeeded only in wounding himself, but he could not be tried. The court acquited Kislov, but sentenced Sidorin and Kel'chevskii to hard labor. Wrangel, wisely, reduced the sentences to exclusion from service and the two generals promptly left the country.[120] He accomplished his task; he brought the Don leadership firmly under control and showed his enemies that he would not tolerate opposition.

When the court tried Count du Chayla in September, it found him innocent. This was a somewhat embarrassing situation for the High Command, since as editor of the paper he was the primary person accused. It made little sense to acquit him and find his superiors guilty for not having stopped him. However, by September the political situation had changed and the trial attracted little attention. Wrangel ordered du Chayla to leave the country. The "innocent" and the "guilty" thus received the same punishment.

After the removal of Sidorin, the Don Cossacks gave Wrangel no more trouble. The reestablished Krug was only a shadow of its former self. An ex-official of the department of finances, Karzhenevskii, formed a government which had been reduced to half of its former size. The government lost its right to issue currency, and Wrangel treated the Cossacks as poor relations, doling out small amounts of money to them now and then.[121]

The Terek Cossacks were without political significance. They had only a few thousand fighters. Ataman Vdovenko never objected to Wrangel's policies, and the government, which was an ephemeral organization, had no impact on the political life of the White movement.

As always, the Kuban Cossacks proved the most troublesome. The bulk of their army remained in the Northern Caucasus, trapped between the Bolsheviks, the Greens, and the Georgians. Wrangel considered it essential to unify his forces by bringing this army to the Crimea. Ataman Bukretov, on the other hand, opposed the transfer, perhaps because he realized that amalgamating his troops into the main army would lead to a loss of independence. But Wrangel was determined. He kept the Ataman under house arrest until he agreed to go to the Black Sea coast and take charge of the operation.[122] The situation of the Kuban army was critical. The Bolsheviks had renewed their attack and the Cossacks panicked: some escaped into the mountains, others asked asylum in Georgia, and many gave themselves up. The Whites managed to evacuate only a segment of the original force. The embarkation, which was completed on May 4, once again took place under difficult conditions. Although the British lent some of their ships, there were not enough boats in the harbor, and the horses and heavy equipment had to be left behind. After this debacle, Bukretov, finding no support either at the headquarters or among the Cossacks, resigned.

The unification of the armies and the resignation of Buketov did not solve the political problems of the Kuban.[123] According to the constitution, the Premier, Ivanis, became acting Ataman. The *rada*, however, sitting in the Crimea, refused to recognize him, and blamed him rather than Bukretov for the events on the Black Sea coast, and in particular for the capitulation of part of the army to the Bolsheviks. The *rada* declared Ivanis a traitor. Ivanis, for his part, rejected the right of a group of politicians to act as a *rada* and did not recognize the validity of its decisions.[124] He hoped to base his authority on an assembly of the radical politicians who had escaped to Georgia because they did not want to continue the cooperation with Russian officers. The Crimean *rada* decided to elect General Ulagai as Ataman, but Ulagai declined the honor. Thus the *rada* succeeded in undermining Ivanis' authority without succeeding in naming a substitute for him.

Wrangel took advantage of this situation and played the two sides against each other. Although he had little respect for Ivanis, he continued to deal with him. Ivanis became his prisoner. No doubt the radical politician hated everything Wrangel stood for, yet he did not dare to oppose the Commander-in-Chief, for his authority depended on the fact that Wrangel regarded him as the Ataman. The difficulties inherent in Ivanis' position became clear in early August, when Wrangel decided to make his understanding with

the Cossacks more explicit. He ordered the atamans to appear at
his headquarters and gave them only a day to consider this new
treaty.[125] In the treaty the atamans reaffirmed their recognition
of Wrangel as the ruler of anti-Bolshevik Russia.[126] He was to be
the unchallenged leader of the armies, have control over the railroad network and other means of communications, and had the
monopoly on issuing currency and on the conduct of foreign relations. Wrangel, in turn, promised autonomy in internal matters to
the voiska and consultations with Cossack representatives, some of
whom he promised to include in his cabinet. This was the type of
agreement which Denikin had wanted for years, but had failed
to get.

Liakhov, the Ataman of the Astrakhan Cossacks, Vdovenko,
and Bogaevskii were irritated by Wrangel's method of presenting
the project, but had no serious objections in principle to signing.
Ivanis, however, had a serious dilemma. He disliked the treaty,
and worse, he knew that if he signed it, he would fatally alienate
the radicals who had taken refuge in Tbilisi. On the other hand, he
recognized that if he did not sign, Wrangel would find someone else
to do so. Ivanis tried to maneuver by submitting a counter-project,
which recognized Wrangel as head of the united armies but rejected his claim to be ruler (*pravitel'*). However, the other atamans
did not support him, and on August 4 he decided to sign the original
treaty. As expected, his political friends in Tbilisi bitterly denounced him.[127]

Wrangel wanted to have an explicit agreement with the Cossacks
because he planned an invasion of the Kuban. He decided to conclude the treaty before any territory was liberated and avoid misunderstandings. He understood that the Cossacks were more pliable
allies as long as they were on alien territory.

Wrangel, who had repeatedly urged Denikin to leave Cossack
territories, only a few months later was ready to return to the Kuban. He realized that in a civil war there can be no period of rest.
He wanted to maintain the momentum of success, because he feared
internal disintegration in a period of inactivity. But in which direction could his troops advance? The only alternative to Cossack territories was the Ukraine, but that presented a number of risks. The
territory on the left bank of the Dnepr was infested with partisan

bands, which were hostile to the Whites. Wrangel, unlike his predecessor, would have been willing to give far-reaching concessions.
He sent an agent to Makhno in the hope of establishing friendly
cooperation. However, the anarchist chief would have nothing to
do with "counterrevolutionaries" and had the emissaries killed.
Petliura, now a puppet of Poland, could no longer maintain an independent policy and was not interested in cooperating with Wrangel. Under the circumstances, the Whites could not have expected
a friendly reception in the Ukraine. The Kuban seemed a much
more promising battleground. Wrangel hoped that the Cossacks
would fight better in liberating their homeland, and victory would
have brought great benefits. The agriculturally rich area with an
anti-Bolshevik population would have been a source of recruits
and food for export. It could have become a staging ground for liberating the other voiska. Wrangel was prepared even to abandon
the Northern Taurida in order to shorten his line of defense and
develop his successes in the east.[128]

News from the Kuban was encouraging. The Bolsheviks never
completely conquered and pacified the region. In some districts the
population accepted the Red Army willingly, hoping that it would
bring peace. However, when it was soon followed by requisition
teams who took everything they could lay their hands on, the Cossacks once again turned against the Bolsheviks.[129]

Guerrillas took advantage of the changing attitudes. General
Fostikov, who with a small detachment had escaped to the foothills
of the Caucasus at the time of the disintegration of the army, had
already formed a partisan force in April 1920, which he called Army
for the Regeneration of Russia. The movement quickly grew and
by the early summer Fostikov had fifteen to thirty thousand fighters, almost all of them Cossacks.[130] The small army operated in the
Maikop, Laba, and Batalpashinsk districts, and consequently Fostikov depended on neighboring Georgia for his contacts with the
outside world. He received very little financial support and had
no clear ideas about events in the Crimea. Nevertheless, he did
learn about Wrangel's plans of invasion and he decided to postpone
his own in order to coordinate his strategy with that of the invading
forces.

Wrangel planned his move for a long time. As acts of diversion,
he sent two small detachments in July to land on the North Coast

of the Azov Sea: a thousand men landed east of Mariupol and occupied Nikolaevskaia *stanitsa*, and another 800 landed west of Taganrog. The first group was destroyed on July 9 by the defending Red army, but the second, under Colonel Nazarov, managed to penetrate inland and attract volunteers. Nazarov soon had 1500 fighters. The Soviet command feared that he might become the focus of a large-scale uprising of the Don Cossacks and sent three divisions against him. Nazarov fought for several weeks against a numerically much stronger enemy, and ultimately he was defeated. He was captured, but, remarkably, managed to escape and returned to the Crimea in September.[131]

In preparation for the invasion, the Commander-in-Chief chose General Ulagai to lead the expedition and General Dratsenko as his chief of staff. Although Ulagai was a popular man and a capable leader, he was disliked by the Cossack left for his past close association with the High Command. General Filimonov, the ex-Ataman, accompanied the forces, hoping to direct the organization of civil administration in the reconquered territories. Everyone expected the operation to succeed. The Cossacks were so confident that most of them took their families with them. As a result, the civilians on the boats hardly left any room for soldiers. In the middle of August three landing parties arrived in the Kuban: 1500 soldiers under General Cherepov landed in the district of Novorossisk; 2900 soldiers under General Kharlamov landed on the Taman peninsula; and the main force of eight thousand under Ulagai successfully attacked and occupied the small settlement of Primorsko-Akhtarskaia.[132]

The Ninth Red army had 24 thousand soldiers, but it occupied a large and unfriendly territory. The Bolsheviks did not have enough forces at the seacoast to prevent the landing.[133] If the Whites succeeded in winning over the population and starting a large-scale rising against the Bolsheviks, and also managed to establish contact with the numerically substantial but ill-equipped forces of General Fostikov, their chances of liberating the entire *voisko* were excellent.

The operation soon turned into a disaster, however. Dratsenko and Ulagai could not work together. Ulagai feared that his lines of communication would be cut and therefore did not dare to move on to Ekaterinodar. He also made no attempt to establish contact with Fostikov. In fact, the partisan chief learned that the invasion had taken place only when it was too late for him to start his planned offensive. Soon the Whites lost the element of surprise, and time was on the side of the enemy. The Bolshevik command took the danger very seriously and sent reinforcements from other fronts: In an important battle on August 22, the Reds forced Ulagai to evacuate Timashevskaia, the largest settlement which he had captured.

On September 1 the Whites started to withdraw from the Kuban, and on September 7 the last soldiers were evacuated.[134] Although the invasion ended as a complete failure, the Whites still evacuated more soldiers than the number of those who had landed at the start of the operation. Many Cossacks were obviously determined to continue the struggle against the Bolsheviks.

General Fostikov held on for some weeks, but his position became increasingly hopeless. In the beginning of October, with the remnants of his force, he retreated into Georgia. The Georgians, who feared the Bolsheviks, did not dare to allow their embarkation into the Crimea until Wrangel presented a show of force. A torpedo boat fired a few shots into the air. The Georgians retreated from the coast and approximately two thousand Cossacks sailed to Feodosia.[135]

The failure of the invasion had far-reaching consequences. Wrangel's army, which had known only victory up to this time, suffered a major defeat, which undermined morale. Had the Whites succeeded in reconquering Cossack lands—and the chances seemed excellent—they could have increased the size of their army and made the Bolsheviks' task of ending the Civil War much more difficult. But since the Whites could not defeat the relatively small Ninth Red Army on friendly territory, the more farsighted among them must have realized at this time that they had no chance of engaging successfully the major Bolshevik forces. The final defeat was only a matter of time.

THE LAST BATTLES

The victories of the Poles against the Red army made Wrangel's early successes possible. Ironically, a few months later and under different circumstances, a new series of Polish victories led to the final defeat of the White movement in South Russia.

Although the close connection between the military fortunes of Wrangel and Marshal Pilsudski were evident even to many contemporaries, only tenuous ties existed between these de facto allies. This was partly because of the difficulties in communications and partly because of the great ideological gap between the two leaders. Since messages between Simferopol and Warsaw went through Paris, at a time when the military situation often changed with startling rapidity, there could be no meaningful coordination of strategies. At the end of June Wrangel named General Makhrov his representative in Warsaw. Makhrov, however, only took up his new duties in September, after the crucial battles at the outskirts of the Polish capital.

Wrangel, acting on the basis of his stated principle of cooperating even with the devil in order to defeat the Bolsheviks, would have liked closer relations with Marshal Pilsudski. The Polish leader, however, remained true to his socialist background, at least to the extent of distrusting a Russian general. He disliked what Wrangel stood for, and he had a low regard for the military value of the White army. He wanted to support representatives of a rather mythical "Third Russia," a category in which he included the Ukrainian socialist and nationalist Petliura and the veteran Social Revolutionary Boris Savinkov. By the time Pilsudski was willing to extend some help to the Whites, it was too late and made no practical difference.

The White Russians watched the changing fortunes in the Polish-Soviet war helplessly. The Polish invasion of the Ukraine soon became a disaster. The value of Petliura as an ally turned out to be slight, for the nationalist leader could no longer attract a sizable following. In Russia, however, the war against Poland aroused nationalist passions, and the Bolsheviks managed to gain support even from some of those who had been hostile in the past. In the middle of May the Red Army launched a counterattack and after a series of victories in June, July, and August, the Reds threatened the Polish capital.

These Polish defeats improved Wrangel's situation temporarily: the Bolsheviks concentrated their energies on the defeat of the foreign enemy, and the French, who were determined not to allow the formation of a communist government in Warsaw, looked on Wrangel more favorably. In order to bolster his strength, on August 10 the French government recognized him as de facto ruler of South Russia. In exchange Wrangel accepted an obligation to repay the Russian state debt, promised land reform, and in time, the convocation of a popularly elected Assembly.[136] In addition, the French successfully pressured the Rumanian government to send to Wrangel at least part of the Russian war materiel which had remained in the country after the end of the First World War. The needed supplies greatly improved the Whites' position, but foreign recognition was even more important. Understandably, the population of the Crimea had no confidence in the permanence of the regime and many refused to cooperate. The establishment of diplomatic ties with France gave a boost to morale, because many Russians regarded it as a guarantee that France would not allow the destruction of the White regime. The middle of August was thus the high point of Wrangel's fortunes. Wrangel, unlike some of his native contemporaries, understood that in the eyes of the French he would remain a useful ally only so long as his armies performed successfully. Therefore he was gravely concerned about the impact on foreign opinion of his failure in the Kuban. He tried to protect himself by pretending that the venture was successful, and that he withdrew not because of defeats but because of strategic considerations. Naturally he and his propagandists emphasized the fact that the army which returned to the Crimea was larger than the one which had set out a few weeks before.

The Whites' defeat in the Kuban coincided with Polish victories. In the middle of August the Poles stopped the Bolshevik advance at Warsaw and in a short time the pursuer became the pursued. The Bolsheviks suffered defeat not only through the strategic errors committed by the Red commanders but also because, contrary to Lenin's expectations, Polish workers and peasants listened to the nationalistic appeals of their leaders rather than to communist propaganda.

When Wrangel learned of the Russian defeats he saw the dangers inherent in them for his own movement. If both the Poles and the Bolsheviks realized that they could not defeat one another, they would be forced to compromise. In that case, nothing would prevent the Bolsheviks from using their vastly superior manpower to destroy the White movement. Wrangel attempted to persuade the Poles to continue the war, but his diplomacy had little success.[137] He did manage, however, to get permission from the Polish government at the end of September to form a "Russian army" on Polish territory. After long and difficult negotiations, the Whites and the Poles agreed to name General Peremykin commander of the newly formed army, which at the time had only six thousand soldiers.[138]

The Whites could no longer afford to be cautious; their military strategy was born of desperation. To avoid facing the entire Red Army unaided, Wrangel decided to lead his army into the Ukraine in order to establish a common front with the Poles. He hoped that his success would encourage the Poles to continue the war, and expected that in case of a link-up his army would incorporate Peremykin's corps.

The Commander-in-Chief prepared for the campaign with his customary thoroughness. Although he had failed to gain the good will of Makhno, he cultivated other partisan chiefs in the Ukraine by promising them money and arms. He received the federalist leader Markotun and discussed with him ways of cooperating.[139] He also reorganized his troops, by dividing them into two armies: the first one was headed by General Kutepov and included the old Volunteer Corps and the Don corps; the second, led by General Dratsenko, included the second and third corps and a Terek-Astrakhan Cossack brigade. It is something of a mystery why Wrangel chose for this important post Dratsenko, who had just conspicuously failed in the Kuban. Wrangel also formed two independent cavalry units, one led by General Barbovich and the other by General Babiev.

At the time of the reorganization the Whites had 43,900 fighting men. According to Soviet observers, the fighting ability of the Whites declined somewhat in the course of 1920. It still contained some superb units like the Drozdovskii division of the old Volunteer Corps, which was made up entirely of officers, but those who had been recently drafted lacked the skill and determination of the volunteers.[140]

Before the Russian Army could move west and cross the Dnepr, it had to strengthen its defenses at the other sectors of the front. In the course of September the Whites fought successfully in the east-

ern and northern sectors. These were their last important victories.
Although official negotiations between the Bolsheviks and the
Poles began only on September 21, at Riga the Bolsheviks had expected even before that day that the war would end with a compromise.[141] This expectation enabled them to regroup their forces and
strengthen their armies on the Southern front. On September 27
M. V. Frunze took command of the front, and established his headquarters at Kharkov.[142] In addition to the Sixth and Thirteenth
armies and the Second Cavalry army, Frunze expected Budennyi's
First Cavalry army to join his forces.

Wrangel saw that the Red Army soon would have an overwhelming superiority and decided to attack before the arrival of Budennyi,
who was expected during the second half of October. On October
6 Dratsenko's army crossed the Dnepr at Khortitsa.[143] The Reds
did not expect a crossing at that spot and the surprise gave a momentary advantage to the Whites. They captured a large number of prisoners and threatened the enemy's line of communications.[144]
Within a few days, however, the operation turned into a disaster:
White communications did not function properly and the generals
did not know where each other's forces were deployed. Dratsenko
committed great errors in deployment. The Red Army brought in
fresh troops and on October 13, after suffering heavy losses, Dratsenko ordered his army to return to the left bank of the Dnepr. The
failure of this operation, combined with the news that on October
12 the Bolsheviks and the Poles had signed a treaty, made it clear
to Wrangel that it was now only a matter of time before the Reds
would be in a position to destroy his armies. Since most people in
the Crimea did not appreciate how much White successes had depended on the course of the Polish war, they did not realize how
close the impending collapse was. Wrangel, for his part, did everything within his power to underplay the magnitude of the defeat
and avoid panic. He, of course, fully realized the seriousness of
the situation. Yet, after consulting with Kutepov and Shatilov,
he decided to defend the Northern Tauride rather than withdraw
all his troops into the peninsula. His decision was motivated not
by strategic considerations but by his determination not to let his
own people or his foreign allies know that his cause was lost.[145] (See
Map 5.)

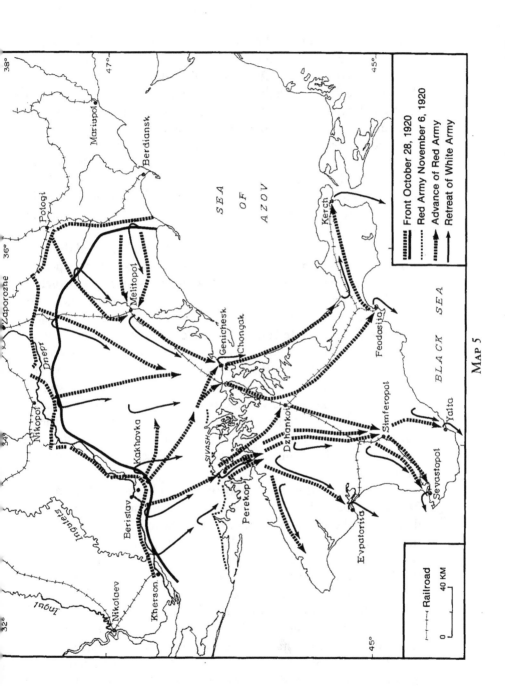

Front October 28, 1920
Red Army November 6, 1920
Advance of Red Army
Retreat of White Army

SEA OF AZOV

BLACK SEA

Mariupol
Berdiansk
Zaporozhe
Potogi
Melitopol
Genichesk
Chongak
Kerch
Feodosia
Dnepr
Nikopol
Kakhovka
SIVASH
Perekop
Dzhankoi
Simferopol
Yalta
Sevastopol
Evpatoria
Berislav
Kherson
Nikolaev
Ingulets
Ingul

Railroad
0   40 KM

MAP 5

The decision to hold the Northern Tauride was a desperate and risky venture, because the Bolsheviks had built up strong forces on the left bank of the Dnepr at Kakhovka and from there could threaten the Perekop Isthmus and the Sivash straits. If the Reds succeeded in capturing those strategically vital points, they could surround the Whites and eliminate their army in the Northern Tauride. Now, for the first time, the Bolsheviks achieved a crushing superiority. On October 28, the first day of the offensive, they had 99,500 foot soldiers and 33,685 horsemen against a 23,070 strong White infantry and 11,795 cavalry.[146] The Reds also had more than twice as many guns and many more machine guns than their enemies.

In a matter of days, the units of the Red Army reached the straits separating the Crimea from the mainland. Wrangel now desperately tried to extricate himself from the dangerous situation which resulted from his foolhardy strategy. He sent all available men to defend Perekop and ordered Kutepov to return and attack the enemy from the West.[147] The Whites succeeded for the last time; Kutepov avoided the danger of encirclement and retreated into the Crimea. The cost was great: the Whites had to leave behind much of their equipment; many units gave themselves up; the fighting spirit of the rest was dangerously undermined by the hasty evacuation. Months earlier, Wrangel had built strong fortifications at the entrance to the peninsula, but at the decisive moment the White troops were too weak in numbers and too demoralized in spirit to take advantage of them.

The attack on the Perekop fortifications began on November 7. No doubt the Bolsheviks were conscious of the symbolism of the date: now the Civil War, which had started exactly three years before, was almost over. The Reds had a superiority of four to one, but the terrain favored the defenders. The narrow isthmus, dotted with lakes and the nearby Chongar peninsula, separated from the mainland by a waterway, made the use of large armies difficult. The weather turned extremely cold, which made attackers and the defenders alike suffer. Within a short time the Reds managed to cross the water and establish themselves in the Chongar peninsula. The Whites were forced to give up one line of fortifications after another. Within five days it became clear that the Red offensive could not be stopped and Wrangel could hold the peninsula for only a very short time.

The task now was not to stop the enemy—that was impossible—but merely to slow down the advance in order to gain time for an orderly evacation. Wrangel's achievement in organizing the evacuation was much more successful than Denikin's performance a few months earlier. To be sure, in November 1920 there was some confusion, and not everyone who wanted to leave Russia was able to. However, the great majority not only of the fighting men but also of the refugees could find places on the ships. Bureaucrats carrying documents and soldiers bringing their weapons were all evacuated.

Wrangel had prepared for this emergency. He avoided panic by pretending that the Crimea would be defended. At the same time he gathered his ships in the harbors. He concealed the purpose of the concentration of ships by pretending to plan a naval attack on Odessa, or on the Kuban.[148] The population, which had great faith in the impregnability of the defenses, was deceived by Wrangel's ruses. Wrangel published his order of evacuation on November 12 and this indeed created panic. However, by this time the evacuation was so thoroughly prepared that embarkation could immediately begin. On November 15 the embarkation was finished and Wrangel himself left Russia. One hundred and twenty-six ships participated in the operation, carrying 145,693 people. All the ships except one, which sank in a storm, arrived safely in Constantinople.[149]

The transformation from soldier to refugee was a painful one for most Russians. Many, including Wrangel, consoled themselves with illusory hopes. They refused to believe that the war was over and that their cause was lost. They continued to hope that when circumstances changed they could return to Russia as members of a victorious army. Wrangel was determined to keep his soldiers together, preferably in close proximity to Russia, and to renew the struggle at the first opportunity.

The French not only did not encourage him, but hindered his efforts. For them the existence of a Russian army was an embarrassment, and they wanted to relocate the refugees as quickly as possible. They persuaded some to return to Russia, and sent others to Brazil. Wrangel was indignant because the French no longer treated him as Commander-in-Chief, but there was nothing he could do. After long months of miserable camp life on Turkish islands, most of the refugees were placed in Bulgaria, Czechoslovakia, and Yugoslavia.

Wrangel spent the last years of his life working for the welfare of his men. He never gave up hope that some day his soldiers might be recalled and once again fight against the hated Bolshevik enemy. He died in Brussels in 1928.

Wrangel was not defeated by his own political and military failures. When he assumed command in the spring of 1920, the White cause was already lost; no politician, however farsighted, and no military man, however able and charismatic, could have turned the tide. As Commander-in-Chief, Wrangel committed errors, such as, for example, not withdrawing from the Northern Tauride to the Crimea in time; these mistakes, however, did not influence the outcome of the struggle.

He was an able politician, diplomat and general. He demonstrated skill and political courage in publishing a land reform law. He handled first the British and then the French with consummate skill. After assuming command, he succeeded in reimposing discipline and giving courage to his demoralized followers. He organized the evacuation of the Crimea brilliantly. And yet, on balance, this able man brought more harm than good to the cause he chose to serve. He weakened the Volunteer Army by undermining Denikin's authority at a time when there was still a chance for victory. He helped the rightists within the White movement to organize and thereby reduced Denikin's freedom of action. Denikin very likely would have pursued a more realistic and enlightened policy if he had not been under constant attack from his conservative followers.

CHAPTER 10

The White Movement in South Russia: Conclusion

The Bolsheviks' decisive victory over the Whites did not immediately assure the stability of the Soviet social and political order.
Makhno continued his struggle in the Ukraine for a few more months,
and a peasant rising in Tambov province assumed major proportions before the Red Army managed to pacify the area. The mutiny
of the Kronstadt sailors in March 1921 aroused near panic in Moscow and persuaded Lenin to introduce major changes in his policies.
But these anarchists, rebellious sailors, and peasants were not part
of the White movement; they had different methods of fighting and
struggled for different goals.

The Whites' defeat was conclusive. The boats which sailed from
the harbors of the Crimea in November 1920 carried defeated soldiers who dreamt in vain of a victorious return. The Whites who for
three years had stood against the new rulers in Moscow—at times
near victors—were destined never again to play an active role in
the political life of their country.

In spite of the passage of almost sixty years, the story of the vanquished has remained elusive and controversial. The White leaders
were not intellectuals or politicians, nor did they want to be; they
had little interest in systematically articulating a program, and no
talent for it. It is true, they issued numerous manifestoes while in

power, and they left to us rich archives containing correspondence, minutes of meetings, and reminiscences. However, their statements and policies lend themselves to contradictory interpretations. It further adds to our difficulties that the White movement was extremely heterogeneous, unified only by a common opposition to the enemy. As a result, we can make only a few generalizations about the movement as a whole.

In conclusion, let us reexamine a few basic issues: Who were the Whites and what did they fight for? How did the Russian people see the two antagonists in the Civil War?

The White movement in South Russia was an uneasy coalition of two groups, the Cossacks and the officers. The officers founded the Volunteer Army and retained leadership in it until the end of the struggle. Their thinking and prejudices profoundly influenced the character of the movement, and therefore they must bear a large share of responsibility for the final defeat. The contribution of the Cossacks was less visible but no less important: they made up the majority of the fighting men, and without their continued participation the army would have soon collapsed.

In view of the length and bitterness of the Civil War, it is ironic that the few thousand officers who came to the Don at the end of 1917 and at the beginning of 1918 decided to take up arms not against the new rulers in Moscow and Petrograd, but against the German army. For a remarkably long time these men persisted in their belief that the Bolsheviks were nothing more than German agents. They wanted to defeat them in order to proceed to the larger and more important task, the resumption of the war. It is easy to see the psychological sources of the officers' naivete. They had fought a bitter and destructive war. They could not have done so without the conviction that winning that war was essential to the future of the motherland. After they had made so many sacrifices in order to defeat Germany, it was impossible for them to see that their Russia, their way of life, now faced a new and far more deadly enemy. They had been taught that politics was a dirty and useless business and that the proper task of a soldier was to fight the foreign enemy. It is understandable, therefore, that the officers denied to themselves that in fact they were fighting for class interest.

Alekseev, Kornilov, and the other officers who came to the Don in 1917 organized the Volunteer Army because they wanted to continue Russia's participation in the World War. But it was increasingly hard for the officers to delude themselves: the Germans repeatedly showed their good will, and for the professional soldiers it was evident that they shared far more with their foreign counterparts than with their revolutionary countrymen. The Bolsheviks were their one natural enemy, and it was natural that the officers came to play a crucial role in the anti-Bolshevik movement in South Russia. Unlike some other potentially anti-Bolshevik groups, they not only knew and trusted one another, but shared a set of common ideas and norms and already possessed a rudimentary form of organization. Since the enemies of the Bolsheviks regarded their tasks as above all military ones, the officers seemed to be ideal leaders.

Furthermore, the officer corps was one of the most conservative institutions of Imperial Russia, and the officers were predisposed to hate and despise everything Lenin and his comrades stood for. Their conservatism had little to do with social background; in fact, before 1917 the army had been one of the best agencies of social mobility. However, the profession naturally attracted those who were willing to defend the existing state. Partially because the prewar intelligentsia had disliked the state and militarism, the officers felt misunderstood and isolated from the educated circles. In these years they had acquired a distaste for politics in general, which in their mind was subversive by definition. Understandably, they especially disliked the socialists and revolutionaries. They were insensitive to the weaknesses and failings of Imperial Russia and had little sympathy for those who wanted to change the country.

Far from being an advantage, the military tradition in the leadership of the White movement turned out to be a major weakness. The officers saw only one aspect of the struggle and therefore grossly misunderstood the nature of the Civil War. Rather ridiculously, while engaged in a life and death struggle, they continued to insist that they stood above politics. But politics could not be simply wished away; the generals could not help but play politics, and they did so very poorly. Nothing in their background prepared them to organize a functioning administration, to articulate their goals and thereby win over the uncommitted, and in general to understand the aspirations of various segments of the Russian people.

Worst of all, in their blind insistence that in the conditions of the Civil War only force mattered, they did not turn for help to civilians. The White movement remained an exclusively military affair. No civilian, with the exception of A. V. Krivoshein, who assumed his duties only in the last months of the struggle, ever possessed any genuine authority. The others—such as the liberal politicians whom Denikin attracted to headquarters, and the reactionary bureaucrats—who participated in the administration of the reconquered provinces—depended entirely on the whim of military men. The officers, foolishly, looked down on all civilians, and the politicians and bureaucrats accepted the idea of military supremacy as natural and even desirable. The Bolsheviks had created a far more successful strategy: the movement was led by civilian revolutionaries who exploited the skills of "military specialists."

The officers shared a great deal with one another. They had attended the same schools, accepted a common code of behavior, and held similar political views. Of course, they did not agree on everything. Denikin, though perhaps no more intelligent than the average officer, was endowed with uncommon integrity and moral sensitivity, and on occasion he sensed that the Russian people did not want to return to the past and that a vast gulf separated the rich and the poor.[1] He would have liked to see old Russia reformed. A few intelligent officers, such as General Makhrov, realized that only basic concessions could save the movement. The majority of the officers, however, were blind reactionaries who gave no thought to reforms. All the leaders of the Volunteer Army, including the most liberal ones, deplored not only the November but also the March Revolution. They all wanted to see old Russia restored, even if some of them would have liked to see it mildly reformed afterwards. Although the Volunteer leaders never articulated their political program, the Russian people understood what it was: a call for the return to the past.

The officers knew their profession. They led their armies well and at times they performed remarkable military feats. The Whites, unlike the Reds, did not have to fear for the loyalty of their senior commanders. No White general ever defected to the enemy. The fine performance of the White armies underscores the fact that in a civil war superior military leadership is far from enough for victory.

Neither historians nor contemporaries have properly appreciated the role of the Cossacks in the Civil War. The Bolsheviks saw their enemies as fighters for an outdated social order and for class privileges, and the Cossacks, many of whom were quite poor, did not quite fit this view. The Whites, on the other hand, hated to recognize the extent of their dependence on the Cossacks. They preferred to see themselves as leaders of the Russian people, and not leaders only of a small and special section of it. Soviet historians have shown little willingness to dispel old myths; and Westerners writing about the Civil War have so overemphasized the role of foreign intervention that they have failed to examine who the Whites were.

The decisive importance of the contribution of the Cossacks to the White cause is evident from the first moment of the struggle to the last. Generals Alekseev and Kornilov decided to start their work on the Don because they understood that there was no other part of Russia where they could safely organize. In the following years Denikin's strategy was often determined by his unwillingness to leave Cossack territories. Consciously or unconsciously he knew that he could not base his movement on the Russian peasantry. Only General Wrangel attempted to continue the struggle without having a foothold on the Kuban or on the Don; but the Cossacks made up as much as half of his army, and he certainly could not have continued the war if they had withdrawn. Fittingly, Wrangel suffered his decisive failure in his attempt to reconquer the Kuban. Had he succeeded, he might have increased the size of his army and survived, at least for awhile, the end of the Polish-Soviet war. When he could not mobilize the Cossacks, it was clear that his cause was lost.

The Cossacks were good soldiers. They had a long and proud military tradition, they were brave, and they knew how to take the initiative. The nature of the fighting in Russia was altogether different from that in France in 1914–1918. The front line moved quickly and the mobility provided by the horse was crucially important. The Cossacks were excellent horsemen and thereby gave the Whites a superiority in cavalry during the first half of the war, which was a major advantage. Nevertheless reliance on the Cossacks proved to be an important source of weakness to the anti-Bolshevik side.

First of all, the Cossacks and the officers fought for different goals. The officers had to overthrow the government in Moscow in order to reconstruct the Russia they loved. They could tolerate no compromise. The Cossacks had a much more parochial point of view. They fought in order to defend their wealth from the *inogorodnie*, the Russian peasantry of their district, and to preserve some of their estate privileges. Although they disliked what the Bolsheviks stood for, they hesitated in making sacrifices to liberate non-Cossack areas. They fought well when the enemy threatened their homes, but lost their morale as they ventured outside their voiska. They would have been satisfied if they could have compelled the Bolsheviks to recognize the independence or autonomy of their districts.

The Cossacks did not want to reconstruct defunct Imperial Russia. They dreamt of reorganizing the country on a federal basis, which would have enabled them to determine their own way of life. The idea of federalism went contrary to centuries of Russian tradition, and in the eyes of the officers, even to talk of decentralization was a revolutionary action, bordering on treason. The more flexible leaders realized that they had to give concessions to the Cossacks, but everyone knew that these were grudging political moves, which could not be trusted.

Furthermore, the Cossacks regarded themselves as democrats. Unlike the rest of the Russian peasantry, most were reasonably well-to-do; they had a pride in their way of life and a tradition of self-government. Their protestations of democracy, however, were hollow because at no point were they ready to share their wealth and power with the fellow inhabitants of their districts, the *inogorodnie*. Ironically, these Cossacks, who were fighting for their essentially feudal estate privileges, were also the most "modern" part of the population: they were better educated and more ready to listen to new ideologies. The "democratic" Cossacks were also the most likely followers of the extreme right. It is quite consistent that twenty years later Hitler found many volunteers among them.

Cossack politicians repeatedly denounced the policy of White headquarters as reactionary. In the beginning of 1920 they succeeded in forcing on Denikin a new and "leftist" course. The Commander-in-Chief gave in because his armies were disintegrating, and he had to grasp at any straw. But it was too late; the ideological differences between Cossacks and officers were not reduced, and in fact were further exacerbated in those traumatic months.

The Cossacks and the officers differed in matters of life style perhaps even more importantly than in ideology. Many Cossacks regarded the officers as unwelcome guests, who performed no useful duties but spent their days idly in cafes and restaurants. The generals and colonels, on the other hand, thought of the Cossacks as little better than bandits, people who interpreted the concept of military booty far too broadly. Contempt and resentment often came to the surface with elemental force; again and again, it seemed that a civil war would break out within the White camp.

The Cossacks could have pressured headquarters far more effectively if they had been unified and well led. Their only leader with vision and moral authority, Ataman Kaledin, was not a charismatic man. In order not to witness the destruction of the *Voisko*, he committed suicide in February 1918. In the summer of 1918 Ataman Krasnov succeeded in building a personal following; he knew how to appeal to the simple Cossacks, but he wanted to pursue extremely reactionary policies which were contrary to the majority view. His conservatism, his vanity, and his adventurism led him to become a German puppet. Naturally, after the Allied victory he could not hold on to his post.

An intelligent and able leader might have enabled the Cossacks to see that there was far more to unite than to separate them. It is true that the Kuban, the Don, and the Terek each had special problems and enemies; nevertheless, the Cossacks, a tiny minority of the Russian people, had to help one another if they were to prevail. The leaders of the Volunteer Army discouraged cooperation; they did not want to be faced with a united front.

The Terek Voisko was too small and had too many powerful enemies to give meaningful help to the Whites. The Don Cossacks were weakened by class struggle: the Northern and poorer districts repeatedly rebelled, causing great harm to the anti-Bolshevik cause. But Kuban politics were the most bitter and confused. Here ethnic hostility was added to the struggle between the rich and the poor.

The Ukrainian and, by and large, the poorer Cossacks wanted a more leftist policy and cooperation with the Ukrainian nationalists, while those Cossacks who spoke Russian were willing to cooperate with Denikin. It is true that division on the Kuban enabled headquarters to intervene successfully, but constant infighting depressed the morale of the armies and lessened their military effectiveness.

Even if the Cossacks and the officers had been united and determined to carry out the struggle, these two small groups could not easily have imposed their will on the large masses of the Russian people. In order to win, the Whites would have had to gain, if not the active support, then at least tolerance and good will from the major segments of society. In this they failed miserably.

Unlike generals, politicians, and revolutionaries, peasants leave no memoirs. Our information about how they perceived the antagonists in the Civil War is based on unreliable reports and conjectures. The party workers and secret service agents who reported on the mood of the villages were outsiders at a time when the people had every reason to conceal their views. The White archives contain a few reports by censors on the content of soldiers' letters. The soldiers wrote of their hatred of the Bolsheviks, but since they knew that their letters were opened, we can hardly take their views at face value.[2]

Sometimes the very fact of Bolshevik victory is adduced as evidence of how the Russian people perceived the antagonists in the Civil War. This is a weak argument, for it is quite possible that the Reds won for reasons other than peasant support, such as superior organization provided by the Party, a better-functioning coercive apparatus, internal lines of communications, abler leaders, greater unity within the Red camp, and so on.

The evidence from desertion rates and peasant risings is ambiguous. There are no reliable figures available about how many people defected, but desertion was an extremely widespread phenomenon. In the conditions of the Civil War it was easy to walk away from the fighting, and at the time of defeats, also very tempting. In any case, even if we had evidence, and we do not, that the peasants were more likely to desert from White armies than from the Bolsheviks, such evidence might prove nothing more than that the Reds were better able to enforce discipline. The activities of peasant partisans greatly harmed both sides. Risings in the spring of 1919 in the northern districts of the Don led to the collapse of the Red front and made possible Denikin's startling successes which immediately followed. Conversely, in the fall of the same year Makhno made a great contribution to Bolshevik victory.

It seems that the peasants quickly understood that both sides in the Civil War fought for goals which were alien to their aspirations. In the elections of November 1917 they overwhelmingly voted for Socialist Revolutionary candidates, proving that while on the one hand little remained of their former monarchism, on the other Bolshevik goals and methods were incomprehensible and unappealing. However, the victors in the elections, the Socialist Revolutionaries, never for a moment had a chance to institute their program. A civil war is not merely a popularity contest. The Socialist Revolutionaries could not win because they possessed neither the ideology nor the organization relevant for the times. They did not know how to turn popular support into divisions, into a functioning administrative machinery; they had no solution to offer for the major problem of the country, which was how to overcome anarchy. Democratic socialism was clearly not the movement which could bring order to the country.

The Socialist Revolutionary leaders wanted to serve the interests of the peasants, but they themselves were intellectuals, removed from the village. As outsiders, they could not mobilize the peasantry. It was different with the partisan chiefs. They themselves were peasants, who not only wanted to benefit their fellow villagers, but who also could express their aspirations better than city-bred intellectuals. Although most of the partisan units were small, the ability of the partisans to melt into the local population in case of need, their excellent knowledge of the terrain, and the support which they received from the people made them militarily important. The partisans, however, could play only a negative role: they could harm their enemies, but they could attain their goals no better than Socialist Revolutionaries. Under no circumstances could the peasants win the war and attain power. They could not long maintain discipline, they could not organize a national movement, and they never even attempted to set up a functioning administration. Makhno was by far the most able and ideologically sophisticated leader, but when he conquered major cities in the Ukraine, his administrative acts were confined to releasing people from jails.

Furthermore, we should not idealize the peasant movement. It was obscurantist, and nurtured a hatred of urban life in particular and modern civilization in general.

For better or worse, the peasants had to choose between the Whites and the Reds. At first glance it would seem that the Bolsheviks had a much better hand to play: the peasants wanted land, and they could give it to them. But we must not overlook some inherent weaknesses in their position. The Whites' base was in the rich South, and so it was incomparably easier for them to feed their armies and their relatively small cities than it was for the Reds to provide for the proletariat of Moscow and Petrograd. Requisitioning is almost invariably cruel, for it is impossible to avoid abuses. White soldiers, especially Cossacks, often brutally mistreated the peasants. There is ample evidence from the Whites' own archives that many villagers regarded both sides as bandits. However, the Bolsheviks came into conflict with the basic interests of the peasants more often. They had no choice. In order to avoid starvation in the cities, and concomitant political suicide, they had to declare war on the peasants. It was the requisitioning detachments of workers, soldiers, and poor peasants which determined the attitude of the countryside toward the Bolsheviks.

The Whites had some other advantages. As the horrors of the Civil War accumulated, the peace and order of the old tsarist days seemed increasingly attractive. The Whites promised to recreate a familiar pattern of life, while the Bolsheviks identified themselves as revolutionaries. However, in 1920 this factor ceased to operate. The people understood that the Reds had won the Civil War, and therefore Wrangel seemed to be an obstacle to peace; nothing hurt him more than the expectation that he would soon be defeated.

The anti-Bolsheviks greatly benefited from the support of the Church. The Reds harmed themselves by anti-religious propaganda, by desecrecating churches and persecuting priests. The Church was the only effective propaganda network the Whites had. The priests knew the mentality of their flocks, and they were strategically placed to be able to reach them. Among other tools, they took advantage of the age-old anti-Semitism of the Russian, but especially of the Ukrainian peasant. It is true that Jews did not live in Russia and therefore the great majority of Russians had little or no contact with Jews. They were, however, not immune to anti-

Semitism. Describing Bolshevik leaders as Jews or as servants of Jews was the most effective propaganda ploy of the Whites anywhere in the country. Some White leaders were more scrupulous than others in exploiting this unattractive method, but they all benefited by it.

The peasantry was stratified, and both sides took account of this fact. Although the Whites deplored class war in their declarations, they did not hesitate to interfere in the struggle between the rich and the poor. All through the Civil War, but especially in the final Wrangel period, White policies favored the rich against the poor, sometimes unconsciously, but mostly consciously. The heirs of Stolypin believed that political stability must be based on the support of the well-to-do and conservative elements. Land reform laws allowed the Kulaks to increase their holdings, and regulations concerning self-government mercilessly excluded the landless. The Bolsheviks took advantage of class struggle far more skillfully. Although they alienated the peasantry as a whole, they successfully recruited cadres among the poorest. Communist ideology appealed to the young and discontented, and the Reds mobilized able and ambitious activists from all segments of society. This way also the Reds carried out a social revolution: they enabled workers and peasants to reach positions of power within a very short time. The Whites wrongly believed that they had all the military and political leaders they needed, and their attitudes and prejudices promised little to those who wanted to make their careers quickly.

The two sides competed for the peasantry because each believed that it should be their natural ally. By contrast, the Whites conceded the workers to their enemies. Indeed, by and large the workers preferred the Bolsheviks to the generals. White intelligence reports almost uniformly complained about hostility in the factories. The proletariat provided recruits for the Red Army quite out of proportion to their numbers in the population, and the Red underground in White territories was largely organized by workers. The Whites made a grave mistake in not trying to win over the working class. Many Menshevik labor leaders hated their Bolshevik competitors so much that they would have cooperated with Denikin had they received understanding and encouragement. Some workers were willing to fight against Lenin's government. The proletariat of Izhevsk, for example, rose against Bolshevik rule. Even such an

320 THE WHITE MOVEMENT IN SOUTH RUSSIA

unsavory character as Kirsta within a few short weeks managed to mobilize thousands of workers in Kiev with a pro-Volunteer Army program. His movement fell apart not because of disillusionment, but because of the victories of the Red Army.

It was the officers' world view which made it difficult for them to win supporters among the proletariat. As conservative populists, they deplored modernity and everything connected with it—cities, factories, and workers. Like many Russians before and after them, they believed in an idealized and mythical image of the wise and unspoiled country folk. Under the circumstances, they were among the first to fall victim to Bolshevik propaganda, which depicted all workers as Bolsheviks. Their instinctive hostility toward the working class, coupled with their lack of political sophistication, prevented them from making distinctions between shades of socialism. To them, all Marxists were equally evil. They accepted Bolshevik propaganda because they were prepared to believe that workers had already been hopelessly corrupted by the forces of modernity.

In March 1917 the Imperial regime collapsed without defenders. The officers, who above all wanted to continue the war, did not come to the aid of the Tsar. The experiences of 1917 further confused and demoralized the anti-revolutionary forces, and therefore the Bolsheviks were able to take power in November almost without bloodshed. It was only in the Civil War that the protagonists of the pre-revolutionary status quo made a concerted effort to reassert themselves.

Not all the participants in the White movement wanted to recreate tsarist Russia. Many desired reforms. In any case, whatever their intentions, the social and political transformation produced by the Great War, the Revolution, and the Civil War could not be undone; even the partisans of the old were bound to create a new Russia. Nevertheless, the Civil War divided those who preferred tsarist Russia to the society which they feared their country was heading toward, and those who hated the old and had confidence that they could build a more just and rational society. After three years of struggle the Whites lost the war, proving that the traditional order had too few defenders, that the old institutions could not be revived, and that Russia would have to be administered by novel methods. The defeat of the Whites was the final and conclusive defeat of Imperial Russia.

Notes

INTRODUCTION

1. Andrew C. Janos, "Authority and Violence: The Political Framework of Internal War," in Harry Eckstein, ed., *Internal War* (New York, 1964), pp. 132–133.

2. The literature on foreign intervention is truly enormous. The most important and best books are: G. F. Kennan, *Soviet-American Relations 1917–1920*, 2 vols. (Princeton, 1956–58); and three volumes by R. H. Ullman on Anglo-Russian relations: *Intervention and the War* (Princeton, 1961), *Britain and The Russian Civil War* (Princeton, 1968) and *Anglo-Soviet Accord* (Princeton, 1972). For my purposes the most useful book was G. A. Brinkley, *The Volunteer Army and Allied Intervention in South Russia, 1917–1921* (Notre Dame, 1966). I relied heavily on Brinkley for my description of the relations between the White leaders and the English and the French.

3. Almost all books on the Bolsheviks in the Civil War suffer from this weakness, but the most extreme examples are the works of E. H. Carr. His three-volume study, *The Bolshevik Revolution, 1917–1923* (London, 1950–53), is still our most detailed and best description of Bolshevik policies. He properly concentrates on institutional developments and social and economic issues. However, his purposeful neglect of all non-Bolsheviks in these years gives his works a curiously distorted quality.

4. For example, S. F. Cohen, *Bukharin, A Political Biography* (New York, 1974).

CHAPTER 1. THE BOLSHEVIKS

1. There is an enormous literature on Leninism. Lenin expressed his views on the importance of organization most explicitly in *What is to be Done?* A particularly insightful and concise study is Alfred G. Meyer, *Leninism* (Cambridge, 1957).

2. T. H. Rigby, *Communist Party Membership in the USSR* (Princeton, 1968), p. 59. Rigby takes this figure from official Soviet sources but adds that party records at this time were not reliable.

3. *Ibid*, p. 78.

4. Leonard Schapiro, *The Communist Party of the Soviet Union*, second edition (New York, 1971), p. 240.

5. A good summary of the Constitution of 1918 can be found in E. H. Carr, *The Bolshevik Revolution*, 3 vols. (London, 1950–1953), I, 134–159.

6. I. A. Kirillov, *Ocherki zemleustroistva za tri goda revoliutsii (1917–1920gg)* (Petrograd, 1922), p. 112.

7. Lazar Volin, *A Century of Russian Agriculture* (Cambridge, Mass., 1970), p. 154.

8. For examples of White propaganda, see Wrangel Military Archives files 146–148, Hoover Institution, Stanford, California.

9. For a summary of the problems of Russian industry in the First World War, see Michael Florinsky, *The End of the Russian Empire* (New Haven, 1931).

10. Alec Nove, *An Economic History of the USSR* (Baltimore, 1972), p. 68.

11. E. G. Gimpelson, *Sovetskii rabochii klass 1918–1920* (Moscow, 1974), p. 26 and p. 341.

12. L. M. Spirin, *Klassy i partii v Grazhdanskoi Voine v Rossii (1917–1920)* (Moscow, 1968), p. 120.

13. On Trotskii's organizational work, see his *Kak vooruzhalas' Revoliutsiia*, 5 vols. (Moscow, 1923–1925); Isaac Deutscher, *The Prophet Armed, Trotskii: 1879–1921* (Oxford, 1954), chapter 12, pp. 405–447; and John Erickson, *The Soviet High Command* (London, 1962), pp. 25–83.

14. A. I. Egorov, *Razgrom Denikina* (Moscow, 1931), p. 47.

15. *Ibid.*

16. *Ibid.*, p. 49.

17. Erickson, *Soviet High Command*, p. 33.

18 *Ibid.*

19. For example, on one occasion Lenin considered dismissing the military specialists. He was surprised to learn from Trotskii that at that time thirty thousand ex-tsarist officers were already serving in the Red army, and that they played such a crucial role that their removal would have been suicidal. L. D. Trotskii, *My Life* (New York, 1930), p. 381.

20. A. P. Aleksashenko, *Krakh denikinshchiny* (Moscow, 1966), p. 180.

21 *Ibid.*, p. 79.

22. Erickson, *Soviet High Command*, p. 60.

23. Deutscher, *Prophet Armed*, Chapter 12, p. 428.

CHAPTER 2. THE ARMY

1. A. I. Denikin, *Ocherki russkoi smuty*, 5 vols (Berlin and Paris, 1921–1925), V, 118. The Whites could never send all their soldiers against the Bolsheviks. Thousands were tied down fighting partisans and protecting the Northern Caucasus from a hostile Georgia.

2. Egorov, *Razgrom Denikina*, p. 43. The role of the Cossacks in the army and their relations with the headquarters will be discussed in detail in Chapter Five.

3. Egorov, *Razgrom Denikina*, pp. 104, 136, 226.

4. P. N. Shatilov, "Zapiski," ms. in Russian Archives, Columbia University, p. 737.

5. N. Kakurin, *Kak srazhalas' revoliutsiia*, 2 vols., (Moscow, Leningrad, 1925), I, 164.

6. Aleksashenko, *Krakh denikinshchiny*, p. 121. Denikin gives different figures, but he includes only the period from March to September 1919 and mentions aid only from England. According to Denikin, his army received 558 cannons, 12 tanks, 1,685,532 shells, and 160 million bullets. *Ocherki*, IV, 86n. Aleksashenko's data was taken from Soviet archives.

7. *Ocherki*, IV, 85. Denikin, who had had no contact with naval circles, had difficulties in finding a commander. On the advice of others, he decided to name Vice Admiral Sablin. Since Sablin was abroad, Denikin appointed Admiral Kanin to take the post temporarily. Kanin soon organized a large naval staff, but the officers had nothing to do since the navy did not yet have ships. Only during the victorious summer of 1919 did the White navy start to play a significant role in the hostilities.

8. By May 1919 thirty hospitals with two hundred beds each and six sanitary trains arrived in the port of Novorossisk. Report of P. P. Iurenev to National Center, Journals of meetings of National Center, May 18, Ekaterinodar, No. 24. Wrangel Military Archives, file 129, pp. 83–88, Hoover Institution.

9. J. Hodgson, *With Denikin's Armies* (London, 1932) p. 140.

10. H. N. H. Williamson, *Farewell to the Don* (New York, 1971), pp. 43–44.

11. Hodgson, *With Denikin's Armies*, pp. 180–181.

12. E. V. Maslovskii, "Nekatorye stranitsy moei zhizni," Columbia University Russian Archives, p. 1351.

13. *Ocherki*, IV, 82.

14. *Ibid.*, 94.

15. P. N. Wrangel, *Memoirs* (London, 1930), p. 59.

16. *Ocherki*, IV, 106–108.

17. For a description of the failure of the Eleventh and Twelfth armies, see Kakurin, *Kak srazhalas' revoliutsiia*, II, 57–72. The same events from the point of view of the Volunteer Army are described in *Ocherki*, IV, 106–113.

18. V. Dobrynin, *Bor'ba s bol'shevizmom na iuge Rossii: uchastie v bor'be donskogo kazachestva* (Prague, 1921) p. 111.

19. Egorov, pp. 69–73.

20. Dobrynin, *Bor'ba s bol'shevizmom*, p. 64.

21. *Ibid.*

22. *Ibid.*, p. 111.

23. *Ocherki*, V, 72–73.

24. Wrangel, *Memoirs*, p. 70. *Ocherki*, V, 79–80.

25. For Soviet evaluations of Denikin's strategy, see Egorov, *Razgrom Denikina*, p. 80, and Kakurin, *Kak srazhalas' revoliutsiia*, II, 97.

26. Egorov, *Razgrom Denikina*, p. 91.

27. Figures from *Ocherki*, V, 75; Kakurin, *Kak srazhalas' revoliutsiia*, II, 98; and Egorov, *Razgrom Denikina*, p. 86.

28. *Ocherki*, V, 73.

29 *Ibid.*, 73–75.

30. Wrangel described him: "If he had not worn uniform, you would have taken him for a comedian from a little provincial theater. He was as round as a barrel, and had a chubby face and a bulbous nose. He knew how to make himself pleasant,

and success had not robbed him of his hearty manner. But his conduct at his headquarters at Rostov aroused the indignation of every honest man. His orgies brought discredit on the Army and on authority in general." Wrangel, *Memoirs*, p. 87.

31. The description of Mai-Maevskii and his strategy is based largely on P. V. Makarov, *Adiutant generala Mai-Maevskogo; iz vospominanii nachal'nika otriada krasnykh partizan v Krymu* (Leningrad, 1929), especially pp. 17-18.

32. *Ocherki*, V, 80-81. Wrangel's refusal to take command was, of course, a remarkable act of insubordination. Such behavior would have never been tolerated in a regular army in time of war.

33. Grigorev's rising is described in great detail in Arthur Adams, *Bolsheviks in the Ukraine; the Second Campaign* (New Haven, 1963).

34. In a report to the Volunteer Army after his defection, Vsevolodov described how he concentrated his troops not in conjunction with the Eighth army, as he was ordered to do, but at some distance, which enabled the Whites to combat them separately. As a result of his actions, a Red Army division was destroyed. Kakurin, *Kak srazhalas' revoliutsiia*, II, 150-151.

35. Dobrynin, *Bor'ba s bol'shevizmom*, p. 74.

36. *Ocherki*, V, 78n.

37. *Ibid.*, 83-84 and 104-108.

38. Wrangel, *Memoirs*, p. 88.

39. Dobrynin, *Bor'ba s bol'shevizmom*, p. 111.

40. *Ocherki*, V, 108-109. Denikin in his memoirs left out point five and part of point six. Mine is a complete translation of what appears in the text.

41. Wrangel, *Memoirs*, p. 89.

42. *Ibid.*, pp. 88-89.

43. Erickson, *Soviet High Command*, pp. 65-67.

44. Aleksashenko, *Krakh denikinshchiny*, pp. 152-153.

45. Wrangel, *Memoirs*, p. 94.

46. Aleksashenko, *Krakh denikinshchiny*, pp. 152-153.

47. General Golubintsev, *Russkaia Vandeia; Ocherki Grazhdanskoi Voiny na Dony 1917-1920* (Munich, 1959), pp. 107-121; and Kakurin, *Kak srazhalas' revoliutsiia*, II, 296-302.

48. *Ocherki*, V, 122. In Kakurin's evaluation Mamontov caused a great deal more harm to the Bolsheviks than Denikin was willing to recognize. Kakurin, *Kak srazhalas' revoliutsiia*, II, 296ff.

49. *Ocherki*, V, 123.

CHAPTER 3. INSTITUTIONS

1. Miliukov, Denikin, Lukomskii, and the other military memoirists agree on this point. It is possible that the monarchists may have projected their own views on the officers, and in fact there was greater heterogeneity of opinion than what appears in primary sources.

2. A. S. Lukomskii, *Vospominaniia*, 2 vols. (Berlin, 1922), II, 1975.
3. A. I. Denikin, *Ocherki russkoi smuty*, 5 vols. (Paris and Berlin, 1921-1925), IV, 202.
4. The political program of the Volunteer Army in the first months of its existence is described in detail in Peter Kenez, *Civil War in South Russia, 1918* (Berkeley, 1971), pp. 73-87.
5. Denikin, *Ocherki*, IV, 211.
6. Lukomskii, *Vospominaniia*, II, 179.
7. Astrov's proposal will be discussed in more detail in Chapter Eight.
8. Denikin, *Ocherki*, V, 85.
9. A. I. Egorov, *Razgrom Denikina* (Moscow, 1931), p. 71.
10. Azbuka report from Kiev, May 19, 1919 (O.S.) Wrangel Military Archives, file 151, pp. 3-4, Hoover Archives, Stanford, California (hereafter WMA).
11. Azbuka report from Manikop district, May 23, 1919 (O.S.), WMA, file 133.
12. Reports of May 1 and May 5, 1919, Ekaterinodar. WMA, file 163, pp. 188-192.
13. Adzhemov reported to a meeting of the National Center. Journal No. 27, May 30, 1919 (O.S.), WMA, file 129. Denikin described the episode in *Ocherki*, V, 95. See also K. N. Sokolov, *Pravlenie generala Denikina* (Sofia, 1921), pp. 129-135.
14. Sokolov, *Pravlenie*, p. 133.
15. Denikin, *Ocherki*, V, 98.
16. Journals of the Special Council, No. 66, June 3, 1919 (O.S.), Wrangel Personal Archives, file 2 (hereafter WPA).
17. Azbuka report, Novocherkassk, June 3, 1919 (O.S.), WMA file 146, p. 190. The agents reported from the Don capital that the *inogorodnie* were enthusiastic about Denikin's order, and now expect a second order to follow in which he would take all power in his hands and thereby destroy the Cossack governments.
18. Denikin, *Ocherki*, V, 100, and Lukomskii, *Vospominaniia*, II, 151.
19. Sokolov, *Pravlenie*, pp. 138-160.
20. *Ibid.*, p. 161.
21. Denikin, *Ocherki*, V, 105.
22. See Denikin's characterization of members of the Special Council in *Ocherki*, IV, 206-210, and also Denikin's letter to Astrov, Nov. 24, 1924. In Panina files No. 5, Columbia Archives. Also Astrov's description in "Vospominaniia," pp. 509-510. Panina files No. 5, Columbia University, and Sokolov, *Pravlenie*, pp. 80-87. The basic law governing the functioning of the Special Council was approved by Denikin on February 15, 1919. The most important paragraphs are reprinted in *Ocherki*, IV, 203, and the entire document can be found in N. M. Mel'nikov, "Grazhdanskaia voina na iuga Rossii," ms., pp. 6-8, Columbia University. In 1919 N. M. Mel'nikov was the President of the Don Government, and in 1920 the head of the South Russian government.
23. Astrov to Denikin, October 23-26, 1924, in Panina files No. 5, Columbia University.
24. *Ibid.*

25. *Ibid.*

26. See the minutes of the Special Council, WPA. No. 1 and No. 2.

27. Kenez, *Civil War, 1918*, pp. 204–205.

28. Lukomskii, *Vospominaniia*, II, 149.

29. Sokolov, *Pravlenie*, p. 181, Mel'nikov, "Grazhdanskaia," pp. 20–29, Astrov, "Vospominaniia," p. 569. D. Kin, *Denikinshchina* (Leningrad, 1927), 72–74.

30. For Astrov's ideas on reconstructing the *zemstvo*, see his letter to Denikin, October 23–26, 1924 Panina files, No. 5, Columbia University.

31. Kin, *Denikinshchina*, p. 76.

32. *Iug Rossii*, July 24, 1919, p. 1.

33. Kin, *Denikinshchina*, p. 76. The percentage of voters who exercised their right in workers' districts was only between 6 and 10 percent.

34. *Ibid.*, p. 80.

35. *Ibid.*

36. Journals of the Special Council, September 19, 1919, WPA file 2.

37. Astrov to Denikin, October 23–26, 1924, Columbia Archives.

38. Journals of the Special Council, No. 54, April 23 (O.S.) 1919, WPA file 2.

39. Lukomskii *Vospominaniia*, II, 197.

40. Tikhobrazov, "Vospominaniia," p. 30.

41. Azbuka report from Novorossisk, March 13, 1919 (O.S.), WMA file 163, p. 125.

42. Azbuka report from Rostov, May 14, 1919 (O.S.), WMA file 146, p. 219.

43. Letter of M. I. A. Shleining to headquarters of Volunteer Army in Taganrog. August 20, 1919 (O.S.), WMA file 147, pp. 159–161.

44. The section of the Azbuka is based on the file the organization collected on itself. WMA file 136.

45. Material on Shulgin's life taken from D. Zaslavskii, *Rytsar' chernoi sotni V. V. Shulgin* (Leningrad, 1925).

46. Letter of Shulgin to Dragomirov, September 5, 1919 (O.S.), WMA file 136, p. 15.

47. *Ibid.*

48. *Ibid.*

49. Journals of the Special Council, No. 32, February 1, 1919 (O.S.), WPA file 1.

50. Shulgin to Dragomirov, May 19, 1919 (O.S.), WMA file 136, pp. 4–5.

51. Journals of the Special Council, No. 28, January 18, 1919, WPA file 1.

52. Shulgin to Dragomirov, May 19, 1919. WMA file 136, pp. 4–5.

53. Shulgin to Denikin, November 5, 1919 (O.S.), WMA file 136, p. 389.

54. From Fita and Zelo to Vedi. April 29, 1919 (O.S.), WMA file 136, pp. 12–13.

55. Azbuka report to head of political secretariat. May 27, 1919 (O.S.), WMA file 136, p. 117.

56. Nemo to Izhe, March 5, 1919 (O.S.), WMA file 136, p. 139.

57. Shulgin to Stepanov, January 6, 1919 (O.S.), WMA file 136, pp. 95–100.

NOTES TO PAGES 70–81

58. Lukomskii to Shulgin, June 15, 1919 (O.S.) and Azbuka to Lukomskii, June 21, 1919 (O.S.), WMA file 136, pp. 305–308.

59. Shulgin to Romanovskii, June 7, 1919, and Pliushchevskii-Pliushkin to Shulgin, June 11, 1919 (O.S.), WMA file 136, pp. 172–173.

60. Shulgin to Stepanov, February 6, 1919 (O.S.), WMA file 136, pp. 132–136.

61. Lukomskii to Shulgin, June 12, 1919 (O.S.), WMA file 136, p. 274.

62. Koiander to Shulgin, December 11, 1919 (O.S.), WMA file 136, p. 403.

63. Zaslavskii, *V. V. Shulgin*, pp. 70–71.

64. On the history of the Osvag, the best source is Sokolov, *Pravlenie*, pp. 93–115, and Melnikov, "Grazhdanskaia," pp. 120–123.

65. Journals of the Special Council, No. 28, January 18, 1919 (O.S.), WPA file 1.

66. Paramonov to Romanovskii, January 4, 1919 (O.S.), WMA file 130.

67. Sokolov, *Pravlenie*, p. 97.

68. Lukomskii, *Vospominaniia*, II, 184.

69. Sokolov, *Pravlenie*, p. 104.

70. *Ibid.*, p. 106.

71. Political summary prepared by the Osvag for the Stavka, May 18, 1919 (O.S.), WMA 133.

72. Sokolov, *Pravlenie*, p. 107.

73. Azbuka report on organizing middle peasants and establishing ties with the villages. Odessa, February 1919, WMA file 130, pp. 1–7.

74. Intelligence report, October 28 Kharkov (O.S.), WMA file 146, pp. 58–61.

75. Journals of the meetings of the Council to the Commander-in-Chief. No. 14, June 4, 1920 (O.S.), WPA file 4. The representative of the Chruch, however, was invited to join the sessions whenever church matters were discussed, and the Chief of Church administration was empowered to report directly to Wrangel.

76. Boris Kandidov, *Religioznaia kontrrevoliutsiia 1918–1920 gg.* (Moscow, 1930), pp. 28–29. When the first foreign ships arrived in Novorossisk harbor in November 1918, the foreigners were greeted with churchbells ringing (p. 37).

77. Journals of the Special Council No. 19, December 14, 1918 (O.S.), WPA file 1.

78. Report of N. N. Lvov to the National Center, No. 26, May 25 Ekaterinodar (O.S.), WMA file 129. Also Denikin, *Ocherki*, IV, pp. 234–236.

79. Azbuka report from the Crimea June 27, 1919 (O.S.), WMA file 183, pp. 263–264.

80. For the Union for Regeneration, see V. Maĭkotin, "Iz nedalekogo proshlogo," *Na chuzhoi storone*, No. 2, 1923, pp. 178–199; No. 3, 1923, pp. 179–193; No. 5, 1924, pp. 251–268; No. 6, 1924, pp. 73–100; No. 9, 1925, pp. 279–302; No. 11, 1924, pp. 205–236; No. 13, 1925, pp. 193–227.

81. Intelligence report from Kharkov, October 19, 1919 (O.S.), WMA file 146, pp. 63–66.

82. Denikin to Astrov, November 24, 1924, Panina files no. 5, Columbia University.

83. The role of the Kadets is described exhaustively by W. G. Rosenberg, *Liberals in the Russian Revolution. The Constitutional Democratic Party, 1917–1921* (Princeton, 1974), pp. 333–356.

84. Petrunkevich to Astrov, March 14, 1919 (N.S.), Gaspra. WMA file 152, pp. 107–108.

85. Denikin, *Ocherki*, V, 155.

86. Intelligence report on the Don. July 1, 1919 (O.S.), WMA file 146, pp. 173–174.

87. Report on monarchist organizations. June 17, 1919 (N.S.), WMA file 150, p. 206.

CHAPTER 4. POLICIES

1. The relationship between the Cossacks and the *inogorodnie* is described in some detail in Peter Kenez, *Civil War in South Russia, 1918* (Berkeley, 1971), pp. 37–44.

2. Azbuka reports on the mood among the peasantry in Wrangel Military Archives, files 130, 131, 136, 145, 146. Hoover Institution, Stanford University.

3. A. I. Denikin, *Ocherki russkoi smuty*, 5 vols. (Paris and Berlin, 1921–1925), IV, 212.

4. M. Mal't, "Denikinshchina i krestianstvo," *Proletarskaia revoliutsiia*, Apr. 1924, No. 4., p. 145.

5. Kolokoltsev's project can be found in WMA file 130, pp. 253–257.

6. Mal't, "Denikinshchina," p. 157.

7. D. Kin, *Denikinshchina* (Leningrad, 1927), pp. 103–106.

8. K. N. Sokolov, *Pravlenie generala Denikina* (Sofia, 1921), pp. 187–189.

9. Denikin, *Ocherki*, IV, 212.

10. *Ibid.*, IV, 224.

11. G. N. Rakovskii, *V stane belykh* (Constantinople, 1920), pp. 41–42.

12. Denikin, *Ocherki*, IV, 212–213.

13. Kin, *Denikinshchina*, p. 90.

14. Journals of the meetings of the National Center, No. 21., Ekaterinodar, Apr. 20, 1919 (O.S.), WMA file 129.

15. Sokolov, *Pravlenie*, p. 189.

16. Denikin, *Ocherki*, V, 155.

17. Journals of the Special Council, June 26, 1919 (O.S.), Wrangel Personal Archives (WPA) file 2. Hoover Institution, Stanford University.

18. Journals of the Special Council, Sept. 12, 1919 (O.S.), WPA file 2.

19. *Ibid.*, June 26, 1919 (O.S.).

20. M. Mal't, "Denikinshchina i krestianstvo," *Proletarskaia revoliutsiia*, Jan. 1924, No. 1., p. 153.

21. *Ibid.*, p. 145.

22. "The economy of South Russia," Intelligence report, March 28, 1919 (O.S.), WMA file 150, pp. 196–205.

23. Journals of the Special Council, March 5, 1919 (O.S.), No. 41, WPA file 2.

24. This was the distribution of Imperial Russia's gold supply: Kolchak had 652 million, the Bolsheviks had 147 million, and the Allies had 320 million. Denikin, *Ocherki*, IV, 226. On the history of Russia's gold reserves, see A. Michelson *et al.*, *Russian Public Finance During the War* (New Haven, 1928), pp. 452–455.

25. Bernatskii described his reform plan in a report to the National Center, May 2, 1919 (O.S.), Ekaterinodar, No. 23. WMA file 129.

26. Denikin, *Ocherki*, IV, 226.

27. *Ibid.*

28. Kin, *Denikinshchina*, p. 138.

29. *Ibid.*, pp. 139–140.

30. Intelligence report, Oct, 19, 1919 (O.S.), WMA file 146, pp. 63–66.

31. Denikin, *Ocherki*, IV, 227; and Kin, *Denikinshchina*, p. 141.

32. "The economy of South Russia," WMA file 150, p. 196.

33. *Ibid.*

34. Kin, *Denikinshchina*, p. 115.

35. *Ibid.*, p. 117.

36. "Economic Report," WMA file 150.

37. Kin, *Denikinshchina*, p. 119.

38. *Ibid.*, p. 135.

39. *Ibid.*, pp. 136–137.

40. Journals of the Special Council, No. 32, February 14, 1919 (O.S.), WPA file 2.

41. Kin, *Denikinshchina*, p. 137.

42. *Ibid.*, p. 123.

43. "Economic Report," WMA file 150.

44. Kin, *Denikinshchina*, p. 129.

45. A. S. Lukomskii, *Vospominaniia* (Berlin, 1922), 2 vols, II, 192.

46. Denikin, *Ocherki*, IV, 229.

47. Kin, *Denikinshchina*, pp. 138–139. One might mention here that the Bolsheviks did not exchange Volunteer Army money. They argued, disingenuously, that while the annulment of Soviet money hurt the poor, the annulment of White money hurt only the rich.

48. Denikin, *Ocherki*, IV, 214.

49. *Ibid.*, IV, 214–215. Denikin remarked in his memoirs that public opinion received his proposals on labor legislation without interest.

50. Journals of the Special Council. Oct. 22, 1919 (O.S.), No. 103, WPA file 2.

51. M. Mal't, "Denikinshchina i rabochie," *Proletarskaia revoliutsiia*, May 1924, No. 5, p. 78; Kin, *Denikinshchina*, p. 161.

52. See, for example, the intelligence report from Novocherkassk, June 13, 1919 (O.S.), WMA file 146, p. 198.

53. B. Kolesnikov, *Professional'noe dvizhenie i kontr-revoliutsiia* (n.p. 1923), pp. 209–210. The memorandum is printed on pp. 384–387.

54. *Ibid.*, 387–390.

55. *Ibid.*, 221.

56. *Ibid.*, 393–395.
57. *Ibid.*, 229–230.
58. Denikin, *Ocherki*, IV, 221.
59. Kolesnikov, *Professional'noe*, p. 231.
60. On Kirsta's movement, see G. Kuchin-Oranskii, *Dobrovol'cheskaia zubatov-shchina. Kirstovskie organizatsii na iuge Rossii i bor'ba s nimi professional'nykh soiuzov* (n.p. 1924); Kolesnikov, *Professional'noe*, pp. 263–286; Kin, *Denikinshchina*, p. 245–256.
61. Kolesnikov, *Professional'noe*, pp. 254–255.
62. Kin, *Denikinshchina*, p. 152.
63. *Ibid.*, 152–153.
64. *Ibid.*, 146.
65. Intelligence report from Kiev, Sept. 8, 1919 (O.S.), WMA file 148, pp. 352–359.
66. *Ibid.*, and Intelligence report from Kiev, Oct. 1919 (O.S.), WMA file 188, p. 128.
67. Kuchin-Oranskii, *Dobrovol'cheskaia*, p. 10.

CHAPTER 5. THE COSSACKS

1. P. N. Shatilov, "Zapiski," ms. in Russian Archives, Columbia University, p. 824.
2. I. Borisenko, *Sovetskie respubliki na severnom Kavkaze*, 2 vols. (Rostov, 1930), I, 23 and 108.
3. G. Pokrovskii, *Denikinshchina: god politiki i ekonomiki na Kubani (1918–1919)*, (Berlin, 1923), p. 42.
4. Peter Kenez, *Civil War in South Russia, 1918* (Berkeley, 1971), p. 230.
5. Pokrovskii, *Denikinshchina*, p. 116; and A. I. Denikin, *Ocherki russkoi smuty*, 5 vols. (Berlin and Paris, 1921–1925), IV, 54.
6. D. E. Skobtsov, *Tri goda revoliutsii i grazhdanskoi voiny na Kubani* (Paris n.d.), p. 68.
7. Pokrovskii, *Denikinshchina*, pp. 130–131.
8. Political survey, August 14–September 14, 1919, Wrangle Military Archives (WMA), Hoover Institution, file 162, p. 117. These surveys were prepared by the political section of the General Staff for the use of the Chief of Staff and Commander-in-Chief.
9. Denikin, *Ocherki*, II, 279.
10. *Ibid.*, IV, 58–59.
11. Pokrovskii, *Denikinshchina*, p. 167; and Political survey, August 14–September 14 in WMA file 162, p. 117.
12. Skobtsov, *Tri goda*, p. 13.
13. Memorandum of the parliamentary delegation of the Kuban Cossacks, Paris, April 16, 1919, WMA file 129.
14. Political survey, May 14–28, 1919, WMA file 162, p. 75.

15. Pokrovskii, *Denikinshchina*, p. 125.

16. Skobtsov, *Tri goda*, p. 72.

17. Political survey, June 14–28, WMA file 162, pp. 36–38.

18. Political survey, June 28–July 14, WMA file 162, pp. 92–94.

19. Denikin, *Ocherki*, V, 191, and A. I. Egorov, *Razgrom Denikina* (Moscow, 1931), p. 56.

20. Intelligence report from the Don, February 1919, WMA file 150, p. 85. Bogaevskii received 239 votes against Krasnov's 52.

21. V. Dobrynin, *Bor'ba s bolshevizmom na iuge Rossii: uchastie v bor'be donskogo kazachestva* (Prague, 1921), p. 69.

22. Denikin, *Ocherki*, IV, 80.

23. Krasnov to unknown correspondent. August 1, 1920 (O.S.), Berlin, Wrangel Personal Archives (WPA) file 36. Hoover Institution.

24. Intelligence report, Novocherkassk, April 10, 1919 (O.S.), WMA file 150, pp. 185–186.

25. Intelligence report No. 6, February 3, 1919 (O.S.), WMA file 150, p. 88. Democratic public opinion blamed the reactionary Rodionov organization for the murder attempt.

26. Pokrovskii, *Denikinshchina*, pp. 232–239.

27. Dobrynin, *Bor'ba s bolshevizmom*, pp. 77–78; L. I. Berz and K. A. Khmelevskii, *Geroicheskie gody; Oktiabrskaia revoliutsiia i grazhdanskaia voina na Donu* (Rostov, 1964), pp. 264–265.

28. Denikin, *Ocherki*, V, 190.

29. D. S. Babichev, *Donskoe trudovoe kazachestvo v bor'be za vlast' sovetov* (Rostov on the Don, 1969), p. 6.

30. Denikin, *Ocherki*, IV, 97.

31. R. E. Pipes, *The Formation of the Soviet Union: Communism and Nationalism, 1917–1923* (Cambridge, Mass., 1957), p. 94.

32. Pipes, *Formation*, p. 95; Borisenko, *Sovetskie respubliki*, II, 23. The per capita ownership of land of the Kabardians was 17.5 *desiatina*. The Ingush average was 5.8 and the Chechen 3.0.

33. Pipes, *Formation*, pp. 195–199.

34. Borisenko, *Sovetskie respubliki*, II, pp. 234–236.

35. Denikin, *Ocherki*, IV, 100.

36. *Ibid.*, IV, 100–105.

37. E. V. Maslovskii, "Nekatorye stranitsy moei zhizni," ms. in Russian Archives, Columbia University, p. 1406.

38. Political survey, August 14–September 14, 1919, WMA file 162, p. 118.

39. A. N. Grekov, "Soiuz kazachikh voisk v Petrograde v 1917 godu," *Donskaia Letopis'*, vol. 2, pp. 229–282.

40. Kenez, *Civil War, 1918*, p. 145.

41. Denikin, *Ocherki*, IV, 55.

42. Skobtsov, *Tri goda*, p. 24. Kharlamov had played a major role in the organization of the Cossack Council in 1917.

43. Denikin, *Ocherki*, V, 202.

44. Lukomskii to Shulgin, June 15, 1919 (O.S.), WMA file 136, P. 305.

45. Pokrovskii, *Denikinshchina*, pp. 148–150.

46. Political survey, June 28–July 14, 1919, WMA file 162, p. 108.

47. Denikin, *Ocherki*, V, 203.

48. K. N. Sokolov, *Pravlenie generala Denikina* (Sofia, 1921), pp. 201–207.

49. *Ibid.*, p. 203; also Political survey, August 14–September 14, 1919, WMA file 162, pp. 127–128.

50. Political survey, WMA file 162, pp. 127–128.

51. A. P. Filimonov, "Razgrom Kubanskoi rady," *Arkhiv Russkoi Revoliutsii (ARR)*, vol. 5, p. 324.

52. Denikin, *Ocherki*, IV, 52.

53. K. N. Sokolov, "Kubanskoe deistvo," *Arkhiv Russkoi Revoliutsii*, vol. 18, p. 239.

54. P. N. Shatilov, "Zapiski," ms. in Russian Archives, Columbia University, p. 798.

55. On the preparation of the coup, see Shatilov, "Zapiski," pp. 797–802; Denikin, *Ocherki*, V, 208; Sokolov, *ARR*, pp. 240–246.

56. Wrangel to Lukomskii, October 14, 1919 (O.S.), Olga Wrangel Archives (OWA) file 2, Hoover Institution.

57. Denikin, *Ocherki*, V, 208.

58. *Ibid.*; Shatilov, "Zapiski," p. 799.

59. Wrangel to Lukomskii, October 27, 1919 (O.S.), OWA file 2.

60. Denikin, *Ocherki*, V, 210; Filimonov, *ARR*, pp. 325–326.

61. Denikin, *Ocherki*, V, p. 210 note.

62. Filimonov, *ARR*, pp. 325–326.

63. At least this is Sokolov's version. There is reason to believe that Wrangel was dismayed. His letters to Lukomskii and Pokrovskii betrayed great pessimism about the loyalty of the soldiers. Sokolov, *ARR*, p. 246. Letters of Wrangel to Pokrovskii and Lukomskii in OWA file 2.

64. Pokrovskii, *Denikinshchina*, p. 240.

65. Filimonov and Kurganskii to Denikin, October 30 (O.S.). Telegram, Ekaterinodar, OWA file 2.

66. Filimonov, *ARR*, pp. 325–327.

67. Romanovskii to Wrangel, October 30, 1919 (O.S.), OWA file 2. The complete text of Romanovskii's telegram was: "You received an order that you should act in consultation with Ataman. Now the Commander-in-Chief orders that in view of the opinions expressed by the Ataman you should act alone."

68. Pokrovskii, *Denikinshchina*, p. 240ff.

69. Wrangel to Pokrovskii, November 6, 1919 (O.S.), OWA file 2.

70. Wrangel's telegram to Denikin, November 8, 1919 (O.S.), OWA file 2, No. 33; Sokolov, *ARR*, p. 25.

71. Filimonov, *ARR*, p. 329.

72. Conversation between Wrangel and Pokrovskii by Hughes teletype. Taganrog-Ekaterinodar, November 11, 1919 (O.S.), OWA file 2, No. 36.

73. Sokolov, *ARR*, p. 247.

74. Conversation between Pokrovskii and Wrangel by Hughes teletype. November 11, 1919 (O.S.), Ekaterinodar-Rostov. OWA file 2, No. 38.

75. According to Denikin, Bukretov was Jewish. *Ocherki*, V, 216.

CHAPTER 6. THE UKRAINE

1. There is an extensive literature on the complex Ukrainian Civil War. My account is largely based on these sources: R. E. Pipes, *The Formation of the Soviet Union: Communism and Nationalism, 1917–1923* (Cambridge, Mass., 1957); J. S. Reshetar, *The Ukrainian Revolution* (Princeton, 1952); Jurij Borys, *The Russian Communist Party and the Sovietization of the Ukraine* (Stockholm, 1960); N. I. Suprunenko, *Ocherki istorii grazhdanskoi voiny i inostrannoi voennoi interventsii na Ukraine* (Moscow, 1966). Henceforth, these four sources will be cited by author and page number only.

2. Borys, p. 54.

3. Pipes, pp. 56–58.

4. Reshetar, p. 66.

5. Suprunenko, p. 127.

6. *Ibid.*, p. 67.

7. *Ibid.*, p. 195.

8. Borys, pp. 225–226.

9. Azbuka report on Greens. June 9, 1919 (O.S.) Wrangel Military Archives (WMA), file 145, p. 46. Hoover Institution, Stanford, California.

10. Peter Kenez, *Civil War in South Russia, 1918* (Berkeley, 1971), pp. 236–240.

11. Report of agent I. P. Demidov from Kiev, Nov. 10, 1919 (O.S.), WMA file 147, p. 135.

12. A. I. Denikin, *Ocherki russkoi smuty*, 5 vols. (Paris and Berlin 1921–1925), V, 143–145.

13. Intelligence report from Kiev, Sept. 8, 1919 (O.S.), WMA file 148, pp. 352–359.

14. Denikin, *Ocherki*, V, 142–143.

15. *Ibid.*, V, 16–17.

16. *Ibid.*, V, 255.

17. *Ibid.*

18. *Ibid.*, V, 255–256.

19. Report from Seventh division, September 4, 1919 (O.S.), WMA file 148, p. 390.

20. A. A. Goldenveizer, "Iz Kievskikh vospominanii," *Arkhiv Russkoi Revoliutsii (ARR)* (Berlin, 1922), vol. 6., pp. 258–261.

21. Denikin, *Ocherki*, V. 258.

22. *Ibid.*.

23. *Ibid.*, V, 256.

24. *Ibid.*, V, 143.

25. Intelligence report from Kiev, Sept. 8, 1919 (O.S.), WMA file 148, pp. 352–359.

26. Denikin, *Ocherki*, V, 143.

27. Intelligence report from Kiev, Sept. 8, 1919 (O.S.), WMA file 148, pp. 352–359.

28. Osvag report from Kiev, Oct. 1919, WMA file 188, p. 127.

29. Denikin, *Ocherki*, V, 140 and 142.

30. According to the intelligence report from the Ukraine of July 6, 1919 (O.S.), WMA file 146, p. 40, the occupying armies found five hundred mutilated bodies. The Bolshevisk also took hostages with them. The Bolsheviks were surprised by the quick collapse of their front. They panicked but were determined to destroy their internal enemies.

31. Intelligence report from Kharkov, no date. WMA file 129, p. 190.

32. Political survey, June 14–28 (N.S.), 1919, WMA file 162, p. 30.

33. *Ibid.*

34. Intelligence report from Kharkov, Aug. 9, 1919 (O.S.), WMA file 146, pp. 130–131. The reporter complained that "the peasants have no feeling of patriotism and that they do not understand the principle of Indivisible Russia."

35. Intelligence report from Kharkov on political life, July 27, 1919 (O.S.), WMA file 146, pp. 178–179.

36. *Ibid.*

37. Intelligence report from Kharkov, Oct. 19, 1919 (O.S.), WMA file 146, pp. 63–66. "Obsofaz," the organization of factory owners, tried to get rid of trade unions and mutual insurance organizations among the workers. The tactless policy of Obsofaz, according to the reporter, sparked a strike among the metallurgists, which lasted for two days, Oct. 17–18.

38. *Ibid.* The people coined the word "shkurinets" from Shkuro to denote a lawless marauder.

39. *Ibid.*

40. Goldenveizer, *ARR*, p. 260.

41. Report from Kiev by I. P. Demidov, Nov. 10, 1919 (O.S.), WMA file 147, p. 135. The illegal paper *Rus'* appeared at irregular intervals, but in several thousand copies. Underground agents also printed posters. *Rus'* became a most popular paper after the occupation of the city by the Volunteer Army.

42. *Ibid.*, p. 262.

43. Demidov's report, written in Nov. 1919, WMA file 147, p. 135, criticizes the Army for not having created a skeletal form of administration before occupying Kiev.

44. Intelligence report from Kiev, September 8, 1919 (O.S.), WMA file 148, pp. 352–359.

45. *Ibid.* People who could not get into Bredov's waiting room were standing in the street, while soldiers kept order among them.

46. *Ibid.*

47. Ataman Grigorev's colorful story is best described in A. E. Adams, *Bolsheviks in the Ukraine; the Second Campaign* (New Haven, 1963).

48. Azbuka report from Kiev, April 29, 1919 (O.S.), WMA file 151, pp. 86–88. Zelennyi said that workers, who made up 6 percent of the population of the Ukraine, had no right to rule the country.

49. Azbuka report from Kiev, May 19, 1919 (O.S.), WMA file 151, pp. 3–4.

50. Denikin, *Ocherki*, V, 132.

51. *Ibid.*, V, 134.

52. My main source on Makhno is P. Arshinov, *Istoriia makhnovskogo dvizheniia, 1918–1921* (Berlin, 1923).

53. *Ibid.*, pp. 48–51.

54. David Footman, *Civil War in Russia* (London, 1961), p. 246.

55. Arshinov, *Istoriia*, p. 51.

56. *Ibid.*, p. 82.

57. At least this was the estimate of White intelligence sources. Report from Ekaterinoslav. September 1919 (O.S.), WMA file 166, pp. 46–47.

58. Arshinov, *Istoriia*, pp. 139–141.

59. J. Hodgson, *With Denikin's Armies* (London, 1932), p. 119.

60. S. Gusev-Orenburgskii, *Kniga o evreiskikh pogromakh na Ukraine v 1919 g.* (Petrograd, n.d.), p. 9.

61. General Tikhobrazov, "Vospominaniia," ms. in Russian Archives, Columbia University, Chapter 26, p. 10.

62. N. I. Shtif, *Pogromy na Ukraine (Period Dobrovol'cheskoi Armii)* (Berlin, 1922), pp. 10–14.

63. Shtif, *Pogromy*, pp. 17–23; Gusev-Orenburgskii, pp. 15; Goldenveizer, *ARR*, p. 267.

64. Zvi Gitelman, *Jewish Nationality and Soviet Politics. The Jewish Sections of the CPSU, 1917–1930* (Princeton, 1972), p. 161.

65. Shtif, *Pogromy*, p. 7.

66. *Ibid.*, p. 16.

67. Goldenveizer, *ARR*, p. 268.

68. Elias Heifetz, *The Slaughter of the Jews in the Ukraine, 1919* (New York, 1921), p. 112.

69. Denikin, *Ocherki*, V, 151.

70. Gusev-Orenburgskii, *Kniga*, p. 14.

71. Ilya Trotzky, "Jewish Pogroms in the Ukraine and in Byelorussia (1918–1920)," in *Russian Jewry* (New York, 1969), edited by G. Aronson, J. Frumkin, A. Goldenveiser, and J. Lewitan, p. 87.

72. Heifetz, *Slaughter*, p. 173.

73. Shtif, *Pogromy*, p. 24.

74. WMA file 146.

75. Report of Olfer'ev, Taganrog, November 14, 1919. WMA File 166, pp. 22–25.

76. I. M. Kalinin, *Pod znamenem Vrangelia* (Leningrad, 1925), pp. 126–127.

77. J. S. Curtiss, *The Russian Church and the Soviet State* (Boston, 1953), p. 101.

78. Shtif, *Pogromy*, p. 71.

79. Goldenveizer, *ARR*, p. 260.

80. *Ibid.*, p. 259.

81. Resolution of the Conference of the Party of People's Freedom. Kharkov, November 3–6, 1919, WMA file 129.

82. Tikhobrazov, "Vospominaniia," p. 10.

83. Denikin, *Ocherki*, V, 145.

84. *Ibid.*, 150.

85. Shtif, *Pogromy*, p. 65.

86. *Ibid.*, p. 84.

87. *Ibid.*, p. 75.

88. Hodgson, *With Denikin's Armies*, pp. 54–55.

89. *Ibid.*, p. 55.

90. Peter Kenez, "A profile of the prerevolutionary officer corps," *California Slavic Studies*, vol. 7 (Berkeley, 1973), p. 148.

CHAPTER 7. INTERVENTION

1. Jean Xydias, *L'intervention francaise en Russie* (Paris, 1927), p. 163. Also quoted in George Brinkley, *The Volunteer Army and Allied Intervention in South Russia, 1917–1921* (Notre Dame, 1966), p. 88.

2. Jurij Borys, *The Russian Communist Party and the Sovietization of the Ukraine* (Stockholm, 1960), p. 62. The figures are from the 1926 census. According to Borys, it is likely that in 1919 the percentage of Ukrainians was even smaller.

3. The Literature on the French occupation of Odessa is enormous. The most detailed description in English is in Brinkley, pp. 113–145. The role of the Kadets in Odessa is discussed in William G. Rosenberg, *The Liberals in the Russian Revolution* (Princeton, 1974), pp. 352–356; Denikin's attitude to events in Odessa can be seen in A. I. Denikin, *Ocherki russkoi smuty* (Berlin and Paris, 1921–1925), 5 vols., V, 8–54. See also Xydias, *L'intervention;* A. S. Sannikov, "Vospominaniia," ms. in Russian Archives, Columbia University; "Ocherk vzaimootnoshenii Vooruzhenykh Sil' Iuga Rossii i predstavitelei frantsuzskogo komandovaniia," *Arkhiv Russkoi Revoliutsii*, vol. 16, pp. 233–262; A. I. Gukovskii, *Frantsuzskaia interventsiia* (Moscow, 1928).

4. Xydias, *L'intervention*, p. 137.

5. Denikin, *Ocherki*, V, 8.

6. Some attributed his russophilia to the influence of his Russian-Jewish wife. E. N. Trubetskoi, "Iz putevykh zametok bezhentsa," *ARR*, vol. 18, p. 165.

7. *Ibid.*, p. 163.

8. Denikin, *Ocherki*, V, 11.

9. Rosenberg, *Liberals*, p. 353.

10. Denikin, *Ocherki*, V, 17. The cabinet had eight departments. The department of communication had a single railroad station under its jurisdiction.

11. *Ibid.*, V, 18.

12. Letter of Shulgin to Stepanov, February 6, 1919, Odessa. Wrangel Military Archives (WMA), Hoover Institution, file 136, pp. 132–136.

13. Denikin, *Ocherki*, V, 20.

14. Col. Novikov, "Bor'ba s bol'shevikami v Novorossiiskom krae," Makhrov files, Russian Archives, Columbia, pp. 5–6.

15. J. S. Reshetar, *The Ukrainian Revolution* (Princeton, 1952), pp. 241–245; Denikin, *Ocherki*, V, 35–36.

16. Trubetskoi, "Iz putevykh," p. 164.

17. *Ibid.*

18. Brinkley, *Volunteer Army*, p. 118.

19. Trubetskoi, "Iz putevykh," pp. 197–199.

20. Rosenberg, *Liberals*, p. 355.

21. Trubetskoi, "Iz putevykh," p. 199.

22. Sannikov, "Vospominaniia," p. 4.

23. Grishin-Almazov's proclamation to officers in Kiev, dated December 25, 1919, in WMA file 132.

24. Sannikov, "Vospominaniia," p. 10.

25. *Ibid.*, p. 14. The Russians expected that the German colonists who lived in the nearby villages would be willing recruits. Indeed, when this area came under White rule in the summer of 1919 many Germans volunteered.

26. Sannikov, "Vospominaniia," pp. 11–12.

27. *Ibid.*, p. 16.

28. *Ibid.*, pp. 44–45.

29. *Ibid.*, p. 19; Denikin, *Ocherki*, V, 40.

30. On Grigorev's advance, see Arthur Adams, *Bolsheviks in the Ukraine; the Second Campaign* (New Haven, 1963), pp. 167–214.

31. Sannikov, "Vospominaniia," p. 27.

32. *Ibid.*, p. 38; Denikin, *Ocherki*, V, 46; Novikov, "Bor'ba s bol'shevikami," pp. 14–15.

33. Ia. I. Kefeli, "S Generalom A. V. Shvartsem v Odesse," Russian Archives, Columbia University, p. 21.

34. Denikin, *Ocherki*, V, 51.

35. *Ibid.*, p. 47.

36. *Ibid.*, p. 51.

37. Xydias, *L'intervention*, pp. 302–205.

38. The description of the evacuation and the march of the Timanovskii brigade is based on the Political survey, April 28–May 14 (N.S.), 1919, WMA, p. 66.

39. The best and most detailed description of the history of the Kadet government in English is in Rosenberg, *Liberals*, pp. 357–381.

40. Richard E. Pipes, *The Formation of the Soviet Union; Communism and Nationalism, 1917–1923* (Cambridge, 1954), pp. 79–81.

41. *Ibid.*, p. 185.

42. V. Obolenskii, "Krym v 1917–1920 gg," *Na chuzhoi storone*, V, 20–24.

43. Denikin, *Ocherki*, III, 44.

44. Rosenberg, *Liberals*, p. 363.

45. M. M. Vinaver, *Nashe pravitel'stvo* (Paris, 1928), p. 7.

46. Rosenberg, *Liberals*, p. 359.

47. Denikin, *Ocherki*, V, 54.

48. Vinaver, *Nashe pravitel'stvo*, pp. 51–52.

49. Documents of the Crimean government, file 18. Hoover Institution.

50. Vinaver, *Nashe pravitel'stvo*, pp. 139–141.

51. *Ibid.*, p. 153. Denikin remained unsatisfied. He criticized the December 20 deadline. In Vinaver's opinion, Denikin's criticism was based on confusing the old and the new calendars.

52. N. N. Bogdanov, "Krymskoe kraevoe pravitel'stvo," pp. 13–14, Documents of the Crimean government, file 19, Hoover Institutions; Vinaver, *Nashe pravitel'stvo*, p. 146.

53. Denikin, *Ocherki*, V, 60.

54. Bogdanov, "Krymskoe kraevoe pravitel'stvo," p. 14.

55. *Ibid.*, p. 15.

56. *Ibid.*, p. 14; Vinaver, *Nashe pravitel'stvo*, pp. 173–176.

57. N. I. Astrov, "Vospominaniia," Panina files No. 5, Russian Archives, Columbia University, pp. 575–583; Vinaver, *Nashe pravitel'stvo*, p. 142. Stepanov, Astrov, and Lukomskii arrived in Simferopol on December 22. Vinaver prepared a draft for discussion, which was based on Denikin's letter to de Bode. Although there was an agreement on basic principles, the discussions were not always friendly. The representatives of the Volunteer Army disliked Nabokov's insistence on trying every Bolshevik; they maintained that there was no time for observing legal niceties. Another disputed issue was the supply of the Volunteer fleet. The Crimean ministers believed that the fleet belonged to the entire country and therefore it was wrong to expect the Crimea alone to feed it. Nevertheless, they accepted this responsibility.

58. S. S. Krym, "Otchet po poezdke v shtab Dobrovol'cheskoi Armii chlenov Krymskogo Kraevogo Pravitel'stva," Documents of the Crimean government, file 17.

59. Crimean government declaration, Documents of the Crimean government, file 18.

60. D. S. Pasmanik, *Revoliutsionnye gody v Krymu* (Paris, 1926), p. 184.

61. Bogdanov, "Krymskoe kraevoe pravitel'stvo," p. 18.

62. Pasmanik, *Revoliutsionnye gody*, pp. 184–185.

63. Borovskii's letter is in file 17, Documents of the Crimean government.

64. Denikin's letter is also in file 17.

65. Obolenskii, *Na chuzhoi storone*, VII, 94–99.

66. Denikin, *Ocherki*, V, 62. Denikin is correct in saying that sending such a small force to the Crimea made absolutely no sense.

67. Pasmanik, *Revoliutsionnye gody*, p. 155.

68. Denikin, *Ocherki*, V, 63.

69. *Ibid.*

70. A. I. Gukovskii, *Frantsuzskaia interventsiia na iuge Rossii, 1918–1919* (Moscow, 1928), p. 214. The government's proclamation asked the *zemstvo* and city organizations to assume administrative functions.

71. Denikin, *Ocherki*, V, 64.

72. Minutes of the meeting of the cabinet, April 16, 1919, Documents of the Crimean government, file 12; Gukovskii, *Frantsuzskaia interventsiia*, pp. 214–215.

73. Vinaver, *Nashe pravitel'stvo*, p. 212.

74. D. Tikhobrazov, "Vospominaniia," chapter 27, p. 7, Russian Archives, Columbia University.

75. The relations between Georgia and the Volunteer Army in 1918 are described in Peter Kenez, *Civil War in South Russia, 1918* (Berkeley, 1971), pp. 240–252.

76. "Kratkaia zapiska istorii vzaimootnoshenii D. A. s Gruziei," a report prepared by the headquarters of the Volunteer Army for General Briggs in February 1919. WMA file 153, pp. 116–123.

77. Denikin, *Ocherki*, IV, 156.

78. *Ibid.*, pp. 161–162.

79. *Ibid.*

80. "Soon Kolchak and Denikin will unite—this is only a matter of weeks. Then the Italians and English will go away, but Russia will remain and therefore it is necessary to establish good relations with it. I give you my advice, if you take it, overcome your vanity and stretch out your hand to Denikin saying, we are with you." Protocol of meeting of the Georgian government with Generals Beech and Briggs. Tbilisi, May 23, 1919. "Demokraticheskoi pravitel'stvo Gruzii i angliiskoe komandovanie," *Krasny Arkhiv*, vol. 25, 1927, p. 106.

81. E. V. Maslovskii, "Nekatorye stransitsy moei zhizni," Russian Archives, Columbia University, pp. 1468–1469.

82. Denikin, *Ocherki*, IV, 137–138. The instructions were prepared by Lukomskii, but Denikin also signed the document.

83. *Ibid.*, p. 139.

84. The description of the attitude of the Georgians toward the Volunteer Army is taken from a report prepared by an Azbuka agent. "Doklad o Gruzii," August 18, 1919, WMA file 141, pp. 57–64.

85. Maslovskii, "Nekatorye stransitsy," pp. 1473–1479. Maslovskii at the time was chief of staff of the Caucasian army whose task was to put down rebellions.

86. *Ibid.*, pp. 1512–1513.

87. Brinkley, *Volunteer Army*, p. 230.

88. Denikin, *Ocherki*, V, 308 note.

89. Brinkley, *Volunteer Army*, p. 231.

90. Maslovskii, "Nekatorye stransitsy," pp. 1512ff.

91. Pipes, *Formation*, p. 206.

92. Erdeli reported to the National Center. Journals of the meeting of the National Center, No. 20, Ekaterinodar, April 12 (O.S.), 1919, WMA file 129. Erdeli had first traveled to Tbilisi. Everywhere he received an unfriendly reception.

93. Denikin communicated with the Azerbaidzhani government by sending an agent, Col. Lazarev, to General Thomson. Lazarev exceeded his instructions

by not indicating that Denikin promised only a temporary recognition. The Baku government, however, was not misled. They knew about Denikin's policies from reading the Russian press. Denikin, *Ocherki*, IV, 171.

94. Z. D. Avalov, *The Independence of Georgia in International Politics, 1918–1921* (London, 1940), pp. 209–210.

95. Political survey, Aug. 14–Sept. 14, 1919 (N.S.), WMA file 162, p. 121. According to this report, members of the Azerbaidzhani parliament were the leaders of the rising.

96. Intelligence report on the Northern Caucasus, August 20, 1919 (O.S.), WMA file 170, p. 69.

97. *Ibid.*, p. 170.

98. Denikin, *Ocherki*, V, 247.

99. R. D. Hovannisian, *The Republic of Armenia. Volume 1: 1918–1919* (Berkeley, 1971), pp. 360–361.

100. Denikin, *Ocherki*, IV, 136.

101. Hovannisian, *Armenia*, p. 362.

CHAPTER 8. DISINTEGRATION AND DEFEAT

1. A. P. Aleksashenko, *Krakh denikinshchiny* (Moscow, 1966), p. 171.

2. A. I. Egorov, *Razgrom Denikina* (Moscow, 1931), p. 134; Also, *Pravda* (October 19, 1919), p. 1.

3. Egorov, *Razgrom Denikina*, p. 144.

4. The most successful Red cavalry leader and future Marshal of the Soviet Union, S. M. Budennyi, came from a poor peasant family from the Don. He was to play a major role in the autumn offensive.

5. Aleksashenko, *Krakh denikinshchiny*, p. 196.

6. A. I. Denikin, *Ocherki russkoi smuty* (Paris and Berlin, 1921–1925), 5 vols., V, 230.

7. Egorov, *Razgrom Denikina*, p. 183.

8. Denikin, *Ocherki*, V, 259.

9. P. N. Shatilov, "Zapiski," ms, in Russian Archives, Columbia University, pp. 819–820.

10. Ulagai to Denikin December 8 (O.S.), 1919, Olga Wrangel Archives (OWA), file 2. Hoover Institution; Denikin, *Ocherki*, V, 261–262. Denikin, reluctantly, decided to support Wrangel's decision to dismiss Mamontov. When Mamontov learned that Wrangel was about to get rid of him, he left the front without waiting for the arrival of Ulagai.

11. Shatilov, "Zapiski," p. 842.

12. N. Kakurin, *Kak srazhalas' revoliutsiia*, 2 vols. (Moscow, Leningrad, 1925), II, 144.

13. Denikin, *Ocherki*, V, 268.

14. Egorov, *Razgrom Denikina*, p. 217.

15. Denikin, *Ocherki*, V, 236.
16. *Ibid.*
17. A report written by Astrov for Denikin (no date, but presumably January 1920), Panina Archives, file No. 5.
18. *Ibid.*
19. K. N. Sokolov, *Pravlenie generala Denikina* (Sofia, 1921), pp. 212–213.
20. Denikin, *Ocherki*, V, 278.
21. Astrov, Panina Archives, file No. 5.
22. Sokolov, *Pravlenie*, pp. 225–226.
23. C. E. Bechhofer-Roberts, *In Denikin's Russia and the Caucasus, 1919–1920* (London, 1921), p. 105.
24. Denikin, *Ocherki*, V, 280.
25. Astrov, Panina Archives, file No. 5.
26. Denikin, *Ocherki*, V, 286.
27. Sokolov, *Pravlenie*, p. 233.
28. Astrov, Panina Archives, file No. 5.
29. G. N. Rakovskii, *V stane belykh: grazhdanskaia voina na iuge Rossii* (Constantinople, 1920), p. 71.
30. V. Cherniavin, "Katastrofa 1920 g. Na fronte Vooruzhennykh Sil luga Rossii i otkhod Protivobol'shevistkikh Voisk v Krym," ms. in Hoover Institution (written in 1938), p. 13.
31. *Ibid.*, p. 98.
32. *Ibid.*, p. 16.
33. *Ibid.*, p. 32.
34. *Ibid.*, pp. 83–84.
35. *Ibid.*, p. 95.
36. The meeitng of the Supreme Krug is described in Denikin, *Ocherki*, V, 292; Sokolov, *Pravlenie*, p. 241; Cherniavin, "Katastrofa 1920," p. 77.
37. Rakovskii, *V stane belykh*, p. 69.
38. Shatilov "Zapiski," p. 854.
39. Denikin, *Ocherki*, V, 295.
40. Rakovskii, *V stane belyki*, p. 74; Cherniavin, "Katastrofa 1920," p. 108.
41. Denikin, *Ocherki*, V, 298.
42. Rakovskii, *V stane belykh*, pp. 80–81.
43. Denikin, *Ocherki*, V, 302.
44. Rakovskii, *V stane belykh*, pp. 81–82.
45. N. M. Mel'nikov, "Grazhdanskaia voina na iuga Rossii," ms. in Russian Archives, Columbia University, p. 146.
46. The discussions are described in Denikin, *Ocherki*, V, 307; Mel'nikov, "Grazhdanskaia voina," pp. 146–147; Sokolov, *Pravlenie*, p. 247.
47. Sokolov, *Pravlenie*, p. 249. The Volunteer Army had come full circle. During the first months of its existence, the generals were willing to tolerate a socialist, Boris Savinkov; in 1920, when defeat seemed near, they once again felt compelled to accept one.

48. Denikin, *Ocherki*, V, 309.

49. Denikin himself did not have a high opinion of the new ministers. He wrote in his memoirs that the majority of the ministers were decent people whose greatest contribution was that they did not try to interfere. *Ocherki*, V, 310.

50. Mel'nikov, "Grazhdanskaia voina," pp. 153–154.

51. Denikin, *Ocherki*, V, 328.

52. *Ibid.*, 315.

53. *Ibid.*, 317–318.

54. N. Voronovich, ed., *"Zelenaia kniga" Sbornik materialov i dokumentov* (Prague, 1921), p. 5.

55. N. Voronovich, "Mezh dvukh ognei," *Arkhiv Russkoi Revoliutsii*, vol. 7 (1922), p. 109.

56. *Ibid.*, p. 111.

57. *Ibid.*, p. 112.

58. *Ibid.*, p. 125.

59. *Ibid.*, pp. 123–132.

60. *Ibid.*, p. 140.

61. *Ibid.*, p. 171.

62. "Orlovshchina" by Ia. M. Shafir in *Antanta i Vrangel' Sbornik Statei* (Moscow, 1923), p. 126.

63. *Ibid.*, p. 127.

64. *Ibid.*, pp. 129–130.

65. *Ibid.*, p. 133.

66. Denikin, *Ocherki*, V, 337.

67. Astrov, Panina Archives, File No. 5.

68. Rakovskii, *V stane belykh*, pp. 38–43.

69. P. N. Wrangel, *Memoirs* (London, 1929), p. 125.

70. Shatilov, "Zapiski," p. 866.

71. Wrangel, *Memoirs*, p. 125.

72. Denikin, *Ocherki*, V, 335.

73. *Ibid.*, p. 336.

74. *Ibid.*, p. 338.

75. Wrangel, *Memoirs*, pp. 128–129.

76. Denikin, *Ocherki*, V, 338.

77. Wrangel to Denikin, February 15, 1920 (O.S.), OWA file 2.

78. Shatilov, "Zapiski," p. 882.

79. *Ocherki*, V, 339.

80. *Ibid.*, p. 344.

81. *Ibid.*, p. 343.

82. P. S. Makhrov, "V beloi armii generala Denikina," ms. in Russian Archives, Columbia University, p. 632.

83. Denikin, *Ocherki*, V, 348.

84. Makhrov, "V beloi armii," p. 641.

85. *Ibid.*, p. 649.

86. Rakovskii, *V stane belykh*, p. 226.

87. W. H. Chamberlin, *The Russian Revolution*, 2 vols. (New York, 1935), II, 288.
88. Dimitry V. Lehovich, *White Against Red. The Life of General Anton Denikin* (New York, 1974), p. 381.
89. Denikin, *Ocherki*, V, 342.
90. *Ibid.*, 352; Makhrov, "V beloi armii," p. 660.
91. Denikin, *Ocherki*, V, 352.
92. Makhrov, "V beloi armii," p. 672.
93. *Ibid.*, p. 633.
94. *Ibid.*, p. 686.
95. *Ibid.*, p. 661.
96. *Ibid.*, p. 691.
97. General Tikhobrazov, "Vospominaniia," ms. in Russian Archives, Columbia University, Chapter 26, p. 30.
98. Wrangel, *Memoirs*, p. 59.
99. V. P. Agapeev, "Ubiistvo gen. Romanovskogo," in *Beloe delo*, vol. 2, p. 113; also Agapeev's report to Wrangel, April 1920, OWA file 2; P. S. Makhrov, "Ubiistvo gen. Romanovskogo," *Russkie novosti*, October 3, 1947, p. 3.
100. Letter of A. I. Denikin to A. M. Dragomirov, Sopron, Hungary, August 7, 1922. Denikin files, Box 12, Russian Archives, Columbia University.

CHAPTER 9. WRANGEL

1. Since the 1930s Soviet historians have attributed the decision not to pursue to Trotskii's treachery. See, for example, I. S. Korotkov, *Razgrom Vrangelia*, (Moscow, 1955), p. 22.
2. P. N. Wrangel, *Memoirs* (London, 1929), pp. 131–132.
3. *Ibid.*, p. 144.
4. *Ibid.*, pp. 147–148.
5. P. S. Makhrov, "General Vrangel' i Savinkov," ms. in Russian Archives, Columbia University, pp. 5–7.
6. Makhrov's report can be found in his memoirs, "General Vrangel'", pp. 29–99.
7. *Ibid.*, p. 109.
8. *Ibid.*, p. 112.
9. Wrangel, *Memoirs*, p. 257.
10. Makhrov, "General Vrangel'", p. 19.
11. V. Obolenskii, "Krym pri Vrangele," *Na chuzhoi storone* (Berlin, Prague, 1925), vol. 9., p. 39.
12. Korotkov, *Razgrom Vrangelia*, p. 31.
13. *Ibid.*, p. 32; Makhrov, "General Vrangel'", p. 103.
14. Wrangel, *Memoirs* pp. 204–205.
15. *Ibid.*, pp. 185–187.
16. *Ibid.*, p. 159.

17. Korotkov, *Razgrom Vrangelia*, pp. 34–35.

18. V. I. Lenin, *Sochinenie*, 4th ed., vol. 31, pp. 305–306.

19. The most detailed description of the negotiations is in P. S. Wandycz, *Soviet-Polish Relations, 1917–1921* (Cambridge, Mass., 1969), pp. 173–189.

20. George Brinkley, *The Volunteer Army and Allied Intervention in South Russia, 1917–1921* (Notre Dame, 1966), pp. 247–254.

21. N. P. Lipatov, *1920 god na Chernom more* (Moscow, 1958), p. 126.

22. These battles are described in Wrangel, pp. 214–217; Makhrov, "General Vrangel'", p. 159; Korotkov, *Razgrom Vrangelia*, pp. 59–66.

23. Obolenskii, "Krym pri Vrangele," p. 7.

24. Makhrov, "General Vrangel'", pp. 131–132.

25. *Ibid.*, p. 10.

26. G. N. Rakovskii, *Konets belykh; ot Dnepra do Bosfora* (Prague, 1921), p. 32.

27. The manifesto is printed in *ibid.*, p. 39; Wrangel, *Memoirs* p. 201; and W. H. Chamberlin, *The Russian Revolution* (New York, 1935), 2 vols, II, 322. Interestingly, the point concerning workers appears only in Rakovskii.

28. Wrangel, *Memoirs*, p. 238.

29. Makhrov, "General Vrangel'", p. 99.

30. *Ibid.*, pp. 139–141.

31. Rakovskii, *Konets belykh*, p. 26.

32. Wrangel, *Memoirs*, pp. 162–163.

33. K. A. Krivoshein, *A. V. Krivoshein (1857–1921) Ego znachenie v istorii Rossii nachala XX veka* (Paris, 1973), pp. 307–308. Elsewhere Krivoshein argues that his father and Wrangel were realistic enough to accept an end to the war without victory, and would have been willing to conclude a treaty with the Bolsheviks which would have left the Whites in control of the Crimea. Krivoshein, p. 315. This point of view is supported by Obolenskii, "Krym pri Vrangele," pp. 6–8, who had conversations with Wrangel on this subject.

34. Makhrov, "General Vrangel'", pp. 25–26.

35. The minutes of the meetings are in Wrangel Personal Archives (WPA), file 4, Hoover Institution.

36. Obolenskii, "Krym pri Vrangele," pp. 9–10.

37. Meeting of April 9, 1920, No. 1, WPA file 4. Wrangel said at the meeting that the cabinet must be careful about giving money to the *zemstva*, because these institutions would not spend it well.

38. Obolenskii, "Krym pri Vrangele," p. 32.

39. May 15, No. 9, WPA file 4.

40. Obolenskii, "Krym pri Vrangele," p. 34.

41. May 7, No. 6 meeting of the cabinet, WPA file 4; also May 11, No. 7. Provisional order about civil departments of army corps; Wrangel, *Memoirs*, p. 205.

42. Order of the Commander-in-Chief, May 10, in WPA file 4.

43. Major General Popov, "Pravosudie v voiskakh generala Vrangelia," WPA file 130, pp. 6–7.

44. *Ibid.*, p. 8.

45. *Ibid.*, p. 9.

46. *Ibid.*, p. 12.
47. *Ibid.*, pp. 12–15.
48. See report on censored letters, Aug. 13–28, 1920, WMA file 240.
49. A. A. Valentinov, "Krymskaia epopeia," *Arkhiv Russkoi Revoliutsii (ARR)* (Berlin 1922), vol. 5., p. 17.
50. An admiring short biography of Kutepov is N. A. Tsurikov, *General Aleksandr Pavlovich Kutepov* (Prague, 1930). For the terror established by Kutepov, see Obolenskii, "Krym pri Vrangele," pp. 37–38; Valentinov, *ARR*, p. 9; and Makhrov, "General Vrangel'", p. 109.
51. Wrangel, *Memoirs*, p. 169.
52. Obolenskii, "Krym pri Vrangele," pp. 37–38.
53. Popov, "Pravosudie," pp. 51–53; Obolenskii, "Krym pri Vrangele," p. 36. For Slashchev's apologia, see Ia. A. Slashchev-Krymskii, *Trebuiu suda obshchestva i glasnosti; oborona i sdacha Kryma: Mamuary i dokumenty* (Constantinople, 1921), and the answer to Slashchev by an anonymous officer, *Otvet generalu Slaschevu-Krymskomu* (Constantinople, 1921).
54. Makhrov, "General Vrangel'", p. 127.
55. Obolenskii, "Krym pri Vrangele," p. 27.
56. *Ibid.*, p. 28.
57. G. V. Nemirovich-Danchenko, *V Krymu pri Vrangele* (Berlin, 1925), p. 26.
58. Obolenskii, "Krym pri Vrangele," pp. 43–45.
59. Makhrov, "General Vrangel'", p. 86.
60. Wrangel, *Memoirs*, pp. 184–185.
61. Makhrov, "General Vrangel'", pp. 148–149.
62. Dorman was saved from an even worse fate by Makhrov's intervention. Makhrov, "General Vrangel'", p. 178.
63. Nemirovich-Danchenko, *V Krymu*, p. 34.
64. *Velikaia Rossiia*, p. 4. Sept. 30, 1920, Simferopol.
65. Nemirovich-Danchenko, *V Krymu*, p. 37.
66. *Ibid.*, p. 41.
67. D. Maslov, "Pechat' pri Vrangele," in *Antanta i Vrangel' Sbornik statei* (Moscow, Petrograd, 1923), p. 174.
68. Makhrov, "General Vrangel'", p. 150.
69. A. Gukovskii, ed., "Agrarnaia politika Vrangelia," *Krasnyi Arkhiv*, vol. 26, pp. 61–62.
70. Obolenskii, "Krym pri Vrangele," p. 29.
71. D. Maslov, "Pechat' pri Vrangele," pp. 186–189.
72. A. I. Denikin, *Ocherki russkoi smuty*, 5 vols. (Paris and Berlin, 1921–1925), IV, p. 214. Wrangel said to Denikin: "It seems to me that those groups which turn to the army for a political program are mistaken. The army, because of its very nature, must stand aside from politics. An army cannot have a political program. We must establish order in which the people, freed from anarchy and oppression, can freely express its will."
73. Krivoshein, *A. V. Krivoshein*, p. 319.
74. Makhrov, "General Vrangel'", p. 30.

75. Obolenskii, "Krym pri Vrangele," p. 11.

76. *Ibid.*, p. 12; also, papers of the Commission for the discussion of the agrarian question, WPA file 6.

77. Wrangel's letter to Glinka, dated March 1920 (O.S.), WPA file 6.

78. The description of debates is based on the minutes of the Commission, in WPA file 6 and Obolenskii, "Krym pri Vrangele," pp. 10–17.

79. See, for example, dissenting opinions of Levshin, Shliefer, and others. Their statement said: "A forced alienation of land, carried out in any form in a country with as little culture as Russia, would lead to fateful consequences. After land reform, demands will start for dividing gardens and later real estate in cities and plants and factories, etc." WPA file 6, p. 79.

80. Nemirovich-Danchenko, *V Krymu*, p. 31.

81. WPA, pp. 20–30.

82. *Ibid.*, pp. 33–34.

83. *Ibid.*, p. 35.

84. *Ibid.*, p. 38.

85. Dissenting opinion of Obolenskii, in *ibid.*, pp. 69–71.

86. Obolenskii, "Krym pri Vrangele," p. 14.

87. Orders of the Commander-in-Chief, May 25, 1920, WPA file 6.

88. Obolenskii, "Krym pri Vrangele," pp. 16–17.

89. Valentinov, *ARR*, p. 15.

90. Gukovskii, *Krasnyi Arkhiv*, vol. 26, pp. 61–62.

91. Report of provincial mediator Shleifer, Sept. 13, to Ministry of Agriculture, *ibid.*, pp. 73–80.

92. Report prepared by Wrangel's government for foreign representatives on the realization of land reform, *ibid.*, p. 63.

93. Report prepared by commission on land reform for Wrangel, WPA file 6, pp. 119–120.

94. Valentinov, *ARR*, p. 15.

95. Journals of the Cabinet, No. 32, Aug. 5, WPA file 4.

96. A. S. Lukomskii, *Vospominaniia*, 2 vols. (Berlin, 1922), II, 216–218. White agents were buying oil, coal and rubber abroad.

97. Wrangel, *Memoirs*, p. 242; report of Russian agent Savitskii in Paris to foreign ministry, June 3, 1920, in *Krasnyi Arkhiv*, vol. 32, p. 139; telegram of Neratov to Paris Embassy, July 20, 1920, in *Krasnyi Arkhiv*, vol. 39. pp. 31–32.

98. Ia. M. Shafir, "Ekonomicheskaia politika belykh," in *Antanta i Vrangel'*, p. 107.

99. On April 9 Vil'chevskii said to the cabinet: "There is enough flour to last until next harvest if we count one pound per person per day. Immediate conservation measures must be taken: (1) forbid baking cakes (2) forbid export grain (3) introduce three meatless days a week (4) buy canned meat and bacon in Bulgaria." Minutes of the sessions of the cabinet, No. 1, April 9, 1920. WPA file 4.

100. Telegram of Struve to Paris Embassy, Sept. 12, 1920. *Krasnyi Arkhiv*, vol. 40, pp. 11–12.

101. Brinkley, *Volunteer Army*, p. 264. Brinkley writes that there is no evidence that the treaty was actually signed by the Russians.

102. Shafir, "Ekonomicheskaia," p. 119.

103. *Ibid.*

104. A. Michelson, P. Apostol, and M. Bernatzky, *Russian Public Finance During the War* (New Haven, 1928), p. 441.

105. Shafir, "Ekonomicheskaia," p. 121.

106. *Ibid.*, p. 115.

107. *Ibid.*, p. 101; The cabinet discussed supplying food instead of giving money to the workers. The idea was rejected because it was calculated that 12,000 workers with their families made up 50,000 people, and that there were no available resources to support them. Sessions of the cabinet No. 1. April 9, WPA file 4.

108. Makhrov, "General Vrangel'", p. 108.

109. Shafir, "Ekonomicheskaia," p. 221.

110. *Ibid.*, p. 225; Nemirovich-Danchenko, *V Krymu*, p. 10.

111. Sessions of the cabinet, June 26, 1920 (O.S.), No. 21, WPA file 4.

112. Richard E. Pipes, *The Formation of the Soviet Union: Communism and Nationalism, 1917-1923* (Cambridge, 1954), p. 189.

113. Grigor'ev (Genker), "Tatarskii vopros v Krymu," in *Antanta i Vrangel'*, p. 234.

114. *Ibid.*, p. 236.

115. *Ibid.*.

116. Rakovskii, *Konets belykh*, p. 27.

117. *Ibid.*, p. 41.

118. *Ibid.*, pp. 44-45.

119. *Ibid.*, p. 50.

120. Makhrov, "General Vrangel'", p. 134.

121. Rakovskii, *Konets, belykh*, p. 102.

122. Wrangel, *Memoirs*, p. 171.

123. Report on Kuban politics prepared by political section of General Staff, July 24, 1920, WMA file 240, pp. 70-72.

124. Rakovskii, *Konets belykh*, p. 105.

125. *Ibid.*, p. 108.

126. Wrangel, *Memoirs*, pp. 143-244.

127. WMA file 240, pp. 70-72.

128. Wrangel, *Memoirs*, pp. 249-250.

129. Rakovskii, *Konets belykh*, p. 116.

130. *Ibid;* Chamberlin, *The Russian Revolution*, II, p. 324.

131. Korotkov, *Razgrom Vrangelia*, pp. 137-138.

132. *Ibid.*, p. 140; Wrangel, *Memoirs*, p. 249. Wrangel gave somewhat smaller figures. According to him the main force had only 4,500 soldiers. The source of the disagreement may be that it was difficult to distinguish the combatants from the non-combatants.

133. Korotkov, *Razgrom Vrangelia*, p. 140.

134. *Ibid.*, p. 142.

135. Wrangel, *Memoirs,* p. 288.

136. Telegram of Neratov to Paris Embassy, Aug. 3, 1920, *Krasnyi Arkhiv,* vol. 39, pp. 39–40; Brinkley, *Volunteer Army,* p. 257.

137. Wrangel, *Memoirs,* p. 275.

138. The idea of setting up a Russian army in Poland had been discussed for a long time. Initially, Wrangel wanted the army to be sent immediately to the Crimea. However, because the Poles were not anxious to help and because the problems of logistics were enormous, Wrangel was willing to accept the idea that this army would initially fight on the Polish front. The Poles agreed to place this army on the right wing of their forces, and in case of a link up of the two anti-Bolshevik fronts, to allow this army to pass under Wrangel's direct command. Wrangel also insisted on calling this army the Third Russian Army. The first two armies were in the Crimea. The Whites hoped that they would be able to build a force of eighty thousand. See telegram of Neratov to Paris Embassy, July 20, 1920, and telegram from Gorlov to Struve, July 12, 1920. *Krasnyi Arkhiv,* vol. 39, pp. 26–33; Brinkley, *Volunteer Army,* p. 269.

139. Wrangel, *Memoirs,* p. 274.

140. Korotkov, *Razgrom Vrangelia,* p. 154.

141. Wandycz, *Soviet-Polish Relations,* pp. 250–258.

142. Korotkov, *Razgrom Vrangelia,* p. 165.

143. Wrangel, *Memoirs,* p. 290.

144. Korotkov, *Razgrom Vrangelia,* p. 177.

145. Wrangel, *Memoirs,* p. 294.

146. Korotkov, *Razgrom Vrangelia,* p. 206.

147. Wrangel, *Memoirs,* p. 308.

148. P. N. Shatilov, "Pamiatnaia zapiska o krymskoi evakuatsii," *Beloe delo,* vol. 4., p. 95.

149. Wrangel, *Memoirs,* p. 236. The French remained ungenerous to the end. They did lend some of their ships, but insisted that all ships must fly French flags. They regarded all Russian ships as their property as compensation for services rendered. Shatilov, "Pamiatnaia zapiska," pp. 101–102.

CHAPTER 10. THE WHITE MOVEMENT IN SOUTH RUSSIA: CONCLUSION

1. A. I. Denikin, *Ocherki russkoi smuty* (Paris and Berlin, 1921–1925), 5 vols., II, 147–148.

2. Wrangel Military Archives, file 240. Hoover Institution.

Bibliography

UNPUBLISHED MATERIALS

Institute for the Study of Russian and East European History and Culture at Columbia University

ARCHIVES

Denikin, A. I. Papers. 26 dossiers. The Collection contains MSS of his publications, speeches, press reports about him, and some unpublished writings.

Makhrov, P. S. Papers. The collection includes the valuable handwritten memoirs "V beloi armii Generala Denikina" and "General Vrangel' i B. Savinkov"; copies of political reports from 1919; correspondence from 1920 with Warsaw, where the General was military representative; and newspaper articles.

Melnikov, N. M. Papers. 44 dossiers. The collection includes reports on the meetings of the South Russian government in 1920.

Panina, S. V. Papers. 9 dossiers. Countess Panina collected the papers of the most prominent Kadet politicians. For the historian of the Civil War in South Russia, the most valuable documents are the writings of N. I. Astrov.

MANUSCRIPTS

Aprelev, Iu. P. "Zametki o sobytiiakh v. Rossii, 1917–1918–1919."
Globachev, N. K. "Vospominaniia."
Golitsyn, A. D. "Vospominaniia, 1917–1920."
Kefeli, Ia. I. "S Generalom Shvartsem v Odesse, osen' 1918—vesna 1919 gg Vospominaniia."
Mandrajy (Mandrachi) Constantin. "Begin at the beginning." Memoirs translated by Vera Mandrajy.
Maslovskii, E. V. "Nekatorye stranitsy moei zhizni."
Melnikov, N. M. "Pochemu belye na iuge ne pobedili krasnykh. Grazhdanskaia voina na iuge Rossii."
Miliukov, P. N. "Dnevnik."
Novikov, Colonel. "Bor'ba s bol'shevikami v Novorossiiskom krae."
Sannikov, A. S. "Vospominaniia, 1918–1919."

Shatilov, P. N. "Zapiski."
Shavel'skii, P. G. "Vospominaniia: v dobrovol'cheskoi armii."
Tikhobrazov, D. "Vospominaniia."

Hoover Institution at Stanford, California

ARCHIVES

Bykadorov, I. Collection of papers concerning the Don Army.
Documents of the Crimean government. 19 dossiers.
Documents of the Terek Cossack government.
Don Cossack Republic. Papers.
Gessen, G. V. Archives. 4 boxes.
Golovine, N. N. Papers. The papers include a translated but unpublished copy of "Russian Counterrevolution, 1917–1918," and minutes of the session of the Russian Academy in Paris devoted to the discussion of S. P. Melgunov's criticism of General Golovin's book.
Lampe, A. A. von. Correspondence and reports of the Russian military agency in Berlin. 9 boxes.
Lukomskii, A. S. Papers. 4 boxes.
Maklakov, V. A. Papers of the Russian Embassy in Paris and Maklakov's personal correspondence.
Melgunov, S. P. Civil War collection. 11 boxes of MSS and newspaper articles.
Nikolaevskii, B. I. Materials on the Russian Civil War. Extracts from various newspapers.
Prikazy i rasporiazheniia po dobrovol'cheskoi i Donskoi armiiam, otnosiashchiesia k periodu grazhdanskoi voiny na iuge Rossii, 1918–1919 gg.
Prikazy, mandaty, tsirkuliary i t.d. otnosiashchiesia k periodu grazhdanskoi voiny na iuge Rossii, 1918–1920 gg (Bolshevik materials).
Relations between the South Russian Volunteer Army and the Georgia Mensheviks, 1919–1920. Compiled by D. P. Dratsenko, 3 dossiers.
Russian newspapers and periodicals pertaining to the Civil War in European Russia.
Rodzianko, M. V. Documents.
Shcherbachev, D. G. Papers, 8 boxes.
Wrangel, P. N. Archives. These archives contain hundreds of thousands of documents which have never been completely catalogued. The materials are relevant for the study of all aspects of the history of the White movement in South Russia, and they are indispensable for the historian. The largest and most valuable section is the Wrangel Military Archives which have 352 dossiers (referred to as WMA in the notes). The other two sections, Wrangel Personal Archives (WPA in the notes) and

Baroness Olga Wrangel's Archives, are restricted until 1979. I am grateful to Mrs. Wrangel for allowing me to use these materials.

MANUSCRIPTS

Cherniavin, V. "Katastrofa 1920 g. na fronte Vooruzhennykh Sil na iuga Rossii i otkhod protivobol'shevistkikh voisk v Krym."

Davis, R. E. Report of the Kuban unit of the American Red Cross, 1917–1919.

Delegatsiia Donskoi Respubliki na konferentsiia mira. Report.

Ergushev, P. "Kazaki i gortsy."

Economic conditions of the Kuban Black Sea Region. Report.

Fedorov, G. "Iz vospominanii zalozhnika v Piatigorskom kontsentratsionnom lagere."

Kutsevalov, B. S. "Ubiistvo Generala Romanovskogo."

Lukomskii, A. S. Letter to General Golovin.

Maximova-Kulaev, A. A. Account of the occupation of Kozlov by Gen. Mamontov's Cossack detachment, a part of Gen. Denikin's troops in August 1919. Interview with N. Lavrova. San Francisco, October 1932.

Vatatsi, M. P. "The White Movement, 1917–1920. Memoirs."

VinaVera, R. G. "Vospominaniia."

PRINTED DOCUMENTS

Bor'ba za pobedu sovetskoi vlasti v Gruzii: dokumenty i materialy, 1917–1921 gg. Tbilisi, Gosizdat G.S.S.R., 1958

Bor'ba za sovetskuiu vlast' na Kubani v 1917–1920 (Dokumenty). Krasnodar Krasnodarskoe knizhnoe izdatel'stvo, 1957.

Cumming, C. K. and Pettit, W. W. (eds.). Russian-American Relations, March 1917–March, 1920: Documents and Papers. New York, Harcourt, Brace and Howe, 1920.

Degras, Jane (ed.). Soviet Documents on Foreign Policy, vol. 1., London, Oxford U.P., 1951.

"Demokraticheskoe pravitel'stvo Gruzii i angliiskoe komandovanie," Krasnyi Arkhiv (abbreviated KA), vol. 21., pp. 122–173, and vol. 22, pp. 96–110 (1927).

"Dnevnik i vospominaniia kievskoi studentki (1919–1920 gg)," Arkhiv Russkoi Revoliutsii (abbreviated ARR), vol. 15, 203–254 (1924).

"Dokumenty k vospominaniiam Gen. Filimonova," ARR, vol. 5 (1922), pp. 322–331.

"Dokumenty k vospominaniiam Gen. Lukomskogo," ARR, vol. 3 (1921), pp. 247–270.

"Dokumenty k vospominaniiam N. Voronovicha," *ARR*, vol. 7 (1922), pp. 321–332.

Georgia, Ministerstvo Vneshnikh Del, *Dokumenty i materialy po vneshnei politike Zakavkazia i Gruzii*. Tbilisi, Tip. Pravitel'stva Gruzinskoi Respubliki, 1919.

Gukovskii, A. I. (ed.). "Agrarnaia politika Vrangelia," *KA*, Vol. 26 (1928), pp. 51–96.

―――. "K istorii iasskogo soveshchaniia," *KA*, vol. 18 (1926), pp. 105–118.

―――. "Krymskoe kraevoe pravitel'stvo v 1918–1919," *KA*, vol. 22 (1927), pp. 92–152.

―――. "Krym v 1918–1919 gg," *KA*, vol. 28 (1928), pp. 142–181, and vol. 29 (1928), pp. 55–85.

Iuzhnyi front. Sbornik dokumentov (mai 1918-mart1919). Rostov on the Don, Rostovskoe knizhnoe izdatel'stvo, 1962.

Meijer, Jan. (ed.). *The Trotsky Papers, 1917–1922*, vol. 1. The Hague, Mouton, 1964.

Mints, I. I. and E. N. Gorodetskii (eds.). *Dokumenty po istorii grazhdanskoi voiny v SSSR*, vol. 1. Moscow, Gospolitizdat, 1940.

Mints, I. I. (ed.). "Vneshniaia politika kontr-revoliutsionnykh pravitel'stv v nachale 1919 g. iz dokumentov Parizhskogo posol'stva," *KA*, vol. 37 (1929), pp. 69–101.

Lenin, V. I. *Polnoe sobranie sochinenii*, 5th edition. 55 vols. Moscow, Gospolitizdat, 1960.

"Ocherk vzaimootnoshenii vooruzhennykh sil iuga Rossii i predstavitelei frantsuzskogo komandovaniia" ("Oranzhevaia kniga"), *ARR*, vol. 16 (1925), pp. 233–262.

"Organizatsiia vlasti na iuge Rossii v period grazhdanskoi voiny, 1918–1920 gg: dokumenty," *ARR*, vol. 4 (1922), pp. 241–251.

Partiia v period inostrannoi voennoi interventsii i grazhdanskoi voiny, 1918–1920 gody: dokumenty i materialy. Moscow, Gospolitizdat, 1962.

Piontkovskii, S. A. (ed.). *Grazhdanskaia voina v Rossii, (1918–1921 gg):krestomatiia*. Moscow, Izdaniia kommunisticheskogo universiteta im. Ia.M Sverdlova, 1925.

"Revoliutsionnoe kazachestvo Dona v bor'be s kontrrevoliutsiei," *KA*, vol. 76 (1936), pp. 24–30.

Shafir, I. M. (ed.). *Secrets of Menshevik Georgia; The Plot Against Soviet Russia Unmasked: Documents*. London, Communist Party of Great Britain, 1922.

Shlikhter, A. G. (ed.). *Chernaia kniga: sbornik statei i materialov ob interventsii antanty na Ukraine v 1918–1919 gg*. Kharkov, Gosizdat Ukrainy, 1925.

Verneck, E., and H. H. Fisher (eds.). *The Testimony of Kolchak and Other Siberian Materials*. Stanford, Stanford U.P., 1935.

"Vneshniaia politika kontr-revoliutsionnykh 'pravitel'stv' v nachale 1919 g.," *KA*, vol. 37 (1929), pp. 69–101.
"Zhurnal zasedeniia soveta ministrov Krymskogo kraevogo pravitel'stva. Apr. 16 1919 g.," *ARR*, vol. 2 (1921), pp. 135–142.

CONTEMPORARY PAMPHLETS

Arefor, S. *Na Rodine*. Rostov on the Don, Narodnaia biblioteka, 1919.
Avramov, P. *Gen. A. G. Shkuro*. Rostov on the Don, Narodnaia biblioteka, 1919.
Baratov, B. I. *Na iug! Na iug!* Moscow, Gosizdat, 1919.
Chirikov, E. N. *Narod i revoliutsiia*. Rostov on the Don, 1919.
———. *Za synom*. Rostov on the Don, 1919.
Denikin, A. I. *Za chto my boremsia?* n.p. n.d.
Dobrovol'skii, N. G. *Gen Shkuro*. Rostov on the Don, 1919.
Donskaia armiia. *Otchet komanduiushchego Donskoi armiei po operativnoi chasti k kontsu sentiabriia 1919 goda*. Novocherkassk, 1919.
Donskaia armiia. *Ocherk politicheskoi istorii Vsevelikogo Voiska Donskogo*. Novocherkassk, Obl. V. Voiska Donskogo Tip. 1919.
Grimm, E. D. *Kak bol'sheviki zakhvatili vlast' na Rusi*. Rostov on the Don, Narodnaia pol'za, 1919.
K kazakam Donskogo, Kubanskogo, Terskogo i Astrakhanskogo voisk. Moscow, Gosizdat, 1919.
Lebedeff, V. I. *The Russian Democracy in its Struggle against the Bolshevik Tyranny*. New York, Russian Information Bureau, 1919.
Makoshin, R. *Chto sdelala Dobrovol'cheskaia armiia?* Rostov on the Don, 1919.
Nevskii, V. I. *Brat'ia kazaki zachem voiuete s nami s rabochimi i s krestianami?* Moscow, Gosizdat, 1919.
Nizhegorodtsev, A. *Pochemu Dobrovol'cheskaia armiia voiuet protiv kommunistov Lenina i Trotskogo*. Kharkov, 1919.
Ostrovskaia, N. *Pro zelennykh*. Moscow, Gosizdat, 1919.
Prezhde i teper'. Rostov on the Don, 1919.
Rostov, B. *Pochemu i kak sozdalas Dobrovol'cheskaia armiia i za chto ona boretsia*. Rostov on the Don, Biblioteka Dobrovol'cheskoi armii, 1919.
Rusakov, P. *Kto takie kontr-revoliutsionery i kak s nimi nado borot'sia*. Moscow, Gosizdat, 1920.
Shchepkin, G. *General-leitenant A. I. Denikin*. Novocherkassk, 1919.
Sosnovskii, L. S. *Tsarskii posledysh baron Vrangel'*. Moscow, Gosizdat, 1920.
Ulianov, I. *Sovetskaia respublika i kazaki*. Moscow, Gosizdat, 1920.

Volin, V. *Don i Dobrovol'cheskaia armiia*. Novocherkassk, Izdanie A.Ia. Vasileva, 1919.

Volkonskii, P. M. *The Volunteer Army of Alexeiev and Deniken*. London, Russian Liberation Committee, n.d.

Volunteer Army, *Kratkaia zapiska istorii vzaimootneshenii Dobrovol'cherkoi Armii s Ukrainei*. Rostov on the Don, 1919.

Volunteer Army, *Sobranie uzakonenii i rasporiazhenii pravitel'stva*. 2 vols. Rostov on the Don, 1918–1919.

Volunteer Army, *The Volunteer Army as a National Factor in the Renaissance of Great Russia, One and Indivisible*. Ekaterinodar, 1919.

Vooruzhennye sily Iuga Rossii, Osobaia komissiia po razsledovaniiu zlodeianii bol'shevikov. *Akt razsledovaniia po delu ob areste i ubiistve zalozhnikov v Piatigorske v Okt. 1918 goda*. Rostov on the Don, 1919.

————. *Akt razsledovaniia po delu o vzryve bol'shevikami bomb na uchebnom sudne "Rion" i t.d.* Rostov on the Don, 1919.

————. *Bol'sheviki v Tsaritsyne*. Rostov on the Don, Osvag, 1919.

————. *Details concerning the crimes of the Bolcheviks in the city of Ekaterinodar and its neighborhood*, n.p. 1919.

————. *Investigation concerning the massacre by the Bolcheviks in the hospitals of the stanitsa Elizavetinskaya of the wounded and sick men of the Voluntary Army*. no. p. 1919.

————. *Svodka materialov po gorodu Khar'kovu i khar'kovskoi gub*. Rostov on the Don, 1919.

BOOKS

Adams, A. I. *Bolsheviks in the Ukraine; the Second Campaign*. New Haven, Yale U.P., 1963.

Agureev, K. V. *Razgrom belogvardeiskikh voisk Denikina. okt. 1919-mart 1920*. Moscow, Voenizdat, 1961.

Agurskii, S. *Evreiskii rabochii v kommunisticheskom dvizhenie 1917–1921*. Minsk, Gosizdat Belorossii, 1926.

Alakhverdov G. G. *Kratkaia istoriia grazhdanskoi voiny v SSSR*. Moscow, Gosizdat polit. lit-ry, 1960.

Alekseev, S. A. *Denikin, Iudenich, Vrangel'*. Moscow, Gosizdat, 1927.

———— (ed.). *Revoliutsiia i grazhdanskaia voina v opisaniakh belogvardeitsev*. Moscow, Gosizdat, 1926–1930, 6 vols.

Aleksashenko, A. P. *Krakh denikinshchiny*. Moscow, Izdatel'stvo Moskovskogo universieta, 1966.

Allen, W. E. D., and P. Muratoff. *Caucasian Battlefields: A History of the Wars on the Turco-Caucasian Border, 1828–1921*. Cambridge, Cambridge U.P., 1953.

BIBLIOGRAPHY 355

Allen, W. E. D. *The Ukraine*. Cambridge, Cambridge U.P., 1940.
Anan'ev K. *V boiakh za Perekop; zapiski uchastnika*. Moscow, Gosvoenizdat, 1935.
Anishev, A. *Ocherki istorii grazhdanskoi voiny 1917–1920 gg*. Leningrad, Gosizdat, 1925.
Antanta i Vrangel' Sbornik statei. Moscow, Petrograd, Gosizdat, 1923.
Antonov, A. E. *Boevoi vosemnadtsatyi god; Voennye deistviia krasnoi armii v 1918 nachale 1919 g*. Moscow, Voenizdat, 1961.
Antonov-Ovseenko, V. A. *Zapiski o grazhdanskoi voine*. 4 vols. Moscow, Gosvoenizdat, 1924–1933.
Anweiler, O. *The Soviets: The Russian Workers, Peasants, and Soldiers Councils 1905–1921*. New York, Random House, 1974.
Arkhiv grazhdanskoi voiny. Berlin, "Russkoe tvorchestvo, 1922.
Arshinov, P. A. *Istoriia Makhnovskogo dvizheniia (1918–1921 gg)*. Berlin, Gruppa russkikh anarkhistov v Germanii, 1923.
Aronson, G., J. Frumkin, Alexis Goldenweiser, and J. Lewitan (eds.). *Russian Jewry 1917–1967*. New York, London, Thomas Yoseloff, 1969.
Aten, M., and A. Orrmont. *Last Train Over Rostov Bridge*. New York, Messner, 1961.
Avalishvili, Z. *The Independence of Georgia in International Politics, 1918–1921*. London, Headley Brothers, 1940.
Azan, P. J. L. *Franchet d'Esperey*. Paris, Flammarion, 1949.
Babichev, D. S. *Donskoe trudovoe kazachestvo v bor'be za vlast' sovetov*. Rostov on the Don, Izd. Rostovskogo Universiteta, 1969.
Baransky, N. N. *Economic Georgraphy of the USSR*. Moscow, Foreign Languages Publishing House, 1956.
Baron, Salo. *The Russian Jew Under Tsars and Soviets*. New York, Macmillan, 1964.
Bechhofer-Roberts, C. E. *In Denikin's Russia and the Caucasus, 1919–1920*. London, W. Collin's Sons and Co., 1921.
Belaia Rossiia. Al'bom No. 1. New York, Izdanie glavnogo pravleniia zarubezhnogo soiuza Russkikh invalidov, 1937.
Beliaevskii, V. A. *Kto vinovat?* n.p. n.d.
———. *Pravda o gen. Denikine; Prichiny prekrashcheniia belogo dvizheniia na iuge Rossii v 1920 g*. San Francisco, 1958.
Berz, L. I. and K. A. Khmelevskii. *Geroicheskie gody; Oktiabr'skaia Revoliutsiia i grazhdanskaia voina na Donu*. Rostov on the Don, Rostovskoe knizhnoe izdatel'stvo, 1964.
Borisenko, I. *Sovetskie respubliki na severnom Kavkaze v 1918 godu*. 2 vols. Rostov on the Don, Severnyi Kavkaz, 1930.
Borisov, S. P. *Partiia v period uprocheniia sovetskoi vlasti*. Moscow, Gosizdat lit-ry, 1959.

Borys, J. *The Russian Communist Party and the Sovietization of Ukraine*. Stockholm, Kungl. Boktryckereit P. A. Nortedt & Soner, 1960.

Brinkley, G. A. *The Volunteer Army and Allied Intervention in South Russia, 1917–1921*. Notre Dame, University of Notre Dame Press, 1966.

Bubnov, A. S., S. S. Kamenev, and R. P. Eideman (eds.). *Grazhdanskaia voina 1918–1921*. 3 vols. Moscow, Gosizdat "Voennyi vestnik," 1928–1930.

Budennyi, S. M. *Proidennyi put'*. Moscow, Voenizdat, 1958.

Buiskii, A. *Bor'ba za Krym i razgrom Vrangelia*. Moscow, Gosizdat, 1930.

Bunegin, M. F. *Revoliutsiia i grazhdanskaia voina v Krymu (1917–20)*. Simferopol, Krymgosizdat, 1927.

Carr, E. H. *The Bolshevik Revolution*. 3 vols. London, Macmillan, 1950–1953.

Chamberlin, W. H. *The Russian Revolution*. 2 vols. New York, Macmillan, 1935.

Chugunov, T. K. *Derevnia na golgofe*. Munich, published by the author, 1968.

Coates, W. P. and K. Zelda. *Armed Intervention in Russia, 1918–1922*. London, W. Gollancz, 1935.

Curtiss, J. S. *The Russian Church and the Soviet State*. Boston, Little, Brown, 1935.

Davis, Norman. *White Eagle, Red Star, The Polish Soviet War, 1919–1920*. London, Macdonald, 1972.

De-Lazari, A. *Grazhdanskaia voina v Rossii v skhemakh*. Moscow, Gosizdat, 1926.

Delert, D. *Don v ogne*. Rostov on the Don, Sevkazkniga, 1927.

Deygas, F. J. *L'Armee d'Orient dans la Guerre Mondiale, 1915–1919*. Paris, Payot, 1932.

Denikin, A. I. *Kto spas' sovetskuiu vlast' ot gibeli*. Paris, Izdanie soiuz dobrovol'tsev, 1937.

———. *Ocherki russkoi smuty*. 5 vols. Berlin, Russkoe Natsional'noe knigoizdatel'stvo and Paris, J. Povolozky et Cie, 1921–1925.

———. *Put' russkogo ofitsera*. New York, Izdatel'stvo im. Chekhova, 1953. (Translated by Margaret Patoski as *The Career of a Tsarist Officer. Memoirs, 1872–1916*. Minneapolis, University of Minnesota Press, 1975.)

A. I. Denikin, *The White Army*. Translated by Catherine Zveginstev. London, J. Cape and Co, 1930. (A greatly abbreviated version of *Ocherki russkoi smuty*.)

———. *World Events and the Russian Problem*. Paris, Imprimerie Rapide C.T., 1939.

Denisov, S. V. *Zapiski: grazhdanskaia voina na iuge Rossii, 1918–1919 gg*. Constantinople. Published by the author, 1921.

Deutscher, I. *The Prophet Armed: Trotsky: 1879–1921.* New York, Oxford U.P., 1954.

Dobrynin, Col. V. *Bor'ba s bol'shevizmom na iuge Rossii: uchastie v bor'be donskogo kazachestva.* Prague, Slavianskoe izdatel'stvo, 1921.

———. *Don v bor'be s kommunoi na Dontse i Manyche Fevr.-Mai 1919.* Prague, 1922.

Donskaia istoricheskaia komissiia. *Kazaki v Chataladzhe i na Lemnose v 1920–1921 gg.* Belgrade, 1924.

Drabkina, E. *Gruzinskaia kontr-revoliutsiia.* Leningrad, Priboi, 1928.

Dreier, V. von. *Krestnyi put' vo imia rodiny: dvukhletniaia voina krasnogo severa s belym iugom 1918–1920 gg.* Berlin, 1921.

Dunsterville, L. C. *The Adventures of Dunsterforce.* London, Edward Arnold, 1920.

Eckstein, H. (ed.). *Internal War.* New York, The Free Press of Glencoe, 1964.

Egorov, A. I. *Razgrom Denikina.* Moscow, Gosvoenizdat, 1931.

Eliseev, F. I. *Labintsy i poslednye dni na Kubani.* New York, published by the author, 1962.

———. *Na beregakh Kubani i partizan Shkuro.* New York, published by the author, 1955.

———. *S Kornilovskom polkom na beregakh Kubani v Stavropole i Astrakhan-skikh stepiakh 1918–1919.* New York, published by the author, 1959.

Ellis, C. H. *The British "Intervention" in Transcaspia, 1918–1919.* Berkeley, University of California Press, 1963.

Erickson, John. *The Soviet High Command. A Military-Political History, 1918–1941.* London, Macmillan, 1962.

Evseev, N. *Flangovoi udar na Voronezh-Kastornuiu.* Moscow, Gosvoenizdat, 1936.

Fediukin, S. A. *Sovetskaia vlast' i burzhuaznye spetsialisty.* Moscow, Mysl', 1965.

Fischer, Louis, *The Soviets in World Affairs: A History of the Relations Between the Soviet Union and the Rest of the World, 1917–1929.* London, J. Cape, 1930.

Florinsky, M. T. *The End of the Russian Empire.* New Haven, Yale U.P., 1931.

Footman, David. *Civil War in Russia.* London, Faber and Faber, 1961.

Gaponenko, L. S. *Rabochii klass Rossii v 1917 g.* Moscow, Nauka, 1970.

Garmiza, V. V. *Krushenie eserovskikh pravitel'stv.* Moscow, Mysl', 1970.

General Kutepov: sbornik statei. Paris, Izdanie komiteta imeni generala Kute-pova, 1934.

Gimpel'son, E. G. *Sovetskii rabochii klass, 1918–1920.* Moscow, Nauka, 1974.

————. *Sovety v gody inostrannoi interventsii i grazhdanskoi voiny.* Moscow, Nauka, 1968.

Gitelman, Zvi. *Jewish Nationality and Soviet Politics. The Jewish Sections of the CPSU, 1917–1930.* Princeton, Princeton U.P., 1972.

Goigova, Z. A. G. *Narody Checheno-Ingushetii v bor'be protiv Denikina.* Groznyi, Checheno-Ingushetii nauchno issledovatel'skii institut, 1963.

Goleevskii, M. M. *Materialy po istorii gvardeiskoi pekhoty i artillerii v grazhdanskoi voiny s 1917 po 1922 god.* n.p. n.d.

Golovin, N. N. *Rossiiskaia kontr-revoliutsiia v 1917–1918 gg.* 5 vols. Paris, Biblioteka "Illiustrirovannoi Rossii," 1937.

Golubev, A. V. *Perekop i Chongar; sbornik statei.* Moscow, Gosvoenizdat, 1933.

Golubintsev, Gen. *Russkaia Vandeia. Ocherki grazhdanskoi voiny na Donu, 1917–1920 gg.* Munich, 1959.

Gordon, A. G. *Russian Civil War.* London, Cassel and Co. 1937.

Gorkii, M., V. Molotov, K. Voroshilov, and others (eds.) *The History of the Civil War in the USSR.* 2 vols. New York, International Publishers, 1938–1947.

Gorkii, M. *O Russkoi krestianstve.* n.p., 1922.

Gukovskii, A. I. *Frantsuskaia interventsiia na iuge Rossii, 1918–1919.* Moscow, Gosudarstvennoe sotsialno-ekonomicheskoe izdatel'stvo, 1928.

Gusev, K. V. *Ot soglashitel'stva k kontrrevoliutsii. Bankrotstva i gibeli partii sotsialistov-revoliutsionerov.* Moscow, Mysl', 1968.

Gusev-Oreburgskii, S. *Kniga o Evreiskikh pogromakh na Ukraine v 1919 g.* Petrograd, Grzhebin, n.d.

Heifets, Elias. *The Slaughter of the Jews in the Ukraine, 1919.* New York, Thomas Seltzer, 1921.

Hodgson, John. *With Denikin's Armies.* London, Lincoln Williams Co., 1932.

Hovannisian, R. G. *The Republic of Armenia. Volume 1: The First Year, 1918–1919.* Berkeley, Los Angeles, University of California Press, 1971.

Hubbard, L. E. *Soviet Labour and Industry.* London, Macmillan, 1942.

Huntington, S. P. *Political Order in Changing Societies.* New Haven, Yale U.P., 1968.

Hurwicz, Elias. *Geschichte des russischen Bürgerkriegs.* Berglin, E. Laubsche Verlagsbuchhandlung, 1927.

Ianchevskii, N. L. *Grazhdanskaia bor'ba na severnom Kavkaze.* Rostov on the Don, Gosizdat, 1927.

Kabakhidze, O. A. (ed.). *Revoliutsionnye komitety Terskoi oblasti v bor'be za vosstanovlenii i uprochenie sovetskoi vlasti (okt. 1919–avg. 1920) Sbornik dokumentov.* Sukhumi, "Alashara," 1971.

Kadishev, A. B. *Interventsiia i grazhdanskaia voina v Zakavkaze*. Moscow, Voenizdat, 1960.

Kakurin, N. *Kak srazhalas' revoliutsiia*. 2 vols. Moscow and Leningrad, Gosizdat, 1925.

———. *Strategicheskii ocherk grazhdanskoi voiny*. Moscow, Leningrad, Gosvoenizdat, 1926.

Kalinin, I. V. *Pod znamenem Vrangelia*. Leningrad, Priboi, 1925.

———. *Russkaia Vandeia*. Moscow, Gosizdat, 1926.

Kandidov, B. P. *Religioznaia kontr-revoliutsiia 1918–1920 gg. i interventsiia: ocherki i materialy*. Moscow, Bezbozhnik, 1930.

———. *Tserkov' i shpionazh; o nekatorykh faktakh kontrrevoliutsionnoi i shpionskoi deiatel'nosti religioznykh organizatsiiakh*. Moscow, Gos. antireligioznoe izd.-vo, 1937.

Kantorovich, V. P. *Frantsuzy v Odesse*. Petrograd, Izdatel'stvo "Byloe", 1922.

Kautsky, Karl. *Georgia, a Social-democratic Peasant Republic*. Translated by H. J. Stenning. London, International Bookshops, 1921.

Kazemzadeh, Firuz. *The Struggle for Transcaucasia, 1917–1921*. New York, Philosophical Library, 1951.

Kenez, Peter. *Civil War in South Russia, 1918; The First Year of the Volunteer Army*. Berkeley, Los Angeles, University of California Press, 1971.

Kennan, G. F. *Russia and the West Under Lenin and Stalin*. Boston, Atlantic–Little Brown and Co., 1960.

———. *Soviet-American Relations, 1917–1920*. 2 vols. Vol. 1: *Russia Leaves the War*. Princeton, Princeton U.P., 1956. Vol. 2: *The Decision to Intervene*. Princeton, Princeton U.P., 1958.

Khachapuridze, G. V. *Bor'ba gruzinskogo naroda za ustanovlenie Sovetskoi vlasti*. Moscow, Gospolitizdat, 1956.

Khmelevskii, K. A. *Krakh krasnovshchiny i nemetskoi interventsii na Donu (apr. 1918–mart 1919 goda)*. Rostov on the Don, Gos. Universitet, 1965.

Kikhtev, S. *Oktiabr'skaia Revoliutsiia i pervye sotsialisticheskie preobrazovaniia v Donetsko-Krivozhskom basseine*. Kiev, Izdatel'stvo politicheskoi literatury Ukrainy, 1969.

Kin. D. *Denikinshchina*. Leningrad, Priboi, 1927.

Kirillov, I. A. *Ocherki zemleustroistva za tri goda revoliutsii (1917–1920 gg)*. Petrograd, "Novaia derevnia," 1922.

Kluev, L. *Bor'ba za Tsaritsyn*. Gosizdat, Moscow, 1928.

Kolesnikov, B. *Professional'noe dvizhenie i kontr-revoliutsiia*. n.p. Gosizdat Ukrainy, 1923.

Kondakov, A. A. *Razgrom desantov Vrangelia na Kubani*. Krasnodar, Krasnodarskoe knizhnoe izd., 1960.

360 BIBLIOGRAPHY

Korenev, D. Z. *Revoliutsiia na Tereke 1917–1918 gg.* Ordzhonikidze, Severo-Osetinskoe kn. izd-vo. 1967.
Korotkov, I. S. *Razgrom Vrangelia.* Moscow, Voenizdat, 1955.
Kovtiukh, E. *Ot Kubani do Volgi i obratno.* Moscow, Gosvoenizdat, 1926.
Krivoshein, K. A. A. V. *Krivoshein (1857–1921) Ego znachenie v istorii Rossii nachala XX veka.* Paris, 1973.
Kritskii, M. A. *Kornilovskii udarnyi polk.* Paris, Imprimerie "Val," 1936.
Kuchin-Oranskii, G. *Dobrovol'cheskaia zubatovshchina. Kirstovskie organizatsii na iuge Rossii i bor'ba s nimi professional'nykh soiuzov.* n.p. Trud, 1924.
Kursell, Otto von. *Pogromshchiki Rossii.* Munich, Germanskoe narodnoe izd.-vo, (192?).
Kuz'min N. F. *Krushenie poslednogo pokhoda Antanty.* Moscow, Gospolitizdat, 1958.
Lampe, A. A. von. (ed.). *Beloe delo; letopis' beloi bor'by.* 7 vols. Berlin, Russkoe natsional'noe knigoizdatel'stvo, "Mednyi Vsadnik," 1926–1928.
Lampe, A. A. von. (ed.) *Glavnokomanduiushchii russkoi armiei general baron P. N. Vrangel'; sbornik statei.* Berlin, knigoizdatel'stvo "Mednyi Vsadnik," 1938.
———. *Prichiny neudachi vooruzhennogo vystupleniia belykh.* Berlin, "Russkii kolokol'," 1929.
———. *Puti vernykh; sbornik statei.* Paris, 1960.
Lang, D. M. *A Modern History of Georgia.* London, Weidenfield and Nicolson, 1962.
Lehovich, D. V. *White Against Red. The Life of General Anton Denikin.* New York, Norton, 1974.
Lipatov, N. P. *1920 god na Chernom more; Voenno-morskie sily v razgrome Vrangelia.* Moscow, Voenizdat, 1958.
Likholat, A. V. *Razgrom natsionalisticheskoi kontrrevoliutsii na Ukraine 1917–1922 gg.* Moscow, Gosizdat polit. lit-ry, 1954.
Lisovoi Ia. M. *Belyi arkhiv: sbornik matrialov po istorii i literature voiny, revoliutsii, bol'shevisma, belogo dvizheniia i t.d.* 3 vols. Paris, 1926–1928.
Luckett, Richard. *The White Generals. An Account of the White Movement in the Russian Civil War.* New York, Viking, 1971.
Lukomskii, A. S. *Vospominaniia.* 2 vols. Berlin, Otto Kirchner, 1922. Translated and abridged by Olga Vitali as *Memoirs of the Russian Revolution,* London, T. F. Unwin, 1922.
Makarov, P. V. *Ad"iutant generala Mai-Maevskogo; iz vospominanii nachal'nika otriada krasnykh partizan v Krymu.* Leningrad, Rabochee izdatel'stvo "Priboi," 1929.
Makharadze, F. *Sovety i bor'ba za sovetskuiu vlast' v Gruzii, 1917–1921.* Tiflis, Gosizdat SSRG, 1928.

Makhrov, P. *Kto i pochemu mog' pokhitet' gen. Kutepova i gen millera?* Paris, 1937.

Margolin, A. D. *From a Political Diary: Russia, the Ukraine and America, 1905–1945.* New York, Columbia U.P., 1946.

Margolin, A. D. *Ukraina i politika antanty.* Berlin, Izdatel'stvo S. Efron, 1921.

Margulies, M. S. *God interventsii.* 3 vols. Berlin, Izdatel'stvo Z. I. Grzhebina, 1923.

Marty, A. P. *The Epic of the Black Sea Revolt.* New York, Workers' Library Publishers, 1941.

Mekler, *V denikinskoi podpole.* Moscow, Molodaia gvardiia, 1932.

Melgunov, S. P. N. V. *Chaikovskii v gody grazhdanskoi voiny: materialy dlia istorii Russkoi obshchestvennosti, 1917–1925 gg.* Paris, Librarie "La Source," 1929.

———. *Grazhdanskaia voina v osveshchenii P. N. Miliukova.* Paris, Rapide Imprimerie, 1929.

———. *The Red Terror in Russia.* London, I. M. Dent and Sons, 1925.

Melikov, V. A. *Stalinskii plan razgroma Denikina.* Moscow, Gosvoenizdat, 1938.

Melnikov, N. M. (ed.). *M. P. Bogaevskii.* Izd. "Rodimogo kraia," 1964.

———. *Kak izvrashchaevtsia istoriia.* Paris, Izd. "Rodimogo kraia," 1963.

Meyer, A. G. *Leninism.* Cambridge, Harvard U.P., 1957.

Michelson, A., P. Apostol, and M. Bernatzky. *The Russian Public Finance During the War.* New Haven, Yale U.P., 1928.

Miliukov, P. N. *Beloe dvizhenie.* Paris, Izdanie Respublikansko-demokraticheskogo obedineniia, 1929.

———. *Istoriia vtoroi Russkoi revoliutsii.* 3 vols. Sofia, Rossiisko-Bolgardskoe knigoizdatel'stvo, 1921–1924.

———. *Russia Today and Tomorrow.* New York, Macmillan, 1922.

———. *Russlands zusammenbruch.* 2 vols. Berlin, Obelisk Verlag, 1926. (*Rossiia na perelome.* 2 vols. Paris, 1927.)

Mints, I. I. (ed.). *Sovetskaia Rossiia i kapitalisticheskii mir v 1917–1923 gg.* Moscow, Akademiia Nauk SSSR Institut istorii. Gospolitizdat, 1957.

Mirkin-Getsevich, B. S. *Les Juifs et la Revolution Russe.* Paris, J. Povolozky, 1921.

Naida, S. F., *et al.* (eds.). *Istoriia grazhdanskoi voiny v SSSR, 1917–1922.* 3 vols. Moscow, Institut Marksisma-Leninisma pri Ts.K. KPSS Gospolitizdat, 1959.

———. (ed.). *Iz istorii bor'by sovetskogo naroda protiv inostrannoi voennoi interventsii i vnutrennei kontr-revoliutsii v 1918: sbornik statei.* Moscow, Gosizdat, 1956.

————. *O nekatorykh voprosakh istorii grazhdanskoi voiny v SSSR*. Mowcow, Gospolitizdat, 1958.

————. (ed.) *Reshaiushchie pobedy sovetskogo naroda nad interventami i belogvardeitsami v 1919g. Sbornik statei*. Moscow, Gospolitizdat, 1958.

Naumenko, V. G. *Iz nedavnogo proshlogo Kubani*. Belgrade. n.d.

Nemirovich-Danchenko, G. *V Krymu pri Vrangele*. Berlin, Tip. P. Ol'denburg, 1922.

Nesterovich-Berg, M. A. *V bor'be s bol'shevikami: vospominaniia*. Paris, Imp. de Navarre, 1931.

Nikulikhin, Ia. *Na fronte grazhdanskoi voiny. (1918–1921)*. Petrograd, Izd. Priboi, 1923.

Nove, Alec. *An Economic History of the USSR*. Baltimore, Penguin, 1972.

Pamiati pogibshchikh. Paris, Imprimerie de la Scoiete nouvelle d'editions franco-slaves, 1929.

Park, A. G. *Bolshevism in Turkistan, 1917–1927*. New York, Columbia U.P., 1957.

Partiia Menshevikov i Denikinshchina. Moscow, Krasnaia Nov', 1923.

Pasmanik, D. S. *Revoliutsionnye gody v Krymu*. Imp. de Navarre, 1926.

————. *Russkaia revoliutsiia i evreistvo (Bol'shevism i iudaism)*. Berlin, Izdatel'stvo Russkaia pechat," 1923.

Pavlov, V. E. (ed.). *Markovtsy v boiakh i pokhodakh za Rossiiu v osvoboditel'noi voine, 1917–1920*. Paris, 1962.

Pipes, R. E. (ed.). *Revolutionary Russia: a Symposium*. Cambridge, Harvard U.P., 1968.

————. *The Formation of the Soviet Union. Communism and Nationalism 1917–1923*. Cambridge, Harvard U.P., 1957.

Pokrovskii, G. *Denikinshchina. God politiki i ekonomiki na Kubani (1918–1919gg)* Berlin, Izd. Z. I. Grzhebina, 1923.

Poliakov, Ia. A. *Donskie kazaki v bor'be s bol'shevikami*. Munich, 1962.

Polovtsov, L. V. *Rytsary ternogo ventsa; vospominaniia o l-om Kubanskom pokhode gen. M. V. Alekseeva, L. G. Kornilova i A. I. Denikina*. Prague Tip. Griunkhut, 1921.

Popov, F. V. *Razgrom denikintsev pod Orlom; iz zapisok kombriga*. Orel, Orlovskie kn. izd-vo, 1959.

Power, Rhoda. *Under Cossack and Bolshevik*. London, 1919.

Pronin, D. *Sed'maia gaubchnaia 1918–1921*. New York, 1960.

Radkey, O. H. *The Election to the Russian Constituent Assembly of 1917*. Cambridge, Harvard U.P., 1950.

Raenko, Ia. *Khronika istoricheskikh sobytii na Donu, Kubani i Chernomore*. Rostov on the Don, Rostovskoe oblastnoe knigoizdatel'stvo, 1939.

Rafes, M. *Dva goda revoliutsii na Ukraine*. Moscow, Gosizdat, 1920.

Rakovskii, G. N. *Konets belykh ot Dnepra do Bosfora.* Prague. Izd. "Volia Rossii," 1921.

———. *V stane belykh: grazhdanskaia voina na iuge Rossii.* Constantinople, Izdat, "Pressa," 1920.

Razgon, I. E. *Bor'ba partizan protiv belogvardeitsev nba severnom Kavkaze 1919–20 gg.* Moscow, Gospolitizdat, 1942.

Reshetar, J. S. *The Ukrainian Revolution. A Study in Nationalism, 1917–1920.* Princeton, Princeton U.P., 1952.

Ribgy, T. H. *Communist Party Membership in the USSR.* Princeton, Princeton U.P., 1968.

Rosenberg, W. G. *Liberals in the Russian Revolution. The Constitutional Democratic Party, 1917–1921.* Princeton, Princeton U.P., 1974.

Rosenfeld, Gunther. *Sowjetrussland und Deutschland, 1917–1922.* Berlin, Akademie Verland, 1960.

Saenko, D. P. *Dmitrii Zhloba.* Krasnodar, 1964.

Samoilov, F. *Delo Borisa Savinkova.* Moscow, Gosizdat, 1924.

Savtchenko, I. *La Guerre des Rouges et des Blancs. Les Insurges du Kuban.* Paris, Payot, 1929.

Savinkov, B. V. *Bor'ba s bol'shevikami.* Warsaw, Izdanie Russkogo politicheskogo komiteta, 1920.

Sazonov, S. D. *Vospominaniia.* Paris. Knigoizdatel'stvo E. Siial'skoi, 1927.

Schapiro, L. B. *The Communist Party of the Soviet Union.* New York, Random House, 1959.

Schmid, A. P. *Churchills privater Krieg. Intervention und Konterrevolution im russischen Bürgerkrieg, November 1918–Marz 1920.* Zurich, Atlantis Verlag, 1974.

Schmiedel, Karl, and Helmut Schnitter. *Bürgerkrieg und Intervention 1918 bis 1922.* Berlin, Deutscher Militarverlag, 1970.

Shabad, T. Geography of the USSR. A Regional Survey. New York, Columbia U.P., 1951.

Shafir, Ia. M. *Belogvardeitsy i krest'ianstvo.* Moscow, Leningrad, Moskovskii rabochii, 1928.

Shchegolev, P. E. (ed.). *Frantsuzy v Odesse; iz belykh memuarov Gen. A. I. Denikina, M. S. Margulies, M. V. Braikevicha.* Leningrad, Izdatel'stvo "Krasnaia gazeta", 1928.

Shestakov, A. V. *Klassovaia bor'ba v derevne.* Voronezh, 1930.

Shkuro, A. G. *Zapiski belogo partizana.* Izdatel'stvo "Seiatel'", Buenos Aires, 1961.

Shteifon, M. B. *Krizis dobrovol'chestva.* Belgrad, Russkaia tip., 1928.

Shulgin, V. V. *Dni.* Belgrad, Knigoizdatel'stvo M. A. Suverin i Ko. "Novoe vremia," 1925.

——. *1920 god: ocherki.* Sofia, Rossiisko-Bulgarskoe Knigoizdatel'stvo, 1921.

Shtif, N. I. *Pogromy na Ukraine (Period Dobrovol'cheskoi armii).* Berlin, Vostok, 1922.

Simonov, B. *Razgrom denikinshchiny; pochemu my pobedili v okt. 1919 g.* Moscow, Gosizdat, 1928.

Skobtsov, D. E. *Tri goda revoliutsii i grazhdanskoi voiny na Kubani.* Paris, n.d.

Slashchev-Krymskii, Ia. A. *Trebuiu suda obshchestva i glasnosti; oborona i sdacha Kryma; memuary i dokumenty.* Constantinople, Knigoizdatel'stvo M. Shul'mana, 1921.

Smolenskii, S. *Krymskaia katastrofa. (zapiski stroevogo ofitsera).* Sofia, 1921.

Sokolov, K. N. *Pravlenie generala Denikina.* Sofia, Rossiisko-Bulgarskoe Knigo-izdatel'stvo, 1921.

Spiridonov, N. *Podpolnaia deiatel'nost' bol'shevikov Kubani v gody grazhdanskoi voiny.* Krasnodar, Krasnodarskoe knizhnoe izdatel'stvo, 1960.

Spirin, L. M. *Klassy i partii v grazhdanskoi voine v Rossii 1917–1920 gg.* Moscow, Mysl', 1968.

Stewart, G. *The White Armies of Russia.* New York, Macmillan, 1933.

Struve, P. B. *Razmyshleniia o russkoi revoliutsii.* Sofia, Russkoe-Bulgarskoe Knigoizdatel'stvo, 1921.

Sukhorukov, V. T. *XI Armiia v boiakh na severnom Kavkaze i nizhnei Volge.* Moscow, Voenizdat, 1961.

Suprunenko, N. I. *Ocherki istorii grazhdanskoi voiny i inostrannoi veonnoi interventsii na Ukraine.* Moscow, Nauka, 1966.

Svechin, Mikhail, *Zapiski starogo generala o bylom.* Nice, 1964.

Svechnikov, M. S. *Bor'ba Krasnoi armii na severnom Kavkaze, sentiabr' 1918–aprel' 1919.* Moscow, Gosvoenizdat, 1926.

Tolmachev, I. P. *V stepiakh Donskikh.* Moscow, Voennoe izdatel'stvo, 1959.

Trotskii, L. D. *My Life. An Attempt at an Autobiography.* New York, Charles Scribner, 1930.

——. *Kak vooruzhalas' revoliutsiia.* 5 vols. Moscow, Vysshii voennyi redaktsionnyi sovet, 1923–1925.

Tsurikov, N. A. *General Aleksander Pavlovich Kutepov.* Prague, 1930.

Turkul, A. V. *Drozdovtsy v ogne.* Munich, Izdatel'stvo Iav i byl. 1948.

Ulam, A. B. *The Bolsheviks.* New York, Macmillan, 1965.

Ul'ianov, I. *Dumy vol'nogo kazaka.* Moscow, Gosizdat, 1920.

Ullman, R. H. *Anglo-Soviet Relations, 1917–1921.* Vol. 1: *Intervention and the War* Princeton, Princeton U.P., 1961. Vol. 2.: *Britain and the Russian Civil War.* Princeton, Princeton U.P., 1968.

V-ov, P. *Otvet generalu Slashchevu-Krymskomu.* Constantinople, 1921.

Val' E. G. *Kak Pilsudski pogubil Denikina.* Tallin, published by the author, 1938.

——. *K istorii belogo dvizheniia: deiatel'nost' General ad"iutanta Shcherbacheva.* Tallin, published by the author. 1935.

——. *Prichiny raspadeniia Rossiiskogo imperii i neudachi russkogo natsional'nogo dvizheniia.* 4 vols. Tallin, published by the author, 1938.

Vasilevskii, I. M. *Belye memuary.* Izdatel'stvo "Petrograd" Petrograd and Moscow, 1923.

——. *A. I. Denikin i ego memuary.* Berlin, Izdanie "Nakanune" 1924.

Vavrik, V. R. *Karpatorossy v Kornilovskom pokhode i Dobrovol'cheskoi armii.* Lvov, Tip. Stavropgiiskago instituta, 1923.

Vinaver, M. M. *Nashe pravitel'stvo: Krymskie vospominaniia, 1918–1919 gg.* Paris, 1928.

Valdimirova, Vera. *God sluzhby "sotsialistov" kapitalom.* Moscow, Gosizdat, 1927.

Vladimirtsev, V. S. *Partiia—organizator razgroma kontrrevoliutsii na iuge.* Moscow, Voenizdat, 1971.

Volin, Lazar. *A Century of Russian Agriculture.* Cambridge, Harvard U.P., 1970.

Wandycz, P. S. *Soviet-Polish Relations, 1917–1921,* Cambridge, Harvard U.P., 1969.

Williamson, H. N. H. *Farewell to the Don.* Edited by John Harris. New York, The John Day Company, 1971.

Vrangel' P. N. *Zapiski,* in *Beloe delo* (ed. by A. A. von Lampe). Vol. 5, pp. 9–306, and Vol. 6, pp. 5–261. Berlin, Russkoe national'noe knigoizdatel'stvo, 1926–1928. Translated and slightly abbreviated by Sophie Goulston. Published in 1930 as *The Memoirs of General Wrangel,* New York, Duffield and Co.; and in 1957 as *Always with Honor,* New York, Robert Speller and Sons.

Xydias, Jean. *L' intervention francaise en Russie, 1918–1919: souverins d'un temoin.* Paris, editions de France, 1927.

Yarmolinsky, Avrahm. *The Jews and Other Minor Nationalities Under the Soviets.* New York, Vanguard Press, 1928.

Zaitsov, A. A. *1918 god. Ocherki po istorii russkoi grazhdanskoi voiny.* Paris, 1934.

Zaporozhets, M. Ia. *Komunisty Makaevki v bor'be za pobedu i ukreplenie sovetskoi vlasti.* Donskoe knizhnoe izdatel'stvo, 1961.

Zaslavskii, D. O. *Rytsar' chernoi sotni. V. V. Shul'gin.* Leningrad, Byloe, 1925.

Zinkevich, M. M. *Osnovanie i put' Dobrovol'cheskoi armii 1917–1930.* Sofia, 1930.

ARTICLES

Arbatov, Z. Iu. "Ekaterinoslav, 1917–1920 gg." *ARR*, vol. 12 (1923), pp. 83–148.

Astrov, N. I. "Iasskoe soveshchanie," *Golos Minuvshego na Chuzhoi Storone*, No. 3 (1926), pp. 39–76.

Biakov, B. "Vospominaniia o revoliutsii v Zakavkaze, 1917–1920 gg." *ARR*, vol. 9 (1923), pp. 91–194.

Cheriachukin, A. V. "Donskaia delegatsiia na Ukrainu i Berlin, 1918–1919 g.", *Donskaia Letopis'*, vol. 3., pp. 163–231.

Dobranitskii, M. "Zelenye partizany," *Proletarskaia Revoliutsiia*, Nos. 8–9 (1924), pp. 72–98.

Drozdov, A. "Intelligentsiia na Donu," *ARR*, vol. 2 (1921), pp. 5–58.

Favitskii, V. "Zelenaia armiia i Chernomor'e," *Proletarskaia Revoliutsiia*, Nos. 8–9 (1924), pp. 43–71.

Filimonov, A. P. "Kubantsy," *Beloe Delo*, vol. 2., pp. 67–102.

———. "Razgrom kubanskoi rady," *ARR*, vol. 5 (1922), pp. 322–329.

Goldenveizer, A. A. "Iz Kievskikh vospominanii," *ARR*, vol. 6. (1922), pp. 161–303.

Grekov, A. N. "Soiuz kazachikh voisk v Petrograde v 1917 godu," *Donskaia Letopis'*, vol. 2, pp. 229–283.

Gurko, V. I. "Iz Petrograda cherez Moskvu, Parizh i London v Odessu 1917–1918 gg.", *ARR*, vol. 15 (1924), pp. 5–84.

Igrenev, G. "Ekaterinoslavskaia vospominaniia," *ARR*, vol. 3 (1921), pp. 234–243.

Karinskii, N. "Epizod iz evakuatsii Novorossiiska" *ARR*, vol. 12 (1923), pp. 149–156.

Kenez, P. "A. I. Denikin," *The Russian Review*, Apr. 1974 (vol. 33), pp. 139–152.

———. "A Profile of the Prerevolutionary Officer Corps," *California Slavic Studies*, vol. 7 (1973), pp. 121–157.

———. "The Relations between the Volunteer Army and Georgia, 1918–1920: a Case Study in Disunity," *The Slavonic and East European Review*, July 1970, pp. 403–423.

Kin. D. (ed.). "K istorii frantsuzskoi interventsii na iuge Rossii," *KA*, vol. 19 (1927), pp. 3–38.

Kritskii, M. "Krasnaia armiia na iuzhnom fronte v 1918–1920 gg.", *ARR*, vol. 18 (1926), pp. 230–254.

L-oi, L. "Ocherki zhizni v Kieve v 1919–1920 gg." *ARR*, vol. 3 (1921), pp. 210–233.

Lehovich, D. "Denikin's offensive," *Russian Review*, Apr. 1973 (vol. 32), pp. 173–186.

Lukomskii, A. S. "Iz vospominanii," *ARR*, vol. 2 (1921), pp. 14–44; vol. 5 (1922), pp. 107–189; vol. 6 (1922), pp. 81–160.

Mal't, M. "Denikinshchina i krest'ianstvo," *Proletarskaia Revoluitsiia* (Jan. 1924), No. 1., pp. 140–157; (Apr. 1924) No. 4., pp. 144–176.

―――. "Denikinshchina i rabochie," *Proletarskaia Revoliutsiia* (May, 1924), No. 5, pp. 64–85.

McNeal, Robert. "The Conference of Jassy: An Early Fiasco of the Anti-Bolshevik Movement," in J.S. Curtiss, ed., *Essays in Russian and Soviet History*. New York, Columbia U.P., 1963. pp. 221–236.

Miakotin, V.A. "Iz nedalekogo proshlogo," *Na Chuzhoi Storone*, No. 2 (1923), pp. 178–199; No. 3 (1923), pp. 179–193; No. 5 (1924), pp. 251–268; No. 6 (1924), pp. 73–100; No. 9 (1925), pp. 279–302; No. 11 (1925), pp. 205–236; No. 13 (1925), pp. 193–227.

"Nachale Vrangelevshchiny," *KA*, vol. 21 (1927), pp. 174–181.

Obolenskii, V. A. "Krym 1917–1920 gg." *Na Chuzhoi Storone*, No. 5 (1924), pp. 5–40; No. 6 (1924), pp. 53–72; No. 7 (1924), pp. 81–110; No. 8 (1924), pp. 5–54; No. 9 (1925), pp. 5–56.

Pokrovskii, M. N. "Memuary tsaria Antona," *Pechat' i Revoliutsiia*, No. 2 (1922), pp. 19–31.

Sokolov, K. N. "Kubanskoe deistvo," *ARR* vol. 18 (1926), pp. 237–253.

Shteinman, F. "Otstuplenie ot Odessy," *ARR*, vol. 2 (1921), 87–98.

Strakhovsky, L. I. "The Franco-British Plot to Dismember Russia," *Current History*, vol. 33 (March 1931), pp. 839–842.

Treadgold, D. W. "The Ideology of the White Movement: Wrangel's Leftist Policy from Rightist Hands," *Harvard Slavic Studies*, vol. 4, pp. 481–498.

Thompson, J. M. "Allied and American Intervention in Russia, 1918–1921," in C. E. Black, ed., *Rewriting Russian History: Soviet Interpretations of Russia's Past*. New York, Praeger, 1956.

Trubetskoi, E. N. "Iz putevykh zametok bezhentsa," *ARR*, vol. 18 (1926), pp. 137–207.

Valentinov, A. A. "Krymskaia epopeia," *ARR*, vol. 5 (1922), pp. 5–100.

Voronovich, N. "Mezh dvukh ognei," *ARR*, vol. 7 (1922), pp. 53–183.

"Vrangelevshchina (iz materialov Parizhskogo 'posol'stvo' Vrem. Pravitel'stav)" *KA*, vol. 39 (1930), pp. 3–46; vol. 40 (1930), pp. 3–40.

NEWSPAPERS

Donskaia Volna (Hoover)   *Novoe Vremia* (Columbia)
Donskaia Rech (Hoover)   *Poslednie Novosti* (New York Public Library)
Iug Rossii (Hoover)   *Signal* (Hoover)
Kievlianin (Hoover)   *Velikaia Rossiia* (Hoover)
Krymskii Vestnik (Hoover)

UPDATED BIBLIOGRAPHY, 1977-2004

Istoricheskie portrety: L.G. Kornilov, A.I. Denikin, P.N. Vrangel
Beloe dvizhenie. Moskva: Astrel', 2003.
Arans, David. *How We Lost the Civil War: Bibliography of Russia*
Émigré Memoirs on the Russian Revolution, 1917-1921. ORI
Russian Bibliography Series, No. 6. Newtonville, MA: Orienta
Research Partners, 1988.
Babine, Alexis Vasilevich, and Donald J. Raleigh. *A Russian Civ*
War Diary: Alexis Babine in Saratov, 1917-1922. Durham, N.C
Duke University Press, 1988.
Bordiugov, G. A., A. I. Ushakov, and V. Churakov. *Beloe delo–*
ideologiia, osnovy, rezhimy vlasti: Istoriograficheskie ocherk
Moskva: Russkii mir, 1998.
Borrero, Mauricio. *Hungry Moscow: Scarcity and Urban Society i*
the Russian Civil War, 1917-1921. Studies in Modern Europea
History, v. 41. New York: Peter Lang, 2003.
Bortnevskii, V. G. *White Intelligence and Counter-Intelligenc*
During the Russian Civil War. Pittsburgh, PA: Center fo
Russian & East European Studies, 1995.
Brovkin, Vladimir N. *Behind the Front Lines of the Civil Wa*
Political Parties and Social Movements in Russia, 1918-1922
Princeton: Princeton University Press, 1994.
_____. *The Bolsheviks in Russian Society: The Revolution and th*
Civil Wars. New Haven, CN: Yale University Press, 1997.
Butt, V. P. *The Russian Civil War: Documents from the Sovie*
Archives. New York: Palgrave Macmillan, 1996; St. Martin'
Press, 1996.
Carley, Michael Jabara. *Revolution and Intervention: The Frenc*
Government and the Russian Civil War, 1917-1919. Montrea
McGill-Queen's University Press, 1983.
Danilov, Viktor P. *Rural Russia under the New Regim*
Bloomington, IN: Indiana University Press, 1988.
Dumova, N. G. *Kadetskaia kontrrevoliutsiia. Ee razgrom: Oktiab*
1917-1920 gg. Moskva: Nauka, 1982.
Figes, Orlando. *Peasant Russia, Civil War: The Volga Countrysia*
in Revolution, 1917-1921. New York: Clarendon Press; Oxfor
University Press, 1989.
_____. *A People's Tragedy: The Russian Revolution, 1891-1924*

London: J. Cape, 1996.

_____ et al. *Interpreting the Russian Revolution: The Language and Symbols of 1917.* New Haven: Yale University Press, 1999.

Foglesong, David S. *America's Secret War against Bolshevism: U.S. Intervention in the Russian Civil War, 1917-1920.* Chapel Hill: University of North Carolina Press, 1995.

Holquist, Peter. *Making War, Forging Revolution: Russia's Continuum of Crisis, 1914-1921.* Cambridge, MA: Harvard University Press, 2002.

Ippolitov, G. M. *Denikin.* Moskva: Molodaia gvardiia, 2000.

Karpenko, Sergei, Anton I. Denikin, and A. S. Lukomskii. *General Kornilov.* Moskva: Golos, 1993.

_____, P. N. Krasnov, and Anton I. Denikin. *Don i Dobrovol'cheskaia Armiia.* Moskva: Golos, 1992.

_____, et al. *Belyi Krym.* Moskva: Rossiskii gos. gumanitarnyi universitet, 2003.

Keep, John L. H. *The Russian Revolution: A Study in Mass Mobilization.* Revolutions in Modern World. London: Weidenfeld & Nicolson, 1976.

Kozerod, Oleg, and Sergei Ia. Briman. *Denikinskii rezhim i evreiskoe naselenie Ukrainy 1919-1920 gg.* Kharkov: 1996.

Kozlov, A. I. *Anton Ivanovich Denikin: (Chelovek, polkovodets, politik, uchenyi).* Moskva: Sobranie, 2004.

Lincoln, W. Bruce. *Red Victory: A History of the Russian Civil War.* New York: Simon and Schuster, 1989.

Mamontov, S. Pokhody i koni. Paris: YMCA-Press, 1981.

Mawdsley, Evan. *The Russian Civil War.* Boston: Allen & Unwin, 1987.

Pearce, Brian. *How Haig Saved Lenin.* New York: St. Martin's Press, 1987.

Pereira, N. G. O. *White Siberia: The Politics of Civil War.* Montreal: McGill-Queen's University Press, 1996.

Pipes, Richard. The Russian Revolution. New York: Vintage Books, 1991.

_____. *Russia under the Bolshevik Regime.* New York: Vintage Books, 1995.

Procyk, Anna. *Russian Nationalism and Ukraine: The Nationality Policy of the Volunteer Army During the Civil War.* Edmonton: Canadian Institute of Ukrainian Studies Press, 1995.

BIBLIOGRAPHY

Raleigh, Donald J. *Experiencing Russia's Civil War: Politics, Society, and Revolutionary Culture in Saratov, 1917-1922.* Princeton: Princeton University Press, 2002.

Robinson, Paul. *The White Russian Army in Exile, 1920-1941.* Oxford Historical Monographs. New York: Oxford University Press, 2002.

Smele, Jonathan. *Civil War in Siberia: The Anti-Bolshevik Government of Admiral Kolchak, 1918-1920.* Cambridge/New York: Cambridge University Press, 1996.

_____. *The Russian Revolution and Civil War, 1917-1921: An Annotated Bibliography.* London/New York: Continuum, 2003.

Somin, Ilya. *Stillborn Crusade: The Tragic Failure of Western Intervention in the Russian Civil War, 1918-1920.* New Brunswick, N.J.: Transaction Publishers, 1996.

Starikov, Sergei, and Roy A. Medvedev. *Philip Mironov and the Russian Civil War.* New York: Knopf, 1978.

Stites, Richard. *Revolutionary Dreams: Utopian Vision and Experimental Life in the Russian Revolution.* New York: Oxford University Press, 1989.

Swain, Geoff. *The Origins of the Russian Civil War.* Origins of Modern Wars. New York: Longman, 1996.

Von Hagen, Mark. *Soldiers in the Proletarian Dictatorship: The Red Army and the Soviet Socialist State, 1917-1930.* Studies of the Harriman Institute. Ithaca, N.Y.: Cornell University Press, 1990.

Wade, Rex A. *The Bolshevik Revolution and Russian Civil War.* Westport, CN: Greenwood Press, 2001.

Index

CPSIA information can be obtained
at www.ICGtesting.com
Printed in the USA
BVHW041515050920
587799BV00004B/23